# Mixed Race Hollywood

# Mixed Race Hollywood

EDITED BY

*Mary Beltrán and Camilla Fojas*

*New York University Press*

NEW YORK AND LONDON

NEW YORK UNIVERSITY PRESS
New York and London
www.nyupress.org

Library of Congress Cataloging-in-Publication Data

Mixed race Hollywood / edited by Mary Beltrán and Camilla Fojas.
p. cm.
Includes bibliographical references and index.
ISBN-13: 978-0-8147-9989-5 (pb : alk. paper)
ISBN-10: 0-8147-9989-2 (pb : alk. paper)
ISBN-13: 978-0-8147-9988-8 (cl : alk. paper)
ISBN-10: 0-8147-9988-4 (cl : alk. paper)
1. Racially mixed people in motion pictures.
I. Beltrán, Mary. II. Fojas, Camilla.
PN1995.9.R23M59    2008
791.43089'05—dc22          2008010949

New York University Press books are printed on acid-free paper,
and their binding materials are chosen for strength and durability.
We strive to use environmentally responsible suppliers and materials
to the greatest extent possible in publishing our books.

Manufactured in the United States of America
c 10 9 8 7 6 5 4 3 2 1
p 10 9 8 7 6 5 4 3 2 1

# Contents

# Introduction
## Mixed Race in Hollywood
## Film and Media Culture

### *Mary Beltrán and Camilla Fojas*

According to mixed race novelist Danzy Senna, we have entered the "mulatto millennium." Other scholars and cultural critics describe it as a new era in which Generation X has passed the baton to "Generation Mix."[1] This certainly seems to be the case in relation to U.S. film, television, and popular culture since the mid-1990s. If you turn on your television, you might happen upon mixed race actors Vanessa Williams in *Ugly Betty* (2006+), Wentworth Miller in *Prison Break* (2005+), Kristen Kreuk in *Smallville* (2001+), models of various mixed racial backgrounds competing on *America's Next Top Model* (2003+), or media coverage of mixed race politician Barack Obama. Similarly, you might see Vin Diesel, Keanu Reeves, or Rosario Dawson's latest film at your local multiplex, hear Mariah Carey talking frankly about her mixed heritage on a talk show, or read about Raquel Welch "coming out" as a mixed race Latina of half Bolivian heritage. Not only has multiraciality, or, in today's vernacular, being "mixed," taken on new meaning in U.S. popular culture, but biracial and multiracial models, actors, and film and television characters seem to be everywhere. This is a far cry from decades past, when individuals of mixed racial descent either were not visible or were construed negatively as tragic and/or villainous figures in cinema and other media.

These images and trends are important to unpack and more fully understand, as the history of mixed race representation promises to reveal a great deal not only about the U.S. media industries but also about the

1

evolution of social norms that historically have divided notions of race in the United States among such discrete categories as white, black, Latino, Asian, Pacific Islander, and American Indian—albeit with the boundaries between these categories always under question. As documented in the work of such scholars as Ella Shohat and Robert Stam, the film, television, and publicity industries that constitute what we think of as "Hollywood" have long been the preserve of stereotypes and social norms about race.[2] Within this framework, portrayals of interracial romance and of individuals of mixed racial and ethnic heritage have served as powerful totems within filmic story worlds, highlighting and challenging fault lines among racial categories and borders. The publicity that has surrounded actors of mixed racial and ethnic descent similarly is linked to cultural attitudes about racial identities and borders and their evolution. Over the decades the ranks of mixed race stars, once filled by such actors as Nancy Kwan, Anthony Quinn, and Rita Hayworth, have been joined by the likes of Jessica Alba, Jennifer Beals, Keanu Reeves, Halle Berry, and Vin Diesel. Mixed race actors also are increasingly likely to foreground their mixed ethnic background as an element in their publicity today, a sign that biraciality and multiraciality are taking on new meanings.

Despite this rich history and the veritable explosion of multiracial imagery in Hollywood film and media culture today, there has been little published scholarship to date on the history or current representation of mixed race individuals, romance, families, or stars on screen. *Mixed Race Hollywood* takes a first step in this regard. Our contributors, who hail from such academic disciplines as film and media studies, ethnic studies, and literary studies, take up the project of interrogating the portrayal of racial mixing in studies of film, television, the Internet, and other popular culture texts. They explore from diverse vantage points how mixed race individuals, romances, families, and stars have fared in media story lines and star publicity and question the implications of these images and trends. Through this work the authors set precedents for theorizing these topics, as well as laying a foundation for the emergent field of mixed race cultural studies.

## Race and Mixed Race: Notes on Terminology

One of the challenges of such a collection is that of terminology. The differing preferred terms with respect to racial formation and identity in various academic disciplines and the slippage between those terms have provided a challenge in the editing of this anthology. We have chosen in *Mixed Race Hollywood* to utilize the terminology most commonly used in film and media studies. Thus we have, for example, encouraged our authors to use the term "race" without scare quotes (such as used here) as are standard in some other disciplines. We do so with the understanding, however, that we consider race always to be socially constructed and contested. As noted by Michael Omi and Howard Winant, race is not a set of biological categories but a social and political construction[3]—the boundaries of which, notably, are challenged by mixed race families and individuals. Racial categories remain markers of difference that are experienced in a material way, however. They are the basis of individual identity and often of life experience and opportunity, as well as serving as persistent bases for social stratification. The socially constructed boundaries between so-called racial categories are unstable and have shifted over time, moreover, while other nations have distinctly different racial categories and methods of classification into these categories. Many Latinos are considered white in Latin American countries, for instance, but are racialized as nonwhite in European and Euro-American contexts.

The terms "race" and "ethnicity" will also at times be used in conjunction in this collection. In a U.S. context, ethnicity denotes a set of cultural distinctions that may involve national ancestry, including but not limited to food, language, dress, and other markers. For instance, the "Asian American" racial category encompasses a wide variety of ethnic and national identities, including, for instance, Filipino, Vietnamese, Korean, Thai, Cambodian, Hmong, Laotian, Chinese, Japanese, Pakistani, and Indian. Notions of ethnicity have often been conflated with those of race in this country, however. This is because race historically has been viewed through a black-white binary in the United States, with Latinos, Asian Americans, Pacific Islander Americans, and American Indians holding shifting, uncertain positions along the continuum. But these groups have in fact been racialized—socially constructed as nonwhite. Adding to the potential confusion, according to current U.S. governmental classification, Latinos are racially white, black, or indigenous, and only ethnically Latino. In contrast, people who identify as white, black, Asian American, or American Indian can claim this identity as their race on the census form. Such contradictions reveal unavoidable slippages between the two terms. While the constitution and meaning of racial categories have changed over time, what might be described as *mixed* race has similarly been in flux. This is evident in the evolution of terms used to designate multiracial peoples, many of which appear in the chapters in this anthology. In current usage, "mixed race," "biracial," and "multiracial" (or "multiethnic") all are used equally to refer to relationships and individuals of two or more of the socially constructed racial categories of the United States. The topic of mixed racial heritage also has generated a lexicon of terms specific to particular racial and ethnic groups and to distinct time periods in U.S. history. A number of these terms may not be familiar to readers. For instance, the term "mulatto" was in common usage by the antebellum period to refer to individuals of both African and European American ancestry, with the related terms "quadroon" and "octoroon" designating a lesser amount of African heritage. "Mulatto" evoked the social disapprobation of racial mixing in its reference, literally, to the hybrid offspring of a donkey and a horse.[4] Although it has fallen out of common parlance, superseded by terms that have a more neutral connotation, it continues to be used in media studies and literary studies to describe characters of half-black ancestry depicted in the early part of the twentieth century because of foundational scholarship in these fields that described such characters as "tragic mulattoes."[5] Early scholars of the tragic mulatto, or, as more commonly was found, tragic mulatta, described her as a bereft, vulnerable figure because of being caught between two worlds, white and black, to which she could never fully belong.

Another term that is utilized here and is part of the contemporary lexicon of mixed race identity is "hapa." This word, which emanates from the Hawaiian language, meaning literally "half," designates someone who is of mixed Hawaiian heritage. Like "mulatto," "hapa" historically had a negative connotation based on social interdictions about racial mixing. "Hapa" has been appropriated more widely, and with a more neutral meaning, to describe individuals with mixed Asian or Pacific Islander and white heritages. Finally, another culture-specific term that is meaningful to this discussion and that appears in the anthology is the Spanish-language word *mestizaje*, which translates roughly to "mixing," or, more specifically, racial mixing. The term "mestizo" is derived from *mestizaje*; it has been used historically to refer to Latinos with mixed Spanish or white and indigenous heritage, while more recently it has at times been used to refer to Latinos of any mixed heritage. Sharing in the history of Spanish colonialism, individuals of mixed Filipino and white descent are also called "mestizo."

## Cultural Shifts: From Fears of Miscegenation to "Generation Mix"

The various ways in which racial categories can be contested hint at how mixed race romantic relationships and individuals historically were seen as disrupting and threatening the white/black (and white/nonwhite) racial binary. In the context of slavery, "miscegenation," or the mixing of what were deemed two races, was made illegal through state laws and local covenants. Meanwhile, half-white progeny existed, typically the result of the rape of female slaves by white slave owners. This potential threat to the social order was managed through establishing a "one-drop" rule of race by hypodescent, which deemed anyone with the slightest hint of African heritage, black, and reinforced the boundaries of white citizenship.[6] Individuals of other mixed heritage, such as those of partial Mexican or American Indian descent, similarly were often categorized, but with less predictability, by hypodescent in many states. Until as late as 1989, in fact, biracial babies were typically assigned the nonwhite race upon classification at birth unless parents intervened for another designation.[7]

The term "passing," signifying an act of pretending to be of only European American ancestry when in fact of partial African or other nonwhite descent, hails from this historical context of the "one-drop" rule. Mixed race individuals, who might have a racially ambiguous appearance, could be motivated to pass for benefits that included education, employment, and housing opportunities. There were risks to such an act, however, including legal covenants against passing. On the other hand, mixed race individuals were and have often been marginalized by nonwhite communities as well. Maria P. P. Root has noted that mixed race Asian Americans have tended to be excluded from Asian American communities as "not Asian enough," for example.[8]

After World War II, race relations underwent considerable transformation. This was the result of a number of developments, including raised awareness of racial discrimination and civil rights activism on the part of individuals and advocacy organizations such as the National Association for the Advancement of Colored People.[9] The desegregation of schools and other public facilities began or took place at an increased tempo in many cities, and films and television at times addressed the unfair treatment of peoples of color and fears of miscegenation in story lines. These changes laid the groundwork for the civil rights movement in the 1960s that would profoundly affect popular cultural representations of marginalized peoples.

By the 1960s, mixed race couples were more prevalent; Root describes the resulting rise in births of mixed race children as the "biracial baby boom."[10] This boom, not coincidentally, coincided with related legislation. In 1964, the Civil Rights Act outlawed discrimination based on such factors as race, color, and national origin. Subsequently, the Supreme Court's decision in *Loving v. Virginia* (1967) overturned remaining state laws against interracial marriage. This decision is often described as inaugurating the boom in biracial families and children. As early as the 1970s, interracial family support groups began to form in cities around the United States and Canada; many ultimately lent their energies to what has been termed the multiracial or mixed race movement. Led largely by parents of mixed race children, the movement has advocated for mixed race and multiethnic children and families and for a reconsideration of racial categories.

These developments led to the first published scholarship on mixed race identity and experience, particularly in the areas of psychology and sociology. Pioneering works in this regard were Paul Spickard's *Mixed Blood* (1991), Maria P. P. Root's edited collections *Racially Mixed People in America* (1992) and *The Multiracial Experience* (1995), and Naomi Zack's edited anthology *American Mixed Race* (1995). These publications laid an important foundation for subsequent scholarship and greater visibility and awareness of mixed race issues. The first college courses on mixed race identity and issues began to be taught, while support groups for mixed race college students also formed on campuses as diverse as Harvard and the University of California–Santa Cruz.

The number of mixed race youth has continued to increase, as mixed marriages and families are increasingly commonplace. By the late 1990s, organizations advocating for mixed race individuals and families were able to successfully lobby the federal government to change the categories on the census to reflect racial multiplicity. In 2000, respondents had the option for the first time of checking more than one racial category. That year, 6.8 million, or 2.4 percent of respondents, indicated that they belonged to two or more races.[11] Given that many multiracial individuals choose to identify themselves by only one ethnic or racial identifier, we can assume that the mixed race population is in fact much larger.

The late 1990s and early 2000s also have witnessed a greater cultural and academic focus on multiraciality.[12] Scholars and cultural critics are debating in particular the implications of the increasing visibility of mixed race in U.S. popular culture and social life. Some, such as Leon E.

Wynter, describe multiraciality as the inevitable solution to racism in this country and argue that race will be nullified in a future when we will all be mixed race.[13] Other scholars, such as Gloria Anzaldúa in *Borderlands/ La Frontera: The New Mestizas*, argue that a multiracial or "*mestiza* consciousness" does not negate racialized histories but can revolutionize U.S. race relations if we can embrace the legacy of our multiple heritages. Most scholars, like the contributors to this collection, fall somewhere between the extremes of "color-blind" and "color-focused" interpretations of the increasing *mestizaje* that characterizes the United States in the future.

## Hollywood's Response: Mixed Race Relationships on Screen

In 2003, Essie Mae Washington-Williams announced publicly not only that she was mixed race, but that she was the biracial daughter of segregationist Senator Strom Thurmond. This lineage, hidden for many decades, was made public only after Thurmond's death. The silence and secrecy that surrounded Washington-Williams's mixed ancestry serve as a reminder of the continuing deep fears in the United States about miscegenation, as well as ongoing taboos against interracial relationships and marriage.

The evolution of the representation of mixed race relationships in film and television has historically reflected and arguably has also impacted such social attitudes. Newly forming notions of whiteness at the turn of the twentieth century, for example, played into how silent melodramas of the first two decades of the twentieth century portrayed mixed race romances between European Americans and characters of partial American Indian, Asian, or Mexican descent. Such melodramas typically based their dramatic conclusions on last-minute revelations of one or both partners' "real" racial status as based on the "one-drop" rule. Examples include *Ramona*, which was released in multiple film versions, the earliest in 1910.

As the major studios began to form and establish dominance over the industry, film stories based on mixed race romances came under heavier scrutiny. The solidification of notions of whiteness and related taboo against mixed race relationships was addressed with the Motion Picture Producers and Distributors of America's "Don'ts and Be Carefuls" guide in 1927 and became official with the enforcement of the Production Code in 1934. Under the Production Code, the representation of sexual relations between people of different races was forbidden. The Code in this regard reflected larger legal, social, and cultural interdictions against marriage between whites and African Americans, and at times between whites and Mexican Americans, Asian Americans, and American Indians, that were reinforced in the U.S. legal arena in this period.

This is not to say that mixed couples were never represented on the screen, particularly given that the Code's stipulations were vague and evaluated by the Production Code Administration on a film-by-film basis. Only a few scholars have engaged in in-depth exploration of Hollywood's portrayal of romantic and sexual relations that crossed inscribed color lines, notable among them Gina Marchetti and Susan Courtney.[14] Both scholars note the deep cultural context that gave rise to anxious portrayals of mixed couples. Needless to say, the Hollywood mixed race couple was typically not allowed a "happily ever after" or depicted marrying or having children, so wary were the studios to suggest any type of positive outcome to the intimate intermingling of the races. Moreover, even as late as the 1960s, these portrayals were often mitigated through casting a white (or half-white) actor to portray the nonwhite character, ensuring that audiences were not viewing *actual* miscegenation on screen. Classic examples include the casting of Natalie Wood as Maria in *West Side Story* (1961) and of Nancy Kwan, of Chinese and Scottish descent, as Suzie in *The World of Suzie Wong* (1960).

As these examples illustrate, mixed relationships that were not classically biracial were not necessarily forbidden by the Production Code but were still circumscribed in ways that reflected social values. For instance, as Marchetti notes, the portrayal of Asian-white relationships evolved in relation to U.S. social and political relationships with Asian countries.[15] U.S. military ventures during World War II brought "exotic" women to the U.S. colonial consciousness, engendering fantasies that were the result of a commingling of heroic nationalism and colonial paternalism. Many World War II films correspondingly made mixed race coupling a major motivation of the plot, following the stereotypes that Asian women are exotic and appealing, the spoils of colonialism. And while mixed Latino and Anglo and American Indian and Anglo relationships are part of the landscape of the Western, notably in such films as *My Darling Clementine* (1946), *High Noon* (1952), and *The Yellow Tomahawk* (1954), they were treated as temporary at best and doomed to end tragically at worst (as in *Duel in the Sun*'s infamous double-shooting conclusion).

The taboo against the portrayal of mixed race relationships, particularly those that ended in marriage or other positive outcomes, began to shift with the waning of the Production Code in the 1950s and the overturning of antimiscegenation laws in the United States in 1967. In *Sayonara*, for instance, evolving attitudes are reflected in the determination of Major Lloyd Gruver (played by Marlon Brando) to marry a Japanese woman despite the army's interdiction against such unions.

Since then, as noted earlier, the number of mixed race couples and families in this country has grown exponentially. Similarly, we have witnessed a blossoming of portrayals of mixed race relationships in film and television that conclude on a neutral or positive note. Such romances were the central focus of such films as *Sayonara* (1957), *My Geisha* (1962), and *Guess Who's Coming to Dinner* (1967), while more recent examples include *Jungle Fever* (1991), *The Joy Luck Club* (1993), *Made in America* (1993), *Fools Rush In* (1997), and *Save the Last Dance* (2001). Television also has witnessed a variety of positive portrayals since such groundbreaking series as *I Love Lucy* (1951–57), *The Courtship of Eddie's Father* (1969–72), and *The Jeffersons* (1975–85) showcased bicultural and mixed race couples among their regular cast of characters. More recently we have seen mixed race relationships explored in relation to such issues as immigration, class, sexual orientation, and nationality, as in the films *Mississippi Masala* (1991), *The Wedding Banquet* (1993), *Lone Star* (1996), and *Chutney Popcorn* (1999) and in the television series *The L Word* (2004+).

## Mixed Race Characters: A Movement from Tragic to Heroic

The spate of diverse and generally positive characterizations of mixed race figures in film and television today demonstrates a dramatic evolution as well. As noted earlier, many of the first mixed race film characters were sympathetic but tragic figures whose lives turned on the discovery of their mixed racial status. More negative portrayals soon followed, moreover, the lineage of which is often traced to D. W. Griffith's *Birth of a Nation* (1915).

*Birth of a Nation*, based on Thomas Dixon's novels *The Clansman* and *The Leopard's Spots*, is a historical fiction of social relations after the Civil War and, as the title suggests, a major foundational fiction of the United States. Some of the earliest film images of mixed race individuals as treacherous, doomed figures that embody the worst characteristics associated with each race in the U.S. consciousness can be traced to this film. These foreboding images of the mixed race figure reflected pseudoscientific ideas about racial mixing that circulated during the era of slavery.

These ideas emanated from a biological argument called "hybrid degeneracy" that continued to have social impact until the 1930s.[16] According to the theory of hybrid degeneracy, racially mixed peoples were emotionally unstable, irrational, and biologically inferior to the "pure" races of their parents. These ideas held sway in the public, which believed that mixed race individuals were the source of social unrest due to an unhappy combination of ambition and racial degeneracy. Indeed, this is the case in *Birth of a Nation*, in which the mixed race character, Silas Lynch—whose very name inscribes the narrative imperative to eliminate him—has self-confidence considered beyond his lot, combined with all the features of racial degeneracy: rapaciousness, immorality, criminality, and moral and emotional instability. In the template the film created, mulatto men are criminal degenerates while racially mixed women are deceitful and sexually promiscuous; and both are threats to proper white society that must be eliminated or marginalized. In his seminal study of African American representation in film, Donald Bogle borrowed the term coined by literary scholars in describing these characters as tragic mulattoes.

Since then, as Bogle and others have documented, the mulatto character became a staple of classical film whose presence was sure to elicit the emotions of tragedy and melodrama.[17] Tragic mulatta characters, or "light-skinned" black characters that arguably are symbolic stand-ins for mulattas, such as featured in *Imitation of Life* (1934 and 1959), *Showboat* (1951), and *Pinky* (1949), continued the precedent of mixed race figures characterized as mentally unstable at best, and deceptive and selfish at worst. All find their paths to happiness and fulfillment stymied within the course of the narrative.

Mixed race American Indian and Latino characters in classical film similarly tended to reflect negative beliefs regarding the emotional and mental stability of mixed race individuals, as well as U.S. policy and cultural attitudes toward native peoples and immigrants. Not coincidentally, the depiction of mixed American Indians and Latinos is most prevalent in the Western genre. For example, such characters appear in *The Searchers* (1956) and *Duel in the Sun* (1946). In contrast, mixed Asian American and white relationships have been more visible than mixed Asian characters in film for the symbolic political alliances they suggest.[18]

In more recent decades, mixed race characters have enjoyed more nuanced and typically more positive representations in film and television. In contrast to the eras of only tragic and shameful *mestizaje*, such figures have been represented alternately as neutral, ordinary, positive, or even heroic. Multiracial action heroes in fact have become a trend in their own right. Such figures often continue to serve as ethnic enigmas but are also now associated with notions of cultural mastery and other positive characteristics.[19] Vin Diesel, Dwayne Johnson (The Rock), Keanu Reeves, and Jessica Alba are a few of the actors of mixed racial heritage whose recent careers have been boosted by their portrayal of such enigmatic and heroic figures. Perhaps unsurprisingly, several chapters in this collection address these actors, given their emblematic significance as reflections of contemporary discourses on mixed race.

These recent roles are part of an overall boom in the casting of mixed race actors in contemporary film and television, as noted at the onset of this introduction. It cannot be determined how audiences "read" these actors and models with respect to notions of race and ethnicity, however, particularly if they portray characters coded as white. As the contributors of this collection underscore, Hollywood traditions of whiteness also continue to serve as potent frames of understanding, even in films and other media texts that foreground mixed race actors and/or a multicultural aesthetic.

Clearly, mixed race imagery has been an enduring and powerful trope of U.S. culture, deployed to convey popular conceptions about national identity, social norms, and political entitlement. While this history and these trends leave more questions than answers, there is much to learn. By beginning to document and interrogate this evolution in Hollywood film and media culture, the contributors to this collection explore these patterns and rethink normative discourses about the representation of race and racial categories. Many argue that the multiracial individual has increasingly become, paradoxically, the racially overdetermined and indeterminate symbol of an "American" multiracial democracy. In addition, they make a clear case for the need to reinterrogate everything we thought we knew about racial and ethnic representation to better apprehend the meanings of these phenomena in film, television, and popular culture.

## The Structure of the Book

For ease of comprehension and to encourage various lines of scholarly inquiry, this anthology is arranged into thematic sections that hone in on major areas of scholarship within mixed race film and media studies. These include (1) mixed race representation and imagined national identities; (2) norms of miscegenation and the portrayal of mixed race romances and families; (3) Hollywood genres and the evolving representation of mixed race; and (4) biracial and multiracial characters and stars in film and media culture.

I

As noted earlier, in classical Hollywood film, mixed race characters typically upset fictions of social order and coherence; in the process they played a major role in how these narratives imagined the United States as a nation in which race was clearly demarcated and white dominance "made sense." While recent decades have brought about an evolution in the portrayal of mixed race, notions of nation and racial identity continue to be constructed and underscored in such portrayals. In the opening part of the anthology, "Miscegenation: Mixed Race and the Imagined Nation," contributors J. E. Smyth, Camilla Fojas, and Lisa Nakamura explore the role of mixed race in the construction of national identity in popular culture texts, from classical Hollywood films to sites of visual and digital culture.

In "Classical Hollywood and the Filmic Writing of Interracial History, 1931–1939," J. E. Smyth examines the representation of the mixed race woman within the context of U.S. literature and film history. She traces the adaptation of female characters from the novels that became templates of Hollywood's portrayal of mixed race. These novels, including Edna Ferber's *Cimarron*, Helen Hunt Jackson's *Ramona*, and Margaret Mitchell's *Gone with the Wind*, inspired such films as *Cimarron* (1931), *Call Her Savage* (1932), *Ramona* (four versions, 1910–36), *Jezebel* (1938), and *Gone with the Wind* (1939). Smyth ultimately argues for a more nuanced interpretation of the racial and sexual discourses circulating in film between 1931 and 1939.

In the next chapter, Camilla Fojas explores another aspect of the construction of U.S. social norms with respect to mixed race through an analysis of classic Westerns that take place on or near U.S. borders. In "Mixed Race Frontiers: Border Westerns and the Limits of 'America,'" Fojas explores the indefinite nationality and social status of mixed race Native American and Latino characters in the post–Civil War era Westerns *Duel in the Sun* (1946) and *Rio Lobo* (1970). Westerns are notorious for presenting Native Americans and Mexicans as racialized outsiders and social problems, an association that circulated during and after the Civil War; less common is the depiction of racially ambiguous or mixed characters with divided loyalties. Fojas argues that in *Duel in the Sun* and *Rio*

*Lobo*, multiracial characters provide crucial opportunities for representing the reunification of a nation in conflict, and that their social integration represents not just the possibility of national reunification but the potential for U.S. dominance on a world scale.

Lisa Nakamura moves the exploration of mixed race and U.S. identities to the Internet in "Mixedfolks.com: 'Ethnic Ambiguity,' Celebrity Outing, and the Internet." In her study, Nakamura focuses on how "closeted" mixed race stars are viewed by fans, particularly through one Web site's construction of a "mixed folks" identity community centered on celebrity mixed race outing. She notes that while the recent vogue for ethnically ambiguous actors might seem a blessing to the multitudes of mixed race actors looking for work, this creates an ironic situation for actors who pass all too well as white. Web sites like Mixedfolks.com attempt to resolve this dilemma by listing actors, musicians, and other mixed race celebrities and connecting them to their "hidden" racial backgrounds, thus outing performers such as Dean Cain (Asian), Jennifer Beals and Vin Diesel (African American), and Madeleine Stowe and Lynda Carter (Latina). Nakamura posits that the site identifies racial heritage as a source of inspiration and identification that must be made to "represent," despite performers' disavowal or failure to acknowledge a nonwhite racial identity.

## II

As noted earlier, the depiction of mixed race relationships has undergone dramatic changes over the decades but still is largely underresearched. In "Identity, Taboo, and 'Spice': Screening Mixed Race Romance and Families," Heidi Ardizzone, Robb Hernandez, and Kent A. Ono make contributions in this regard, in chapters that explore the history and contemporary portrayals of interracial romantic and sexual relationships and families in a variety of contexts.

Heidi Ardizzone opens this part with "Catching Up with History: *Night of the Quarter Moon*, the Rhinelander Case, and Interracial Marriage in 1959." In this chapter, Ardizzone argues that the film typically pinpointed as groundbreaking for its portrayal of interracial romance, *Guess Who's Coming to Dinner* (1967), was preceded by an equally important film eight years prior, Hugo Haas's *Night of the Quarter Moon* (1959). As she notes, it was the first Hollywood portrayal of an interracial marriage in which no one passes, no one dies or suffers a tragic downfall, and the couple touches passionately. She explores this landmark film in the legal and social context and in relation to other portrayals of black-white marriage in the 1950s and 1960s, declaring *Night of the Quarter Moon* the first to present interracial marriage as a democratic right.

In "A Window into a Life Uncloseted: 'Spice Boy' Imaginings in New Queer Cinema," Robb Hernandez explores the evolution of cinematic representation of mixed race couples in gay-oriented independent films. He explores how what has been dubbed New Queer Cinema of the 1990s portrayed interracial gay couples in which one partner was Latino in *Billy's Hollywood Screen Kiss* (1998) and *Trick* (1999), as well as conducting a reception study with Latino gay male viewers to illuminate how they interpreted the pairings in these films. He argues that New Queer Cinema, dominated by white male directors, often deployed a Spice Boy archetype, a pan-Latino exotic other, as the object of desire of the Anglo male. Notably, Hernandez found that Latino gay male viewers who participated in the study uniformly identified with the white protagonists in the films, demonstrating their embeddedness within a "gay marketplace of desire." He posits that such viewers adopt a disidentificatory position to negotiate mixed raced desire on and off screen.

This is followed by Kent A. Ono's exploration of a contemporary mixed race family in "The Biracial Subject as Passive Receptacle for Japanese American Memory in *Come See the Paradise*." In this chapter, Ono focuses in particular on the narrative function of the half-Japanese child in Alan Parker's film *Come See the Paradise*, released in 1990. Ono asserts that in the film Mini, the child of a Japanese American woman and an Irish American man, serves as the witness to a particular Nisei (second-generation Japanese American) scenario, that of the incarceration of Japanese Americans in the United States during World War II. He argues that in this regard Mini is both a receptacle for Japanese American memory and the salve that can heal the scarred divide between Japanese America and white American society. Ono asserts that Mini otherwise is devoid of agency, however. Her position as a child and the version of history stressed in the story line—which emphasizes the heroism of white men in saving powerless Japanese Americans—construct the biracial subject not only as vulnerable and naïve but also as having no distinct or unique consciousness.

## III

Genre criticism offers an important avenue for the examination of mixed race representation and performance. In particular, it offers the opportunity to explore films and television programs in relation to the social concerns and norms of the era in which they were produced and consumed. As socially constructed racial boundaries have shifted in the United States, so naturally have the representations of race and mixed race in genre films. And as noted by the authors in this part, "Genre, Mixed Race, and Evolving Racial Identities," certain genres, such as science fiction and action film, have offered particularly fruitful forums for depicting and exploring mixed race and its ramifications.

In "Race Mixing and the Fantastic: Lineages of Identity and Genre in Contemporary Hollywood," Adam Knee argues that fantasy films have functioned as a significant popular means of working through cultural tensions and aspirations regarding racial and ethnic mixing, given the singular latitude their narratives offer for dramatizing interactions and amalgamations among all manner of beings. In illustration, Knee conducts a comparative analysis of how issues of racial, ethnic, and cultural mixing have been articulated in three films within the realm of the fantastic, the horror film *Jeepers Creepers* (2001), the vampire film *Underworld* (2003), and the cinematic remake of the popular magic-themed television series *Bewitched* (2005).

Jane Park continues the exploration of mixed race and genre in "Virtual Race: The Racially Ambiguous Action Hero in *The Matrix* and *Pitch Black*." In this chapter, Park examines the role of the racially ambiguous hero in two science fiction action films released at the turn of the millennium: *The Matrix* (1999) and *Pitch Black* (2000). Park explores the popularity of these characters in the context of the history of nonwhite and mixed race actors in Hollywood. She argues that these multiracial representations offer new ways of thinking about racial identity, difference, and discrimination.

Finally, in "From Blaxploitation to Mixploitation: Male Leads and Changing Mixed Race Identities," Gregory T. Carter explores connections between Blaxploitation films of the 1970s and contemporary action films that he terms "Mixploitation" through analysis of the careers and public images of three mixed race actors whose careers span two decades, Ron O'Neal, Vin Diesel, and The Rock (Dwayne Johnson). As he notes, Ron O'Neal played the lead in the Blaxploitation classic *Super Fly* (1972). In accordance with the times, his racial makeup was never an issue; he was merely black, even if his physical appearance indicated a mixed racial background. Vin Diesel and The Rock rose to fame two decades later; Carter argues that, in contrast, these stars' mixed heritage is as central to their public images as their film roles. In his explication of the changes and constants that connect these two periods and genres, Carter notes that both Blaxploitation and Mixploitation purvey exceptional masculinities for their times, shackle actors with narrow racial identities, and feature unmistakably mixed, (part-) black men, even if the latter genre avoids focus on racial issues.

## IV

In the final part, "Generation Mix? Shifting Meanings of Mixed Race Figures," we compile the work of scholars whose work interrogates the mediated depiction of mixed race characters and actors in film and television. While all discern an evolution of representation since the era of the tragic mulatta, they also uncover ambivalence in contemporary depictions in film and media culture.

Aisha D. Bastiaans revisits the mulatta figure in her contribution, "Detecting Difference in *Devil in a Blue Dress*: The Mulatta Figure, Noir, and the Cinematic Reification of Race." In her investigation Bastiaans focuses on the character of Daphne Monet, played by biracial actress Jennifer Beals in the film *Devil in a Blue Dress* (1995). She explores Monet's significance within the context of the neonoir film genre and the 1990s backlash against civil rights gains, as well as the implications of casting Beals in the role of Monet. Bastiaans argues that we, the audience, are detectives who actively participate in decoding the mystery of the mixed race character passing for white. She concludes that the film ultimately reinscribes historical anxieties over post–Civil War race relations, with the mulatta character playing a crucial role in this regard.

While contemporary shifts in representation have provided opportunities for mixed race actors, color lines arguably still exist in Hollywood. In "Mixed Race in Latinowood: Latino Stardom and Ethnic Ambiguity in the Era of *Dark Angels*," Mary Beltrán examines this phenomenon in relation to stars of partial Latino descent. What are the implications of the popularity of a number of mixed Latino stars with respect to imagined racial borders and notions of what it means to be Latino today? Beltrán takes up this question in an analysis of the career and promotional discourses that have surrounded Jessica Alba (of Mexican, French, and Danish heritage) and Rosario Dawson (of Puerto Rican, Afro-Cuban, Irish, and Native American heritage). As she argues, the two stars' careers illustrate the media industries' continued privileging of actors seen as assimilable to standards of whiteness, while they also demonstrate a confusion regarding how to utilize mixed race performers, and the racialization of even actors who attempt to embrace a multiply-raced identity in their public image.

In "Mixed Race on the Disney Channel: From *Johnnie Tsunami* through *Lizzie McGuire* and Ending with *The Cheetah Girls*," Angharad N. Valdivia explores the evolution of mixed race figures with regard to how it is manifest on children's television today. Valdivia presents the results of a comparative analysis of the construction of race and ethnicity in contemporary Disney television programming featuring mixed race characters. These shows and characters include *Johnnie Tsunami* (1999), in which a Hawaiian father forces his son to separate from all things Hawaiian; *The Cheetah Girls* (2003), in which the cheetah print functions as a signifier for mixed race; racially mixed characters in *That's So Raven!* (2002); and the racially diverse casts of *Lizzie McGuire* (2001) and *Sister, Sister* (1994–99). Through close readings of these shows in relation to Disney's historical depiction of race, for example, in *Dumbo* (1941) and *Song of the South* (1946), Valdivia ponders the implications of recent televisual reflections on the emotionally loaded conceptions of mixed racial heritage.

Finally, LeiLani Nishime considers the evolution of the mixed race figure in relation to the cinematic storyworld of *The Matrix* trilogy (*The Matrix* [1999], *The Matrix Reloaded* [2003], and *Matrix Revolutions* [2003]) and its Eurasian star, Keanu Reeves. In "*The Matrix* Trilogy, Keanu Reeves, and Multiraciality at the End of Time," Nishime analyzes representations of bi- and multiraciality in the science fiction trilogy. As she notes, *The Matrix* ends with a monologue by Reeves as the protagonist, Neo, in which he promises that he will show everyone caught in the matrix "a world without rules and controls, without border or boundaries. A world where anything is possible." This fluid world of possibilities is also the world promised the filmgoer in promotional texts, while Reeves himself provided a visual metaphor for the hybrid future. Nishime argues that the trilogy is unable to ultimately transcend boundaries into a utopic future "without rules and controls," however. She posits that it instead illustrates the contradictions inherent in current debates wherein fear of the catastrophic results of racial mixing exists at the same time as utopic predictions that racial mixing will make race, and all attendant problems, disappear. Her reading of the popular film trilogy provides a snapshot of the contradictory ways in which mixed race people are represented and repressed, exploited and celebrated in contemporary film.

This collection documents the emergence of a new era in the popular cultural depictions of race and racial relations. Mixed race characters and relationships have gained more favorable positions in Hollywood film and media culture, but they have also become more useful to a nationalist portrait of the United States. That is, depictions of multiraciality are often instrumentalized as symbols of the liberal democratic culture of the United States in which the mixing of races and cultures is used to present the United States as a model of multiculturalism and globalism. But the depiction of multiraciality also opens up the possibility for new models of identification, new understandings of race and ethnicity, and new models for racial and ethnic relations. As these chapters indicate, the status of racial mixing is continually changing, and each new cultural representation and media event adds another angle and another level of meaning to the complex history of race and ethnicity in the United States. We hope that this collection will contribute to emerging discourses and discussions of racial mixing and become a template for further work and new studies on the topic.

## NOTES

1. Danzy Senna, "The Mulatto Millennium," in *Half and Half*, ed. Claudine O'Hearn (New York: Pantheon, 1998), 12–27. "Generation Mix" was coined by the MAVIN Foundation, a nonprofit organization that advocates for mixed race individuals and families and aims to raise awareness of racial identity issues. See www.mavinfoundation.org.

2. Ella Shohat and Robert Stam, *Unthinking Eurocentrism: Multiculturalism and the Media* (London: Routledge, 1994).

3. Michael Omi and Howard Winant, *Racial Formation in the United States* (London: Routledge, 1994).

4. Ursula M. Brown, *The Interracial Experience: Growing Up Black/White Racially Mixed in the United States* (Westport, CT: Praeger, 2000), 36–37.

5. For more information on tragic mulatto/mulatta figures in nineteenth- and twentieth-century literature, see Suzanne Bost's *Mulattas and Mestizas: Representing Mixed Identities in the Americas, 1850–2000* (Athens: University of Georgia Press, 2005); and Eva Allegra Raimon, *The Tragic Mulatta Revisited: Race and Nationalism in Nineteenth-Century Antislavery Fiction* (New Brunswick, NJ: Rutgers University Press, 2004).

6. Further information on the enforcement of the "one-drop" rule can be found in Ian F. Haney Lopez, *White by Law: The Legal Construction of Race* (New York: NYU Press, 1997).

7. Maria P. P. Root, *The Multiracial Experience: Racial Borders as a Significant Frontier in Race Relations* (Thousand Oaks, CA: Sage, 1996), xviii.

8. Maria P. P. Root, "Multiracial Asians: Models of Ethnic Identity," in *Race, Identity, and Citizenship: A Reader*, ed. Rodolfo D. Torres, Louis F. Mirón, and Jonathan Xavier Inda (Malden, MA: Blackwell, 1999), 158–68.

9. Clint C. Wilson II and Félix Gutiérrez, *Race, Multiculturalism, and the Media* (Thousand Oaks, CA: Sage, 1995), 87.

10. Root, *The Multiracial Experience*, xiv. As Root notes, the 1960s boom now "practically guarantees that anyone living in a large U.S. city knows someone who is racially mixed."

11. U.S. Census Bureau, "The Two or More Races Population: 2000," November 2001, www.census.gov/prod/2001pubs/c2kbr01-6.pdf.

12. Recent works include—but are not limited to—Ursula M. Brown's *The Interracial Experience*; Rachel F. Moran's *Interracial Intimacy: The Regulation of Race and Romance* (Chicago: University of Chicago Press, 2003); Marion Kilson's *Claiming Place: Biracial Young Adults of the Post–Civil Rights Era* (Westport, CT: Bergin and Garvey, 2001); Werner Sollors's *Interracialism: Black-White Intermarriage in American History, Literature, and Law* (New York: Oxford University Press, 2000); Renee C. Romano's *Race Mixing: Black-White Marriage in Postwar America* (Cambridge, MA: Harvard University Press, 2003); Jon Michael Spencer's *New Colored People: The Mixed-Race Movement in America* (New York: NYU Press, 2000); and the edited collections *The Sum of Our Parts: Mixed-Heritage Asian Americans* (Philadelphia: Temple University Press, 2001), ed. Theresa Williams-Leon and Cynthia Nakashima; '*Mixed Race' Studies: A Reader* (London: Routledge, 2004), ed. by Jayne O. Ifekwunigwe; *New Faces in a Changing America: Multiracial Identity in the 21st Century* (Thousand Oaks, CA: Sage, 2002), ed. Loretta I. Winters and Herman Debose; and *Mixed Race America and the Law: A Reader* (New York: NYU Press, 2003), ed. Kevin R. Johnson.

13. Leon E. Wynter, *American Skin: Pop Culture, Big Business, and the End of White America* (New York: Crown, 2002).

14. Gina Marchetti, *Romance and the "Yellow Peril": Race, Sex, and Discursive Strategies in Hollywood Fiction* (Berkeley: University of California Press,1994); Susan Courtney, *Hollywood Fantasies of Miscegenation: Spectacular Narratives of Gender and Race* (Princeton, NJ: Princeton University Press, 2004).

15. Marchetti, *Romance and the "Yellow Peril."*

16. Brown, *The Interracial Experience*, 37.

17. See Donald Bogle, *Toms, Coons, Mulattoes, Mammies and Bucks: An Interpretive History of Blacks in Films*, 4th ed. (New York: Continuum, 2001), 9; Jane M. Gaines, *Fire and Desire: Mixed-Race Movies in the Silent Era* (Chicago: University of Chicago Press, 2001); Freda Scott Giles, "From Melodrama to the Movies: The Tragic Mulatto as a Type Character," in *American Mixed Race: A Culture of Microdiversity*, ed. Naomi Zack (Lanham, MD: Rowman and Littlefield, 1995), 64;

Susan Courtney, *Hollywood Fantasies of Miscegenation*; Claudine C. O'Hearn, ed., *Half and Half: Writers on Growing Up Biracial and Bicultural* (New York: Pantheon, 1998);

18. In fact, mixed race Asian actors have typically performed roles as Asians. Some notable examples are Nancy Kwan and more recently Russell Wong.

19. Mary Beltrán, "The New Hollywood Racelessness: Only the Fast, Furious (and Multi-racial) Will Survive," *Cinema Journal* 44, no. 2 (Winter 2005): 50–67; LeiLani Nishime, "The Mulatto Cyborg: Imagining a Multiracial Future," Cinema Journal 44, no. 2 (Winter 2005): 34–49.

‖‖‖‖‖‖‖‖‖‖‖‖‖‖‖‖‖‖‖‖‖‖‖‖‖‖‖‖‖‖‖‖‖‖‖‖‖‖‖‖‖‖‖‖‖‖‖‖‖‖‖

# Part I

# Miscegenation
## *Mixed Race and the Imagined Nation*

‖‖‖‖‖‖‖‖‖‖‖‖‖‖‖‖‖‖‖‖‖‖‖‖‖‖‖‖‖‖‖‖‖‖‖‖‖‖‖‖‖

# Classical Hollywood and the Filmic Writing of Interracial History, 1931–1939

## J. E. Smyth

For decades, film historians have argued that classical Hollywood cinema portrayed the past as "male, white, and American."[1] This does have a certain relevance for studio-era biopics (*Abraham Lincoln*, 1930; *Alexander Hamilton*, 1931; *The Mighty Barnum*, 1934; *Diamond Jim*, 1935; *The Story of Alexander Graham Bell*, 1939), which deftly transposed the nineteenth-century heroic discourse of masculine biography to the screen. It was a historical genre dominated, with a few rare exceptions, by more white American men.[2] During the 1930s, however, Hollywood adapted the historical novels of several prominent American women, from the classic work of Helen Hunt Jackson to the popular novels of Edna Ferber and Margaret Mitchell. Hollywood's adaptation of this genre not only borrowed the "mixed" historical attributes of the imagined past (accuracy of detail, sociocultural histories "from below," and fictional protagonists) but also frequently structured the vision of that past around the experiences of mixed blood Americans. In 1931, the top-rated American historical film, an adaptation of Ferber's *Cimarron*, had a mixed race hero, half-Cherokee newspaperman and adventurer, Yancey Cravat (Richard Dix). As the decade wore on, Hollywood increasingly experimented with racially transgressive heroines drawn from the classics of American literature like Jackson's Ramona Moreno (*Ramona*, Twentieth Century-Fox, 1936). But the studios had a wider range of contemporary resources in the historical fiction of best-selling novelists Edna Ferber (*Show Boat*, 1926; produced by Universal in 1936) and Margaret Mitchell (*Gone with the Wind*, 1936; produced by Selznick International/MGM in 1939). Broadway, Hollywood's other major story market, served as the testing ground for both the Oscar Hammerstein/Jerome Kern musical version of Ferber's novel and Owen Davis's antebellum narrative of New Orleans belle Julie Marston (*Jezebel*, 1933; produced by Warner Brothers in 1938).

These narratives would become icons of Hollywood's Western and Southern film genres. However, rather than exemplifying the racial binarism endemic to these genres (red versus white on the frontier, black versus white in nineteenth-century Southern society), many of these classical Hollywood films subverted traditional notions of national history, gender, and race and classic "tragic mulatto" stereotypes.[3] Film and cultural historians from Robert Berkhofer to Richard Slotkin have identified two roles for the Native American in Hollywood—the vicious redskin and the passive, "vanishing American"—yet these characters of partial indigenous descent do not conform to either type.[4] Similarly, film and cultural historians from Thomas Cripps to Linda Williams have cataloged the racist Hollywood offenses directed at black Americans onscreen, yet the mulatto women depicted in these films are neither motherly Aunt Jemimas nor silent servants.[5] The classic trope of the "tragic" mixed race woman, first formulated in 1937 by African American literary critic Sterling Brown,[6] was sexualized, passive, doomed. In contrast, these mixed race protagonists are not historically doomed—they are active survivors.

Bibliographies on Hollywood censorship and ethnic and racial stereotyping have established the studio era's conservative, even racist attitudes, yet they cannot explain the surprising presence of mixed race film protagonists who destabilize traditional racial hierarchies.[7] Although the Production Code was vigorous in its suppression of themes of miscegenation and sexual aberrance,[8] unlike the contemporary race film, *Imitation of Life* (1934), historical films *Cimarron, Ramona, Show Boat, Jezebel,* and *Gone with the Wind* all escaped rigorous racial censorship.[9] These films may be five exceptions to the Hollywood rule, but they were A-feature, prestige productions by five different major studios. Screenwriters adapted scripts from texts that, in all but one case, were the work of female historical novelists. In a genre supposedly dominated by the writing and experience of white men, the narratives focused on the experience of women and mixed race Americans.

This study of mixed race heroines in classical Hollywood questions the critical symbiosis that has linked classical Hollywood cinema to traditional white patriarchal narratives, and instead underscores the film industry's unique engagement with the history of American race and sexuality at the height of the so-called classical Hollywood era.[10] Hollywood's interracial history was written not only in the texts of popular historical fiction, scripts, production and publicity records, and reviews but also with purely visual historiographical tools specific to cinema—editing, lighting, color, costume design, and makeup. This mixed, filmic writing of interracial history drew on both textual and cinematic modes, creating a predominantly feminine hybrid strong enough to unravel America's racial and sexual norms.[11]

## Biracial Fictions

Although until the late twentieth century, mainstream historians virtually ignored the experiences of mulattas and mestizas, biracial women have a long history as protagonists in American literature. As Suzanne Bost pointed out in her study of mixed race literary representation, "Throughout popular culture and literature, debates about the nature of mixed-race identity are mapped out on the body of a woman because thinking about racial mixing inevitably leads to questions of sex and reproduction."[12] Women also have the unique ability to embody the past, present, and future of American multiracialism. Mixed race women not only are the product of white male rape and the exploitation of Native and African American women, but also have the potential to bear mixed race children. Over time, racial mixture is therefore rendered a natural, integral component of American development and not a result of aberrant male violence.

In American literature, light-skinned, "mixed" heroines are frequently indistinguishable from their white sisters, challenging the validity of race as a visual and cultural category. Many mixed race heroines in nineteenth-century literature act in contemporary dramas about slavery and the myth of racial purity structuring American "exceptionalism" (*Clotel*, 1853; *Zoe*, 1859, etc.). But others are set distinctly within the American past. The first mixed race heroine in American literature was Cora Munro, James Fenimore Cooper's tragic West Indian–Scottish heroine in *The Last of the Mohicans: A Narrative of 1757*. Hollywood filmmakers have had a long-standing attraction to *The Last of the Mohicans*; it was adapted for the screen in 1909, 1936, and 1992. However, beyond director Jacques Tourneur's projection of the innocent romance between Cora and the Mohican brave Uncas in the 1920 version, none of the other three feature film adaptations directly addressed Cora's biracial ancestry.[13]

For the majority of literary critics, Cooper's novel is the definitive American racial myth. Although Cora and the Mohican warrior Uncas are the most attractive characters in the novel, *The Last of the Mohicans* appears to sanction their deaths and to celebrate the birth of a new, white America.[14] Despite Cora's eventual death, she figures as Cooper's most successful "historian" within the novel. In the novel's second half, Cooper employed multiple narrators, each inflected by racial and sexual perspectives excluded from traditional frontier historiography. Magua, Chingachgook, Uncas, and Tamenund are the principal historians after the massacre of Fort William Henry. Yet it is the biracial Cora Munro who recounts to the Delaware elder, Tamenund, the only true "mixed" oral history of events leading to her capture.[15] While Hawkeye and Magua present irreconcilable perspectives on the abductions, Cora admits the cruelty of her European people while appealing to the superior justice of Tamenund to free her sister. With Cora, Cooper created a new form of historical interpretation, one that acknowledged multiple versions of and attitudes toward the past.

Although Cooper's doomed Cora helped to create the myth of the "tragic mulatta" in American literature, mixed race heroines were not always punished for their racial transgression, eradicated from the narrative of American history, or excluded from Hollywood's adaptations. Like *The Last of the Mohicans*, *Ramona* is one of Hollywood's most enduring literary resources, filmed in 1910, 1916, 1928, and 1936. Helen Hunt Jackson's Ramona Moreno lives through the expulsion of the California Indians from their land, her eviction from her farm, and the death of her Native American husband, Alessandro. Like Cooper, Jackson was preoccupied with the history of racial mixing and the expulsion of Native Americans and focused on the experiences of a mixed race woman to destabilize traditional narratives of the West. The history of *Ramona* began in 1881 with the publication of Jackson's history of the U.S. government's policy toward Native Americans, *A Century of Dishonor*.[16] It was one of the first attempts to indict the government's policy with the tools and rhetoric of a thoroughly researched and argued history. But Jackson's book was largely ignored by the public, and she later adopted the form of the novel to capture her audience, writing *Ramona* (1884).[17] As she wrote to her friends Antonio and Mariana Coronel in November 1883, "I am going to write a novel, in which will be set forth some Indian experiences to move people's hearts. People will read a novel when they will not read serious books."[18]

In writing her novel, Jackson adhered closely to a number of obscure personal histories from Southern California's recent past.[19] From local stories of mixed race unions, ill-fated love affairs, and racial prejudice, Jackson chronicled the life of Ramona, ward to the rich Morenos, a Californio ranching family. But Ramona is neither white nor Spanish-Mexican; she is half California Indian. When Senora Moreno tells her this, Ramona leaves her protected existence and the love of the Morenos' only son for life with her native people. She marries Alessandro, an Indian chief's son, sees their land taken by white settlers, her people killed by those same "Americans," and her husband shot by another white man for horse stealing. Ramona's life captured the attention of an American public indifferent to traditional histories and exposés of government abuse. However, as historian Dydia DeLyser has pointed out, Jackson's historical structure appealed to the public's sense of nostalgia for the old Spanish Californio days rather than to a contemporary sense of racial injustice.[20] Jackson's biracial heroine connected white Americans to their Native American predecessors, making the racial "other" less strange.

Cooper's and Jackson's twentieth-century descendants, Edna Ferber and Margaret Mitchell, were two women who once dreamed of attending college to study dramatics and history before poverty and family obligations restricted their futures. During the 1920s and early 1930s, Edna Ferber was one of America's most financially successful novelists. She had a proclivity for writing generational narratives set in America's past, such as *So Big* (1924; filmed in 1925, 1932, and 1953) and *Show Boat* (1926; filmed in 1929 [partial silent], 1936, and 1951), and for constructing semibiographical stage hits with George S. Kaufman like *The Royal Family of Broadway* (1928; filmed 1930). In 1926, she created Julie Laverne, the tragic biracial actress in *Show Boat*.[21] A "passive" beauty married to a white man, Julie is forced to leave the showboat troupe when outsiders discover her black ancestry and transgression of the southern antimiscegenation laws. Yet in Ferber's novel, Julie's history of racial discrimination and her close relationship to young, white Magnolia Hawks are incidental to Magnolia's ensuing struggle for independence and financial security. Ferber's next historical novel, *Cimarron* (1929), was more active in its detonation of American myths. She created a multiracial hero, mixed-Cherokee/white pioneer and Indian rights crusader, Yancey Cravat.[22]

Margaret Mitchell once admitted that she had initially wanted to write a history of Georgia during the Civil War and Reconstruction eras.[23] However, she knew that it would never sell or be read beyond her circle of friends. Like Douglas Southall Freeman, Pulitzer Prize–winning author of the biography *Robert E. Lee* (1934), she had worked as a news reporter, often combining her historical and literary interests by writing Civil War articles for her Atlanta paper.[24] But unlike Freeman, she had little money and no university degree. She was also a woman. The worlds of the public and academic historian were closed to her, so she did her best to please herself and her potential public, constructing a fictional narrative to support her historical knowledge. In her letters to friends, colleagues, and fans, Mitchell emphasized both her meticulous research and her historical arguments about the Civil War and Reconstruction.[25] In the end, Mitchell's interviews of aging veterans, her treks though the old battlefields of the Army of Tennessee, and her years in the archives produced a heroine who preferred the company of black slave children, who was better understood by her Mammy than her mother, who consistently flouted sexual conventions, and whose most sympathetic friendships were with two racial and class hybrids, the "mustee" (mixed African American and Cherokee) slave woman Dilcey and southern cracker Will Benteen. Scarlett O'Hara was nobody's idea of a magnolia-white belle.

In Ramona Moreno, Yancey Cravat, and Scarlett O'Hara, three of America's most prominent female historical novelists created protagonists who transgressed racial boundaries supporting eighteenth- and nineteenth-century American history, Manifest Destiny, and the discourses of racial supremacy, difference, and slavery. Their marginal stories are central to these "classic" histories of westward conquest and slavery. Moreover, racial ambiguity is amplified in the film adaptations through narrational strategies, cinematography, and costume, until the interracial protagonist ultimately discloses the performed nature of the nation's most deeply cherished racial and sexual myths of frontier and antebellum society.

## Race and Manifest Destiny in Hollywood

RKO's *Cimarron* (1931) was the first major prestige Western to have a mixed race hero.[26] From the beginning of her historical epic of nineteenth- and twentieth-century Oklahoma history, Edna Ferber complicated the racial discourse of the frontier and its heroes. She wrote of Yancey Cravat, "They say he has Indian blood in him. They say he has an Indian wife somewhere, and a lot of papooses. Cherokee. . . .They said evidences of his Indian blood were plain; look at his skin, his hair, his manner of walking."[27]

*Still from* Cimarron.

When screenwriter Howard Estabrook read Ferber's novel, he under-lined and annotated the passages that hinted at this racial mixture, de-termined to focus on them.[28] Estabrook's script emphasized both Yanc-ey's Cherokee ancestry and his active sympathy with his people. Yancey was remarkable for other reasons. He was a major force in the shaping of Oklahoma history, literally helping to write it with his newspaper, the *Oklahoma Wigwam.* Although his wife, Sabra, had an equal role in con-structing the headlines and organizing news for public consumption, it was Yancey who actively criticized the government's policy toward the Native American tribes of Oklahoma. *Cimarron* was unique to Ameri-can western historical fiction in actually portraying two groups tradition-ally excluded from the profession of making and writing western history, mixed blood Native Americans and women.

Yancey's racial identity is contested and redefined throughout the nar-rative. His dark complexion and Cherokee war whoops function with his white hat and expansionist rhetoric. "Just what does 'Cimarron' mean?" one character asks Sabra derisively. The film confronts the term's spectrum of multiracialism when Isaiah, a young black boy who has stowed away from Wichita and idolizes Yancey, comes to church in Osage dressed up as a pint-sized version of his hero, right down to the heeled boots, coat, and hat. Yancey laughs at his youthful mirror image, but Sabra, schooled in the post–Civil War South, does not find this racial mixing amusing.

What does it mean to be an interracial hero on the frontier? Consider first the theoretical structure of the Western, both as a representation of the national past and as a genre. Rather than interpreting or critiquing the past, classical Hollywood Westerns allegedly reflect a mythic view of the history of frontier conquest and settlement.[29] Myths are founded on binary opposites, and Westerns (garden and wilderness, civilization and savagery, cowboy and Indian) are no exception. These narrative elements, set in perpetual conflict, also form the structure of genre. Despite occasional changes in audience taste, film genres are remarkably resilient, and the Western in particular seems to have an inherent, mythic resistance to change.[30] In terms of the rigid tenets of film genre and the structure of the Hollywood Western, there is little room to consider interracial heroes, figures who transgress not only racial barriers but also the distinct categories of western myth. They are at best marginal figures beside the pure-blooded western archetypes of cowboy and Indian, embarrassing reminders of the consequences of racial expansion and the underside of Manifest Destiny. But *Cimarron*'s hero is neither the archetypal, pure-blooded Anglo gunfighter cleansing the West of Indians nor the noble, equally pure-blooded Indian condemned to extinction in a changing nation. He also lives beyond the circumscribed boundaries of traditional frontier myths and historical periodization, playing an active part in Oklahoma history through the state's oil boom at the turn of the century and the Great War.[31]

Although the film was the most honored of 1931, winning awards for best picture and screenplay, no other Western of the Depression era pursued *Cimarron*'s historical experiments with interracial heroes. Instead, interracial women dominated the box office. In 1932, Fox reconsidered the biracial Western woman in *Call Her Savage* and later in 1936 with the prestigious Technicolor version of *Ramona*. *Call Her Savage* has an extensive covered wagon sequence narrating the illicit relationship between the heroine's white mother and Native American father; *Ramona* was the classic narrative of the transition from Californio to white society. Portraying Clara Bow as a mixed race woman certainly resonated with slander campaigns in the *Coast Reporter* and *Photoplay*'s more subtle hints of the actress's alleged sexual "aberrance,"[32] but reviewers like Mordaunt Hall of the *New York Times* only referred to Nasa Springer's (Bow's) race cautiously, emphasizing her "fiery temper" and attraction to "half-breeds" and closing mysteriously, "How Nasa came by her fiendish temper and her choice for a second husband [a mixed blood] are retailed in the closing scenes."[33]

Visually, Native American ancestry did not show in the white faces of actresses Clara Bow and Loretta Young (Ramona). There was no physical visual marker to distinguish them from their white cohorts. According to film historian Gwendolyn Audrey Foster, "The [Hollywood] cinema is . . .the garment center of white fabrication."[34] Yet in spite of the Hollywood cinema's alleged construction and preservation of whiteness, the filmmakers made no attempt to paint racial difference on the faces of these "mixed blood" protagonists. When these women discovered and adopted their heritage, they simply dressed the part. Race was therefore something to be performed through costume, and is presented as an essentially unstable visual and historical construct. More than the three earlier black-and-white versions, Darryl F. Zanuck's Technicolor version of *Ramona* (1936) heightened the theme of racial injustice through the use of color. Ramona's skin is no darker than that of any of the other Anglo women in the film; without the justification of "color" difference, the discourse of Manifest Destiny falls apart and the vicious expansion in California is revealed as capitalist theft.

That same year, producer Edward Small had the opportunity to project African American and Anglo interracial mixing in his adaptation of Cooper's *Last of the Mohicans*, but screenwriter John Balderston sublimated Cora's biracial ancestry in order to focus on the more established historical conflicts of the French and Indian War. Race was evidently not serious enough for traditional historical epics or too serious for the censors (Stahl's contemporary "miscegenation" narrative, *Imitation of Life* [1934] had raised a furor with the Production Code Administration [PCA] two years earlier).[35] While Hollywood whitewashed Cora Munro's mulatta identity, filmmakers were evidently less worried about mixed blood mestiza (mixed Indian or Latino and white) heroines. As film historian Thomas Doherty mused about the mixed blood heroine in *Call Her Savage*, "In limited quantities, Indian blood added a sexually potent spice to pioneer stock."[36] But Darryl Zanuck had claimed, "I was severely criticized by my associates as well as by the newspaper columnists for imagining that Young could play a half-Indian."[37] Was Young too popular a Fox star to risk her career on a potentially damaging role? Was she too white? Was she just too inexperienced for the role? Or was her star persona, lacking Clara Bow's uninhibited, even transgressive reputation, too mild and uninteresting? Contemporary reviews acknowledged both *Ramona*'s overt criticism of American frontier policies and its portrayal of racial hybridity, but were not hostile. The film reviewer for *Time* wrote: "Ramona herself is half-historical, half fictional, half-white and half Indian, but there is nothing half-way in the manner in which Twentieth Century-Fox has handled her biography. It has used the simple framework as a bitter disquisition on the traditional white methods of dealing with Indians, civilized or raw."[38]

With the publication of *Gone with the Wind* in the summer of 1936 and the release of James Whale's adaptation of *Show Boat*, Hollywood's emphasis on the biracial woman in U.S. history shifted south. As Thomas Cripps has noted, whereas the 1929 partial sound version of *Show Boat* "muted" the interracial marriage between Julie and Steve, Whale gave it "high relief."[39] In fact, the 1929 version excised any mention of miscegenation. In Charles Kenyon's script, it is Parthy's maternal jealousy of her daughter's close relationship with Julie that causes all the trouble.[40] In 1936, Hammerstein and Whale followed Ferber's original and the musical's original libretto, focusing on the miscegenation crisis. Like mestiza heroines Nasa Springer and Ramona Moreno, there were no physical markers to darken and distinguish Julie (Helen Morgan) from the rest of the white show-boat boat troupe. As Linda Williams notes, it is only her knowledge of an African American slave song that makes Queenie (Hattie McDaniel) and the audience suspect her of "passing."[41] Julie is a classic tragic mulatta who "pays" for her attempts to thwart the racial system; when her mixed race status is uncovered, she submits to expulsion from the Hawks troupe and later slides into a self-destructive lifestyle in Chicago. But a few years later, Hollywood truly problematized race in two of the most prestigious historical films to date, *Jezebel* and *Gone with the Wind*. With Julie Marston and Scarlett O'Hara, filmmakers broke the racial and sexual molds on more than a narrative level; cinematic elements of script, costume, staging, and cinematography all worked to create a powerful new image of the American woman.

## Jezebels and Rebels

For years, critics of Margaret Mitchell's novel *Gone with the Wind* and David O. Selznick's 1939 production have claimed that both the book and the film preserved racist discourses and color barriers. Historians Catherine Clinton and Elizabeth Fox-Genovese have focused on *Gone with the Wind* as a complex reinscription of racism, laden with demeaning stereotypes and a paternalistic view of slavery, and have dismissed Mitchell's historical claims as a potential way of "whitewashing" the novel's problematic racial stereotyping.[42] Tara McPherson's most recent cultural "reconstruction" of Mitchell and Selznick's work, while acknowledging Scarlett's challenges to the prevailing sexual order in Southern society, has concluded that the heroine's subversion "is possible because it is situated within a scenario that romanticizes the Old South, revamping plantation mythologies."[43] Sarah Gardner has claimed that Mitchell reproduced the prevailing myths about Reconstruction cherished since the nineteenth century and "many of the overtly racist policies" of Populists.[44]

Mitchell's historical perspective on Reconstruction was allegedly patterned after the two most popular racist texts of the early twentieth century, Thomas Dixon's *The Clansman* (1905) and D. W. Griffith's film *The Birth of a Nation* (1915). However, though skeptical of Reconstruction, she did not demonize her black characters as had Dixon. Instead, through a reconfiguration of the family and Scarlett's own physical appearance, Mitchell consistently questions the rigid racial and sexual construction of the white Southern protagonist at the heart of the Civil War epic.

Although Mitchell asserted the primacy of women as historical novelists of the Civil War, citing Mary Johnson (*Cease Firing, The Long Roll*) as her greatest influence, she was a public admirer of the work of Thomas Nelson Page. Page's Reconstruction novel, *Red Rock* (1898), far from anticipating the racism in Thomas Dixon's work, projects a view of a multiracial Southern family/region, both before and after the war. While Dixon envisioned American identity through the consolidation of white solidarity in the North and South, excluding blacks from the new nation, Page's blacks are true family members of the Southern community and unite against the threat of white Northern intervention.[45] Mitchell would bring Page's multiracial family to a new level, emphasizing both the cultural and blood ties between black and "white" Southerners to such an extent that her heroine embodied this Southern hybridity. Via Page, Scarlett is literally part of their family, and Mitchell actively emphasizes Scarlett's ties to the biracial Dilcey.

In *Gone with the Wind*, Mitchell's Scarlett was closer than family to Mammy, Pork, and Dilcey. Though short-tempered with everyone while she struggles for survival at Tara in the winter of 1864, Scarlett treats the stoic and courageous Dilcey, a mustee, as an equal. While Mammy is in despair at the death of Scarlett's mother, Ellen, Dilcey, like Scarlett, grimly

*Bette Davis in* Jezebel.

endures. With her father insane, Scarlett may identify herself as "head of the family," but it is Pork, Dilcey's husband, who becomes the man of the house. Scarlett and Dilcey share Pork in a makeshift Southern household, but one in which traditional patriarchal roles and familial control shift among the three of them. Later, when Scarlett gives Pork her dead father's watch (a man more worthy of inheriting the token symbol as head of house than Scarlett's own son), Pork tells her, "'Ef you wuz jes' half as nice ter w'ite folks as you is ter niggers, Ah spec de worl' would treat you bet-ter.'"[46] Scarlett is both a sexually and racially transgressive force in *Gone with the Wind,* and her kinship and understanding of blacks embody blood and cultural ties that in many ways make her the most powerful biracial heroine in American historical literature.

Scarlett's mixed racial status, though metaphoric, is not unique in contemporary Southern period literature. U.S. literature has a long tradition of popular mulatta heroines, from *Clotel* (1853) to Zora Neale Hurston's *Their Eyes Were Watching God* (1937). Owen Davis's play *Jezebel,* produced on Broadway in 1933, hinted that the emotional kinship between New Orleans belle Julie Marston and black folks was more than skin deep. Race, gender, and rebellion are fused in Julie, who is more at home with her black servants than with her white family. Julie and her maid even favor the same clothes. From the moment she sees that red dress in the New Orleans shop, Julie wants and wears it, making her fiancé remark in horror, "Why, it's more fit to be seen at the Quadroon Ball."[47] She wears a dress only a mulatta, an African American woman, or a prostitute would wear, defies her fiancé, and, in the play, is quite at home watching a cockfight with mulatto and black riverfront "trash." In 1938, with Robert Buckner, John Huston, and director William Wyler's adaptation of Davis's work for Warner Brothers, the cinematic medium made Julie's racial border crossing even more evocative; on screen, Julie's red dress is black

When Jack Warner refused to buy *Gone with the Wind* for Bette Davis, he allowed Hal Wallis to develop *Jezebel* for her instead. As Thomas Schatz has pointed out, by 1938 Davis had established a star reputation built upon "powerful and provocative" screen roles (Mildred in *Of Human Bondage*, 1934; Joyce in *Dangerous*, 1935), but *Jezebel* represented an even more radical change in her work at Warner Brothers.[48] It was a prestige move from modern narratives to the more lavish world of historical productions, and Julie's varied rebellions against the Southern system were as dramatic as Davis's own well-publicized fights with the Warner studio system over the quality of her roles. Screenwriter Robert Buckner brought the time period forward from 1830 to 1852 to emphasize the impending crisis of the Civil War and to capitalize on Julie's obvious resonance with Scarlett O'Hara.

Warner Brothers handled *Jezebel* as its major American prestige effort of 1938.[49] It had all the structural credentials of a major historical film, including Warner Brothers' massive research bibliographies and background for both screenwriters and set designers.[50] Studio publicity took two forms. On the one hand, it emphasized the filmmakers' historical research. *Jezebel*'s research bibliography was extensive, with references to everything from Charles Gayarre's *History of Louisiana* (1866) to Lyle Saxon's more recent popular history, *Fabulous New Orleans* (1928).[51] On the other hand, the film's advertising in the press book indicates that the publicists were wary of marketing *Jezebel* as a full-blown historical film. In order to avoid any highbrow historicism that might keep the average filmgoer away, they stressed the contemporary nature of the story, the heroine's modern outlook, and the up-to-date love scenes. "She's a modern miss in an old-fashioned setting," wrote one of Bette Davis's Julie.[52] So Warner Brothers followed two paths, emphasizing the historical content and relevance and the heroine's modern appeal. But in fusing Julie's modern sexual rebellion against the period conventions with the studio's public claims of historical

accuracy, Warner Brothers made Julie, the embodiment of Southern rebellion, the character with whom most twentieth-century filmgoers could
clearly identify.

*Jezebel* placed the seductive and transgressive power of the South
within national history in the character of Julie Marston; her personal rebellion becomes emblematic of the South's own rebellion against Northern economic repression. Because she flouts sexual conventions by wearing a dress only a black woman or a prostitute would wear, Julie is a true
spokeswoman for all Southern women. Her impassioned descriptions of
the South and her bewitching attempts to lure Preston Dillard, the South-
ern-born Boston banker, back home to her, are some of the film's most
persuasive sequences. When they stand alone in the moonlight, Julie sees
him waver in his devotion for his Northern wife and Northern bank and
cries triumphantly, "We're in your blood, and you'll never forget us."

This was as close as Hollywood filmmakers could get to suggesting Julie's mixed ancestry. Censors, working with scripts, would cut obvious lines
with more direct racial implications. But more often screenwriters could
imply racial mixture through purely visual forms, thus escaping the net of
the Production Code. When Julie performs the Southern belle for Dillard's
wife, she gathers her plantation's black slave children to her on the porch,
and is the only "white" Southerner to join in their songs. Her vividly white
dress not only contrasts with the skin of the slave children but also darkens
her own. Just as in *Ramona*, costume becomes the basic cinematic signifier
of race. Eventually Dillard rejects this appeal of tainted Southern womanhood, even when it is deceptively clad in white. His rejection of Julie's South
and his decision to marry a pure, "untainted" Northern woman signify his
faith in racial purity and industrial order and his rejection of the past. The
decision nearly costs him his life at the end of the film.

Hal Wallis originally assigned Edmund Goulding to direct *Jezebel* before
replacing him with William Wyler. Goulding recorded his view of the film
in some production notes, describing the film as a tale of powerful women
and the perils of "petticoat government."[53] Goulding ignored the fundamental elision of Southern history and the dangerous female that John Huston's
final script and Wyler's direction bring out. Julie is dangerous, a Jezebel, impure, combative, obsessed with memories of her Southern childhood and
love of Preston Dillard; she has a power impossible to exorcise. It is she
who walks out, resolute, fearless, and healthy, to face the pestilence of yellow fever. Just as in *Cimarron*, a biracial protagonist serves as history's most
compelling figure and the living embodiment of its mythic creation.

One cannot simply dismiss Julie as a cinematic embodiment of Sterling Brown's "tragic mulatta." But Brown's work on mixed race protagonists in American literature was unique in the 1930s. *Jezebel's* racially transgressive heroine was virtually unknown to 1930s historiography. William Dunning, Ulrich Phillips, Claude Bowers, and Thomas Dixon still dominated professional and popular historical opinion on race and slavery.[54] W. E. B. Du Bois's *Black Reconstruction* (1935) presented a radically different view of U.S. race relations, but it was not until C. Vann Woodward's *Tom Watson: Agrarian Rebel*, published within months of *Jezebel*, that mainstream American historians began to challenge traditional racial history.[55] However, Woodward dealt with Populist challenges to segregation; he did not question the white symbol of antebellum Southern womanhood.

## *The Black Irish of* Gone with the Wind

Like Julie, Scarlett O'Hara was closer to her black servants than to her white family. While her mother never perceived her rebellious character, Mammy saw and understood. During Scarlett's return to Tara and the impoverished, agonizing months that followed, Mitchell describes her doing tasks that slaves consider beneath "house niggers." *She* captures and ties up a cow for Melanie's baby, *she* goes to Twelve Oaks to gather food, *she* hunts for the animals in the swamp, *she* hoes and plows and picks cotton. In the process, she even begins to look like Mammy, Dilcey, and Prissy. In their 1939 adaptation of *Gone with the Wind*, producer David O. Selznick, screenwriter Sidney Howard, director Victor Fleming, cinematographer Ernest Haller, and designer Walter Plunkett showed an awareness of this racial transformation—Scarlett's skin has darkened from sunburn and exposure; her thick, black hair has frizzled in the heat; her clothes have become patched and filthy. She even wears Mammy's sunbonnet in the fields. Walter Plunkett, famed costume designer specializing in historical films, made Prissy and Scarlett's dresses after the siege out of the same cheap fabric. Melanie wore an apron made out of a burlap sack, and Suellen and Careen wore cotton print dresses that had obviously once belonged to slaves.[56]

The "black" Irish's unstable status as white immigrants during the nineteenth century is well documented, as is the Southern poor white tenant farmer's position in the racial hierarchy.[57] In losing her prewar economic status, Scarlett is also in danger of losing her "whiteness" and slipping too close to the position of her former slaves. Many Southerners during the 1930s faced a similar racial transformation. Selznick and Sidney Howard's decision to eliminate cracker Will Benteen and mustee slavewoman Dilcey from the script may indicate their desperate efforts to streamline *Gone with the Wind's* complex narrative, but also to mask Scarlett's close friendships with two racial and class hybrids—the poor white and the Cherokee–African American. The fact that Scarlett's only unguarded relationships were with Will and Dilcey marks her own status as a racial and class hybrid after 1864. But visual traces of Scarlett's hybridity remain in the film. Undoubtedly *Gone with the Wind's* pivotal and most powerful scene in both the novel and film involves Scarlett and the Old South's rebirth on the Negro soil in the slave quarters. In Mitchell's novel, Scarlett has just returned home to Tara and realizes that she must run the plantation, care for her family, and save them all from the destruction and famine of Sherman's invading army. The ghosts of her ancestors and the memory of their struggles in Europe and the New World lull her into a dreamless sleep, but in the morning she is still haunted by hunger and the ruin of that old world she loved but took for granted. Scarlett walks to John Wilkes's Twelve Oaks in search of food and sees Southern history in charred ruins at her feet.

Twelve Oaks, more than the rambling, immigrant-built Tara, exemplified the powerful racial myth of the antebellum South. Scarlett gets no sustenance there but finds food in the slave gardens near the ruins. She pulls a radish from the earth, eats it, and then vomits, falling in the dirt. When she rises at last from the slave earth, purged and grim, a Southern phoenix rising from the ashes, she swears an oath, showing no loyalty to principle or memory, but only to herself and her family's salvation. The new South is literally born from the ashes of the old; Scarlett draws new life from the soil of her former slaves. She has worn their clothes, eaten their food, slept on their earth, and her kinship is now total.

Selznick recognized the overarching importance of this sequence, and Scarlett's oath (restaged at Tara) concludes the first half of the film.[58] Ironically, the first time one sees the mythical Southern moonlight is when it illuminates for Scarlett the charred ruins of Twelve Oaks and the ravaged facade of Tara. Victor Fleming and Ernest Haller turned the full force of American cultural myth on the devastation of Sherman's March to the Sea. Scarlett finds death and madness inside her home, and as she staggers outside, she sees the ravaged expanse of slave gardens and houses that once held life. Haller shot into the harsh red light of predawn, turning Scarlett into a near-black silhouette, a symbol of all struggling Southern women, regardless of color, in 1864. With her dark, frizzled hair and ragged, hoopless dress, Scarlett looks like not only a poor-white Southerner but also a black woman, as she limps toward the slave gardens. In one of the longest unbroken close-ups in classical Hollywood cinema,[59] Fleming and Haller followed her descent to the slave earth and her extraordinary and brutal refusal to bow to defeat before tracking out on her rigid silhouette, echoed by the remains of a charred oak. Here, in this allegory of the course of Southern history (defeat, purge, recovery, revenge), the filmmakers recast the iconic image of rebellion as an almost biracial woman.[60]

This was the pivotal moment of historical transition for both Mitchell and David O. Selznick, one that confronted the myth of Southern history and the shadowy future of the reconstructed Southern woman. Although production documents reveal Selznick and Howard feared historicizing the Reconstruction era in the film's second part,[61] causing them to emphasize the melodramatic romance, their film did not ignore questions of race and history. Film historian Thomas Cripps has documented Selznick's deference to African American groups worried about the film's possible negative images of blacks, while Howard was very wary of portraying the Ku Klux Klan sympathetically: "I hate to indulge in anything which makes the lynching of a negro in any sense sympathetic."[62] Unlike *The Birth of a Nation, Gone with the Wind* was not a traditionally racist film narrative that defined black and white Americans through rigid genre typologies and binary oppositions. Instead, through film's historiographical tool, cinematography, racial mixing left its trace on the historical narrative. At the heart of both the historical novel and the film, a dark-skinned, frizzle-haired woman pushed herself up from the slave earth and swore to forget the past.

Hervey Allen, one of the most popular historical novelists of the last century, had this to say of the distinction between historiography and historical fiction: "Neither historian nor novelist can reproduce the real past," but historical novelists can give "the reader a more vivid, adequate, and significant apprehension of past epochs than does the historian."[63] In other words, historical fiction's less rigid structure may generate new discoveries and attitudes toward the past often suppressed by the discourse of traditional historiography. Jackson, Mitchell, and Ferber made their careers in part by presenting obscure, overlooked, and potentially controversial characters and viewpoints. But the market for popular history during the first half of the twentieth century extended beyond the historical novel. Studio-era

Hollywood's complex view of national history included mixed race Americans and reconsidered the role of the mixed race woman, her subversive past acting in counterpoint to traditional history's accepted racial categories and biography's patriarchal canon of heroes. Some of Hollywood's most popular actresses competed for and played these roles, and after Vivien Leigh's success as Scarlett in *Gone with the Wind*, newer stars like Ingrid Bergman (Edna Ferber's *Saratoga Trunk*, Warner Bros., 1942), Jennifer Jones (*Duel in the Sun*, Selznick International, 1946), and Jeanne Crain (*Pinky*, Twentieth Century-Fox, 1949) would play mixed race American women in major prestige productions. Unfortunately, in its acceptance of the so-called mythic discourse of classical Hollywood, allegedly supported by the Western and Southern plantation genres, film scholarship has effaced the more complicated surfaces of racial history in American cinema.

### NOTES

1. George F. Custen, *Bio/pics: How Hollywood Constructed Public History* (New Brunswick, NJ: Rutgers University Press, 1992), 109.

2. Julie Des Jardins, *Women and the Historical Enterprise in America: Gender, Race and the Politics of Memory, 1880–1945* (Chapel Hill: University of North Carolina Press, 2003).

3. On the Western: Will Wright, *Six-Guns and Society: A Structural Study of the Western* (Berkeley: University of California Press, 1975); and Richard Slotkin, *Gunfighter Nation: The Myth of the Frontier in Twentieth-Century America* (Norman: University of Oklahoma Press, 1992). On the plantation epic: Jim Cullen, *The Civil War in Popular Culture: A Reusable Past* (Washington, DC: Smithsonian Institute Press, 1995); and Tara McPherson, *Reconstructing Dixie: Race, Gender, and Nostalgia in the Imagined South* (Durham, NC: Duke University Press, 2003).

4. Robert F. Berkhofer, *The White Man's Indian* (New York: Vintage, 1979); Slotkin, *Gunfighter Nation*.

5. Daniel Bernardi, ed., *The Birth of Whiteness: Race and the Emergence of U.S. Cinema* (New Brunswick, NJ: Rutgers University Press, 1996); Daniel Bernardi, ed., *Classic Hollywood, Classic Whiteness* (Minneapolis: University of Minnesota Press, 2001); Richard Dyer, *White* (London: BFI, 1997); Linda Williams, *Playing the Race Card* (Princeton, NJ: Princeton University Press, 2001). See also Donald Bogle, *Toms, Coons, Mulattoes, Mammies, and Bucks*, 2nd ed. (New York: Continuum, 2003); and Thomas Cripps, *Slow Fade to Black* (Oxford: Oxford University Press, 1993).

6. Sterling Brown, *The Negro in American Fiction* (Washington, DC: Association of Negro Folk Education, 1937), 43–44.

7. Randall M. Miller, ed., *The Kaleidoscopic Lens: How Hollywood Views Ethnic Groups* (Englewood, NJ: Ozer, 1980); Peter C. Rollins and John E. O'Connor, eds., *Hollywood's Indian* (Lexington: University Press of Kentucky, 1998); Leonard J. Leff and Jerold Simmons, *The Dame in the Kimono* (Lexington: University Press of Kentucky, 2001).

8. See the PCA's prohibition of themes of interracial sex (1930–34) in Leff and Simmons, *The Dame in the Kimono*, 285–300.

9. Censorship records of *Ramona, Show Boat, Jezebel, and Gone with the Wind* (PCA Files, Academy of Motion Picture Arts and Sciences [AMPAS]; *Cimarron's* file does not exist) all indicate that PCA head Joseph Breen was far more interested in covering cleavage, limiting kisses, and excising scenes of childbirth than in issues of race.

10. See J. E. Smyth, *Reconstructing American Historical Cinema: From Cimarron to Citizen Kane* (Lexington: University Press of Kentucky, 2006), for a broader look at the history and implications of "classical" Hollywood scholarship and the unique historical practices during the 1930s that conform to no conservative, classical norm.

11. My suggestion of a "filmic writing of history" in Hollywood takes issue with Marc Ferro, who coined the expression and argued that it was impossible on two counts: one, that verbal and visual historical discourses were too different to be reconciled, and two, that Hollywood in particular lacked the capability of rendering serious history on screen; (Ferro, *Cinema and History* (Detroit, MI: Wayne State University Press, 1988), 161–63).

12. Suzanne Bost, *Mulattas and Mestizas: Representing Mixed Identities in the Americas, 1850–2000* (Athens: University of Georgia Press, 2003), 2. See also Judith R. Berzon, *Neither White Nor Black* (New York: NYU Press, 1978).

13. Martin Barker and Roger Sabin, *The Lasting of the Mohicans: The History of an American Myth* (Jackson: University of Mississippi Press, 1995).

14. Richard Slotkin, *The Fatal Environment: The Myth of the Frontier in the Age of Industrialization 1800–1890* (Norman: University of Oklahoma Press, 1985), 81–106; Cassandra Jackson, *Barriers between Us: Interracial Sex in Nineteenth-Century American Literature* (Bloomington: Indiana University Press, 2004).

15. Cooper, *Last of the Mohicans: A Narrative of 1757* (1826; New York, 1986), 303–5.

16. Helen Hunt Jackson, *A Century of Dishonor* (New York: Harper, 1881).

17. See introduction to Helen Hunt Jackson's *Ramona* (Boston: Little, Brown, 1913) by A. C. Vroman.

18. C. C. Davis, *The True Story of Ramona* (New York: Dodge, 1914), 15. See also A. C. Vroman and T. F. Barnes, *The Genesis of the Story of Ramona* (Los Angeles: Press of Kingsley-Barnes and Neuner, 1899).

19. Davis, *The True Story of Ramona*, 33–42.

20. Dydia DeLyser, *Ramona Memories: Tourism and the Shaping of Southern California* (Minneapolis: University of Minnesota Press, 2005). See also Chon

Noriega, "Birth of the Southwest: Social Protest, Tourism and D. W. Griffith's *Ramona*," in Bernardi, *The Birth of Whiteness*, 203–26.

21. Edna Ferber, *Show Boat* (New York: Doubleday, 1926).

22. Edna Ferber, *Cimarron* (New York: Doubleday, 1930).

23. Mitchell, letter to Mrs. Julia Harris, April 28, 1936, in *Margaret Mitchell's "Gone with the Wind" Letters, 1936–1949*, ed. Richard Harwell (New York: Macmillan, 1976), 2–3.

24. Ibid., 5.

25. *"GWTW" Letters*, passim, but especially Mitchell's letters to Harry Stillwell Edwards, June 18, 1936, 13–15; to Julia Collier Harris, July 8, 1936, 26–27; and to Stephen V. Benét, July 9, 1936, 36.

26. Several prominent films with Native American protagonists were made in the silent era, most notably *The Vanishing American* (1925) and *Red Skin* (1929).

27. Ferber, *Cimarron*, 11.

28. Estabrook's annotated copy of Ferber's *Cimarron*, Howard Estabrook Collection, Academy of Motion Pictures Arts and Sciences Library, 10–11, 61, 88; Estabrook, "Adaptation and Structure of Screen Play," May 22, 1930, A20; first draft, June 19, 1930, 35; shooting script, August 27, 1930, A23.

29. Slotkin, *Gunfighter Nation*. For a study of the enforced division of racial categories in frontier discourse, see Reginald Horsman, *Race and Manifest Destiny* (Cambridge, MA: Harvard University Press, 1981).

30. Rick Altman, *Film/Genre* (London: BFI, 1999), 19–29.

31. Frederick Jackson Turner, "The Significance of the Frontier in American History" [1893], in *Rereading Frederick Jackson Turner*, ed. John Mack Faragher (New York: Henry Holt, 1994), 31–60.

32. David Stenn, *Clara Bow: Runnin' Wild* (New York: Doubleday, 1988), 209–34.

33. Mordaunt Hall, "Clara Bow as a Termagant in a Film of a Novel by Tiffany Thayer," *New York Times*, November 25, 1932.

34. Gwendolyn Audrey Foster, *Performing Whiteness: Postmodern Reconstructions in the Cinema* (Albany: SUNY Press, 2003), 2.

35. See Production Code Administration files, *Imitation of Life* (1934), AMPAS.

36. Thomas Doherty, *Pre-Code Hollywood: Sex, Immorality and Insurrection in American Cinema, 1930–1934* (New York: Columbia University Press, 1999), 263.

37. Darryl F. Zanuck to Neil McCarthy, 28 April 1936, in *Memo from Darryl F. Zanuck*, ed. Rudy Behlmer (New York: Grove Press, 1993), 10.

38. *Time*, 5 October 1936, 28.

39. Cripps, *Slow Fade to Black*, 293.

40. Charles Kenyon, *Show Boat*, adaptation and continuity (19 April 1928), 149 pp., 25–33, Box 2876, f 1063, MGM Script Collection, AMPAS.

41. Williams, *Playing the Race Card*, 176. When MGM remade the film in 1951, scripts excised this sequence (see *Show Boat*, 1951, MGM Script Collection, AMPAS).

42. Elizabeth Fox-Genovese, "Scarlett O'Hara: The Southern Lady as New Woman," *American Quarterly* 33 (Autumn 1981): 391–411; Laura F. Edwards, *Scarlett Doesn't Live Here Anymore: Southern Women in the Civil War Era* (Bloomington: Indiana University Press, 2000); McPherson, *Reconstructing Dixie*; Sarah Gardner, *Blood and Irony: Southern White Women's Narratives of the Civil War, 1861–1937* (Chapel Hill: University of North Carolina Press, 2004).

43. McPherson, *Reconstructing Dixie*, 54.

44. Gardner, *Blood and Irony*, 242.

45. See Walter Benn Michaels's illuminating discussion of the historical divide between Page and Dixon: *Our America: Nativism, Modernism, Pluralism* (Durham, NC: Duke University Press, 1995), 16–23.

46. Margaret Mitchell, *Gone with the Wind* (New York: Macmillan, 1936), 722.

47. Robert Buckner, *Jezebel*, temporary script, 30 April 1937, 11, Warner Bros. Archive, University of Southern California.

48. Thomas Schatz, "'A Triumph of Bitchery': Warner Bros., Bette Davis, and Jezebel," in *The Studio System*, ed. Janet Staiger, 74–92 (New Brunswick, NJ: Rutgers University Press, 1995), 75.

49. See Schatz for a basic production history and contextualization of *Jezebel* within Davis's career in the 1930s.

50. Warner Bros. research—"Bible," Warner Bros. Corporate Archive.

51. *Jezebel* research log, Warner Bros. Archive.

52. *Jezebel*, press book, 4, Warner Bros. Archive.

53. Edmund Goulding, *Jezebel* production notes, July 7, 1937, 3, Warner Brothers Archive.

54. See William A. Dunning, *Reconstruction, Political and Economic, 1865–1870* (New York: Harper and Brothers, 1907).

55. W. E. B. Du Bois, *Black Reconstruction* (New York: Harcourt and Brace, 1935); and C. Vann Woodward, *Tom Watson: Agrarian Rebel* (New York: Macmillan, 1938).

56. Olivia de Havilland, letters to the author, 2000–2001.

57. Noel Ignatiev, *How the Irish Became White* (New York: Routledge, 1995); David Roediger, *The Wages of Whiteness: Race and the Making of the American Working Class* (New York: Verso, 1999); Neil Foley, *The White Scourge* (Berkeley: University of California Press, 1997).

58. Sidney Howard, "Preliminary Notes to a Screen Treatment of *Gone with the Wind*," 14 December 1936, 50 pp., esp., 32–34, David O. Selznick Collection, Harry Ransome Center, University of Texas, Austin.

59. Lasting well over a minute, the close-up rivals the length of the final shot of *Queen Christina* (1933).

60. Although Williams described this sequence, she ignored the biracial "rebirth" and connections to Southern history, and instead focused on Scarlett's realignment with her father's immigrant Irish philosophy (207); see Smyth,

*Reconstructing American Historical Cinema from Cimarron to Citizen Kane*, 158–65. For more on Irish links, real or imagined, with African Americans, see Catherine M. Eagan, "'Still "Black" and "Proud"': Irish America and the Racial Politics of Hibernophilia," in *The Irish in Us*, ed. Diane Negra (Durham, NC: Duke University Press, 2006), 20–63.

61. Howard, "Preliminary Notes," 1.

62. Thomas Cripps, "Winds of Change: Gone with the Wind and Racism as a National Issue," in *Recasting: Gone with the Wind in American Culture*, ed. Darden Pyron (Miami: University Presses of Florida, 1983), 137–52; Howard, "Preliminary Notes," 39.

63. Hervey Allen, "History and the Novel," *Atlantic Monthly*, February 1944, 119–20.

II

# Mixed Race Frontiers

## Border Westerns and the Limits of "America"

### Camilla Fojas

> Mexican on one side, Irish on the other, and me in the middle.
>
> —Bernardo Reilly in *The Magnificent Seven*

Many Westerns take place in the border region between the United States and Mexico, which accounts for the prevalence of titles like *Rio Grande* (1950) and *Rio Bravo* (1958), all referring to the use of the river as a natural demarcation between nations rather than the result of war. The Western, the most enduring Hollywood genre, has always been associated with U.S.-style masculinity, the battle between civilization and barbarism, and the dramatization of the founding values of the early nation. But Westerns might also be examined for shared provenance, the preoccupation with Native American nation formation and immigration, the relationship to Mexico, the presence of Mexicans and Mexican Americans, and the ever-present threat of racial miscegenation.[1] Though the "frontier" typically connotes its Western incarnation and the uncivilized "Indian" territory beyond it, the southern frontier, Mexico, and the Mexican past of the United States are of equal relevance in the construction of the moral universe of the Western. The popularity of the border as a symbol of national order and control coincides with political concerns along the border, particularly the control of the national labor market, immigration from the south, and the troubled relationship with Mexico.

Mexico carries various meanings: it represents a victorious sign of territorial expansion—since the United States expropriated much of its land mass in 1848—but it also represents the possibility of loss, of the need to continually defend the national frontier from hostile invasion or reannexation. Mexico is often depicted as a racialized and primitive wilderness where Western male heroes go to reinvigorate their masculinity—often with the help of Mexican or "Indian" women; where mixed race characters and relationships are common; and it often represents the uncivilized past of the United States, the idyllic land that, during post–Civil War era stories, replaces the terrain just beyond the Western frontier. In this chapter, I explore two border Westerns, *Duel in the Sun* (1946) and *Rio Lobo* (1970), in which racial mixing and the mixed raced characters are central to the plot development. *Duel in the Sun* is about mixed Indian-creole Pearl Chavez, who, born and raised in the borderlands, is depicted as a primitive savage who drives the white men around her crazy with lust. *Rio Lobo* also features a mixed race character, white-Mexican Pierre Cordona, whose racial and ethnic flexibility and adaptability enable the execution of post–Civil War justice. These characters represent both the national character in racial terms and the political boundaries of the nation in geographic terms. Though nominally "Westerns," these films traverse the divisions separating genres while they constitute the subgenre of the border Western or the Western that makes use of the borderlands to emphasize a story about U.S. prominence in the region.

## Racial Borders in the Southwesterner

King Vidor's *Duel in the Sun*, otherwise known as "Lust in the Dust" and often referred to as a Texas ranch epic,[2] is a cross between a Western and a psychosexual melodrama centered on mixed race Indian-Mexican creole Pearl Chavez. Pearl's story is tragic from beginning to end. Her mother is a debauched Indian dancer in a border town cantina, and her father, the "white half,"[3] is a gambler. Her father is derogatively referred to as a "squaw man" in a manner reminiscent of the treatment of the protagonist of the play *The Squaw Man*, shot for the screen in 1914, 1918, and 1931. Her father murders her mother for infidelity and is executed for it. Pearl, left parentless, is sent to live with her father's second cousin and ex-betrothed, Laura Belle McCanles, and her family on a Texas ranch. The threat of incest or of "unnatural" intimacies across the family generations is a constant refrain in the story.

*Lewt McCanles (Gregory Peck) eyes Pearl Chavez (Jennifer Jones) as his mother, Laura Belle McCanles (Gish), gazes upon him in* Duel in the Sun.

Thomas Schatz calls *Duel in the Sun* a "prototype New Hollywood Block-buster" that combined top stars, a big budget, an epic story line, and high-gloss production values.[4] Producer David O. Selznick was hoping to exploit his success with *Gone with the Wind* (1939) by drawing on an all-star cast of Jennifer Jones (Selznick's future wife), who had just won an Academy Award as best actress for *The Song of Bernadette* (1943), Gregory Peck, Joseph Cotton, Herbert Marshall, Lillian Gish, Lionel Barrymore, and Walter Huston.[5] Perhaps this parade of Hollywood pedigree is what lured audiences to the box office to watch a rather unusual story featuring a mestizo character with a Spanish surname, Pearl Chavez, as the lead protagonist.[6] A review of the film in *Time* magazine contemporary with its release sums up the Hollywood moral concisely: "The audience learns (thanks to the Johnston office) that illicit love doesn't really pay in the long run but for about 134 minutes it has appeared to be loads of fun."[7] Indeed, the story follows the dictates of the antimiscegenation laws that were in effect until 1967, as well as the interdiction of the Hays Production Code against interracial relationships.

As mentioned earlier, the story begins in a Mexican border town out-side the limits of the United States, but immediately shuttles Pearl to a Texas ranch, ignoring the legal implications of this international move. We might presume that Pearl has binational citizenship, but the real ques-tion is whether or not she also has binational identification and belong-ing. She is literally invited into the micro-national formation of the bar-ricaded Texas Ranch—symbol of U.S. victory in the U.S.-Mexican war to secure its borders—but her mixed race presence is the catalyst for havoc and unrest that disrupt the domestic tranquillity of the Anglo McCanles clan. Upon her arrival at the ranch, Jesse, the older McCanles son, intro-duces it as "a million acres of McCanles empire," to which Pearl responds "empire? Isn't this still Texas?" Indeed, within Western mythology, Texas is the center and source of the larger national empire, within which the migration of the southern border ensured the geographic and economic expansion of the United States in the 1840s. By the 1880s, large ranches like the McCanles ranch—a reference to the McAllen ranch and its epon-ymous town—were becoming major industrial engines and, as depicted in *Giant* (1956), centers of oil wealth.

*Duel in the Sun* might be best described as a hybrid generic formation, with this hybridity reflected in both the form and the meaning of the nar-rative. The melodramatic tone sets the emotional pitch high and turns on a more intense identification on the part of the viewer. The characters, especially the "bad" ones, evoke the Western outlaw while on the surface the story seems to depart entirely from the defining features of the West-ern myth, especially regarding how racialized sexuality and overwrought sentimentality seem to dominate all other plot preoccupations. Unlike other Westerns, marginal themes are central. A mixed race Native Ameri-can woman is at the center of the plot, but her centrality serves a specific purpose. Typical of the melodrama, she is the center of a cautionary tale about the fateful consequences of racial mixing.

*Duel in the Sun* was one of the first films to depict intimacy and ir-repressible attraction between Anglo and mixed blood Indian characters. Unlike other mixed race melodramas in which the major drama centers on the female characters' issues of identity, this film is a drama of attrac-tion and ambivalence to the Indian character—played by Anglo-American actress Jennifer Jones in brownface—that reflects a national drama over the role and status of Native Americans. Philip Deloria, writing about the status of Native Americans in U.S. popular culture, argues that the In-dian and "playing Indian" has long been a major trope of narratives of

U.S. identity. Hollywood has been at the center of the performance of the Indian and constitutes one of the largest archives of demeaning stereotypes that serve white mastery. In Jacquelyn Kilpatrick's analysis of Native American representation from early Hollywood to the present, she finds that there are three basic stereotypes: primitive and of lesser intelligence, sexually promiscuous, and heathen or spiritually closer to the earth.[8] It is not surprising that Pearl embodies all three types at once and is thus eliminated as a social menace. This scenario resounds after World War II, when there was considerable public concern about the political fate of Native Americans regarding their potential for either assimilation or self-governance.

For Laura Mulvey, *Duel in the Sun* is fundamentally a Western whose generic space is transformed by the core narrative preoccupation with Pearl Chavez, "a girl caught between two conflicting desires."[9] Stanley Corkin also argues that the film transforms the Western genre, shifting its central terms to the feminine. Yet neither critic acknowledges the mixed race dimension of the erotic tension among the characters and how this might affect its critical interpretation and cultural meaning. Pearl Chavez is recognizable as a mixed race character seemingly modeled on the tragic mulattoes of melodramas like John Stahl's *Imitation of Life*—though for mixed Indian and Latino characters of Westerns, passing for white is never an option, since ethnic and national identifications are often played for high nationalist drama. The mixing of the Western and melodramatic genres reflects the thematic concerns about the mixing of races—implying that such mixtures lead to a demise perpetuated by the "weaker" term: "Indian" passion overwhelms Anglo morality just as the feminine melodrama erodes the stoic masculinity of the Western. The film itself has a clear moral imperative to reestablish boundaries between all the various tributary meanings and symbols of its two guiding terms: civilization (U.S.) and barbarism (Mexico and Native America).

The prelude to *Duel in the Sun* frames the story in national terms—a voice-over narration, ominously delivered by Orson Welles, offers the following preface to the film, which

two years in the making, is a saga of Texas in the 1880s when primitive passions rode the raw frontier of an expanding nation. Here the forces of evil were in constant conflict with the deeper morality of the hardy pioneers. Here, as in the story we tell, a gray fate lay waiting for the transgressor upon the laws of god and man.

The story is full of the language of fate and fatedness, of chance and misfortune, and of the laws of nature or forces beyond human control that are posed against the force of human will. On the side of will are the Anglo "hardy pioneers" and the hardworking Texan ranchers, and on the side of fate are all the racialized and foreign characters who exhibit degenerate traits and a lack of control. The former are heroes and nationalists who are to be celebrated, and the latter are outlaws who must be corralled, exiled, or extinguished. This opening gambit establishes the terms that justify an exclusionary nationalism within a story set after the Chinese Exclusion Act of 1882 and when, in Texas, the era of the cattle drives and the open range was replaced with that of enclosed and secure ranches lined with fences. For instance, a major subplot is that of the railroad trying to lay tracks across the McCanles ranch lands; the railroad is considered a trespassing invasion and the Chinese workers a nuisance. The laying of the railroad symbolizes both a racialized immigrant invasion and the linking of lonestar Texas to the rest of the United States, which in turn allegorizes the linking of the United States to the rest of the world.

Thus, behind the salacious characterization of mixed race Pearl Chavez is a story about the status of Texas in the United States and a dazzling portrait of a border town just beyond the state limits. The setting of Texas in the 1880s is crucial to the framing of mixed race Pearl. The state was experiencing growing pains in these years as it increased in size largely through Anglo settlement, and there was considerable uncertainty about the future role of its Mexican and native cultural heritage. By 1881, the Indian question had been settled with the Texas Rangers' violent expulsion of the majority of the Apache and Comanche natives of the borderland region.

*Duel in the Sun* has the curious imprint of a historical circumstance involving a cross-racial liaison that caused considerable disquiet. One of the major ranches of the Texas Ranger period, the McAllen ranch, was inhabited by James McAllen and a young Mexican woman, Santos Tijerina; the intimate mixed race relationship between McAllen and Tijerina was a scandal for the town and for the young woman's family in Mexico.[10] According to some sources, her family sent a troop of Mexican hit men to seek revenge on James McAllen, which resulted in an Alamo-esque night of shooting that McAllen miraculously survived. The Texas Rangers were sent in to police the situation. Although they could not find the men responsible, they killed two innocent Mexican men in their place—a common practice of "revenge by proxy" among the Rangers.[11] The McAllen Ranch is haunted by this interracial relationship and perhaps served as material for the writers of *Duel in the Sun*, which recalls a doomed and embattled mixed race relationship that ends in a bloody shoot-out. It is certainly possible that the McAllen ranch, with its history of interracial romance and treachery, returns in *Duel in the Sun* as the anagrammatic McCanles ranch. *Duel in the Sun* shifts the story, if in fact it is citing it, to concerns that were more prevalent in the period just following World War II: concerns about the role of the United States in the hemisphere, about the southern boundary, and about the social and political place of Native Americans in U.S. society.

After World War II, Native Americans had a deeply contested status. Many postwar Westerns, including *Duel in the Sun, Rio Grande, The Searchers* (1956), and *The Comancheros* (1961), contributed to the cultural attitudes and policy toward Native Americans that established key terms of U.S. national identity. Native Americans have had a dual position in U.S. culture and policy; they are regarded as either enemies of the state or potentially assimilated members of mainstream culture, depicted as either warring Indians or "Indian scouts," as in the case of *Rio Grande*. These border Westerns deploy the border to set limits and delineate citizen from alien while also depicting Native Americans as unfit for North American national terrain. *Rio Grande*, for instance, is about the proper kind of family formation as a necessary allegory for the need for a militarized and protected nation. The threat to nation formation in this instance is a racialized and primitive internal alien whose sovereignty and freedom threaten the firm establishment of core American values around family and military, synthesized and encoded in the "Americanism" of "homeland security." *The Comancheros* is about the vice-ridden and rapacious Indians and the North American Comancheros who furnish them with all manner of contraband from their exile outpost in Mexico. The Comanche Indians cross the border without incident. Like their Apache kin, they are without limits and enjoy liberal freedoms that threaten U.S. national security. But worse yet are the Comancheros, who shirk their patriotic duties and sense of civilization to aid and abet the consolidation of outlaw Indian nations. These Westerns encode ambivalence about Native Americans during their increased political and social visibility in the period following World War II. *Rio Grande* and *The Comancheros* entertain this cultural ambivalence about Indians while using the border to assert the boundaries of national identity, to delimit between characters who reflect the national line and those who do not, between good and bad Indians. *Duel in the Sun* transcends this discourse of good and bad Indian to present a cautionary tale about the moral pitfalls of full Indian integration through lack of limitations on racial miscegenation. It also evokes fears of deracination of the white man that had become central to the laws of the era.

Though *Duel in the Sun* is set in the late 1880s, when federal Indian policy tended to advocate autonomy, the film is addressed to post–World War II audiences at a time when the government is systematically terminating Native American rights to political autonomy. Thus relevant to the story is an 1888 law regulating marriage between white men and Indian women, which sought to limit the expansion of Indian communities through marriage: "Be it enacted . . . , that no white man, not otherwise a member of any tribe of Indians, who may hereafter marry, an Indian woman, member of any Indian tribe in the United States, or any of its Territories except the five civilized tribes in the Indian Territory, shall by such marriage hereafter acquire any right to tribal property, privilege, or interest whatever to which any member of such a tribe is entitled."[12] These five tribes—Cherokee, Choctaw, Chickasaw, Creek or Muscogee, and Seminole Indian—were considered "civilized" because they were more assimilated to Euro-American ways of life, mostly as farmers and planters. They were also more likely to mix with Euro-Americans to produce "mixed blood" offspring. The fear that energized the preceding policy was that marriages with the noncivilized tribes might result in reverse assimilation or the Indian-ization of white men and further consolidation of maverick Indian nations. This is not explicitly addressed in *Duel in the Sun*, though some aspect of the fear of reverse assimilation is coded as the deleterious influence of Pearl's character. Her love interest, Lewt, is already a bad character, but he becomes worse around Pearl, whose presence initiates and secures his demise.

In the opening scene, we are introduced—in a matter of minutes—to the entire depraved Chavez family, who partake of every vice available in the Mexican border town.[13] Pearl, mirroring her mother, dances on a platform outside a saloon while her mother dances inside on the bar. Also inside the saloon, Pearl's father is playing a game of chance; it is here, in this dysfunctional family portrait, that we make the association of chance, misfortune, and fate with Pearl's character. She is fated to mime her family history, suggesting that her racial makeup is a congenital weakness. She is doomed to embody the erotic life of her mother and to exhibit the murderous impulse of her father. She will replay both histories when, through her sensual weakness, she attracts a lover whom she is fated to murder. The whole scenario will play out in the high emotional tones of melodrama.

Linda Williams designates melodrama as one of the "body genres" that evoke intense bodily reactions in the viewer, enacted in identification with the obscene display of intimate emotions and a body literally rapturously "gripped" by an excess of affect.[14] Melodrama has a particular temporality structured by its central fantasy around loss, which Williams describes as "too late!" In *Duel in the Sun*, the title refers to this fated scene of a double loss, of a duel that leads to the tragic death of the protagonists. Our affect is pulled from this tragic scene of being "too late," of knowing the fate of the lovers, as foreshadowed by the history of Pearl, and yet not able to do anything to forestall it. We arrive late, having failed to heed the warning clearly forecast by the original scene of miscegenation at the border.

*Duel in the Sun* is the film that inspired Laura Mulvey to build upon her schema regarding the "masculinization" of the spectator in Hollywood film. In her original formulation, the gaze is defined as male and the woman on screen is objectified for a male voyeuristic pleasure. Female and male spectators alike are shuttled into this masculine spectatorial position. Yet, she rethinks the position of the female spectator through the sexual crises of Pearl as the central character in the Texas ranch melodrama.[15] Mulvey takes as a point of departure the instability of the sexual identity of the female character as a symptom of the tensions of sexual difference. According to psychoanalytic theory, women arrive at sexual difference through repression of sexual instincts. She finds liberation of the sexual instinct for women in genre films: "Hollywood genre films structured around masculine pleasure, offering an identification with the *active* point of view, allow a woman spectator to rediscover that lost aspect of her sexual identity, the never fully repressed bed-rock of feminine neurosis" (142). A film like *Duel in the Sun* shifts the narrative terms by placing a woman at the center and making her story of internal conflict the central drama. For Mulvey, the two brothers represent aspects of Pearl's identity and the two poles of her internal conflict and sexual ambivalence. She must choose either the ordered and civilized world of Jesse, which would entail a passive feminine identification, the proper course toward marriage, or the sexual expressivity and passion of Lewt, which Mulvey describes as "not based on maturity but on a regressive, boy/girl type of mixture of rivalry and play" (148). Both choices represent annihilation for Pearl, but the latter, with Lewt, is less oppressive, thus enabling the expression of her repressed desires.

In this analysis, there is no attention to the racial constitution of sexual identity and the sexual relations among characters. For instance, it recalls a history of Latinas in Westerns—Chihuahua of *My Darling Clementine* or Helen Ramirez of *High Noon*—who intensify the rivalry between white men. Race constitutes another major point of reference in the dueling oppositions in Pearl's crises of identity. The racial position of her character shuttles between the "proper" repression of passing for white and the abject and primitive racialization represented by her mother and the post-slavery servants of the McCanles ranch. As a mixed race character, her position is one of racial instability presented by the impossibility of being neither the one nor the other. The blind spots of the Oedipal narrative are more numerous than at first appearance; the scandal of desire is energized not just by the mysteries of sexual difference but by the obscurities and paradoxes of racial fetishism.

The sexual fetish and the racial fetish are built upon the same logic. For Freud, fetishism corresponds to a precise moment in the formation of the young boy's psyche when he sees his mother's genitalia. At this moment, rather than embracing or acknowledging her difference, he immediately fears that the same fate might befall him. He masters this fear by disavowing his mother's lack and replacing the missing penis with something close at hand: a fetish object in the form of a foot, a shoe, or some other suitable substitute. The fetish is a useful explanatory mechanism, since it contains a paradoxical logic in which something is both the same and the opposite at once. The fetish points to an attempt to control and master difference out of anxiety about loss: loss of power and control. According to Mulvey, the mastery of the male gaze indicates the power to deny a frightening difference by turning the woman into an object of control. Likewise, racial difference is opaque and associated with some anxiety-provoking occult powers; the racialized other is feared as powerful and alluring at the same time. The white subject assuages his or her fear by denying the racialized subject's difference. That is, the racial other is a source of fear and anxiety, and his or her difference is neutralized as simply less evolved or primitive to better facilitate domination. In the case of Pearl, she is feared both as a woman and as a mysteriously racialized being. She is alluring to the white brothers for her difference, but ultimately is deemed too uncivilized, sensual, and unsettling and must be eliminated. For Frantz Fanon, the irrationality of racial fetishism is a direct result of its basis in ideologies of nationalism and colonialism.[16]

Pearl is a symptom of the postwar nationalist consolidation of the United States in the struggle to redefine citizenship and belonging after the war. Postwar film and media depictions of peoples of color tended to highlight the irrationality and cruelty of racism within a society sensitized by the atrocities of World War II. In keeping with this postwar liberalism, *Duel in the Sun* is wrapped in a vague ideological veneer of antiracism that is critical of the injustice faced by Pearl from Lewt's bigoted father and the tragic duel in the sun between the doomed lovelorn characters.

Pearl symbolizes the difficulties and paradoxes of race; she enters the McCanles ranch as an exotic stranger and as a distant member of the family—like Native Americans who are both the foundation of the nation (as in Disney's *Pocahantas*) and its excluded margins. This familiarity and difference at once disrupts the domestic coherence and tranquillity of the McCanleses, who must either make Pearl assimilate to their ways or eliminate her as a threat. The problem with Pearl is her refusal to be dominated and subjugated, reflecting a similar social fear about Native Americans as unassimilable. This ignites a secondary fear about too much intimacy between the native other and members of the Texas empire, between Pearl and the McCanles sons.

Pearl is in all instances constituted as inferior to the white women around her and slightly superior to the African American maid, Vashti. Mulvey describes Jesse's "perfect" fiancée, an Anglo ingenue with blond hair and perfect poise, as "a phantasmagoria of Pearl's failed aspiration" to become a lady. Yet Mulvey does not describe the other important term in this dialectical crisis of identity. The African American maid represents another more threatening reality for Pearl, who is caught in a racial dialectic between white and black. Vashti and Pearl share many of the same characteristics, yet Pearl has more agency and free choice by virtue of her proximity to Anglo culture. Yet she is not far from the African American maid in her moral standing and intellectual capacity; tragic ending aside, she stakes her claim on the white men around her despite her bad reputation—emanating entirely from her status as mixed race.

Pearl's mixed race embodiment allegorizes the various sexual and racial dialectical oppositions between characters: good/bad, racialized/white, pure/impure, and civilized/savage. In one of the early scenes, there is an obvious triangle of identification among Laura Belle, the African American maid played by Butterfly McQueen, and Pearl. The entry of the maid immediately introduces a racial continuum of identification along with the gradations of melodramatic intensity. The dark women are associated with the overwrought emotions and excessive expressivity of melodrama, while the white women—Laura Belle and Jesse's fiancée—are depicted in subtle affective and aesthetic tones. In this scene, Laura Belle, the embodiment of civility and culture, is at the piano when the maid, Vashti, interrupts this tranquillity with seemingly childish questions—questions that are actually a sign of her limited legal rights ("Can I get married?"). The camera follows Laura Belle to establish her dominant vantage onto the maid. Pearl is in the background watching with a wry grin, indicating her disidentification with Vashti and desire to identify with Laura Belle. As Pearl and Laura Belle reposition themselves alongside each other, Pearl articulates her desire to "be like" Laura Belle, but the visual contrast between the two, in skin color and aesthetic tones and mood, undermines this identification. Pearl vacillates between the two poles of Anglo assimilation and racialized other, but eventually settles into the grinding determinism of race; for example, when Senator McCanles first happens upon her, he comments on her unusual clothing, which he interprets as either a sign of the high breeding of her father or the "latest in wig-wam fashion."

Jennifer Jones's obvious "brownface" underscores the fiction of the mixed race character and precludes any possible threat of actual racial and interracial depictions. Also, as a fictional character, Pearl is not threatening, since her only desire is to "be good," even though her racial degeneracy sabotages these efforts. Pearl is also bereft of all the signifiers of Native American community and politics; she is entirely disenfranchised from her parents and ethnic heritage, and even her borderland provenance obviates the larger questions of land rights and self-rule for native peoples. The borderlands are many things for Pearl. They are the natural home for a mixed race character, as well as the origin of her degraded moral values. She is alone without community or family, and her mixed race status isolates her further from both national belonging and ethnic communities. Her lack of political encumbrance makes Pearl a desirable plaything of the Texan capitalists. She is depicted as both too ignorant and too foolhardy to contribute to native self-governance, a right established by the Wheeler Howard Act of 1934 but that had come under contest after World War II. The borderlands function as a kind of purgatory and no-man's-land from which her only salvation is isolation from the Latino and Native communities and full integration into Anglo Texan society. This redemption encodes the postwar initiatives of full Native American mainstream assimilation. According to Donald Fixico, these initiatives were led by "mixed bloods," who were able to forge closer ties to mainstream society by virtue of their mixed heritage.[17]

Border films have always concerned immigration and assimilation in terms of the "costs" to U.S. citizens. In *Duel in the Sun*, the cost is represented as the most extreme expense, that of human life. True to the Western form, Pearl meets her death in the final showdown with Lewt. The film begins as a salacious tale of exotic beauty and eroticism but ends as a cautionary moral story.

## Mestizo America

Racial mixing was likely more prevalent in the old West than indicated in Westerns, yet the mestizo character is most often depicted as singular and unique, as presenting extraordinary characteristics. Mixed race female characters like Pearl are too volatile and unproductive to aid in the consolidation of the nation and often were eliminated, while mixed race men were less popular during this era. However, by the liberal and racially conscious late 1960s, the racially mixed male character had become a topic of public discourse as a figure representing the possibility for national reintegration.

*Rio Lobo* (1970) features a male mixed race character, Pierre Cordona, within the more liberal civil rights and postfeminist atmosphere of "melting-pot America." Pierre Cordona, described as half French and half Mexican, is also "American" and fighting for the Southern Confederates. *Rio Lobo* is set after the Civil War. John Wayne, portraying Union colonel Cord McNally, has to track down a group of Confederate rebels among whom are some Union traitors selling information about gold shipments. McNally is in charge of getting gold to the North to fund the war effort while bringing the traitors to his own style of justice. He will soon discover that the information about the gold shipments was sold to a couple of Confederates, including Pierre Cordona, by one of his own men. In typical Wayne fashion, McNally will bring Cordona back to the side of justice. He does this simply by his exemplarity: he leads the way with his moral rectitude, and others follow.

Mixed race male characters might exhibit ethnic and racial characteristics but might be considered white enough to be deemed acceptable objects for an Anglo female audience. Of course, as part of the convention of Hollywood mulatto and mestizo characterizations, these roles were often played by white performers. The character of Pierre Cordona, played by heartthrob Mexican actor Jorge Rivero, is a notable exception. Hollywood trafficked in racial types, which were undermined by these mixed race characters played by white actors. With these characters, attractive by dominant standards of beauty, the race question could be addressed and dramatized in portraits that were pleasing to the eyes of the audience. For instance, in the press junket around the original release of *The Searchers* (1956), the actor Jeffrey Hunter, who plays the quarter Indian character Martin Pawley (whose brown-tinted skin only emphasizes his blue eyes), is introduced as a promising young screen hero—suggesting that his Anglo good looks remain untarnished by this racialized role.

In *Rio Lobo*, Pierre Cordona is mixed racially and nationally. He is a key figure of the opposition who combines two problematic former pieces of other nations, the French empire, as represented by Louisiana, and the former Mexican territory that constitutes more than one-third of the United States. During this era, the French represented a threat to U.S. sovereignty and imperiousness in the hemisphere; they were responsible for coining the term "Latin America," where "Latin" referred to the common cultural heritage of the French and the Spanish. The presence of "Americans" from New Orleans during this time of French imperialism in Mexico is a defiant reminder of the victory of the Louisiana Purchase from France that consolidated the southern territory of the United States. Thus the conflict represented in Mexico is that of an empire striking back, a ridiculing of French arrogance and imperial chauvinism.

*Rio Lobo* was Howard Hawks's last film before his death in 1977, and it continues many of the thematic concerns of his earlier work, particularly that of a strong female lead. Hawks maintains a reputation for strong female protagonists whose roles often shore up the insufficiencies and paradoxes of masculine social norms. Yet for Robin Wood, the "Hawks woman," though often self-possessed, never ceases to be a "male-determined" embodiment of male fantasy who is depicted without female bonds or friendships and always represented in relation to men.[18] Laura Mulvey describes the Hawks woman as a symptom of cultural "ambivalence about female sexuality."[19] Women are independent, yet they are sources of anxiety, challenges to male authority and gender norms, and often depicted as a threat to male friendships. *Rio Lobo* maintains this tradition in the character of Shasta, played by Jennifer O'Neill, who is independent and self-possessed and upsets expectations about her presumed social role. Yet her challenge to masculine norms has distinctly racial and ethnic overtones. In the triadic rivalry among Cordona, McNally, and Shasta in which McNally is the defining center, Shasta gains leverage by virtue of her shared whiteness and North Americanness with McNally. For instance, when inquiring about Cordona's romantic timing, she asks,

"Are all Mexicans as sudden as he is?" This comment amuses McNally and draws her into his intimacy as they bond over Cordona's racial and ethnic peculiarities.

Cordona's masculinity is undermined in his relation to Shasta, a dynamic that serves to reinforce McNally's authority. For instance, when Shasta first meets Cordona, he has just run out of his room to engage in gun battle without his pants on; he is literally caught with his pants down. The violence of the scene causes Shasta to faint; upon waking, she too finds herself in her underwear. Both characters, Cordona and Shasta, are presented as potentially denuded sexual objects while McNally maintains an authoritative (and fully clothed) vantage onto them.

Cordona's mixed French and Mexican heritage makes him foreign and different and thus ripe for treason. This idea circulated widely in the eugenics-based ideology so prevalent during and after the Civil War, when the mixing of races was viewed as the cause of the war. Cordona is the incarnation of the boundary between the United States and Mexico at the same time that he represents the separation and divisiveness created by the Civil War. Unlike Pearl, who cannot be trained to be a "lady" and is thus unassimilable, Cordona can be trained to assimilate and flourish as an "American." Though he shuttles between the designations of "Frenchy" and "Mexican," his difference will eventually be absorbed within a liberal discourse of melting-pot nationalism.

*Rio Lobo* begins with Cordona and his men capturing McNally and using him to safely traverse Union territory, but McNally outstrategizes them and leads them into the midst of a Union camp. The situation reverses, however, so that McNally has in his charge the two Confederate soldiers responsible for his capture: Captain Pierre Cordona and Sergeant Tuscarora Phillips. But this situation does not last for long; the war, they discover through a newspaper headline, has come to an end. Pierre Cordona opines, in a sentiment that resounds across these post–Civil War Westerns, "all this for nothing." Although the war is over, McNally's sense of justice is not; he continues to seek the men who committed treason and sold the information about gold shipments to the South. It is not long before all three men meet up again in Rio Lobo, where they find that one of the men is guilty of treason and is terrorizing the town by forcing its inhabitants under violent duress to sell their land at less than a third of its worth. This violent imperialist, Ketchum, will not stop until he has amassed all the land and property of the town, where the family of Cordona's good pal Tuscarora stands to lose their land and livelihood. McNally's mission is clear; he must go to Rio Lobo with Cordona in tow and liberate the town from its tyrannical imperialist—recalling the cold war era references to the "evil empire" of the Soviet Union.

Shasta, a woman they meet in a neighboring village, offers to guide Cordona and McNally to Rio Lobo. Strangely, the town seems full of single, young, attractive women who make it clear that they are interested and available; the appearance of these women seems to be a strategy of divergence from an increasingly convoluted plot. The semiclad women of Rio Lobo are of different races and ethnicities. One is Mexican, and the other two are visibly white Anglo, but all are wearing wildly incongruous outfits of long skirts and wraparound bikini-style tops, which seem misplaced in the old West and better suited to an Elvis beach film. To varying degrees, the Anglo women show their attraction to Cordona with an aggressivity usually reserved for men. For instance, upon his arrival in a small town, Cordona slips into a house to hide, whereupon he finds a topless woman who suggestively invites him to stay. She fixes her gaze on him and flirts provocatively but to no avail; he neither looks nor flirts in return. He is a Latin lover whose stoicism makes him a nonthreatening and desirable object for Anglo women. They can express their desires without the possibility that they will be actualized. The only Mexican woman shows no interest in Cordona. Notably, any interest on her part would represent a threat to his full assimilation.

Pierre Cordona's mixed race heritage proves useful; he appeals equally to all women, and his "Latinness" is sensual and seductive enough to lure these single women into his and McNally's liberation cause. The mixed race male presents this strategic initiative to attract and assimilate both postfeminist and civil rights era subjects, women and peoples of color. In the end, Cordona and McNally, with the help of these women, succeed in ridding the town of the imperial and tyrannical Ketchum.

The mature Wayne is no longer the asexual romantic lead as in other films of his corpus like *Rio Grande* or *Rio Bravo*, but the aging and benevolent father figure. His role is to father the younger, more handsome lead, to socialize him, make him a more honest and mature man and potential husband, as well as someone who might carry on the John Wayne American way. The antihero turned hero surrogate son is represented as foreign, of a mixed racial and national heritage that represents both histories of the Southwest, French and Mexican. He is a "stepchild" who is taught the ways of the father to better assimilate.

Most Westerns end with a final showdown, a kind of war between the good forces and the bad, which, in this case, is also the last stage in the crossover assimilation story. Cordona has become one of Wayne's men. Here the mixed race character represents the noble mission of assimilation and national cohesion against the forces of empire. Whereas Pearl signifies the race-based dissolution of the United States, Pierre Cordona represents its protection.

Both films, *Duel in the Sun* and *Rio Lobo*, present a popular discourse about the role and status of racial mixing and immigrant assimilation through the mixed race character, and each proposes a different solution. Pearl represents the volatile condition of Native Americans and racialized immigrants in the 1940s, during a time of heightened nationalism. If she were considered simply "Indian," she might be relegated to the separate Indian nations on reservations, but she is literally orphaned between cultures. The film suggests not just that she does not have a place in mainstream U.S. culture but that she is a bad influence for white Americans. Thus if Pearl and her like are not contained, they will cause the degeneration of the U.S. social order. On the other hand, *Rio Lobo* reflects some of the gains of the civil rights era but remains a cold war narrative of intervention and assimilation. The film seems to make the case that mixed race characters like Pierre Cordona are the best disseminators of the "American way," since they are able to cross racial and ethnic lines to gather a larger audience and garner more support. Moreover, the hope of assimilation is placed on mixed race characters who might effectively lead on both sides of the racial divide. By the 1960s, racialized and foreign figures like the adopted Indian son in *The Undefeated* (1969), the French character in *The Comancheros* (1961), and of course Pierre Cordona are taught the ways of the father, John Wayne, and thus are brought into the fold of mainstream U.S. culture.

The prevalence of similar tropes and themes among border Westerns are part of a larger ideological picture and framing of the relationship of the United States to Mexico in particular and to Latin America in general. The historical period of many of these Westerns, the mid–nineteenth century, was a crucial time for nation-building and for rethinking the relationship across the Americas. After the crucial shift in the focus of expansion in the mid–nineteenth century, from the Western to the Southern frontier, the United States would begin to enlarge its imperial campaign and political influence in the hemisphere and the Pacific. These border Westerns may have resonance for a cold war audience preoccupied with

Korea, Cuba, and Vietnam, but they also distill a national origin story out of a more recent and accessible past, one that is geographically local and distinct, from the Alamo to the Civil War to the French invasion of Mexico, all occurring somewhere along the shifting line between the United States and Mexico.

NOTES

1. See Thomas Schatz, *Hollywood Genres* (Austin: University of Texas Press, 1981); Jack Nachbar, ed., *Focus on the Western* (Englewood Cliffs, NJ: Prentice Hall, 1974); Richard Slotkin, *Gunfighter Nation* (New York: HarperPerennial, 1992); Gaylyn Studlar and Matthew Bernstein, eds., *John Ford Made Westerns: Filming the Legend in the Sound Era* (Bloomington: Indiana University Press, 2001); André Bazin, "The Western, or the American Film *par excellence*," in *What Is Cinema?* vol. 2 (Berkeley: University of California Press, 1971); Stanley Corkin, *The Cowboy as Cold Warrior: The Western and U.S. History* (Philadelphia: Temple University Press, 2004); James K. Folsom, ed., *The Western: A Collection of Critical Essays* (Englewood Cliffs, NJ: Prentice Hall, 1979); Jane Tompkins, *West of Everything: The Inner Life of Westerns* (New York: Oxford University Press, 1992).

2. Albert J. Griffith, "The Scion, the Señorita, and the Texas Ranch Epic: Hispanic Images in Film," *Bilingual Review/Revista Bilingue* 16, no. 1 (1991): 15–22.

3. According to Lewt McCanles, Pearl's father is the "white half"; yet the name Chavez and the border town location seem to suggest that he is a creole Mexican of Spanish descent.

4. See Thomas Schatz, "The New Hollywood," in *Film Theory Goes to the Movies*, ed. Jim Collins, Hilary Radner, and Ava Preacher Collins (New York: Routledge, 1993), 11.

5. Luis Reyes and Peter Rubie, *Hispanics in Hollywood: A Celebration of 100 Years in Film and Television* (Hollywood: Lone Eagle, 2000), 110-12.

6. Reyes and Rubie remark on this unique feature of the story, the centrality of a Spanish-surnamed character; see ibid., 111.

7. Quoted in ibid., 112.

8. Jacquelyn Kilpatrick, *Celluloid Indians* (Lincoln: University of Nebraska Press, 1999), xvii.

9. Laura Mulvey, "Afterthoughts on 'Visual Pleasure and Narrative Cinema,'" in *Popular Fiction: Technology, Ideology Production, Reading*, ed. Tony Bennett (London: Routledge, 1990), 147.

10. See *Border Bandits: A True Tale of South Texas,* directed by Kirby Warnock (Trans-Pecos Productions, 2004).

11. See Américo Paredes, *With a Pistol in His Hand* (Austin: University of Texas Press, 1958).

12. Francis Paul Prucha, ed., *Documents of United States Indian Policy* (Lincoln: University of Nebraska Press, 2000), 175.

13. The town is immediately recognizable as a Mexican border town for its post-Prohibition history of supporting vices unavailable in the United States.

14. See Linda Williams, "Film Bodies: Gender, Genre, and Excess," in *Film and Theory,* ed. Robert Stam and Toby Miller (Malden, MA: Blackwell, 2000), 207-21.

15. See Mulvey, "Afterthoughts on 'Visual Pleasure and Narrative Cinema.'"

16. Frantz Fanon, *Black Skin, White Masks,* trans. Charles Lam Markmann (New York: Grove Weidenfeld), 1967.

17. Donald L. Fixico, *Termination and Relocation: Federal Indian Policy, 1945-1960* (Albuquerque: University of New Mexico Press, 1986), 10-11.

18. Robin Wood, "Retrospect," in *Howard Hawks: American Artist,* ed. Jim Hillier and Peter Wollen (London: BFI, 1996), 163-74.

19. Laura Mulvey, "Gentlemen Prefer Blondes: Anita Loos/Howard Hawks/ Marilyn Monroe," in *Howard Hawks: American Artist,* ed. Jim Hillier and Peter Wollen (London: BFI, 1996), 214-29.

‖‖‖‖‖‖‖‖‖‖‖‖‖‖‖‖‖‖‖‖‖‖‖‖‖‖‖‖‖‖‖‖‖‖‖‖‖‖‖‖‖‖‖‖‖

# 3

# Mixedfolks.com
## *"Ethnic Ambiguity," Celebrity Outing, and the Internet*

### *Lisa Nakamura*

> I am mixed with black and white and proud of it. I am
> glad that there is a site like this around.
> —"Clint," mixedfolks.com

> Huey uses the peace and quiet of vacation to tackle the
> great mysteries of our day:
> "Yeah—Vin Diesel's black."
> —"The Boondocks"[1]

Multicultural, multiracial, or "multiculti" actors were reported as enjoying a newfound vogue in a December 2003 *New York Times* article entitled, "Generation E.A.: Ethnically Ambiguous." In it, Ruth La Ferla writes that racially mixed actors are now "perceived as good, desirable, successful" because they possess "a face whose heritage is hard to pin down."[2] In 2001, Paul Spickard wrote that "multiculturalism is all the rage" and that "in the last decade and a half, a multiracial movement has emerged in the U.S.," resulting in a booming business in multiracial autobiographical narrative.[3] In recent years the popular press has paid particular attention to racial hybridity or multiraciality, the space where races previously seen as separate converge in the space of a single body.

Simultaneously with this development, the rapid adoption of Web 2.0 technologies that allow users to create and distribute their own content has given rise to a vast body of text and images on films, television shows, stars, and industry gossip by fans and other media enthusiasts. Scholars like Henry Jenkins have seen film and Internet convergence as a generally positive development, because it enables grassroots media production in digital media to democratize the film industry. Do-it-yourself amateur cultural production such as machinima and fan-produced moving image additions to the diegetic universes of *Star Wars* and other familiar narratives "affirm the right of everyday people to actively contribute to their culture."[4] Jenkins concludes that the Internet has given rise to new opportunities for a user-produced folk culture based around digital media creation to create a new "convergence culture."

While users are creating new bodies of folk media on the Web, hybrid texts composed of disparate elements taken from all types of digital sources and composited into new forms of "grassroots" media, a new social awareness of racial "hybridity" also is being created at the grassroots level. This "convergence culture" encompasses both racial regimes and media taxonomies. Media convergence and racial hybridity, or "ethnic ambiguity," are both old things that are "new again"; just as the development of earlier media technologies such as the photograph, printing press, and phonograph permitted the development of convergent media such as "talking books" and illuminated photography, so too has racial hybridity had an earlier, socially marginal characterization as "race-mixing" or miscegenation. However, at the turn of our century, a limited type of rehabilitation of both terms has taken place; at least for now, both are celebrated as democratizing, novel, and ultimately part of a narrative of technological and social progress.

Little has been written about the Internet as a channel for information on mixed race stars, which is in a way unsurprising, for the Web has always been a suspect method for getting at the "truth" about anything, especially stars. Indeed, early fears of the Internet had much to do with the lack of accountability that users had in regard to telling the truth and establishing correct attributions for statements. However, an analysis of user-produced Web sites on race and film stars can offer unique insight into what users *want* from stars in regard to public articulations of racial identity. This presents an interesting counterpoint to the tendency of new media theory to claim the Internet as a raceless space, since users' bodies are invisible while they use it. Much mainstream scholarship about the Internet notes that its most salient distinguishing feature is its ability to conceal identity markers such as gender and race.[5] This is its utopian promise and claim to adding something genuinely new to user experience.

As Burnett and Marshall write, "Part of the allure of the Web is that one's identity may not be attached to one's physical body on the Web. One can transform . . .in the anonymous web."[6]

The Web is unlike film because its interactivity and collaborative authoring tools permit, indeed depend upon, participation and authorship by users. Thus, the Web has a peculiar and privileged relationship to gossip. The Web content permits anonymous publication, making attribution difficult to establish. And when it comes to the matter of race and stars, the Web works like a tremendous gossip mill, but one with a difference. For when stars leave the matter of their race purposely ambiguous, the Web steps in to fill this gap in knowledge with speculation, assertion, and opinion. Celebrity Web sites speculate endlessly about all aspects of star identity, and in the case of stars defined as "mixed race" by mixedfolks. com, like Vin Diesel, Jessica Alba, Cameron Diaz, The Rock, and Jennifer Beals, at least some of this speculation has to do with race.[7] The Black Entertainment Network posits that the nature of this speculation changes depending on the race of the audience as well; in an article posted in 2004 on the bet.com Web site, writer James Hill noted that white audiences are unaware of and unable to see black multiraciality: "What I found amazing was the filmmaker's assumption that the average White viewer would understand the subtlety of bi-racial features that let Black folks know Vin Diesel and Jennifer Beals had 'something in 'em,' where most White folks didn't seem to notice at all."[8] Hill asserts that black audiences are differently enabled when it comes to perceiving the distinctive features of mixed race actors; the "open secret" of Diesel's and Beals's biraciality is not a secret to them, but only to "White folks."

Both black and white fans are intensely aware of race, albeit in different ways and with different perceptual understandings of it, and multiracial fans identify strongly with multiracial stars. In this chapter I will discuss the Web as a technology that can work to out mixed race stars, to fix their identities or at least encourage stars to claim them. This digital medium also evidences users' intense interest in what stars "are" and lets them broadcast these opinions. Mixedfolks.com is a Web site whose community of fans and users claim their right to participate in how stars ought to be represented racially. In this sense, they are intervening to rewrite star identities to solidify the sense of a distinctive mixed race identity that encompasses everyday people as well as stars. The site's design provides a gathering place for users to share their mixed race personal narratives, thus going far beyond its overt purpose as an outing site for celebrities. Users themselves come "out" on the site by sharing their stories of misunderstanding, classificatory confusions, racial anxieties, and ultimate sense of identification as "mixedfolks" that arise from accepting and understanding the nature of mixedness as a "third" identity.

In 2003 La Ferla asked the reader to "consider the careers of movie stars like Vin Diesel, Lisa Bonet, and Jessica Alba, whose popularity with young audiences seems due in part to the tease over whether they are black, white, Hispanic, American Indian or some combination."[9] Diesel has proven so far to be the master of this particular tease, and the mystery of his actual racial heritage has given rise to a great deal of speculation on the Web and elsewhere. Though the black media industry has been eager to claim him as one of their own—he was featured in an *Ebony* magazine article as one of "Hollywood's Top Black Moneymakers," and his film *The Fast and the Furious* has aired on the Black Starz! Cable network—he refuses to claim his blackness outright in any medium. When Diesel was featured on the cover of *Entertainment Weekly*, the accompanying article emphasized its subject's carefully tended racial ambiguity: "Diesel isn't being coy, he's being clever. He's not hiding from the public, he's courting it. By stripping away all identifying marks, presenting himself as a blank slate—particularly when it comes to his racial background—he's found a way to market himself to the broadest possible audience. He's selling himself as a multiethnic Everyman, a movie star virtually every demographic can claim as its own. "If you're Hispanic, you look at Vin and see a Hispanic," Cohen notes. "If you're Italian, you see an Italian. If you're African American, you see an African American. He could probably even play a Jewish character." *Boiler Room* director Ben Younger sees Diesel the same way. "People seem to make him into whatever they want him to be," he says. "Which is maybe one of the reasons why he's so popular. 'He's our boy.' Which is kind of funny because a lot of the people doing that wouldn't necessarily get along with each other. Italian Americans and African Americans? Not exactly a match made in heaven."[10] The fluidity of Diesel's race is matched only by the diversity of his roles; he has played several Italian and Latino characters, and even his "blackest" role, that of a mysterious science fiction hero in *Pitch Black*, Diesel would only describe in an interview as "urban."[11]

While Diesel, perhaps the most high-profile E.A. actor of recent years, steadfastly refuses to address the issue of his own racial background and identity, this is a relatively recent development. His independently produced short film *Multi-Facial* (1995) poignantly depicts racial passing as an occupational necessity for actors with ethnically ambiguous looks. *Multi-Facial* portrays mixed race actors as having no identities at all rather than enjoying a "third" identity, and thus having no effective way to market themselves to the film industry. The industry itself is blamed: when Diesel's character is rejected after reading for a dramatic role as a Latino, a compassionate Latina actress volunteers information about a soap opera that might hire him, and a black actor offers to help him get into an "industrial." "Industrials" such as music videos, infomercials, and training videos rely on the use of racial and gender types to hail diverse audiences. These "bread-and-butter" parts, as they are referred to in *Multi-Facial*, benefit greatly from the use of multiracial actors who can simultaneously hail many audiences.

However, the ambitious protagonist rejects these roles as unworthy of a "great actor," since great actors transcend type. Unfortunately, the roles available to him as a struggling young actor are all of this kind. He is asked to rap and to perform other types of minstrelsy to audition for roles as a Spanish-speaking Latino, as an Italian "Guido" wearing a porkpie hat and a sleeveless undershirt, and as a "mad homeboy." *Multi-Facial* strongly critiques racial film casting that forces mixed race actors to adopt broadly typecast performances of racial types; the scene in which Diesel channels Al Pacino's performance as Tony Montana in *Scarface* to get a part as a Latino ends painfully when he is unable to answer an actress's impassioned burst of Spanish with one of his own.[12] However, Diesel's efforts to pass as Latino, Italian, and black are depicted as surprisingly successful: the attractive Latina actress asks him after the interview, "Don't you know Spanish?" implying that he would have learned it at home as she had, and that he has at least "gotten over" with her. Thus, the film depicts racial passing as an occupational necessity for mixed race actors that can bleed over into aspects of their personal lives.

*Multi-Facial* was screened at the Sundance Independent Film Festival, and Diesel credits it with landing him his first role in a Hollywood film as an Italian American soldier, Adrian Caparzo, in Steven Spielberg's *Saving Private Ryan*. In an interview that accompanies the DVD version of *Multi-Facial*, Diesel says that the film is fictional but based on his own life, and he is quick to claim groundbreaking status for himself as a director and writer. He says that he realized after viewing the finished twenty-minute film that "I had just done something that might not have been done before. The stars had very clear origins; very clear nationalities, and mine has always been in question." He claims that the film was success-ful because it introduced "something new": the multiracial actor. Diesel's entrepreneurial spirit is much in evidence in this interview; he relates that he had to make his own film in order to get the right kind of role as a multiracial character, and that in doing so he "introduced to the film world someone whose origins weren't as clear as others actors and stars." Indeed, the film makes a poignant case for the humiliations and discomforts of racial passing for multiracial actors in the film industry. However, Diesel's trajectory as a star has relied on a different but related strategy for getting the "right kind" of roles. Instead of declaring himself to be white and denying himself as a "black actor," a category that he notes as a particularly distinctive and formidable one when he lists "Danny Glover, Sidney Poitier, Morgan Freeman" as role models for his black actor father, he refuses to identify as anything at all other than mixed. In so doing, he avoids the self-hating identity of a black man who refuses to admit that he is black and avails himself of a different racial strategy for assimilating to white society: that of *covering*.

According to Yale legal scholar Kenji Yoshino, minorities of all kinds are compelled to "cover—to minimize the race-salient traits that distinguish [them] from the white mainstream."[13] In a version of the neoliberal strategy adopted by President Bill Clinton's so-called don't ask, don't tell policy in regard to gay soldiers in the military, covering requires that race become a subject individuals of color are forbidden to articulate. "Color-blind" social policies require the cooperation of the individual, who is compelled to suppress or "cover" her racial identity as much as possible. While passing usually requires action, covering requires inaction. Just as the ethnic assimilation model allowed nonwhites to join American society despite their skin color and differing phenotypes so long as they were willing to act differently, or change those aspects of their exotic identities that *could* be changed, color-blind policies need individuals themselves to act blind to their own color.

There are subtle yet extremely important differences between passing and covering. If passing was the strategy of individuals who could not be assimilated to white privilege because of their colored bodies, and who thus chose to rewrite them as white, covering is the recourse of those who live in a "multicultural" world that values the exotic and does allow people of color to gain positions of power but requires them to cover in order to get it. Neoliberalism dictates that it is acceptable and sometimes good for an individual to *be* black but unacceptable for them to *perform their blackness* in specific institutional settings such as work, school, or other instances of the public sphere. Light-skinned multiracial actors such as Diesel, Dean Cain, Keanu Reeves, Kristin Kreuk, and The Rock who play nominally white roles are able to manage their skin color and body far more actively than other stars do or are *able* to do; they are indeed "multifacial."[14] Muteness or vagueness about race, a refusal to declare a *specific* connection to a nonwhite racial group, is a strategy to *cover* race. Yoshino describes the landmark case of a United Airlines flight attendant who was fired for wearing cornrows to work. This case exemplifies the ways that racial identity must be suppressed if it can be characterized as *elective*. The flight attendant's unsuccessful lawsuit for unlawful termination on the basis of racial discrimination was rejected because it was determined that her cornrows were elective, that she was responsible for her decision to wear them. The court maintained that it was disciplining her behavior, which she could change, rather than her race, which she could not. The compulsion to *cover* creates a dilemma that is different from but just as confounding as that of light-skinned black people in the early twentieth century.

Paul Spickard claims that the recent popularity of biracial biography reflects a concept of identity that is distinctly postmodern, in contrast to earlier narratives about racial passing that appealed to a modernist sense of identity. He writes, "Gates . . .notes that 'the thematic elements of passing—fragmentation, alienation, liminality, self-fashioning—echo the great themes of modernism.' One might go a step further and say that the themes of multiraciality—constructedness, contingency, paradox, multiplicity—are among the themes of postmodernism."[15] I would modify that formulation to say that while *passing* is modernist, *covering* is postmodernist. The requirement to cover is a form of racial governmentality that works to punish expressions of race but does not require an individual to pass muster as a *different* race. Although it is an equally rigorous but less "modern" technique than passing, it is close enough to attract criticism on the same grounds.

In her landmark essay "Passing for White, Passing for Black," Adrian Piper elegantly details the anatomy of passing as a tempting but shameful act. And if passing is despised within the black community, outing is perhaps even more so. Piper writes, "In the African American community, we do not 'out' people who are passing as white in the European American community. Publicly to expose the African ancestry of someone who claims to have none is not done."[16] Piper further explains that "a person who desires personal and social advantage and acceptance within the white community so much that she is willing to repudiate her family, past, history, and her personal connections within the African American community in order to get them is someone who is already in so much pain that it's just not possible to do something that you know is going to cause her any more."[17] While Diesel has never denied that he is black or part black, his refusal to own his blackness in public is read as a betrayal or at least a disappointment by many of his African American critics. The "black community" has expectations regarding star conduct in terms of racial identity, and Diesel has failed to meet these. And nowhere has this criticism been more vocal than on the Internet.

From the civil rights movement's earliest days, its African American leaders in the United States have promoted a discourse of racial uplift that *required* outstanding individuals, members of a so-called talented tenth, to represent the race in a positive light to society at large. This discourse of racial rehabilitation is alive and well today, as users create Web content that makes urgent claims for stars and celebrities of color to take up the burden and responsibility to represent their racial and ethnic identities for the good of all people of color. Mixed race fans are no different, and have similar requirements for their chosen stars: as is asserted in Mengel's article "Triples: The Social Evolution of a Multiracial Panethnicity: An Asian American Perspective," multiracial people often fail to identify strongly with any one of their races of origin, but rather form a separate collective identity based on "panethnicity which is based on mixedness *per se*."[18] The notion that mental health and self-esteem—surely an entitlement in the American context—can only be attained through viewing role models that permit positive racial identifications informs the design and content of mixedfolks.com. This site's creators and users, its virtual community, believe that stars have a social duty and an implicit obligation to represent their minority heritage when they gain a place in the public eye. They demand, sometimes respectfully and sometimes not, that stars acknowledge their nonwhite racial heritage, even when or perhaps especially when this star is a multiracial person who plays white roles. This is because racial ambiguity demands articulation and clarification by viewers; in cases in which a star's race is not phenotypically obvious, the star has the opportunity to disavow her race. And just as the main stumbling block to hybrid new media is the copyright law that requires users to attribute every piece of their creation to its original source, so too are multiracial movie stars compelled by their fans to "attribute" themselves. Multiracial fans have a unique stake in multiracial stars acknowledging their "darker" racial heritage.

It has been more than ten years since *Multi-Facial* brought Vin Diesel to the attention of mainstream Hollywood, and he is now the star that he says he always wanted to be, as well as an actor who is respected more than most of his peers who perform in action-hero roles. Why has Diesel maintained this racial tease during his long and successful career as an actor and star? Beyond the rhetoric of transcendent individualism espoused by the self-made man and entrepreneurial auteur lies the imperative of global marketing. Multifaciality is crucial for consolidating popularity in a global marketplace of celebrity. Other multiracial stars like Jennifer Lopez have followed a now-familiar trajectory from "ethnic" star appearing in "ethnic" films to "global" star by taking roles that are racially unmarked or, rather, marked as nominally white. (In her 1999 video "If You Had My Love," the viewer witnesses a remarkably literal example of this movement in the space of three minutes; Lopez appears as a cornrowed hip-hop girl, a Latina flamenco dancer, and a white-clad blonde with stick-straight hair.)[19] Celebrity mixed race identity that aspires to global standing needs to claim and *defend* a position of unmarked racial otherness: while it will not admit or allow its identity as belonging to a particular race (thus excluding particular audiences from the pleasures of identification), it is equally zealous about eschewing *normative* whiteness. This makes it impossible for any specific racial group to claim the star as a role model. This has been Diesel's strategy; he is an actor who has had to work very hard at disavowing blackness after his mainstream success in films like *The Fast and the Furious* and *Pitch Black* made him a desirable role model for the black community.

Mixedfolks.com subordinates star gossip to a specific political goal: that of promoting the visibility and rights of mixed race folks who are not necessarily stars. Ironically, it accomplishes this by subverting the carefully maintained and modulated identities of mixed race stars by outing them *as* mixed. It also provides extensive bulletin board space for users to post pictures of themselves and personal narratives and to form connections based on sharing a pan-ethnic mixed identity, a "third" identity. The site attempts to resolve the problem of missing role models for mixed race "folks" by identifying some from the popular culture. The site lists actors, musicians, and other mixed race celebrities who are often assumed to be white by many viewers and connects them to their "hidden" racial backgrounds. There are three categories of "mixedfolks" that organize the list of stars and other famous people such as athletes and musicians: "African/African American, Hapa/Asian (entire Asian continent) and Hispanic and

*Vin Diesel's profile on mixedfolks.com*

Native American." Users who did not know that comedian Rob Schneider is part Filipino, that actresses Jennifer Beals, Halle Berry, and Mariah Carey are part African American, and that Mercedes Ruehl, Madeleine Stowe, and Lynda Carter are part Latina are set straight on the site's home page. These people are all claimed as "mixedfolks," whether or not they identify themselves in that way. The way in which these actors and public figures are identified as "African/African American," "Asian," or "Hispanic or Native American" without their consent or most likely knowledge characterizes this form of information dissemination as "outing." Rather than simply giving true or untrue information about stars, the site works by revealing the hidden and slightly scandalous *racial* truth about these figures, a truth they are at times anxious to hide or at least choose not to publicize. Raquel Welch, born Jo Raquel Tejada, is listed under mixed race "Hispanic" actresses as Bolivian and white. The site links to a *New York*

*Times* article that describes her decision to come out as a Latina after having been seen as a generic white bombshell (but always an "exotic" one, as viewers who remember her fur bikini in *One Million Years B.C.* will attest). In this article, cited as well by Thrupkaew, Welch says, "I'm happy to acknowledge [being Latina] and it's long overdue and it's very welcome. There's been kind of an empty place here in my heart and also in my work for a long, long time."[20] Welch is thus framed as a model of mixed race identification, one that the site encourages other actors to emulate.

The site's creators are very careful to deflect criticism of their site's mission to out stars by posting an explanation on the home page that they beg users to read before e-mailing them with complaints. It reads:

About MixedFolks.com
(Please read before e-mailing me)

1.) First of all let me state that the purpose of MixedFolks.com is simple, to celebrate your multiracial heritage. I try to provide information that multiracial people will find relevant and interesting. It is not meant to be divisive.

2.) You will notice that most of the people on this site are mixed with African or African-American and something else. The reason for this is that when I first started the site it was just going to feature half White and half Black people because that's what I am. But as I started working on the site I decided to add anybody who was half Black to add diversity. Once the site went up I got a lot of e-mail from people asking me to add other people who were of Mixed race origin but not necessarily Black. At first I wasn't going to do that because I thought it would be too much work adding all those people and also because I felt that I could only relate to issues affecting those who were half Black. But as I talked with more and more biracial people of other races I learned that we all have similar issues, both positive and negative.

3.) I realize that some of the people on this site choose not to identify with being biracial and that is their prerogative. I'm just stating that they happen to be of mixed race heritage, what they choose to call themselves and identify with is their business and I respect that. I'm not trying to tell anyone what they should identify with, it's none of my business.[21]

The site's stated mission to serve *all* mixed race people, not just stars, means that its creators must overtly concern themselves with user feedback. While some Web site creators can tend toward hostility or

*Site organization of mixedfolks.com*

defensiveness when confronted with user criticism, this one tries hard to be or at least appear responsive to challenges from community members regarding unclear or inconsistent racial definitions, the exclusion of particular racial groups (like non–African Americans), and accusations of "divisiveness." The site proprietor takes pains to note that he has changed the site to reflect their preferences and complaints. Though he claims that the issue of mixed racial definition is "much to complex" [*sic*] to resolve on the site, he does assert the right to convey racial truth *despite* stars' individual preferences. Though stars may wish to pass or at least cover, he is "just stating that they happen to be of mixed race heritage, what they choose to call themselves and identify with is their business and I respect that." This is a tricky position to take, for revealing someone else's "business" by just stating what they "are" is a peculiar way to "respect" their identifications. However, the site's ultimate goal, which is to provide a virtual community for "mixedfolks," coalesces around the pleasures of star identification in at least two senses of the word: the identification and consequent reclassification of formerly perceived white stars as "people of color," a process that allows them to be rehabilitated as role models, as well as the identification with the star by the viewer. The site's design encourages both of these processes, particularly in its "community" pages.

The site offers a rich array of resources for its users. Though the celebrity outing page is set as the default home page, on its left-hand side a menu listing "MF Community," "Chat," "Library," "Multimedia," "Links," "Comics," "Names," and "Message Board" offers several modes of interactivity that encourage learning and further exploration. The "library" link leads to four pages of bibliographic information, listing critically respected mixed race memoirs such as James McBride's *The Color of Water* and Rebecca Walker's *Black, White and Jewish: The Autobiography of a Shifting Self*, along with fictional accounts of mixed race identity and passing such as Lalita Tademy's novel *Cane River* and William Faulkner's *Light in August*. These are mingled with more culturally marginal titles like *Six Black Presidents: Black Blood, White Masks U.S.A.*, which outs several American presidents as mixed race African Americans. The section also includes an extensive list of children's books on mixed race identity, such as Marguerite Davol's charming *Black, White, Just Right!* Scholarly books on the topic of mixed race identity are also much in evidence here: Maria P. P. Root's *Racially Mixed People in America* and Ursula M. Brown's *The Interracial Experience* are listed along with screenshots of their covers. The emphasis on self-education and research evidenced in this part of the site demonstrates the intention to move beyond gossip about stars and into a more self-reflective and analytical mode regarding interracial identity. Significantly, the site does not link to other celebrity gossip pages or Web sites about the film industry. The celebrity outing content listed on the front page teases the reader into entering the site and hopefully becoming interested in some of the resources likely to promote self-education, reflection, and community.

Mixedfolks.com thus gives the lie to the notion that E.A.'s satisfy "a desire for the exotic, left-of-center beauty that transcends race or class," as Amy Barnett, editor of *Teen People*, asserts, since it works to reattach racially mobile bodies to their "proper" racial categories. However, the Web site claims a socially positive identity that attempts to hail its audiences as politically active group of "mixedfolks" by describing its mission as follows:

"These pages are for all the rest of us. Mixedfolks who may not be well-known but we still want to represent."[22] Rather than exposing the hidden facticity of race in order to shame or embarrass the actors, the site identifies them as hidden sources of inspiration and identification that must be *made* to "represent" on the Internet despite their disavowal of (or failure to acknowledge) a nonwhite racial identity in film and television. There is a complex interplay between the site's construction of a "mixedfolks" identity community within its bulletin boards and areas for user participation, the visual culture of celebrity mixed race outing, and the intermedial connections between the celebrity Web site and filmic and televisual media. Rather than "transcending race or class," bracketing these identity categories as outmoded or beside the point, the site and its community assert that "E.A. beauty" arises from the mutual recognition of hybridity, both in shared mediaspaces and in virtual community spaces.

A vibrant community of users has grown up around this celebrity outing site, creating an interracial palette of mixedfolks that is very different from what Hollywood produces as models of mixedness. On the post–YouTube Web, everyone is potentially a star, and the site encourages users to "out" themselves just as it outs movie actors, musicians, athletes, and "others." The pages linked to "MF Community" contain personal profiles put up by users. Each page has sixteen slots for photographs submitted by users, as well as a paragraph that explains the ways that they are "mixedfolks." This form is designed exactly like that of the main site that identifies the stars, with spaces for pictures and short bios. The link between users' mixed racial identity and mixed star identities is overtly stressed not only by the site's designer, who set up this template, but also by the community members themselves. In "Carolyn's" profile, which includes a photograph of herself smiling at the camera in a chin-on-hand pose, she writes, "My mother is Italian, my father is Black/Rican. I love being mixed, I don't claim to be one or the other. I am 29 years old and love playing the 'spotting game' with my husband. You know the game, . . . where you see a star or just someone off the street and say, 'I know that person has a lil' somethin' somethin' up in 'em.'"[23]

The use of photographic headshots of both stars and community members in this site is vitally important to creating a visual culture of mixed race identity, for the photos invite the viewer to visually verify the existence of a "little somethin' somethin' up in 'em," to quote mixedfolks.com community member Carolyn. Users are invited to gratify the desire to racially profile others by playing the "spotting game" in digital mediaspace.

This use of the Internet as part of a scopic regime of understanding mixed race identity has its roots in earlier visual media, in particular, photography and film. Courtney asserts that film, in particular, played a crucial role in solidifying the notion of race as visible and apprehensible to the naked eye. In this sense, film technology was only following up on a custom established by the legal system as early as the nineteenth century; as she notes, the "scopic rule" of racial identification was in force as early as 1806.[24] As she writes in her persuasive genealogy of racial regimes of vision, "Conceptions of race as something the eye can see are by no means unique to the twentieth century," though visual media technologies like film intensified them. She also notes that the scopic rule whereby an observer was empowered to determine a person's race solely by visual observation was only "one of two methods by which the court attempts to determine racial identity (the other is bound up with ancestry and racial names)."[25] Mixedfolks.com only asks that community members provide first names in order to protect their privacy, thereby giving them the chance to hide their ancestral names—this is de rigueur in most virtual communities. Remarkably, many members provide their full names as well as their photographs, thus demonstrating an openness that has become increasingly rare as identity theft and scams have become more prevalent. Users of mixedfolks.com are eager to claim and represent their mixed race status through personal photographs, biographical narrative, and disclosure of their real identities.

It is probably not surprising that the biggest surprises on mixedfolks. com have to do with the number of celebrities who have a "hidden" Asian heritage. Asian multiracial people have long had the privilege of choosing to claim whiteness through passing as well as through covering. Unlike for mixed race black people, who were subject to  hypostatic rules of blood quanta, such as the "one-drop rule," the classification system of mixed race identity has been much looser in the case of multiracial Asian Americans. The elaborate taxonomic language of "black" and "white" ancestry such as "quadroon," "octoroon," and "mulatto," to which multiracials of African descent have been subjected, does not apply to Asian multiracials: the term "Eurasian" seems to have sufficed for all admixtures.[26] While some viewers may know that Dean Cain, Keanu Reeves, Kristin Kreuk, and the Tilly sisters are part Asian, it is unlikely that they are aware that Nia Peeples, Paula Abdul, Norah Jones, Ben Kingsley, and Shannyn Sossamon are.[27]

The "names" link on the site provides several lists of names describing different types of multiracial people. The majority of these refer to African

American ancestry, but the site's community-creating mission gives equal time and space to a list of terms contributed by community members. The first list's terms, which include "mulatto" and "octoroon," are attributed to the *American Heritage Dictionary*. The second list, however, includes eighty-six terms, including "Blackamese," "Blackipino," "chexmex," "Blatino," "Mexicoon" (described as "an offensive term for someone of both Mexican and black ancestry"), "wigger," "Oreo," "wood chips," "Halfrican," and "rice cracker."[28] The flagging of only *some* of these terms as "offensive" implies that the rest of them are not. Both nonoffensive and offensive terms are listed on the same page as the first and better-known list of terms, as if they were just as legitimate. This transmission of vernacular, on-the-ground knowledge of mixed race identity exemplifies the Internet's affinity for spreading folk culture, for it broadcasts a counterdiscourse regarding mixed race identity that can be read alongside and in opposition to the *American Heritage Dictionary* and Dictionary.com. The problematic language of hypostatic descent that has its roots in the slave trade is opposed to a new vernacular of hybridity that contains a great deal more complexity and humor. In addition, it recognizes the existence of other, non-African races as components of mixed racialized identities.

Mixedfolks.com also recognizes shades of white. Just as the site's language of classification tends to identify stars' racial heritage in terms of which parent is which race (e.g., "His father is black, his mother is Irish" in Vin Diesel's profile), in keeping with this emphasis on detail, it also taxonomizes whiteness in terms of ethnicity and nation. Italians, Irish, Scandinavians, Scots, Germans, and especially Jews are listed as parents of "mixedfolks," just as Koreans, Japanese, Chinese, Mexicans, and Indians are all listed specifically. This desire to make distinctions between whites, in a sense to treat them as "mixedfolks" as well, resonates with earlier, now forgotten struggles by Jews and other former people of color to assimilate into whiteness. As Eric Goldstein and David Roediger write in their insightful historical treatments of whiteness as a social construct and contested identity, whiteness was achieved by ethnic Europeans rather than simply conferred.[29] Mixedfolks avoids a monolithic view of whiteness by acknowledging its different varieties in its genealogies of mixed race stars.

The Internet has always provided a space for transformations of various kinds. Diarists become bloggers and publishers, and amateur camera users become photographers whose work is reproduced widely in all sorts of contexts, thanks to Blogger and Flickr. The transformation of media professionalism by the Internet is paralleled by transformations in racial identity representation. Internet users have availed themselves of their power within the new participatory medium of the Internet to revise the story of celebrities and race, to color-in racial blankness or default whiteness by uncovering narratives of mixed racial identities. Vin Diesel is a transformative, convergent, and contradictory figure as well. He is an entrepreneur and self-made man who was nonetheless "discovered" by a major Hollywood director, an actor who cares about his craft yet appears primarily in spectacle-driven genre films dubbed "video games" by film reviewers, a black public figure who will not claim blackness. The promiscuous production of digital communication about stars guarantees that all kinds of virtual communities, including communities of multiracial "thirds," will continue to shape media narratives about mixed race.

## Acknowledgments

I owe many thanks to my colleague Mary Beltrán for her patience and support while I completed this chapter, as well as for the opportunity to write it. She knows how I feel about Vin Diesel. Camilla Fojas provided useful suggestions for revision. Thanks as well to Lynn Spigel for her invitation to present some of this work at her excellent "Electronic Elsewheres" Symposium at Northwestern University in the fall of 2003. Though this chapter turned into something very different from what I presented there, I am still grateful to Lynn and to Mimi White for providing some extremely useful commentary.

NOTES

1. Aaron McGruder, "The Boondocks" (Universal Press Syndicate, 2002).

2. Ruth La Ferla, "Generation E.A.: Ethnically Ambiguous," *New York Times*, December 28, 2003.

3. Paul Spickard, "The Subject Is Mixed Race: The Boom in Biracial Biography," in *Rethinking "Mixed Race*," ed. David Parker and Miri Song (London, VA: Pluto Press, 2001), 76

4. Henry Jenkins, *Convergence Culture: Where Old and New Media Collide* (New York: NYU Press, 2006), 132. Machinima is "a hybrid of machine and cinema . . . 3-D digital animation created in real time using game engines" (152). These visual narratives exploit the characters, sets, and other visual apparatus of

preexisting popular game repurpose such as Halo or Grand Theft Auto to create new narratives. See his chapter in *Convergence Culture* entitled "Quentin Tarantino's Star Wars? Grassroots Creativity Meets the Media Industry" for some excellent examples and an extended discussion.

5. Robert Burnett and P. David Marshall, *Web Theory: An Introduction* (London: Routledge, 2003), 78.

6. Ibid., 175

7. This is of course true as well about star sexuality. See in particular Michael d'Angelis's wonderful book on celebrity outing, *Gay Fandom and Crossover Stardom: James Dean, Mel Gibson, and Keanu Reeves* (Durham, NC: Duke University Press, 2001).

8. James Hill, "What's It All About? 'Alfie' Doesn't Seem Sure," *Bet.com*, November 5, 2004.

9. La Ferla, "Generation E.A."

10. Benjamin Svetkey, "Vin at All Costs," *Entertainment Weekly*, August 2, 2002.

11. "Urban" often stands in for "African American" or "black" in the entertainment and fashion industries.

12. While there is a long history of white actors in nonwhite roles, such as Pacino in *Scarface*, Luise Rainer and Paul Muni as O-Lan and Wang in *The Good Earth*, and Richard Barthelmess in *Broken Blossoms*, the racial identity of the actor remains clear to audiences. This is not the case when mixed race actors portray whites, hence the mission of mixedfolks.com.

13. Kenji Yoshino, *Covering: The Hidden Assault on Our Civil Rights* (New York: Random House, 2006), 133. Yoshino takes this term from sociologist Erving Goffman, who defines it as follows: "It is a fact that persons who are ready to admit possession of a stigma (in many cases because it is known about or immediately apparent) may nonetheless make a great effort to keep the stigma from looming large. The individual's object is to reduce tension, that is, to make it easier for himself and the others to withdraw covert attention from the stigma . . . this process will be referred to as *covering*." Erving Goffman, *Stigma: Notes on the Management of Spoiled Identity* (Harmondsworth: Penguin, 1968), 102.

14. Vin Diesel's active management of his facial and bodily representation extends to areas other than movie roles: according to Fametracker.com, director John Frankenheimer claims that on the set of *Reindeer Games*, Diesel refused to show his "guns," or extremely muscular arms, in pictures in which he was not the star. "Vin Diesel: Fame Audit," www.fametracker.com/fame_audit/diesel_vin.php (accessed October 8, 2006).

15. Spickard, "The Subject Is Mixed Race," 81.

16. Adrian Piper, "Passing for White, Passing for Black," in *Passing and the Fictions of Identity*, ed. Elaine K. Ginsberg (Durham, NC: Duke University Press, 1996), 246.

17. Ibid.

18. Laurie M. Mengel, "Triples: The Social Evolution of a Multiracial Panethnicity: An Asian American Perspective," in Parker and Song, Rethinking "Mixed Race."

19. See Mary Beltrán, "The Spitfire, the Airbrush Artist, the Trainer, and the Diva: Racializing and Class-ifying Moreno and Lopez as Star Bodies" (paper presented at the symposium "Latino/a Studies in the Midwest," Ohio State University, Columbus, April 2004), for an excellent historical discussion of race-changing in the service of marketing.

20. Noy Thrupkaew, "The Multicultural Mysteries of Vin Diesel," Tolerance. Org, August 23, 2002. The link to this article from mixedfolks.com is no longer active.

21. The rest of the disclaimer reads as follows:

4.) I realize that most all Blacks in America have some mixed ancestry. But there is clearly a difference between someone who has parents of two different races and someone whose great great grandmother was White but everyone else in their family is Black. This does not mean that there are not people who are multigenerational mixed but in order to narrow the focus of this site (due to limited time and resources) many of them are not included. This should not be seen as a dismissal of those who are multigenerational mixed, or that they are any better or worse than other mixed people.

5.) So the next question is, how do you determine who is mixed? First of all, I don't determine who is mixed, but for the purposes of this site (Except the MixedFolks.com Community) I can only add someone to this site if they have parents of two different races (in other words first generation mixed, I have made a few exceptions though). The only reason for this rule is that I simply don't have time to research and add everyone who ever had some race mixing in their past. Again, this does not mean that there are not people who are multigenerational mixed but in order to narrow the focus of this site (due to limited time and resources) many of them are not included. Unfortunately I have to clarify this because to some it is not understood. Realistically this site is for enjoyment and information, it is not intended to be the final word on the definitions of race or who is mixed and who isn't. That is a question much too complex for me or this site."

22. This text appears on the "MF Community" page.

23. http://mixedfolks.com/community.htm (accessed July 8, 2006).

24. Susan Courtney, Hollywood Fantasies of Miscegenation: Spectacular Narratives of Gender and Race, 1903-1967 (Princeton, NJ: Princeton University Press, 2005).

25. Ibid.

26. Though Eurasian identity lacks a taxonomic set of terms to describe it, there has been a long-standing obsession with identifying *any* admixture of white and Asian blood; this is especially evident in narratives depicting Indian and British relations in the context of empire. See Kipling's story "His Chance in Life" and others from *Plain Tales from the Hills* for an example of racial anxiety about the infiltration of "half-caste" Eurasians into government positions. Rudyard Kipling, *Plain Tales from the Hills*, ed. Godfrey Cave (London: Penguin, 1994).

27. See LeiLani Nishime on the mingled pleasure and guilt of identifying mixed race stars in her wonderfully titled "Guilty Pleasures: Keanu Reeves, Superman, and Racial Outing," in *East Main Street: Asian American Popular Culture*, ed. Shilpa Dave, LeiLani Nishime, and Tasha Oren (New York: NYU Press, 2005).

28. See http://mixedfolks.com/names.htm for the full list.

29. See Eric L. Goldstein, *The Price of Whiteness: Jews, Race, and American Identity* (Princeton, NJ: Princeton University Press, 2006); David R. Roediger, *Working toward Whiteness: How America's Immigrants Became White; the Strange Journey from Ellis Island to the Suburbs* (New York: Basic Books, 2005).

III

# Identity, Taboo, and "Spice"
## *Screening Mixed Race Romance and Families*

||||||||||||||||||||||||||||||||||||||||||||||||||

# 4

# Catching Up with History
## Night of the Quarter Moon, *the Rhinelander Case, and Interracial Marriage in 1959*

*Heidi Ardizzone*

In 1925, defendant Alice Jones Rhinelander partially disrobed before a jury in White Plains, New York, to prove she had not misrepresented her racial identity to her husband, as charged. Leonard Rhinelander, the son of a leading New York family, was suing his wife for an annulment, claiming he had thought she was white when he married her. Showing the judge and jury portions of her torso and legs supported her lawyers' claims that Alice's nonwhite ancestry was visible on her body, evidence which her husband had had many opportunities to view during their three-year relationship before marrying. Although no reporters were present, the imagined scene created a new wave of scandal, media attention, and speculation near the end of a monthlong trial that made near-daily headlines in New York City and consistent newspaper coverage throughout the country. In 1959 the film *Night of the Quarter Moon*, loosely based on the Rhinelander case, reconstructed the scene.[1] Actress Julie London, playing Ginny Nelson, wiped nervous sweat from her brow as she hesitantly began to remove her clothing, determined to prove to the California court that she had not tricked her rich white socialite husband into marrying her.

Both the historical Alice and the fictional Ginny were willing to bare their bodies to defend their marriages, trying to preserve a union that was threatened by interfering white in-laws. The interracial marriages presented by the historical trial and by the film version thirty-four years later were seen by whites as tests of social equality, challenges to the entire system of segregation. That Alice and Ginny were of ambiguous appearance

*This illustration and caption were the most common advertising image and slogan for* Night of the Quarter Moon. *Notice the fist tearing the woman's bodice.*

only highlighted one problem posed by black-white intermarriage: how to categorize and identify people of mixed ancestry.

With the 1959 film, director Hugo Hass finally turned the Rhinelanders' "sensational love story" into "screen dynamite!"—at least in the minds of MGM's ad campaigns. A promotional "tabloid" marketing the film to the general public featured provocative photos of Julie London, at various stages of undress, and John Drew Barrymore, alternately cavorting with her and protecting her from "hoodlums" and other mysterious attackers. Society and his "blue-blood" family all objected to their love. Nothing in the images or captions explained exactly why there was so much violence and opposition to their romance, exactly what "unwritten law" they had defied. Nat King Cole appeared several times, always at a piano or singing, and Indian actress Anna Kashfi was featured prominently as a barelegged "exotic dancer." But what did they have to do with the story line?[2]

Julie London's lightly tanned skin allowed visual promos to keep up the ambiguity. "I don't care what she is . . . she's mine!" lobby cards and posters proclaimed without explanation.[3] But "what she was" was one-quarter black-Angolan, and the "unwritten law" (actually still written law in many states in 1959) was against interracial marriage. The Bantam paperback, published in the same year and written by one of the film's screenwriters, was more explicit: "She's my wife! I don't give a damn about the color of her skin!"[4]

Despite the vagueness of some of its promotional materials, *Night of the Quarter Moon* was the first Hollywood film that not only depicted a black-white interracial marriage but also made that marriage the center of its plot. It was, as *Variety* noted, a "miscegenation-themed romance and courtroom melodrama."[5] The translation of the historical Rhinelander case of 1925 to a late 1950s story and audience highlighted some of the historical shifts in Americans' understanding of black-white interracial relations, civil rights, and racial identity. But my primary interest here is to place the film within the context of American film treatment, as well

John Drew Barrymore rushes to aid his wife, Julie London, as attorney James Edwards rips her dress in a sensational trial.

M-G-M Presents "NIGHT OF THE QUARTER MOON" in CinemaScope

*John Drew Barrymore, Julie London, and James Edwards in* Night of the Quarter Moon *pivotal moment.*

as legal perspectives and popular understandings of interracial marriage in the 1950s and 1960s. The film has been largely forgotten by critics and ignored by scholars, just as the Rhinelander case was largely forgotten by moviegoers in 1959. Its topic put it on the list of movies that would not be shown in southern states like Mississippi; contemporary and later critics cited its weak script, quick shooting schedule, maudlin melodrama, and heavy-handed moralizing. (Ironically, one of the harshest critics—who summed up the film as "outrageous bilge"—found aspects of the plot that followed the historical detail the most unbelievable.) Although it was released internationally and rereleased in the United States (first under the title *Flesh and Flame*, then *The Color of Her Skin*), it reportedly played primarily to "exploitation grind houses." It did, however, stay in movie theaters in New York and Washington, D.C., for several months and reappeared on television through the 1960s.[6]

But *Night of the Quarter Moon* represented a significant transitional moment between the "passing" films of the late 1940s and 1950s and the films of the late 1960s usually cited as the first treatments of interracial marriage. Furthermore, *Quarter Moon* positioned interracial marriage as an aspect of civil rights. Five years after *Brown v. the Board of Education*, we might hope for a stronger indictment of racial discrimination—*Quarter Moon*'s challenge is limited, to say the least. Produced and set in a period when the civil rights movement was moving into the foreground of American consciousness and legal prohibitions of black-white marriage were weakening, *Quarter Moon* made a contribution that merits serious attention.

Appearing after well-publicized civil rights boycotts and sit-ins, *Night of the Quarter Moon* had to catch up with history in several senses. With the civil rights movement under way but still struggling, *Quarter Moon* had a message to hammer home: discrimination is bad. More subtly, it used interracial marriage as a vehicle to portray conflicts over civil rights. Set in California after that state had overturned antimiscegenation laws, *Quarter Moon* further placed itself within the history of post–World War II challenges to racial segregation and discrimination. (In another sense, history still had to catch up to the film: much of its audience—and most of the film's characters—objected to interracial marriage even if they claimed to support civil rights.) In addition, this now-obscure film was the first major motion picture to depict a black-white interracial marriage. It certainly predates *One Potato, Two Potato*, which has been given that title.[7] In its placement of interracial marriage as both a civil rights issue and a vehicle for intrafamily drama, *Night of the Quarter Moon* falls into an extended trajectory between the much more well-known *Birth of a Nation* (1915) and *Guess Who's Coming to Dinner* (1967). It also represents an important link between the passing, "tragic mulatta" films of the 1940s and 1950s and the interracial marriage as "race problem" films of the 1960s. Finally, *Night of the Quarter Moon* was made and released thirty-four years after the events of the Rhinelander marriage and annulment trial from which it drew narrative inspiration. Much of the initial Rhinelander story translated well; some significant details had to be updated.

When news broke in 1924 that Leonard Rhinelander, wayward heir to millions in New York real estate, had married Alice Jones, daughter of a "colored cab driver," newspapers across the country picked up the story. Under the sudden glare of media, the nervous groom stood by his wife and her family for two reporter-stalked weeks. He even gave an interview, claiming that he did not care what color Alice was. Then he disappeared with lawyers dispatched by his father, resurfacing only as a signature on an annulment suit. Interracial marriage had never been illegal in New York, nor was there ever any legal "blood quantum" definition of who was black and white.[8] The annulment suit, then, charged that Alice had misrepresented herself as white, hiding the fact that she "had colored blood" from Leonard prior to their marriage. The Rhinelander lawyers based their actual case on misrepresentation, and the assumption that no sane, intelligent white man would knowingly marry a nonwhite woman. For the year between her husband's disappearance and the start of the annulment trial, Alice and her family proclaimed faith that Leonard was still in love with Alice and wanted to remain married to her. He was, they charged, clearly under the influence of, if not held against his will by, his father, lawyers, and bodyguards. Perhaps he would not even show up to personally make his charge in court.

But Leonard Rhinelander did appear in court, with his lawyers and bodyguards, to provide weeks of testimony regarding his relationship and marriage. Now covered by every major American newspaper, the trial pulled out details of the couple's courtship, sexual relations, forced separations, and passionate love letters written over their three-year relationship. Well aware of his father's disapproval, Leonard had waited until he aged into a trust fund from another family inheritance to marry Alice, staying with her for long periods of time before and after their wedding at her parents' home in New Rochelle, New York.

There was some evidence that Alice and her family had tried to live in the margins of racial categories, as neither black nor white. But she was consistently depicted in newspapers as "black," "Negro," "mulatto," or "colored." These terms were sometimes synonyms, sometimes subcategories of each other, but always seen as related. And, at the start of the trial, her lawyers had conceded that Alice "had some colored blood in her veins," denying only that she had misrepresented herself.

Scandal followed scandal in the trial, and the highlights and melodrama seemed unending. Leonard's lawyers portrayed their client as a nervous, naïve, tongue-tied boy, lured into marriage by the sexually promiscuous, streetwise, gold-digging Alice. Conversely, her lawyers portrayed Leonard as an elite child of wealth, raised to presume he was entitled to take advantage of a working-class, mixed race woman. He had seduced her and left her hanging while he traveled the world. Of course she wanted him to marry her; what respectable woman wouldn't? The battle lines were drawn, and the dirt began to fly.

However perfect the historical case might have seemed to Hollywood writers and producers, a movie version would have to wait until the social climate and industry policy had changed. For almost forty years, Hollywood had avoided the topic of interracial romance, especially between blacks and whites.[9] Romance between blacks and whites had been only one of many socially undesirable topics prohibited or limited in a series of codes followed by the Hollywood film industry. The "Thirteen Points of the National Motion Picture Industry" (1921) did not specify interracial relationships, although their warning against illicit love affairs would have included any interracial romance in more than half of the United States by 1921. The 1927 list of "Don'ts," however, as well as the 1930 Production Code of the Motion Picture Producers and Directors of America, which superseded it, both proscribed miscegenation, defined as "sex relationships between the white and black races."[10] But in the post–World War II era, Production Code control over movie content gradually weakened. In an industry that had always followed the letter more than the spirit of the restrictions, film producers and movie distributors began to directly challenge the Production Code Administration. In fact, one of the first plot treatments of passing, *Pinky* (1949), resulted in a legal scuffle over its distribution. However, this was only one of many such disputes. Overall, the challenge was aimed at the general issue of censorship, far more than the specific themes that were under contention. The Production Code tried to keep up with the times while maintaining control by allowing for greater freedom throughout the 1950s on many previously proscribed topics, including miscegenation.[11]

In addition to the relaxation of the Production Code, the rise of a new wave of civil rights activism in the wake of *Brown v. the Board of Education* presented a new political context for film depictions of African American experiences and racial issues. Writing in 1959, black film critic Albert Johnson suggested that the *Brown* decision had renewed Hollywood's interest in "Negro-white relationships" in general, but that the politics and response to the desegregation ruling seemed too dangerous for film or theater portrayal yet. Instead, Johnson observed, "It was apparently decided by various Hollywood producers that a *gradual* succession of films about Negro-white relationships would have a beneficial effect upon box-office returns and audiences as well."[12] Although Johnson discussed romantic relationships in recent films, he also included portrayals of friendships and social interactions between blacks and whites. In this context of loosening restrictions and increased studio interest in race, Hollywood inched closer and closer to depicting interracial black-white marriage, using many hedges and deflective devices along the way.

I consider two groups of movies in my analysis of *Night of the Quarter Moon*'s historical significance. The first set resurrected the question of how much black ancestry made one black and actually predated *Brown* by several years, in the post–World War II era. *Lost Boundaries* (1949) told the true story of a married couple, both of mixed ancestry, who lived as white until their black ancestry was discovered.[13] And a series of films, beginning with *Pinky*, featured apparently white women whose black ancestry must be either hidden or proved untrue. Similar plots were found in *Band of Angels* (1957), *Kings Go Forth* (1958), a very successful remake of *Imitation of Life* (1959), *I Passed for White* (1960), and *Shadows* (1961).[14] For all these films' female leads, having actual or suspected black ancestry posed an obstacle in their pursuit of happiness and their romance with a white man. The well-worn "tragic mulatta" character, then, moved back into center stage, although now in a new political context. It was a relatively safe way to reintroduce black-white interracial romances as Hollywood began to abandon the Hays Codes. White readers and audiences had long accepted such stories in fictional writing and on stage.[15] And showing a seemingly white woman in a relationship with a white man deflected some of the charge, and therefore negative response, to a story line of interracial romance.[16]

With few exceptions, the tragedy of the mixed race woman in 1950s American cinema centered in part on her desire to live freely and marry the man she loved, who generally happened to be white.[17] Still, film scholars have pointed out the potential challenge these films posed to American racialism in the postwar era. Historian Renee Romano considers this "wave of movies featuring interracial couples" in the middle to late 1950s "exploited the melodramatic possibilities of interracial love to titillate their audience; they were designed to entertain by walking carefully around the edges of a social taboo."[18] Film scholar Gina Marchetti further points out that even the earlier films' destabilization of racial categories suggested that "racial differences are not 'natural' but culturally constructed and subject to historical change."[19] This challenge converged uneasily with a struggling civil rights movement, which asserted a goal of political and social equality for African Americans long subverted by decades of segregation and legalized discrimination. That movement never prioritized interracial marriage as a valued right but did—when pressed—define marriage as an individual right, and prohibitions on interracial marriage as discriminatory.[20]

What little scholarly attention *Night of the Quarter Moon* has received has placed it in the context of these movies.[21] It certainly did conform to their formula in several ways: it features a woman of mixed ancestry who appears white and is in love with a white man. White actress Julie London, with a makeup tan, played the female lead, thus visually muting the "daring" of its portrayal.[22] But the film transgressed the tragic mulatta device by having the female lead openly aware of, proud of, and more than willing to publicly acknowledge that she is "one-quarter" black. Unlike the other female leads, Ginny Nelson never deceives her husband, never actively tries to pass. She is not sure if her one black grandmother makes her Negro or white or something else, but she never denies that grandmother or other darker-skinned family members. (The "exotic" dancer Anna Kashfi is her cousin Maria, married to piano playing Cy, played by Nat Cole.) This is a particularly important point because it is also a departure from the Rhinelander case: Alice Jones Rhinelander was much more ambiguous and ambivalent about her father's nonwhite ancestry. In other words, this new twist cannot be explained by the film's link to the historical trial. It may represent a conscious step in the gradual movement of Hollywood portrayals of interracial relationships. The second transgression of the "tragic mulatta" formula is that the white man Ginny loves marries her, knowing full well she has black ancestry. He is not the first on-screen white man willing to do so, but he is the first to actually do it, and to agree not to try to hide his wife's racial identity. Finally, *Quarter Moon* was the only one of these films to directly address the question of interracial marriage as a civil rights issue, and it has not been recognized in this context.

In general, "tragic mulattas" in films of the late 1940s through the early 1960s did not connect their individual desires for freedom and rights and love to any broader political cause. The second group of films I want to consider as a historical context for *Night of the Quarter Moon* focused more explicitly on interracial marriage without the vehicle of a character of ambiguous racial identity. When scholars call *One Potato, Two Potato* (1964) the first movie treatment of an interracial marriage, they may mean it was the first to show a black man married to a white woman.[23] *One Potato* was also the first to *not* bring racial identity and ambiguous racial appearance into the narrative. However, reviewers in 1959 recognized the new focus on marriage that *Quarter Moon* added to the pool of film flirtation with "miscegenation." They noted the "bold" theme of marriage between a white man and a black or "one-fourth Negro" woman, the narrative that "belabors the question of intermarriage."[24] Indeed, the Nelsons' marriage is the central issue of the film.

The primary obstacle in *Quarter Moon* is social and family opposition to the Nelsons' interracial marriage. Ginny's admission of black ancestry circumvented the primary racial issue involved in the historical Rhinelander case: What was the definition of blackness, and how could one "tell" if an apparently white person was black or white? Most of the film's plot deals with the repercussions to the news that the wealthy white man's wife is "colored." As one reviewer noted, the "cruelly victimized couple" confronted "some mighty mean people," and the film delivered its social lesson "rather shrilly."[25] It is from this perspective, then, that I will focus the remainder of my analysis. The most important films to consider in this second school are *Birth of a Nation* and *Guess Who's Coming to Dinner*. *Night of the Quarter Moon*'s treatment of interracial marriage as a challenge to white liberal racial ideologies resonates with these two much better-known film treatments of the political significance of interracial marriage. Like them, *Quarter Moon* reflects the politics of the place and time of its setting and making.

With the story translated into film and set in the late 1950s, Leonard Rhinelander became Roderic "Chuck" Nelson (John Drew Barrymore), the son of a high society San Francisco family. Once the energy behind the family business, Chuck is a Korean War veteran who had spent two years as a prisoner of war where he had been tortured and "brainwashed." Traumatized by these experiences, he is a shadow of his former self even after months of rehabilitation. His worried brother takes him on a fishing trip in Mexico, where he falls in love with the daughter of their Irish fishing guide. Virginia "Ginny" O'Sullivan is beautiful and shapely in her short-shorts and bikini tops. She swims nude and soaks up the sun, apparently the source of her even tan.

However, Ginny knows what's what, and she tells Chuck early in their flirtation that she is only Irish on her father's side. Her mother's father was Spanish, and her mother's mother "pure Portuguese Angolan." Reminding him that Angola is in Africa, and Angola is "90 percent black," she makes sure he understands: "Chuck, I'm one quarter." As the movie posters promised, Chuck doesn't care "what she is," as long as she's his. After a few more weeks of sun and fishing and kissing, they are in love, and it is time for him to leave. Her father confronts a distraught Chuck about how his high society family will respond: "Do you have the courage to present them with a bride whose mother is the daughter of Portuguese Angolans?" He does.

They marry, and Chuck brings Ginny home to California to start their life together. Neither is truly prepared for how they will be received, but when the new Mr. and Mrs. Roderic Nelson land in San Francisco, they both know what her ancestry is. Still, her appearance is ambiguous, and the reporters who meet them do not question her ethnicity except to ask about her Irish maiden name and father's occupation. The newlywed couple laughs over the paper as they nuzzle in their hotel room the next morning. Front-page headlines read, "Fisherman's Daughter Hooks Nelson Millions."[26]

This is not enough to deter his mother's approval. The haughty Cordelia Nelson (Agnes Moorhead) welcomes the young bride and brushes off any concerns about her humble family background. Cordelia is so taken with the beautiful and polite Ginny that she encourages her other son to find a bride just like her, even if she's a "Ubangi."

The headlines have also caught the attention of Ginny's cousin Maria (on the Angolan side), who owns a nightclub in town with her husband, Cy Robbins (Nat Cole). The newlyweds drop in at the club, and introductions are awkward as Maria confesses she was not sure if she should call. "I have no secrets from Chuck," says Ginny. "Well, no secrets now," laughs Cy, and he excuses himself to sing. Champagne arrives; Maria announces the newlyweds and jokes, "This is the night the Social Register does a flip!"[27] The next day, the headlines read, "Social Leader's Bride Revealed as Quadroon."

Enter American racism: it is "society's" responses that frame the narrative of this "racial love story."[28] The vivid depiction of "frightful and shocking experiences" due to "racial bigots" was also highlighted, although not always lauded, by reviewers. Cordelia rushes to save her son from his unfortunate marriage, eventually managing to sequester him, medicated and traumatized, in his childhood home. (One reviewer described Cordelia as "understandably though not sympathetically vindictive.") In short order, the Nelsons are removed from their hotel, then attacked by white neighbors soon after they move into a segregated area. In fact, this attack opens the film, framing the love story in the context of white racist violence.[29] Depictions of racism make regular appearances in passing films as well, but here the primary issue is the fate of an interracial marriage, not the choice of a person of ambiguous racial appearance to identify as black or white. Ginny's rights and privileges as Chuck Nelson's wife are at stake. Her narrative dilemma involves whether and how to exercise this right.

Even the opening scene sets up this dilemma. As the credits and opening music fade, we see a woman (Ginny) in a robe and housedress happily and industriously hanging framed artwork in her living room. It is a scene of idealized 1950s domesticity. The room and the woman appear to be typically middle-class in postwar white suburbia. The walls are tastefully wallpapered; a large multipaned window looks out on bushes, a small lawn, and a neighboring home. Within seconds, however, the scene is interrupted by a group of white youth outside throwing rocks at her window. Hit with flying glass, Ginny makes a panicked call to her husband at work, who rushes to her rescue. All expectations of middle-class marital normality are quickly upended as the teenagers begin attacking her roses and pulling up small trees. Her husband is soon arrested for fighting with the neighbor boys. At the police station the last vestiges of Ginny's image as a white middle-class housewife fall away. She is accused of trying to seduce the boys, prevented from seeing her husband, and forced to submit to newspaper photographers. When she objects to this treatment, she is told if she doesn't like it she should "go back to Mexico."

Meanwhile, Cordelia Nelson begins to mobilize her own formidable privileges to usurp her wayward son's basic civil rights. Mother, brother, a lawyer, and the family doctor surround Chuck at the police station, trying to convince him to admit he had not known Ginny was colored. Chuck sees the parallels with his war prison experiences from the beginning of the episode, but he physically collapses. Under the influence of a sedative, to Chuck the four questioners seem to become North Korean military officers, and he breaks. He confesses that he thought Ginny was white, that capitalists had started the war to make money; he starts sobbing and begging for a blanket, clearly reliving his war trauma. The scene leaves no doubt who the bad guys are. The image of Cordelia and the three men who follow her lead is literally overlaid with Chuck's fevered memory of his North Korean torturers, their faces fading into and out of each other.

Finally released from the police station, Ginny tries to contact her husband, now sequestered at his mother's palatial home. She continually asserts her rights as a wife to see him, to no avail. Unable to gain access, she jumps the gate and starts to storm the front door. Cordelia heads her off and, while waiting for the police to arrive, confronts her unwanted daughter-in-law:

> Cordelia: "You're a very stunning girl, Ginny. It's not difficult to understand why my son felt obliged to marry you. Where did he propose to you? On a beach or in a cotton field?
> Ginny: "You're unbelievable."
> Cordelia: "I always thought we should have equality for all the people in the world, until it happened to me. No, Ginny, it isn't easy when it happens to you.
> You want to have a baby, you want to have a family. Well, do you think it's fair to subject it to what you are going through?"

In the book version, Cordelia elaborates even further: "I joined all the causes, I worked for them too."[30]

The supposedly liberal white woman cannot stand up to that ultimate challenge of her ideals of equality when "it" happens to her: a black woman marries her son. But Cordelia's defense is not very credible. If she anguishes over this shaking of her ideals, it is off screen. On screen she has little time to consider the philosophical ironies of her situation as she hustles to control medical care, publicity spin, and legal options. With the righteousness of motherhood, Cordelia Nelson uses her power of attorney to initiate an annulment suit on her son's behalf.

Still, Cordelia's limited defense connects the issue of interracial marriage to the broader context of racial equality. The link between marriage and racial politics had always been present in the public debate over intermarriage and segregation. Segregationists, after all, used intermarriage as the final argument against racial equality.[31] It was perhaps the issue that encapsulated most concisely white Americans' fears about the gender and race implications of an egalitarian society: What if a black person married *your* child?

Not since the landmark *Birth of a Nation* in 1915 had the challenge of "what if a black person married your child?" been so directly confronted on screen by a white liberal parent, albeit with a completely different political agenda.[32] D. W. Griffith's blockbuster narrative of post-Reconstruction racial politics infamously depicted two narratives of black or mulatto men threatening white women with "forced marriage" as an extension of their newly won political rights. The narrative that parallels both *Guess Who's Coming to Dinner* and *Night of the Quarter Moon* features a white liberal parent who does not realize the implications of his liberal racial politics for his child until it is (almost) too late. Senator Stoneham, a northern white, is in the South supporting African American politicians and voting rights for former slaves. Although the widowed Senator Stoneham is seen keeping house with a mixed race woman, when his mixed race protégé kidnaps and tries to forcibly marry his daughter Elsie, the senator finally sees the error of racial equality.[33]

*Birth of a Nation* premiered during the height of anti-intermarriage laws and sentiment and has been credited with helping inspire the resurrection of the Ku Klux Klan it valorized. Anti-intermarriage laws, enacted or strengthened in more than half of the United States in the first few decades of the twentieth century, focused on preventing legal unions between blacks and whites. But the film's reception was as controversial as it was successful. African American activists objected to its depiction of blacks and Reconstruction, and white audiences were highly disturbed at seeing their greatest fears so vividly depicted in a new and overwhelming medium. The myth of the black rapist victimizing white women continued to fuel white racism and violence throughout the post–World War II era. Hollywood, however, considered film portrayal of a threatening or even physically aggressive black man too controversial until the 1970s. After *Birth of a Nation*, depictions of African Americans would focus on safer stereotypes of servants, entertainers, and slow, subservient characters. Even the black filmic response did not aim to show consensual, loving unions between blacks and whites. Instead, filmmaker Oscar Micheaux challenged the mythic portrayal of black men sexually threatening white women with a far more historically accurate portrayal of white men sexually threatening black women.[34]

Little surprise, then, that virtually every "near-white" in film in the 1940s and 1950s was a woman; every interracial couple until 1964 featured a white man and a black, usually mixed race, often white-appearing and white-acting woman. Film pairings of white females and black males between 1915 and 1964 were carefully nonsexual. For example, film historian Donald Bogle has called the popular pairing of child actress Shirley Temple with the nonthreatening servant/dancer Bill "Bojangles" Robinson the "perfect interracial love match" for Hollywood.[35]

In the intervening half century between *Birth of a Nation* and *Guess Who's Coming to Dinner*, much had changed, of course, although the basic question remained the same. What if a black *man* wanted to marry your (white) *daughter* is the very question posed to two other white liberal parents played so famously by Spencer Tracy and Katherine Hepburn in the classic *Guess Who's Coming to Dinner*, eight years after *Night of the Quarter Moon*.[36] When their daughter brings home as her fiancé the unambiguously black Sydney Poitier, they (particularly the father) struggle to overcome their own lingering prejudices despite their political commitment to the idea of social equality. The filmmakers manipulated Poitier's character in numerous ways to dampen the stereotypes and fears white audiences brought to the story. The black fiancé is a doctor, a Nobel Prize winner, handsome, wealthy, and "cultured." He refuses the white daughter's premarital sexual advances and promises her white father he will not marry her without her parents' consent. In fact, one common critique of *Guess Who* was that only one kiss between the couple survived the final edit.[37] And they plan to live outside of the United States, avoiding the problem of American racism that Ginny and Chuck find threatening their marriage. Many of these gyrations were no doubt deemed necessary because he is a he: a black man in love with a white woman. This evoked the weight of centuries of American racial ideas that focus a particular fear and rage on black male sexuality and the imagined need to protect white women from that sexuality.[38]

By 1967 it was possible to depict a beautiful, young white woman joyfully choosing an intelligent, handsome black man as her husband. And by 1967, the moral impetus was to accept the couple's joy and their love, although the parents, black and white, struggled with their internal prejudices and fears of how society will treat their children. And in 1967 any state laws that still prohibited such marriages would be overturned by the Supreme Court decision *Loving v. Virginia*. Mildred Loving, it should be noted, was (like Ginny Nelson and Alice Rhinelander) a woman of mixed ancestry and one who did not simply identify as black.[39]

In 1959, however, the makers of *Quarter Moon* advanced the same moral impetus to support the Nelsons' love and marriage. But Cordelia's response to having "it happen" to her is far closer to the reaction of *Birth of a Nation's* white liberal father than to the parents of *Guess Who's Coming to Dinner*. Cordelia even has the power to intervene and does so. It is she who keeps the married couple separated, keeps her own son unnecessarily sedated (for his own good, of course), and manipulates the lawyers and doctors so the trial can proceed without the plaintiff's presence. (This is essentially the situation that Alice Rhinelander believed Leonard to be in when his father's lawyers took him away from her and convinced him to sign an annulment suit they had already drawn up.) She does so by subverting Ginny's marital rights with her own power of attorney over her son. Her response allowed the writers to get to an annulment trial, the main feature of the Rhinelander case, and still have a suspenseful love story. However, Cordelia is unambiguously the villain in *Night of the Quarter Moon* because of her opposition to her son's interracial marriage and her hypocrisy. Conversely, Senator Stoneham is the villain because he opens the door to intermarriage by supporting civil rights.

Moving *Night of the Quarter Moon's* story line to a California location in the late 1950s further emphasized its political resonances. California had been the first state to overturn its antimiscegenation laws on the basis of civil rights, marking the beginning of a legislative push that would eventually culminate with *Loving v. Virginia* (1967). Unlike New York, California had had such a clause in its civil code since 1850, when it became a state. The legislation proscribed "all marriages of white persons with negroes, Mongolians, members of the Malay race, or mulattoes." Like many such statutes, the same section also set blood quantum definitions of racial categories: "Every person who shall have one-eighth part or more of Negro blood shall be deemed a mulatto."[40] Had the story been set in this California, just a few years earlier, a woman with Ginny Nelson's family history (one African grandparent) would have been categorized as a mulatto. The Nelsons' marriage would have been void, and a trial unnecessary.

But in 1948, the California high court had overturned that century-old civil code section when *Perez v. Sharp* reached the California Supreme Court. After World War II, and particularly after the U.S. Supreme Court declaration in 1954 that segregation was discriminatory and unconstitutional, states began to independently dismantle these laws. Prior to the California decision, thirty states still had anti-intermarriage laws. By 1959, twenty-two states still outlawed marriage between blacks and whites, and only sixteen states still banned interracial marriages by the time of *Loving v Virginia* in 1967.[41]

Lawyers for the Los Angeles county clerk who had denied a marriage license to Andrea Perez (white) and Sylvester Davis (Negro) based their case on scientific racism. Using social and physical studies of race, they argued that nonwhite races were inferior, that "amalgamation" was "not only unnatural, but is always productive of deplorable results." Prohibition of interracial marriage, therefore, was for the public good, which outweighed the individual's right to marry whom he or she wishes. In its decision rejecting these arguments, the court noted that the current laws allowed some people of mixed ancestry to marry whites and allowed marriages between nonwhite races, as well as marriages between "Caucasians and others of darker pigmentation, such as Indians, Hindus, and Mexicans." It also rejected theories of racial superiority, pointing out that much of the defendant's evidence drew on and paralleled Adolf Hitler's theories of Aryan supremacy. Finally, the court declared that marriage was an individual right, and prohibition on the basis of race was discrimination.[42]

Ginny is not interested in making her case about race or equality. In fact, she is not entirely sure what racial category she fits in. Maria is, and she gives her lighter, un-American cousin a quick lesson on American racial ideology: "When you have one little drop of African blood in you, just one little drop and they find out, you're a Negro." At least, she concludes consolingly, Ginny could get some money out of the Nelsons. But Ginny does not want money; she wants her husband, and now she needs a lawyer to help her. When she turns to Cy, he is suspicious of her motives. In a rare dramatic scene for Cole, Cy rages at the idea of her using the image of the "downtrodden Negro" for personal gain: "I won't get a lawyer for anyone who wants to exploit color; there's been enough of that!" When Ginny retorts that she does not want to exploit color, she gets sidetracked for a moment: "I'm not Negro, I'm white, or mostly white." But that is not the main issue: she just wants her husband back. Cy knows a guitarist, Asa Tully, a black lawyer who cannot find real legal work. Tully takes on Ginny's case, which ends up in a trial.[43] Ginny, Maria, and Cy may not have been ready to make her case a civil rights suit, but the film still manages to give that impression. When Ginny arrives at the courthouse, a woman shouts out of the mostly white crowd milling around: "We're with you Ginny! This is America! You can marry anybody you want!" But few whites in the audience would have agreed. Gallup polls in 1959 found that 97 percent of white Americans opposed interracial marriage. By 1959, Hollywood was ready to make a film about a marriage between a black person who did not deny having black ancestry, and a white person who knew his or her spouse was not white. But audiences were not yet ready.

Reviews of the film suggest that it was well received artistically but not ideologically. *Harrison's Reports* deemed it well produced but warned that "its theme of miscegenation is highly controversial" and probably unsuitable for southern audiences. Its plot summary stressed Chuck's knowledge that Ginny was "one-fourth Negro" and ignored the roles of Maria and Cy altogether.[44] The *Catholic Review* ignored the film, except to list in its "B" category. (Interracial marriage was not a reason for church censorship.) *Variety* offered a cursory plot summary and judged the film "an attempt at controversy, fairly well premised but burdened with a trite story." Finding only James Edwards's performance as Asa Tully worthy of praise, the reviewer predicted "only spotty biz" with the "miscegenation theme . . . likely to militate against general acceptance."[45] The black-published *Chicago Defender* considered the film a "frank and daring treatment of an unconventional subject," one of the best of the new crop of "interracial releases."[46] The *New York Times* review was the most positive, critiquing the jumbled narrative and overly dramatized plot but complimenting the lead actors and the merciful final reunion.[47]

Still, in the racial wake of World War II and the legal ripples of *Brown*, interracial marriage was receiving more serious consideration. Some Americans came to see it as a "solution" to the problems of racial prejudice, and more, including the majority of the California State Supreme Court, understood that it was a part of the larger picture of civil rights. While refusing to directly take on the issue of interracial marriage as a right, *Night of the Quarter Moon* did connect civil rights to the marriage question in several ways. Cordelia demonstrates the connection in her own stunned realization that her support of equality had gone too far (a textbook response of segregationist warnings). So, too, does the anonymous voice reminding audiences that America is, as the saying goes, a free country and Ginny should be able to marry whomever she wants.

When Cordelia takes the stand, she repeats her opposition, uncomfortably explaining to Asa Tully: "My only thought was for my son's happiness and I don't believe in today's society . . . that he could find happiness with one of your race." Any (white) parent faced with her situation would feel and do the same, she asserts. She cannot, however, defend her comment about her son proposing marriage "in a cotton field." Embarrassed but defiant, she ignores Tully's queries as to her implications about "wanton slave girls" seducing white men.

It is, indeed, an embarrassing moment for the film as well. It was not, apparently, part of the film's message to challenge such racist stereotypes of black women. Indeed, the film depends on stereotypes for much of its character and plot development. Ironically, despite Cordelia's implications and the historical precedent of the Rhinelanders' three-year premarital affair, the Nelsons had waited until their marriage to have sex. Unlike Alice Rhinelander's lawyers, then, Asa Tully did not have to deal with premarital sex marring his client's image. Still, Ginny's character is highly sexualized. They may have been sexually restrained before marriage, but the newlyweds are clearly happy in their newfound sexual relationship in the days between their arrival in San Francisco and their forced separation. Her robe slips alarmingly, her voice purrs and teases, and when she is dressed, her clothes are tight and low-cut, accentuating her figure.

As the courtroom drama continues, Chuck finally wakes up from his drug-induced coma and goes looking for his wife. Maria and Cy confront him with the same set of questions that failed to deter Ginny. In this scene the unambivalently black people in the film literally stop dancing and singing for a few minutes (they have been rehearsing) to explain American racial definitions and racism to Chuck, as they tried to with Ginny.[48] Chuck, too, has been thrown into a new landscape of race that most white Americans have the privilege to ignore or avoid. But Maria and Cy have been living there. The light-skinned Maria sympathizes—she too came to this country as a child, and she might have tried to pass, but instead she grew up watching her mother work as a maid for whites. As she explains, "We call it the black curtain. There are some people who sneak behind it, some who sneak back away from it, and others who try to make believe it doesn't even exist. But it does, Chuck, and like it or not you're on one side and Ginny's on the other." Where will they live? How can he make her happy in the racist land of America? Maria implores him that if he truly loves her, he will "make her hate you and let her go."

Cy, without the skin tone to consider passing, chimes in with his own indictment of racism—and his solution: "Doesn't make sense, does it, Chuck? It's like some crazy off key beat. Does the color of her skin really make that much difference? Why does life have to be like this? I get filled up myself, and when I do I just shrug it off . . . take it out on music." He sits at the piano and begins pounding out a discordant jazz tune, which gradually slows and becomes more melodic.

Chuck has been given a fast course on American racism from those most affected by it. And he takes the lesson to heart, showing up in court to support his mother's case—he testifies that he wants the annulment and he thought Ginny was white. This time, we all know he is lying. And because he lies, Ginny must now partially disrobe in order to prove that Chuck, having seen her skinny-dip before their marriage, would have known she was not white. The narrative is stretched far to accommodate this scene, as the participants argue over tanning, nighttime versus daytime nude bathing, and the propriety of a disrobing. In the Rhinelander trial, the purpose had been to prove that Leonard, having seen Alice's body during premarital sex, should have known she was not white. The mores of the 1950s required a more innocent explanation for Chuck's prenuptial familiarity with his wife's unclothed body. But how could Hollywood make a film version of the famous trial without its most infamous scene? And so, Tully convinces the judge the color of Ginny's skin has become the key issue in the case and that there was "a definite legal precedent" for a disrobing to "sweep away the veil of lies that has obscured the simple truth." The judge reluctantly agrees and clears the courtroom of all nonparticipants. Reporters, especially female reporters, object strongly but leave, and Ginny begins to slowly and dramatically unbutton her tight bolero jacket.

This disrobing scene confused contemporary and recent reviewers alike. The *New York Times* reviewer "fail[ed] to get the point" of it, and the *Los Angeles Times* called it "as crude as it is improbable."[49] And contemporary online reviewers poke endless fun at "the most ridiculous courtroom climax in memory," where the disrobing serves "some cloudy plot point about skin pigmentation and tan lines."[50] One reviewer at the time, however, did praise Hugo Hass for the "careful suspense" of the scene, as Ginny alternately falters, assures her father, wipes nervous sweat from her brow, and continues with the long row of buttons. Will she do it? Her lawyer does not wait to find out. In a scene that Albert Johnson called "one of the most incredible courtroom sequences in film history,"[51] Asa Tully impatiently reaches out a dark brown hand and tears Ginny's bodice entirely off her back. It was a shocking visual image, one that the *Chicago Defender* expected would "stir up a bit of controversy."[52] Within the film's narrative, Asa Tully's motive is intended to spur Chuck into action. This it does. The young husband leaps to his feet, throws his arms around the cowering Ginny, trying to hold her bodice over her chest, and yells at Tully to take his hands off her.

These two images of Ginny disrobing—her lawyer exposing her back and her husband shielding her as she clutches her torn top to her chest—were among the most popular in advertising for the film, book, and associated sound track. Of these the latter was the most popular. One MGM catalog sent to theaters to offer a variety of posters and suggest publicity approaches and tie-ins, provided seven reproductions of the "I don't care what she is" image, with John Barrymore protecting the vulnerable Julie London. (Unlike the publicity targeting audiences, the theater catalogs were very clear that the issue was interracial marriage.) The ripping scene sometimes included Asa Tully's entire body, more often just his hand or arm reaching into the frame and ripping the woman's dress. Sometimes it was clear that the arm tearing her dress was darker, sometimes it was not.[53]

Perhaps the most fundamental narrative shift between the Rhinelander case and the film is that Ginny Nelson has her happy ending. She is not tragic, sacrificing neither her love nor her identity. What ordeals she has gone through have served their purpose: she has her husband back again. Chuck explains to the judge that he only did what he thought was right, and the Nelsons drive off, literally, into the sunset. The overall message of the narrative supports the love between Ginny and Chuck, agreeing with him that her race does not matter—or at least that it should not matter. But the ending leaves Maria and Cordelia's shared question unanswered. "Where will you go?" asks a reporter as the Nelsons leave the courthouse for their ride off into the sunset. They do not know, but they will be together.

Alice Jones Rhinelander was still very much alive, living alone as Alice Jones two decades after the final legal dissolution of her marriage, when *Night of the Quarter Moon* opened in New York. She was still there when it began to show up in local television listings in the early 1960s. What would she have thought of the overlaying of the civil rights issue only the tragedy of her life? Like Andrea Perez and Mildred Loving, she had had to fight in court to defend her marriage to a man of another racial identity. But Alice's fight had been against her husband (although she continued to believe for much of the trial that he was only following his father's wishes and wanted her to win). And she ultimately lost her fight. By the 1950s, however, an interracial marriage contested in a courtroom was part of a much larger legal and political struggle to dismantle the carefully erected codes and practices of segregation.

Scholars of race have long lamented the lag between social experience of race and mainstream film portrayals. Catching up with history is still under way. As limited as they were, the handful of films on passing and racial identity that came out between 1949 and 1961 were the first steps. *Night of the Quarter Moon* pushed the envelope even further, mitigating the element of pretense or racial passing, and focusing its entire narrative on a mixed marriage and the social responses to it. It was an important step, and one that has been overlooked. In its presentation of the Nelsons' reunion as a typical Hollywood ending, and those who oppose them as racists and hypocrites, it was a precursor to the films of the mid-1960s that have been heavily analyzed. It presented an interracial marriage five years before *One Potato, Two Potato* and made that marriage the center of its plot eight years before *Guess Who's Coming to Dinner*. Granted, these later films featured a black man married to, or potentially marrying, a white woman. Having a woman of color and a white man would have been less shocking to white audiences, but its racial and gender arrangement reflected not only the historical Rhinelander marriage but also the couples whose marriages or attempted marriages ultimately overturned the legality of antimiscegenation laws in the United States. And the explicit references to intermarriage as a positive aspect of civil rights challenged audiences to transfer the sympathy they were expected to feel for Ginny Nelson into a broader support for political and social equality. Here history lagged behind the film, but in most other ways this was an on-screen attempt to catch up with the past of the Rhinelander case, and the present California's legalization of mixed race marriages. *Night of the Quarter Moon* deserves its own place in this history.

NOTES

1. Literary scholar Mark Madigan first noted the connection between the Rhinelander case and *Night of the Quarter Moon*. Mark J. Madigan, "Miscegenation and the 'Dicta of Race and Class': The Rhinelander Case and Nella Larsen's *Passing*," *Modern Fiction Studies* 36 no. 4 (Winter 1998): 532-28.

2. *Night of the Quarter Moon*, promotional tabloid (New York: Cato Show Printing, 1959). All promotional materials cited are in the author's possession.

3. "Night of the Quarter Moon," Loew's Incorporated, 1959, Cards 1, 59-77; "Night of the Quarter Moon," MGM Press Book, London: MGM Pictures, Limited Metro House, 1, 6–8.

4. Franklin Coen, *Night of the Quarter Moon: A Provocative Novel Based on the Daring MGM Motion Picture Release* (New York: Bantam Books, 1959), cover. Indeed, the line "I don't give a damn . . . " is closer to the Rhinelander case than to anything in the movie. One of the most damning pieces of testimony came from

Leonard's chauffeur, who swore he had warned Rhinelander that his girlfriend was colored. "I don't give a damn," was Leonard's response. Earl Lewis and Heidi Ardizzone, *Love on Trial: An American Scandal in Black and White* (New York: Norton, 2001), 188-89. Unless otherwise specified, all information on the Rhinelander case is taken from this source. Although we were aware of this film while writing the book, I did not locate a copy of the film until after its publication.

5. "Night of the Quarter Moon," *Variety*, February 11, 1959, 6.

6. Thomas Cripps, *Making Movies Black: The Hollywood Message Movie from World War II to the Civil Rights Era* (New York: Oxford University Press, 1993), 283-84; "Q.T. Boycott of Negro Films: Mississippi: 'No Dixie Traitors,'" *Variety*, March 25, 1959; Richard L. Coe, "Well, Night Has Fallen," *Washington Post and Times Herald*, March 12, 1959, B10; Charles Stinson, "Quarter Moon Now on Many Area Screens," *Los Angeles Times*, April 3, 1959, A10; "Television Programs," *New York Times*, September 15, 1963, 146; see also October 28, 1964, 91; June 7, 1965, 75; February 25, 1966, X25, December 28, 1968, 75; *Washington Post*, July 17, 1967, D9; January 29, 1969, 180; October 19, 1969, 198; *Los Angeles Times*, April 17, 1975, N13.

7. Donald Bogle, *Toms, Coons, Mulattoes, Mammies, and Bucks: An Interpretive History of Blacks in American Film*, 3rd ed. (New York: Continuum, 1994), 201.

8. While some states did not offer a definition of racial terms like Negro, white, Mongol, and so forth, those that did usually used a blood-quantum fraction or term that described how much ancestry made one black rather than white. The most common were one-fourth and one-eighth, which  also had their own terminology: quadroon and octoroon, respectively. (The title reference to the "quarter moon" is partially a play on the one-quarter Negro ancestry of the film's leading female character, who is a quadroon by blood-quantum definitions.)

9. Film depictions of white-Indian and white-Asian romances appeared earlier and were generally less objectionable to American audiences than those featuring black-white relationships. For analyses of these films and their significance for American racial and gender ideologies, see Gina Marchetti, *Romance and the "Yellow Peril": Race, Sex, and Discursive Strategies in Hollywood Fiction* (Berkeley: University of California Press, 1993); Eugene Franklin Wong, *On Visual Media Racism: Asians in the American Motion Picture* (New York: Arno Press, 1978); Jacquelyn Kilpatrick, *Celluloid Indians: Native Americans and Film* (Lincoln: University of Nebraska Press, 1999).

10. Garth Jowett, *Film: The Democratic Art* (Boston: Little, Brown, 1976), appendix III and IV, 467, 469; Thomas Whartenberg, *Unlikely Couples: Movie Romance as Social Criticism* (Boulder, CO: Westview Press, 1999), 5.

11. Jowett, *Film*, 393-427. See also Gregory Black, "Hollywood Censored: The Production Code Administration and the Hollywood Film Industry, 1930-1940," *Film History* 3, no. 3 (1989): 167-89.

12. Albert Johnson, "Beige, Brown or Black," *Film Quarterly* 13, no. 1 (Fall 1959): 39.

13. According to Allyson Hobbs, while the reception of the Johnsons' story was lauded at the time as a civil rights triumph (the all-white New Hampshire town in which they lived continuing to accept and embrace them after their racial identity became public), the documentary *Lost Boundaries* complicated this image. Allyson Vanessa Hobbs, "Boundaries Lost and Found: The Meaning of Racial Passing in the Early Civil Rights Era" (paper presented at the annual meeting of the American Historical Association, Atlanta, Georgia, January 6, 2007). For a discussion of Hollywood's postwar shift in depictions of race, see Cripps, *Making Movies Black*, 151-73.

14. Two films produced during this period that do not fit this pattern were Orson Welles's *Othello* (1952) and *Showboat* (1951). With little else in common, both the Shakespearean tragedy and the long-popular musical stand out for their portrayal of interracial marriage. *Showboat* featured Ava Gardner as the apparently white Julie, who has some black ancestry but is passing for white. When her racial identity is discovered, her white husband avoids arrest by drinking some of her blood so that he and all their white coworkers can honestly swear he has colored blood in him, too. Despite this loyalty, he eventually leaves her, and she reappears later in the film, a downwardly spiraling alcoholic willing to sacrifice herself further to aid the film's white heroine. Her downfall and tragic ending were typical of nineteenth-century and early twentieth-century depictions of mixed race women and men.

15. There is much scholarship on literary depictions of people of mixed ancestry, particularly women. See, for example, Judith Berzon, *Neither Black Nor White: The Mulatto Character in American Fiction* (New York: NYU Press, 1979); Werner Sollors, "'Never Was Born': The Mulatto, an American Tragedy," *Massachusetts Review* 27 (Summer 1986): 293–316; Anna Shannon Elfenbein, *Women on the Color Line: Evolving Stereotypes and the Writings of George Washington Cable, Grace King, Kate Chopin* (Charlottesville: University Press of Virginia, 1989); Jacquelyn McLendon, *The Politics of Color in the Fiction of Jessie Fauset and Nella Larsen* (Charlottesville: University Press of Virginia, 1995); Siobhan Somerville, *Queering the Color: Race and the Invention of Homosexuality in American Culture* (Durham, NC: Duke University Press, 2000).

16. A similar deflection may be said to be at work in *A Patch of Blue* (1965). While the film audience would clearly see a dark-skinned black man befriending a young white woman, the woman's blindness provided a multilayered hedge for the portrayal of interracial love. She is literally blind and does not know the man is black until she has already fallen in love with him. He chooses not to tell her, leaving her to assume he is white—a nonvisual form of passing? When this knowledge does not sway her, her blindness becomes a symbol for the white liberal ideal of a color-blind society in which skin color is literally not seen and race is not acknowledged as meaningful.

17. Hernán Vera and Andrew M. Gordon, *Screen Saviors: Hollywood Fictions of Whiteness* (New York: Rowan and Littlefield, 2003), 130.

18. Renee C. Romano, *Race Mixing: Black-White Marriage in Postwar America* (Cambridge MA: Harvard University Press, 2003), 166-67. Romano briefly mentions *Night of the Quarter Moon* as one of these films.

19. Marchetti, *Romance and the "Yellow Peril,"* 176. Similarly, Donald Bogle suggests that some of the later films "picked up the old tragic mulatto theme and turned it inside out." Bogle, *Toms, Coons, Mulattoes, Mammies, and Bucks*, 200. (Bogle is referring specifically to *Shadows* here.)

20. Peter Wallenstein discusses the attempts to bring other miscegenation law challenges to the Supreme Court during the 1950s and early 1960s in *Tell the Court I Love My Wife: Race, Marriage, and Law—An American History* (New York: Palgrave Macmillan, 2002), 173-86.

21. Bogle, *Toms, Coons, Mulattoes, Mammies, and Bucks*, 201; Romano, *Race Mixing*, 167; Daniel Leab, *From Sambo to Superspade: The Black Experience in Motion Pictures* (Boston: Houghton Mifflin, 1976), 213-14.

22. Scholars have noted that this device allowed the portrayal of interracial romance even during the period the Hays Code prevailed. See, for example, Elspeth Kydd, "'The Ineffaceable Curse of Cain': Racial Marking and Embodiment in *Pinky*," *Camera Obscura* 43, 15, no. 1 (2000): 99.

23. See Leab, *From Sambo to Superspade*, 216-17.

24. "Night of the Quarter Moon," *Harrison's Reports*, February 14, 1959; Richard L. Coe, "Oscar Nominations Do Provoke Thought," *Washington Post and Times Herald*, March 8, 1959, H2. (*Quarter Moon* did not receive an Oscar nomination, but its release on the East Coast coincided with the announcement of the nominees, and several articles ran photos from the film along with reports on the Oscars, in part perhaps to highlight the prevalent themes of race.)

25. Howard Thompson, "Racial Love Story," *New York Times*, March 5, 1959, 35.

26. This is another parallel with the Rhinelander case, in which first headlines emphasized only the class difference between the two while reporters scrambled to confirm reports that the bride was colored.

27. Alice Rhinelander actually has the historic position of being the first known nonwhite listed in the New York Social Register. The following year, however, not only she but also Leonard disappeared from the listing.

28. Thompson, "Racial Love Story," 35.

29. In the book version, a white couple—also neighbors—comes by to offer support and eventually friendship. They continue to support Ginny but never appear in the film version as released. In the film version, the neighbor boys harassing Ginny chant, "Einie, meenie, minie, moe, catch a tiger by the toe," letting audiences speculate about more explicitly racist renditions of that rhyme—as in the book version, which uses the phrase "catch a nigger," instead. Coen, *Night of the Quarter Moon*, 70.

30. Ibid., 96.

31. Marriage itself had been categorically denied to enslaved African Americans, one of many civil rights so prohibited. Tera Hunter, "Til Death or Distance Do You Part: African American Marriage in the Nineteenth Century" (public lecture, University of Notre Dame, November 13, 2006).

32. Other scholars and cultural critics have noted the many parallels between these two films. James Baldwin notes the almost exact role of black maids who each defend "their" white families against intruding black men. *The Devil Finds Work* (New York: Dial Press, 1976), 71-72. Baldwin also discusses the role and image of the mulatto and black characters in *Birth of a Nation*. Baldwin, *The Devil Finds Work*, 45, 47-48.

33. In the other narrative a black former slave, Gus, chases a sheltered young white girl through the forest as she flees, terrified, from his marriage proposal and eventually falls to her death. Gus pays with his life, becoming, in the film's racist narrative, the first victim of the heroic Klansmen who save the white South from black and Northern tyranny.

34. While white segregationists had always employed fears of and aversion to interracial relationships as leverage against political equality, civil rights activists and African Americans had very different views. Interracial marriage was never at the forefront of any mainstream civil rights campaign or organization. Most African American leaders and white civil rights workers would have agreed with a statement Maria made in the book version of *Night of the Quarter Moon*: "The Negroes got enough on their hands right now, a big enough fight without taking on intermarriage. We do that, we're playing right into their hands." Coen, *Night of the Quarter Moon*, 138.

35. Bogle, *Toms, Coons, Mulattoes, Mammies, and Bucks*, 47.

36. Although *One Potato, Two Potato* predates *Guess Who's* in its portrayal of a black man married to a white woman, the driving narrative issue was whether the couple could successfully raise the woman's white child by a previous marriage. Portrayals of interracial romance or near romance, most notably *Patch of Blue*, are also relevant here, but none address the specific challenge of interracial marriage in the context of a political movement toward racial equality.

37. There have been numerous analyses of *Guess Who's Coming to Dinner*. In addition to those cited here, see "Racism as a Project: *Guess Who's Coming to Dinner*," in Vera and Gordon, *Screen Saviors*.

38. Two classic analyses of the relationship between race, gender, and tensions over interracial sex are Jacquelyn Dowd Hall, "The Mind That Burns in Each Body: Women, Rape and Racial Violence," in *Powers of Desire: The Politics of Sexuality*, ed. Ann Snitow, Christine Stansell, and Sharon Thompson (New York: Monthly Review Press, 1983); and Darlene Clark Hine, "Rape and the Inner Lives of Black Women in the Midwest: Preliminary Thoughts on the Culture of Dissemblance," *Signs* 14 (August 1988): 913–20. More recent treatments include Toni Morrison, ed., *Race-ing Justice, En-gendering Power: Essays on Anita Hill, Clarence*

*Thomas, and the Construction of Social Reality* (New York: Pantheon, 1992); and Devon W. Carbado, ed., *Black Men on Race, Gender, and Sexuality: A Critical Reader* (New York: NYU Press, 1999).

39. Despite the continued social taboos against interracial marriage, it is notable that the *Loving* decision did not result in widespread outrage. For segregationists, the battle had already been lost. For a stunning reanalysis of Mildred Loving's self-identity as "Indian," see Arica Coleman, "'Tell the Court I Love My [Indian] Wife' Interrogating Race and Self-Identity in Loving v. Virginia," *Souls* 8, no. 1 (Winter 2006): 67-80.

40. The initial code only prohibited marriages between whites and Negroes or mulattoes. Malay and Mongolian races were added later. Each was defined as someone of one-half Malay or Mongolian ancestry, or more. Opinion, Supreme Court of California in re *Perez v. Sharp* (October 1, 1948), 32 Cal. 2d 711, 198 P.2d 17), 712-13. California's law was considered relatively mild because it did not criminalize mixed marriages and did not void interracial marriages licensed in other states. Romano, *Race Mixing*, 47.

41. Romano, *Race Mixing*, 186.

42. *Perez v. Sharp*, 730-40.

43. Asa Tully calls Ginny "Alice in Wonderland," a reference to her having entered the bizarre world of American racial ideas. ("Alice in Wonderland" was also the theme of a popular black editorial on the Rhinelander case.) "Alice in Wonderland," *Amsterdam News*, August 2, 1925.

44. "Night of the Quarter Moon," *Harrison's Reports*, February 14, 1959.

45. *Variety*, February 11, 1959, 6. For more praise of Edwards, see also Charles Stinson, "'Quarter Moon' Now on Many Area Screens," *Los Angeles Times*, April 3, 1959, A10.

46. "Nat Cole, Julie London, Barrymore Star in Film on 'Interracial Theme,'" *Chicago Defender*, February 14, 1959.

47. Thompson, "Racial Love Story," 35.

48. Thomas Cripps has noted the effect of casting musical stars as reducing the plot "to a string of vaudeville turns" in *St. Louis Blues*.

49. Thompson, "Racial Love Story," 35; Stinson, "'Quarter Moon' Now on Many Area Screens," A10.

50. www.phoenixnewtimes.com/extra/dewey/moon.html.

51. Johnson, "Beige, Brown, or Black," 42.

52. "They Said No! But Here's Real Proof That It Can Be Done," *Chicago Defender*, February 14, 1959.

53. In the book version, Asa Tully falls in love with Ginny Nelson. They become close enough that she briefly considers giving up her fight for her marriage. There is no overt sign of this incipient romance in the film.

II

# A Window into a Life Uncloseted
## *"Spice Boy" Imaginings in New Queer Cinema*

### *Robb Hernandez*

In the summers of 1998 and 1999, *Billy's Hollywood Screen Kiss* (1998) and *Trick* (1999) were eagerly anticipated by the popular gay and lesbian national news publications the *Advocate*[1] and *Out* magazine.[2] They were touted not as only the "big gay film" of their respective year (and featured as the opening- or closing-night films of international gay and lesbian film festivals), but also as films that might bridge the gap between homosexual and heterosexual viewers. In particular, each movie was commended for its marketing scheme, strategically advertising gay romantic comedy to gay and straight audiences years before industrial insiders had endorsed gay-based narrowcasting, a programming practice that later placed struggling networks like Bravo and Showtime on the map.[3] In fact, the *Advocate*'s cover story on *Billy's Hollywood Screen Kiss* by Edward Guthmann reported that Trimark Pictures planned a campaign that would speak to both gay and straight moviegoers. Neither *Billy's Hollywood Screen Kiss* nor *Trick* was a commercial "blockbuster," even when they had produced gay media fervor. Both films' merchandise included sound tracks and put young actors and filmmakers on Hollywood's radar of the "up-and-coming" (might anyone remember a less than fey Sean P. Hayes in the lead role of "Billy" prior to his Emmy Award–winning turn as Jack Mc-Farland in NBC's *Will and Grace*?). Meanwhile, the mainstream and gay media's subscription to an essentialized and homogeneous "gay audience" perpetuated a monocular conception of spectatorship as uniform, stable, and white.

This chapter is interested in recuperating this moment and reevaluating the burgeoning wave of what is otherwise called the New Queer

Cinema movement. By acknowledging its cultivation of a marketable white gay film audience, this study emphasizes the reciprocal racialized "Other," namely, U.S. queer Latino men, as both critical readers and character constructs. In several films within New Queer Cinema, queer Latino men emerged as "Spice Boy" archetypes, paired with heroic and lovelorn white gay protagonists, punctuating interracial same-sex desire as a crucial, recurrent, and often overlooked image.

Film festival favorites, *Billy's Hollywood Screen Kiss* and *Trick* take viewers on a sojourn into gay male relationships situated in urban city centers, Los Angeles and New York City, respectively, although populated by a monochromatic white diegesis. Los Angeles photographer Billy Collier may be pursuing a perfect Hollywood screen kiss with a possibly straight waiter in *Billy's Hollywood Screen Kiss*, but he consummates his desires only with exotic Spice Boy Fernando. A frivolous erotic encounter is the impetus for another interracial relationship in *Trick*, in which playwright Gabriel Bloom cruises go-go boy Mark Miranda on a late night New York subway ride. Together, they spend the rest of the evening looking for a place to "get off."

Through textual analyses, I examine the formations of Spice Boy and white gay male relationships in these films and elucidate how reception of such interracial same-sex images impacted queer Latino men as media consumers in their everyday lives. These interpretations are also tested through a reception study with U.S. queer Latino viewers, using ethnographic research methods, including interviews, surveys, and focus group film screenings of *Billy's Hollywood Screen Kiss* and *Trick*. The participants' interpretations of these interracial couples offered productive points of entry into queer Latinos' reading practices, viewing habits, and even their personal relationships with white gay men.

From this audience study four primary concepts thematized their critical readings: acceptance and rejection, language, identity formation, and confrontations with gay whiteness and power. This study speaks to the difficult and complicated process of media reception in relation to interracial desire in its contradictory and inconsistent realities. U.S. queer Latino men must negotiate the intersections of race, class, sexuality, and, more specifically, gender expression. This complex positionality has quite significant material implications in everyday life. This is particularly true for young men who have yet to be accepted and embraced without question or judgment by their birth *familias* (families), by the predominantly white gay male community, or even by each other.

*"Spice Boy" Archetypal Imaginings: Latinos in New Queer Cinema*

In 1993, feminist filmmaker and critic B. Ruby Rich announced the makings of what at the time was called Queer New Wave Cinema, a cycle of films directed and written primarily by white gay men programmed in internationally renowned film festivals and picked up for mainstream distribution in the United States. And although Rich lamented the displacement of lesbian directors and women-based films, this film movement's very heterogeneity suggested a great potentiality to conceptualize this proliferating new cinema.[4] Unlike Brazilian Cinema Novo or Italian Neorealism, there was no one "single aesthetic vocabulary" to comprehend its significance but rather common use of such postmodern elements as pastiche, irony, social history, and emphasis on minimalism, excess, and pleasure.[5] In Michele Aaron's retrospective assessment, these dissimilar works "share an attitude" of defiance, give voice to the invisible, remain unapologetic of flawed and imperfect protagonists, revise a heteronormative past, defy traditional Hollywood convention, and resist the closure of death. She writes, "Cynically put, [New Queer Cinema] kick-started Hollywood's awareness of a queerer audience (a combination of the 'pink profit' zone and the general public's current delectation) and its appropriation and dilution of queer matters."[6] Including films like *Jollies* (1990), *My Own Private Idaho* (1991), *Swoon* (1992), and *Zero Patience* (1993), Hollywood's absorption of stylish "queerness" perpetuated a series of successful mainstream commercial releases, including *Philadelphia* (1993), *To Wong Foo, Thanks for Everything Julie Newmar* (1995), *The Birdcage* (1996), and *In and Out* (1997).

Although Rich in 1993 remained hopeful that lesbian filmmakers and filmmakers of color (she makes particular note of the work of a pre–*Watermelon Woman* Cheryl Dunye) would intervene in the movement's predominant white gay male auteurism, writer Daniel T. Contreras stresses the displacement and limitations queer of color cultural producers faced at this time. Marlon Riggs's *Tongues Untied* (1990) and Jennie Livingston's *Paris Is Burning* (1990) remain demonstrative of highly regarded queer and racialized achievements in this movement. Critical racial subjectivity and, in the case of this chapter, queer Latino film and video production in the United States remained largely outside this burgeoning cinematic field, however. As Contreras notes, "It would be difficult to argue, more than ten years on, that the New Queer Cinema developed a critical *racial* perspective, but it would also be difficult to argue that the space it inhabited did *not* contain a racial component at all."[7]

It is at the same juncture Contreras examines that the invention of the Spice Boy archetype lies. Despite the exclusion of U.S. queer Latino cultural productions throughout the 1990s (aside from the Frameline, Outfest, and The Mix gay and lesbian film festivals in San Francisco, Los Angeles, and New York City), gay Latino men occupied the diegesis of several independent and Hollywood commercially based New Queer Cinema films. Depicted as pool boys, hustlers, go-go dancers, and marauding cads, Spice Boy exotics emerged as secondary characters to faulted but heroic white gay male protagonists. Often portrayed as hypersexualized hypermasculines, these Latinos hail from foreign lands like Puerto Rico or Guatemala and sometimes entire continents like all of South America, speaking with exaggerated foreign accents.

*La lengua* (the tongue) becomes a common typifying characteristic suggesting the sexual promiscuity, availability, and disregard for white gay male coupledom of Spice Boys. It is unsurprising that the first glimpse of Fernando in *Billy's Hollywood Screen Kiss* is a close-up shot of his tongue probing Billy's ear. The Spice Boy incites and stimulates white male arousal and excitement, enough to upturn relationships and disturb insecure white partners of their white lovers. He is a cinematic plot device that reminds the central heroic protagonist of the lusts of the body and the moral importance of commitment, romance, and mostly love, all of which the Spice Boy is incapable of providing.

Of course, the persistent reinscription of Latina/o hot-blooded exoticism in relationship to white heterosexual Hollywood romance is nothing new in the American cinematic imaginary. Perhaps it is a historical burden this film movement assumed, the traces of reductive stereotypes plaguing the careers of the earliest brown faces on celluloid—ranging from Lupe Velez's fiery sexual hunger to Ramon Novarro's aristocratic charm. Latina/o film scholars continue to propose a trajectory of images in the U.S. media that organize dark men as greasers, bandidos, and drug lords, while light men are Latin lovers, Casanovas, or swashbucklers.[8] Latinas culturally situated within a virgin/whore dualism emerge on film as spitfires, temptresses, and cantina girls. In regard to the implications of these stereotypical taxonomies for women of color, cultural critic Alberto Sandoval-Sánchez writes,

Such degrading and sexist labels clearly signal the exploitation of the female body and its commodification in patriarchal voyeuristic and misogynist practices. "Latin" women, or "senoritas," are objects of desire, available for romance, to satisfy the male gaze and sexual desire, they are registered in the Anglo-American cultural imaginary in the form of woman-as-spectacle.[9]

The consequence of this spectacularization reoccurs in contemporary Hollywood, reverberating in recent star studies of Rosie Perez, Selena, and Jennifer Lopez and their well-publicized curves. The sexual availability and anxieties punctuating these stereotypical taxonomies, though cognizant of similar allegories in African American and Asian American film portrayals, fail to consider the exploitation and commodification of queer racialized subjects in the white gay cinematic imaginary. The heteronormative assumptions framing studies and traditional approaches to Latinidad in Hollywood film continually reassert a heteropatriarchal Latin Lover/Spitfire dichotomy. For Spice Boy archetypes, these images cannot be easily categorized or situated in conventional straight Hollywood narratives in which the cantina girl lures a white cowboy for an evening of pleasure or a swashbuckler sweeps a noble daughter off her feet.

This examination of U.S. queer Latino filmic character construction submits that Spice Boys exist according to Gloria Anzaldúa and other Chicano scholars' notion of a *Nepantla* state of becoming, a hybridic in-between space for mestiza or mixed blood people.[10] This Nahautl term, which describes the "central interface between [the] different realities,"[11] generates creative acts and conditions for people situated within collisions between different political, geographic, gendered, cultural, and psychic borders. The *Nepantla* of the Spice Boy is a filmic example of creativity in which a Latino cinematic image is neither wholly Latin Lover nor Spitfire. Arguably, this queer "stereotypical blend" traverses a borderland where Latino masculinity and femininity converge.[12] The Spice Boy contains a weakness for white men like Dolores Del Rio, a spectacular accented feminized appeal like Carmen Miranda, and a sensual charm like Ramon Novarro. Hence, the Spice Boy traverses racialized, sexualized, and gendered vectors, becoming a seductive and fetishized object imbued with an exoticism that satiates white gay male sexual appetites.

### Harvesting Spice: Extracts of Interracial Desire in
### Billy's Hollywood Screen Kiss *and* Trick

Although a content analysis of several films from New Queer Cinema is warranted, this chapter will examine the coupling of Fernando and Billy Collier in *Billy's Hollywood Screen Kiss* and Mark Miranda and Gabriel Bloom in *Trick*. These films offer two same-sex, interracial couplings with different narrative ends that share qualifying attributes common to Spice Boy textuality, namely, the exchange of racialized bodies, labor, and desire. This phenomenon in New Queer Cinema is worthy of further investigation.

Both films position lonely, hopeless white romantics as central protagonists. Billy Collier (Sean P. Hayes) is a down-on-his-luck photographer documenting his life, friends, and intimates through grainy Polaroid snapshots. His confidante, "fag hag" Georgina (Meredith Scott Lynn), criticizes him for his uninspired photo essay on vacuum cleaners and for his choice in men. He's bedding Fernando (Armando Valdes-Kennedy), a superfluous Latino exotic uninterested in long-term monogamy.

*The perfect screen kiss? Brad Rowe (left) and Sean P. Hayes star as Gabriel and Billy in Billy's Hollywood Screen Kiss (1998). Photo courtesy of Jerry Orlinger's Movie Materials.*

When famed artist and mentor Perry (Richard Ganoung) commissions Billy to produce a series of campy and sardonic reinterpretations of classic Hollywood movie kisses, a chance encounter with waiter Gabriel (Brad Rowe) propels Billy's sexual fascination. Billy casts Gabriel to star in his photo series as a Burt Lancaster type, despite being disappointed that this musician–turned–"Kate Moss" male model has a girlfriend. As they grow closer, Billy's fixation accelerates, until he puts Gabriel to the test and discerns if there is any chance that sexual curiosity may give way to the perfect "Hollywood screen kiss."

*Trick* also features an evening of sexual pursuit, erotic glances, and mixed messages. Gabriel Bloom (Christian Campbell) is an American musical playwright and pianist portrayed as a dimpled adoring "boy next door" put out of his apartment by his overzealous straight roommate and used by an overbearing best friend (Tori Spelling). Frustrated by the poor reception of his latest musical number at a songwriting workshop, Gabriel attends the opening of a new gay club, where he happens upon a cast of characters, including go-go boy Mark Miranda dancing on the bar. Mark's objectification, the "looked-at-ness" of his spectacular ethnic desire, continues into the following scene.

Riding the subway home, Mark enters the same car, passively closing his eyes, inviting Gabriel's gaze through director Jim Fall's use of a subjective camera. After an exchange of knowing glances, Mark goes home with a nervous Gabriel, astounded by his luck ("He's a go-go boy!" Gabriel declares in one scene). When the men are met with a series of obstacles that disallow any private time for a hot sexual encounter (surprising that private space is even needed for the young men, given Mark's hypersexual availability), their initial erotically charged meeting gives way to a reciprocal understanding of their insecurities. Might this be more than a one-night stand? As the narrative comes to a close, Mark troubles Gabriel's assumption that he is "just another little phone number on a dirty cocktail napkin shoved into the bottom of his pocket." Mark reveals that he has had his heart broken by a Yale choirboy, further undoing his "Casanova" typing. Hand in hand, they passionately kiss at the end of the film, suggesting that even "tricks" have happy endings.

Although the Spice Boy in *Billy's Hollywood Screen Kiss*, Fernando, and his coupling with Billy Collier fall short of the well-developed Mark Miranda–Gabriel Bloom story line, they share similar narrative characteristics. At the opening of the film, Fernando and Billy are nearly naked in bed, suggesting their sexual encounter from the night before. In fact, Billy

*Mark Miranda (left, J.P. Pitoc) and Gabriel Bloom (Christian Campbell) as the white-Latino interracial couplet in* Trick *(1999). Image courtesy of 2007 New Line Cinema Productions.*

says exasperatedly, "I picked you up at Rage, for Christ sakes," demonstrating the sexual impetus between the interracial pairings in both films. When Billy is outraged by Fernando's open relationship with his white boyfriend, Peter, he accuses him of being unfaithful. This accusation also prevails in *Trick* when Gabriel assumes that go-go boy Mark is a playboy. As the narratives suggest, these couplings originate in gay clubs, inferring the significance of gay male social spaces as the sole location for same-sex interracial interactivity. Moreover, it is erotic pleasure rather than a U.S. ideology of romance that is sought at the fruition of these Spice Boy–white male pairings. The racialized implications of this desire result in each couple ultimately meeting different narrative ends.

From their first scenes on screen, these Spice Boys are typed by their nearly naked, well-sculpted bodies. In a tight close-up shot, it is Fernando's exotic tongue that opens the film and indicates their highly sexual encounter from the night before. When Gabriel sees Mark for the first time in a club, he is go-go dancing in a thong on top of the bar. Mark's image is projected onto a series of television screens, offering an ambient display of racialized homoerotic voyeurism. Though the laborious orientation of

Fernando is trivial and unclear, perhaps suggesting that it is his prowess and sexual availability that is at work, Mark is a sex worker, a fascinating subject for the white gay man lucky enough to converse with—much less bed—this Adonis figure.

These mixed raced pairings may suggest a queer colonial encounter in which the primitive ethnic Other is discovered by the civilized explorer. This is argued similarly by Ana M. López's treatment of Latina images in film; she posits Hollywood as a cultural ethnographer creating, integrating, and translating "Otherness." She adds, "Thinking of Hollywood as ethnographer, as co-producer in power of cultural texts, allows us to reformulate its relationship to ethnicity. Hollywood does not represent ethnics and minorities: it creates them and provides its audience with an experience of them."[13] In her analysis, Carmen Miranda's static frivolity and self-conscious spectacularity subverted Hollywood authority over the Latina body. The case can be made that New Queer Cinema evokes its own referents to a colonial fantasy; Spice Boys are objectified and consumed in the text and even in the marketing and exhibition of the films (*Billy's* Fernando is disproportionately featured in the film's trailer

*J.P. Pitoc as 'Spice Boy' Mark Miranda in* Trick *(1999). Image courtesy of 2007 New Line Cinema Productions.*

compared with his actual screen time, for example).[14] Tempting as it is to equate this filmic archetype to what Latina feminist cultural critics call Malinche iconography,[15] it is important to note that this coupling is not a linear conquest of first world/third world or explorer/explored, nor does it have the same procreative and biological preoccupations and consequences (miscegenation laws, color hierarchies, intermarriage, etc.). Unlike López's critical insights into Latinas in Hollywood film, Spice Boys are not the product of the Good Neighbor Policy (Carmen Miranda), nor do they likely incite anxiety over racial mixing (Dolores Del Rio) or reciprocal implications for the family (Lupe Velez), particularly in a white gay male cinematic context.[16]

Similar to Lopez's observations, Gina Marchetti's discussion of the construction of "yellow peril" in classical Hollywood film also examines the colonial ideological imperative behind Asian cinematic images that serve as metaphors for East-West relations. The seductive female of the Orient emerges in these films, embodying unexplainable powers to provoke Western white male travelers to do their bidding. These interracial romances typically found an unfortunate, sacrificial, or fatal end, in narrative patterns shared with the "tragic mulatto" or "mulatta" figure in Hollywood film. According to Marchetti, the "tragic mulatta's" attempt to pass as white was typically portrayed as tainting white racial purity, similarly to how Asian-white romances were an allegory for the encroaching "taint" of the West by the East.[17]

The emergence of Spice Boys in New Queer Cinema similarly posits racialized queer desire as the central impetus between Latino-white pairings. Unlike heteronormative racialized subjects' attempts to pass or assimilate into a white patriarchal American mainstream, Spice Boys operate in a white same-sex erotic currency of what Dwight McBride calls the "gay marketplace of desire."[18] Passing is not an option for Spice Boys, as their exotic visual cues both are crucial to their place within the marketplace and provide them a unique location in this economy as desired commodities. For the white gay male protagonists in these films, to bed a Spice Boy is an achievement.

Unlike classical Hollywood portrayals of white American men succumbing to and conquering female ethnic Others, white gay men in these films are persuaded, enchanted, and penetrated by the Spice Boys' hypersexual and hypermasculine seduction. Again, the *Nepantla* conditions of this image permits the Spice Boys' archetypal hybridity, including their seductive female mystique and penetrable macho capabilities. It is perhaps this in-betweenness that proves an important counterpoint to previous studies of heteronormative mixed raced pairings in early and contemporary Hollywood cinema.

Rather than attempting to assimilate into a white American mainstream as a "tragic mulatto" figure or pose a danger to the heterosexual family order, these sexual objects are in high demand in this marketplace. Their assigned role is to be desired, consumed, and fetishized, but never to be loved. After all, as Billy's drag queen friend Deidre flippantly suggests to him in one scene, "If you're in the mood for a little Latino love tonight, Francisco's here." By intentionally changing Fernando's name throughout the film, this Spice Boy's own subjectivity is undermined and redetermined in the marketplace as an available and interchangeable sex object, penetrating Billy's ear but never his heart.

Hence, Spice Boy portrayals within this film movement birth their own fragmented and contradictory realities for young queer Latino men as filmic manifestations, active cultural critics, and consumers. Spice Boys are neither degraded passive possessions nor allegorical colonized Others, but rather active contributors and actors in this fetishized erotic visual economy. These multiple locations necessitate an intersectional lens, remaining cognizant of young U.S. queer Latino men's diverse racialized, sexualized, gendered, and classed positionalities. By examining images and reception, this study evaluates how interracial desire and the marketplace operate in these young men's lives.

## Screening Spice: U.S. Queer Latinos as Cultural Readers

When five young Latinos gathered at the University of Colorado at Boulder to screen *Billy's Hollywood Screen Kiss* and *Trick*, they varied in their exposure to New Queer Cinema. The sample group consisted of Alex, Che, Justin, Lorenzo, and Mario,[19] young men from the Boulder County–Denver Metro area. Each participant was born in the United States and only one was born in a state other than Colorado (Alex was from Texas). The oldest person in attendance, Justin, was twenty-two years of age; the youngest was Lorenzo, at age nineteen. Participants contended that they were partially if not entirely proficient in Spanish, but only Lorenzo identified Spanish as his first language. Many of these young men "came out of the closet" at different periods of their lives—some in high school and others in college.

While these lauded films were promoted in film festivals and publications like the *Advocate* and *Out*, Che was just a sixteen-year-old high school student in Denver, and Mario was eighteen and preparing for a graduation celebration in Longmont, a small town in Boulder County. For these young adolescent men discovering their same-sex attractions, these films became important markers of personal exploration.

Only Justin reported attending a screening of one of the films, in this case *Trick*. More commonly, some participants had to watch the films in the sometimes dangerous seclusion of their parents' home or under the watchful eyes of family members. This was certainly the case for Alex. He was only able to see fragments of *Billy's Hollywood Screen Kiss* on cable in his parents' living room, fearful of the consequences should he be caught. He comments:

> My mom was there in the room and I didn't want [her] to see the movies so, because "they were gay," so I was like, okay, change it [the channel]. But actually I did see some of it . . . and I heard about "Trick" but I didn't have anyone to see it with and I couldn't rent it because I didn't have a Blockbuster account and I would have to use my mom's and I didn't want to do that.[20]

For Alex and his mother, the underlying fear remained. Had he watched a film like *Billy's Hollywood Screen Kiss* and derived pleasure from the images, he might confirm his gay identity for himself and his family. It was this anxiety of exposure that drove him to intervene, stop the film, and turn the television off. Similarly, Che embarked on this "dangerous" territory and consciously sought these films out to understand his own sexual desires. He, too, had to be aware of his home life and immediate surroundings:

> So I was just watching TV, they had a queer movie on every Sunday night. So when my parents would go to bed I'd stay up and watch it. Just kind of getting a window into a life uncloseted. You know that's what I was looking for, a life uncloseted, where people could be who they are and that's what those movies are.[21]

A way to consume the gay and trendy diegetic spaces of West Hollywood in *Billy's Hollywood Screen Kiss* and New York City in *Trick*, these films became "windows" into fantasy worlds.

Recalling Lynn Spigel's significant work on television technology installation and its gendered meanings for post–World War II housewives, study participants' responses underscore how television's promise to be a "window on the world" is fraught with its own sexual and gendered anxieties. "Conspicuous consumption" became an oppositional media habit for post–World War II America;[22] it is also relevant to these queer Latino men's viewing habits in a racialized and sexualized contemporary context. The domestic viewing environments for these men in U.S. Latino households are critical locations that offer clues into the meaning and interpretations they assigned to these fantasy worlds. Although many young queer men may adopt similar "conspicuous consumptive" maneuverings, it is significant that the media engagement occurs in, to some degree, Latino homes arranged according to Catholic dogma, heteronormative orders of *la familia* (the family), Spanish language usage, and, in most cases, working-class realities (financial limitations in the number of consoles, DVD player affordability, and access to oppositional media devices such as TiVo, remote control, or digital cable). Queer film images in the home may offer "windows" into a homoerotic and racialized go-go boy bar mise-en-scène, but they simultaneously invite self-surveillance, self-policing, and exposure. To view queer media content is a "conspicuous" survival strategy, and these young Latino men were all too aware of parental location, remote control channel switching, viewer/receiver distanciation, and temporal limitations (the time available to privately consume).

The desire for affirmation, acceptance, and a place to belong goes beyond these metonymic "windows" and manifests itself in terms of racial authenticity. According to their personal interviews, most study participants recalled painful moments of scrutiny, prejudice, and blatant rejection by their straight Latina/o peers. Many longed to be accepted but questioned whether or not the primarily heterosexual Latina/o community would repudiate them because they desired men, forfeiting the possibility of being "Latino enough."

What it means to be Latino thus was a source of conflict for study participants. After watching the two films, the young men completed surveys; during a focus group debriefing, they were asked to identify the Latino characters. With regard to *Billy's Hollywood Screen Kiss*, they identified Fernando as Latino, recording a series of racial cues typifying his ethnic Otherness. In his survey, Justin reports, "Fernando was very sexual . . . the Latino Lover stereotype appears in films whether gay or straight and Latinos are often exotic or erotic and promiscuous."[23] Additionally, subjects observed Fernando's thickly accented aphorisms and Spanish bilingualism as racialized markers. However, in the case of *Trick*'s Mark Miranda, participants, though noting his obvious "sexual prowess," debated whether his inability to speak Spanish made him white or an ethnic Other:

> Lorenzo: The other main character [referring to Mark Miranda], I don't think he is [Latino].
>
> Mario [observing Lorenzo]: Yeah, me, too . . .
>
> Lorenzo: Just because he has dark hair, dark eyes, doesn't mean he's Hispanic. There are a lot of Hispanics who have blond hair and blue eyes.
>
> Che: But he has a Latino last name . . .
>
> Justin: Yeah, that's why—with a name like Miranda, but I just guessed, because it was possible, I just thought with Miranda, *Mark Miranda* [his emphasis].
>
> Lorenzo: I think there's more to it than just because you have a last name that's Hispanic, so that means you're Hispanic?
>
> Che: A lot of people are identified as Hispanic by their skin tone, I'm interracial, but I'm not seen as white because my skin tone is brown, I'm seen as Chicano first, and nobody else recognizes that I'm part Yugoslavian and part Finnish either, you know? A lot has to do with your last name and your skin color. Unfortunately, I know it shouldn't be like that because people who speak Spanish are classified as Hispanics; [they] are of every single color and background.
>
> Mario: I didn't hear him utter one Spanish word throughout the whole thing.
>
> Justin: I know a lot of Latinos who don't speak their language.

Although they did not reach a definite conclusion about Mark's racial character construction, in many ways, their analysis about what qualifies a person to be seen and identified as Latino drew on personal experiences. For instance, Che remarked that though he is a child of mixed raced parentage, he is no less Chicano simply because he does not speak Spanish fluently. By understanding language as a site of authenticity, some subjects measured these characters by their native tongues. This was particularly true for Lorenzo, the only participant to identify Spanish as his first language. However, the remaining subjects contested this notion of language and instead emphasized color, physique, and sexual prowess as sufficient determinants of racial characterization. By turning to other visual cues of

Latino identity, these young men implicitly suggest the constructed nature of the Spice Boy archetype. The casting of actors Armando Valdes-
Kennedy and J. P. Pitoc inspired productive personal insights into queer
and Latino identity formations.

Earlier study participants reported that they "conspicuously consumed"
New Queer Cinema in a strategic effort to view and to reenvision themselves in metropolitan urban spaces far from the mundane happenings
of Boulder, Colorado. Interestingly, subjects did not passively embrace all
characters portrayed in the films but instead held important criticisms
of Spice Boy depictions. In fact, they actively differentiated messages regarding queer Latinoness from whiteness. During the focus group, Justin stressed, "What defines the white guy versus the brown guy was the
white guy seems to be a little more normal, your Average Joe. . . . I think
in both of these films the sexual prowess was definitely with the Brown
boys."[24] Similarly, Che also criticized the racial applications of whiteness
within the diegetic constructs of the two narratives. He states, "[White
gays] are seen as the 'normal' ones in the GLBT [gay, lesbian, bisexual,
and transgender] communities. . . . [Latinos are] deviants of their culture,
that's what I thought they were portrayed as in the movies. You know,
there's only one of them here because their culture is so against it."[25] To
varying degrees these young men documented the differential portrayals
of white-Latino interrelatedness. Each subject read these images similarly,
contesting the filmmakers' archetypal Spice Boy, and also applied their
lived experiences to these cultural readings.

> Mario: I hear it a lot, like if I go out with somebody Caucasian usually,
>    they try to make me say something in Spanish and its sparks their
>    fire or something like that. And it really pisses me off, but it's per-
>    ceived more sexually, and romantic, and flows off your lips and your
>    tongue makes weird noises . . .
> Lorenzo: Why does it piss you off? Is it because we're a sideshow? Like
>    a little circus. . . . We're a freak or something . . .
> Mario: Yeah, a novelty.
> Che: And I don't think it's necessarily a conscious thing.
> Mario: It turns them on.
> Che: Yeah, and they don't understand that.

The filmic commentary on queer Latino male sexuality led to a greater
personalized criticism of Spice Boy–white gay male interracial pairings

in New Queer Cinema. These young men began to identify a similarly lived experience, the fetishism of their bodies, tongues, and skin color. They interpreted these filmic messages and made them applicable to their own lives. By naming familiar interactions with white gay men, participants escaped being primarily sexualized racial objects and coterminously enjoined their interracial sexual experiences with Spice Boy film representation.

During their one-on-one debriefing interviews, the participants reported an overall impact after the focus group conversation. Che reportedly made a personal connection between his past relationships with white gay men and the visual analysis of Spice Boy racial objectification in film:

> Che: My first boyfriend wanted me to speak Spanish to him when we were just making out or you know, because he thought it was sexy. And I don't think he really appreciated the language but he . . . I think that's one of the things he liked about me, a perk, that we were talking about, is that I would speak Spanish and that's "oh, so romantic," you know?
>
> RH: And did you?
>
> Che: Yeah, just because when you think you're in love you want to please the other person for the most part. And at the time I really didn't see it as a mockery of my culture as "oh, well that's neat, let me look at that!" But after retrospect, hindsight is always twenty-twenty. And definitely, I can see it now as a mockery of who I was, you know, just subconscious racism. . . . "Oh, it's different, it's me."[26]

As critical interpreters of racial visual cues, study participants ruptured the silences about their sexual objectification and fetishism. No longer rationalizing or dismissing the actions of white male sexual desires as frivolous or "in the heat of the moment," these young men questioned this "sideshow" treatment. Upon further inquiry, subjects talked about a gay community in which they voluntarily serve as activists and event organizers and about the racism (to varying degrees) they simultaneously endured. At this juncture, if these men were besieged with racial prejudice particularly among their own sexual partners, lovers, and boyfriends, then why did they remain, sustain, and participate in these spaces?

In the audience survey, participants were asked to identify one character in these films in which they saw themselves. Subjects unanimously named Billy Collier (Sean P. Hayes), the protagonist of *Billy's Hollywood*

*Screen Kiss*, as a marker of common identification. The love-starved Billy is an artist at his "peak" of creative and artistic inspiration. Though caught in the sexual entanglements of resident Spice Boy Fernando, Billy believes in the great couples of conventional romantic melodramas and the magic of a Hollywood screen kiss. Regarding his own "Billy" identification, Mario wrote, "[He's] still looking for love, nervous, always expecting things to turn out negatively."[27] Similarly, Lorenzo contended that he sees himself as Billy because he "seems to only be attracted to straight men, which is what I feel sometimes."[28] During his interview, Justin expanded, "The hopeless romantic in Billy I think is what I identified with most. . . . I like picture-perfect things."[29] For participants, Billy was a sympathetic hero. They, too, wished Billy would find love, companionship, and the great Hollywood screen kiss. For these young men Billy became a symbolic character with whom they could identify, as he also longed to "find the one."

These romanticized notions of the perfect kiss spoke to all of the young men interviewed, though some still remained suspicious of this fantasy. Che contends,

> I don't know, my search for love is based on a lot of the things I was presented with as a child like everything ends happily ever after and that's what the majority of the people in the United States grow up thinking, that everything is going to end up happily ever after. That you're going fall in love and ride off into the sunset. . . . And it's hard to find people who are perfect because nobody's perfect, you know. I am really starting to doubt if . . . there is that one true love out there. There's nothing [*sic*] true, I'd have to say, but you got to believe that there is.[30]

All the young men involved in the study reported a deep concern with finding love, sustaining love, and being perceived in film as racialized exotics with the inability to love. As Che stresses, his desires for "the one" are also rooted in a U.S. ideology of love, the promise that if immigrant ethnic Others work hard enough they achieve national citizenship and fairy-tale endings. Despite the racist cinematic constructions of Spice Boys in these films, the filmmakers' commentary on Latino-white gay male interracial relationships, and participants' personal experiences with racial objectification or "sideshow" perception, they remained committed to these existing social structures.

Rather than condemn or directly confront this complex racialized "marketplace of desire," these men negotiate between their lived experience and their pursuit of partnership. Ultimately, they are conflicted between their realized sense of self and their idealized sense of self. As realized subjects, they fully recognize the material consequences of racism they must contend with in the club, the movie theater, or the bedroom. Mario cannot forget incidents when white gay men have flirtatiously lured him to speak Spanish. Che cannot ignore moments when his boyfriend asked him to coo Spanish into his ear. Lorenzo cannot erase the fact that these "Sizzling Summer Films"[31] portrayed him like a "sideshow." These lived experiences speak to the historic circumstances portraying Spice Boy exoticism, in the words of gay film historian Vito Russo, as "yardsticks" to white gay male sexual normativity.[32]

Ironically, the idealized sense of self permits these young men enough agency and "empowerment" to cultivate a fantasized self-vision: to find "the one." Each of these young men, despite recognizing the intense racial codifications visualized on screen, identifies with Billy Collier not because of his "blue eyes" per se (though not disputing this possible reading) but because of his perpetual search for love. Although Billy rejects the seductive Fernando for the hallowed Gabriel, these young queer Latino men empathized with him unanimously. As Justin observes, like Billy, he too believes in a "picture perfect" partner. Ultimately, these men negotiate between aspects of their identity and lived experiences in order to accommodate their longings for partnership, love, and "the one," no matter where and with whom that love may be found.

Because of the contradictory and fragmented elements in their own media engagement, it is necessary to adapt another theoretical lens to reconceptualize U.S. queer Latino viewing practices. José Esteban Muñoz proposes "disidentifications" as a queer of color survival strategy in which ideology is neither assimilated nor resisted but "scrambles and reconstructs the encoded message of a cultural text in a fashion that both exposes the encoded message's universalizing and exclusionary machinations and recircuits its workings to account for, include, and empower minority identities and identifications."[33]

It is important to acknowledge that "empowerment" is a complicated expression, and it can occur contradictorily. Muñoz emphasizes the migratory nature of the disidentificatory subject, submitting, "The negotiations that lead to hybrid identity formation are a traveling back and forth from different identity vectors."[34] What is occurring in these young men's viewing practices is a disidentificatory subscription to a predominantly white gay marketplace of desire. As Muñoz argues, this "rethinking" does not assure a resistant or subversive reading of the cultural text. Perhaps the "empowering" gains for these young men are in their migratory negotiations of Spice Boy visual representation, and the interplay between white desire and racial fetishism within the marketplace. There is something to be gained from these young men's interpretative acts of New Queer Cinema: their recircuiting of film texts and self-tropicalizing "spicy" performances in their everyday erotic exchanges with white gay men.

## Surviving Queer Mixed Race Coupling: The End of New Queer Cinema

The Spice Boy–white gay male couplet does not survive in most film narratives, opening the possibility for the white protagonist to fall in lust with the desired ethnic Other but to fall in love with another white man. The sexual predication of the interracial coupling certainly occurs in the pairing of Fernando and Billy, as the former could not bear more than mere erotic seduction. Although Billy does not get Gabriel in the end, the last scene of the film introduces Joshua, a handsome white gay man interested in photography, suggesting a same-race, same-sex happily ever after. However, Gabriel Bloom and Mark Miranda in *Trick* escape these narrative expectations. Nearing the close of the third act, Gabriel and Mark find themselves alone in a men's room. Gabriel approaches him suggestively and in turn, coaxes Mark. Yet Mark coyly smiles and teases, "What kind of a girl do you think I am?" and walks out of frame. In the film's last moments, the camera follows the boys on the street. They kiss as the sun rises over New York City while the camera envelops them in a 360-degree turn. It is clear that their interracial pairing is certified.

Though Mark's Spice Boy typification shares a variety of common characteristics with Fernando and other Spice Boys, he breaks with the archetypal form. He is the first lead Latino character in New Queer Cinema who "gets the guy" in the end, though his lack of pronounced racial visual cues, including no satirical accent and no racial point of origin, further troubled study participants' readings of his Latinidad. Actor J. P. Pitoc, who played Mark Miranda, is reportedly of mixed Hungarian and Columbian heritage; though "lacking" an authentic "Latinoness," he has endeared himself to queer U.S. Latino audiences, signing autographs and giving out free *Trick* DVDs as a special guest at the San Francisco Gay Latino Pride Parade in 2000.[35] As Mary Beltrán observes in her reading of "multiculti"

action film heroes, the casting of mixed race lead actors offers a potentially raceless aesthetic, reassuring an "uneasy white audience" with an un-
determinable racialized body prescribed in "symbolic whiteness."[36] Hence,
the racelessness of J. P. Pitoc potentially catalyzed ambiguous readings for
queer Latino cultural readers in this study and other viewers, while also
reassuring his cinematic survival in the film text. He became a Spice Boy
dark enough to diversify the film as the fetishized sex object consumed by
the invited voyeuristic gazes of white gay men, and yet he was tamed by a
diluted "spice" embodying symbolic white codes. As such, *Trick*'s strategic
use of an indeterminable racialized queer body defied the cinematic ends
confronting a Spice Boy like Fernando, permitting Mark and Gabriel's safe
passage along Christopher Street. In part, this film was a precursory end
point for New Queer Cinema as a movement.

The U.S. "Latin Boom," characterized by the Ricky Martin phenomenon in the late 1990s, the commercial reappropriation of Sundance and
independent cinema, the growing reliance on corporate sponsorship for
gay and lesbian film festival programming, and a less than "defiant" mainstream Hollywood interpretation of queer cinema, changed low-budget
queer film production, exhibition, and distribution in the United States.
Although ethnic tourism of sexually available exotics continued to re-
emerge in queer Hollywood and independent films located (to some degree) in Latin American countries, such as *The Fluffer* (2001), *Testosterone*
(2003), and the Academy Award–winning *Brokeback Mountain* (2005),
Spice Boy and white gay male couplings appear to be of little significance in more recent U.S. queer film productions in the early twenty-first
century.

By circumventing the obvious interracial politics of representation in
New Queer Cinema, researchers failed to consider what these films meant
to perhaps an entire generation of young U.S. Latino men in the 1990s. In
tandem with the brutal and violent costs of "coming out" as evidenced by
the murders of Matthew Shepard, Brandon Teena, and Gwen Araujo, New
Queer Cinema was an important point of entry and release for young Latinos "looking for a life uncloseted."

As cultural readers, they longed to be a part of these fantasized cinematic worlds (to varying degrees) and, in reaction, adapted consumptive
maneuverings in their parents' homes. Interpreting Spice Boy representations, these young men named common experiences and collectively
opposed the racial fetishism echoed in their personal, social, and sexual
relationships with white gay men. Surprisingly, they did not criticize or

resist their own participation and commodification as Spice Boys in a "gay marketplace of desire." The disidentificatory potential of these young men suggested an "empowering" position—consumed by white gay male desire and consented to by these young queer Latino men.

Asserting their own pleasurable gains in real-life interracial couplings, their readings of the Spice Boy archetype trouble a colonizer/colonized allegory. Without the procreative and intermarriage consequences of heterosexual interracial relationships, queer Latino men as cultural readers offer new theoretical conceptions in audience studies accounting for queer and racialized film viewing. Demonstrating the complicated attainment of "happily ever after," these young men refused to confront the white gay male marketplace for its racial currency. If they did so, they might complicate the Spice Boy fantasy and surrender not only the possibility of finding "Prince Charming" but also their picture-perfect Hollywood screen kiss.

NOTES

1. Edward Guthmann, "Lights, Camera, Attraction," *Advocate* 9 (June 1999): 38-43.

2. Stephen Saban, "Tricky Business," *Out*, July 1999, 44-49.

3. For an important discussion of the rise of gay-based narrowcasting in U.S. network television, see Ron Becker, *Gay TV and Straight America* (New Brunswick, NJ: Rutgers University Press, 2006).

4. B. Ruby Rich, "New Queer Cinema," in *New Queer Cinema: A Critical Reader*, ed. Michele Aaron (New Brunswick, NJ: Rutgers University Press, 2004), 22.

5. Ibid., 16.

6. Michele Aaron, "Introduction," in Aaron, *New Queer Cinema*, 8.

7. Daniel T. Contreras, "New Queer Cinema: Spectacle, Race, Utopia," in Aaron, *New Queer Cinema*, 127.

8. For more on Latino film stereotypes, see Charles Ramírez Berg, "Stereotyping in Films in General and of the Hispanic in Particular," in *Latin Looks: Images of Latinos and Latinas in the U.S. Media*, ed. Clara Rodríguez (Boulder, CO: Westview Press, 1997), 104-20.

9. Alberto Sandoval-Sánchez, *Jose, Can You See? Latinos On and Off Broadway* (Madison: University of Wisconsin Press, 1999), 28-29.

10. Constance Cortez, "The New Aztlan: Nepantla (and Other Sites of Transmogrification)," in *The Road to Aztlán: Art from a Mythic Homeland*, ed. Virginia M. Fields and Victor Zamudio-Taylor (Los Angeles: Los Angeles County Museum of Art, 2001), 367.

11. Ana Louise Keating, ed., *Gloria E. Anzaldúa: Interviews/Entrevistas* (New York: Routledge, 2000), 176.

12. Ramírez Berg, "Stereotyping in Films," 117.

13. Ana M. López, "Are All Latins from Manhattan? Hollywood, Ethnography and Cultural Colonialism," in *Mediating Two Worlds: Cinematic Encounters in the Americas*, ed. John King, Ana M. López, and Manuel Alvarado (London: BFI Publishing, 1993), 68.

14. "Special Features," *Billy's Hollywood Screen Kiss*, DVD, directed by Tommy O'Haver (Trimark Pictures, 1998).

15. By "Malinche iconography," I am referring to images, fictions, and cinematic allegories representing a Mexican/Chicana sexuality through the white heterosexual colonizer's active exploration, conquest, and domination of the passive Aztec indigenous woman. The image, story, and myth of Malinche, based on the historical figure Malintzín Tenepal, reduces Mexican/Chicana desire to the "sinful" betrayal of her race as she chooses, willingly receives, and procreates with first world European authority over Chicano patriarchy. Within Chicano nationalist discourse she is a cautionary tale for assimilation, feminism, lesbianism, and interracial desire. See the work of Norma Alarcón, Alicia Gaspar de Alba, Catriona Rueda Esquibel, and Cherríe Moraga.

16. López, "Are All Latins from Manhattan?" 69.

17. Gina Marchetti, *Romance and the "Yellow Peril": Race, Sex, and Discursive Strategies in Hollywood Fiction* (Berkeley: University of California Press, 1993), 69.

18. Dwight A. McBride, *Why I Hate Abercrombie & Fitch* (New York: NYU Press, 2005).

19. These names are pseudonyms to protect the confidentiality of research participants.

20. Alex, personal interview, March 15, 2002.

21. Che, personal interview, March 7, 2002.

22. Lynn Spigel, "Installing the Television Set: Popular Discourses on Television and Domestic Space, 1948-1955," in *Private Screenings: Television and the Female Consumer*, ed. Lynn Spigel and Denise Mann (Minneapolis: University of Minnesota Press, 1992), 26.

23. Justin, personal interview, March 17, 2002.

24. Ibid.

25. Che, personal interview, March 7, 2002.

26. Ibid.

27. Mario, personal interview, March 12, 2002.

28. Lorenzo, personal interview, March 6, 2002.

29. Justin, personal interview, March 17, 2002.

30. Che, personal interview, March 7, 2002.

31. Guthmann, "Lights, Camera, Attraction," 38.

32. Vito Russo, *The Celluloid Closet: Homosexuality in the Movies* (New York: Harper and Row, 1987), 59.

33. José Esteban Muñoz, *Disidentifications: Queers of Color and the Performance of Politics* (Minneapolis: University of Minnesota Press, 1999), 31.

34. Ibid., 32.

35. Andrew J. Wysocki, "J. P. Pitoc Events," www.jppitoc.com/gay_pride_2000.htm (accessed January 1, 2006).

36. Mary Beltrán, "The New Hollywood Racelessness: Only the Fast, Furious, (and Multiracial) Will Survive," *Cinema Journal* 44, no. 2 (Winter 2005): 63.

# The Biracial Subject as Passive Receptacle for Japanese American Memory in *Come See the Paradise*

## *Kent A. Ono*

When Alan Parker's *Come See the Paradise* premiered in U.S. theaters on December 22, 1990, it had been approximately forty-five years since the release of John Sturges's film *Bad Day at Black Rock* (1955), starring Spencer Tracy. That film was Hollywood's last substantial foray into the subject of Japanese Americans' incarceration during World War II,[1] when, by executive presidential order, 120,000 Japanese Americans were either imprisoned or forcibly uprooted and then transported from their homes on the West Coast to inland "assembly centers" and then later to ten concentration camps in isolated parts of the midwestern and western United States.[2] A film critic comparing the two films might be expected to comment on the obvious differences between them, since, after all, important civil rights activism and legislation took place between their release dates, historically altering the racial horizon. The notion that racial or gendered discrimination is a contestable and grievable offense could legitimately be assumed in the post–civil rights era film *Come See the Paradise* whereas, in the pre–civil rights time frame of *Bad Day at Black Rock*, contesting racial discrimination, for instance, not only could not be assumed outright but might be considered to be an unpopular and unwinnable position to take, given the nation's stage of white supremacy at the time. One notable similarity between the two films, however, is the role that absence plays. The reason Spencer Tracy's character goes to Black Rock is to investigate the death of Komoko, a Japanese American man we later find out has been murdered in a racially motivated crime. While Komoko is the narrative's raison d'être, Komoko never appears; the narrative action *conveniently* takes place after his death.[3] Similarly, as I argue in this chapter, in *Come See the Paradise*, Mini, the child born of Japanese American Lily Kawamura and Irish American Jack McGurn, is a mixed race girl whose personality, hopes, fears, desires, and passions—in a word, her subjectivity—the film evacuates. Although, unlike Komoko, Mini is present in the film, instead of paying attention to Mini or her experience, the film uses both her existence as a concept (analogous to Komoko's death in *Black Rock*) and the image of her body to facilitate the development of other characters and ultimately to propel the narrative forward.

Hollywood films such as *Come See the Paradise* that center white people and (re)read them as individual antiracist heroes during former periods of virulent white racism are a staple of the industry.[4] In this chapter I argue Mini is central to this (re)reading of Japanese American racial history in *Come See the Paradise*, even as she and her mixed race perspective are sublimated to the film's narrative. Mini is primarily a function within the film, not interesting in her own right but rather useful in advancing claims about social issues. Mini is the passive onlooker of events that happen around her and the receptacle for a subjective historical account of Japanese American incarceration. One key role she plays in the film, therefore, is to register and record the facts of incarceration. Additionally, as the product of miscegenation automatically loved by her parents and grandparents, she serves as the salve that helps heal the wounding divide between Japanese America and white society, by the end of the film marking the possibility of a successful cross-racial white–Japanese American relationship. In all these ways, Mini both literally and figuratively embodies the film's perspective on the future of race relations in the United States, a perspective that acknowledges, but then—in large part through the depiction of a mixed race figure—transcends the historical fact of the racist incarceration.

Mini's vantage point within the film as mixed race renders her a unique character within the film, indeed within incarceration films as a whole, where mixed race Japanese Americans hardly figure,[5] and thus her character offers tremendous potential. Yet the film constructs her without agency of her own, and her position as a child situates the mixed race subject not only as vulnerable and naïve—indeed infantile—but also as having no particular or unique consciousness. Because of an implicit fear of dilution or a washing away of the history of Japanese Americans altogether that Mini as a mixed race subject might portend, Mini is tutored throughout the film about a particular version of Japanese American incarceration. This version of the incarceration, thus, paternalistically relies upon the nonagency of Mini and on the bracketing of her mixed race subjectivity, her readiness to consume the narrative's ideological content, and her imagined willingness to carry forward the narrative perspective inculcated in her by her mother about incarceration, one that emphasizes the heroism of white men, and both the helplessness and appreciation of thankful, but agentless, Japanese Americans.

But, why the mixed race child as the ideal subject through which to imagine the memory of the incarceration? Despite having been incarcerated herself, Mini is constructed as a tabula rasa—a blank slate—on which the memory of incarceration her mother (i.e., the film) tells can be imprinted. And, her ability to be the model student to learn about the tried-and-true lessons of the incarceration rests on her mixed racial identity. Hence, her *model minoritarian* subject position in the film is closely interconnected with her mixed race identity.[6] Specifically, it is both because of her lack of (full?) (complete?) Japanese American identity—for if she were monoracially Japanese American (like her mother, aunts, and uncles with whom she was incarcerated), the logic goes, she would *already know* her history—and because she is not (fully?) (completely?) white that she is more likely to be empathetic within a racially and economically divided society, and thus can be the blank slate for the new era: the next generation, the future that is the spectator's present. Mini has none of the racist baggage that white people have of the past, nor is she somehow jaded as a Japanese American by the cumulative effects of historical racism against her people; hence, she can learn about what happened to Japanese Americans with a fresh, open, and objective mindset. In short, her mixed raceness, as opposed to her whiteness, Irish Americanness, Japanese Americanness, or Asian Americanness individually, renders her a perfect conceit for this nostalgic pedagogical narrative told through individualized romance.

This chapter both examines the representation of Mini as a mixed race Japanese American, Irish American character and laments the haunting absence of the development of her character within the film. In order to build my argument, I show how Mini's character is a narrative conceit that allows for comparisons between her and other characters and for the development of character relations throughout the film. I also illustrate that little information about her, such as information about her experience of being a mixed race child, is offered in the process. Thus, she serves as a strategic element of comparison, an important narrative nodal point, useful in her ability to help shed light on other characters, on character relations, and on filmic purpose, but of little value or worth as a subject in her own right. Mini exists as a function and is useful to the degree that she helps develop the film's overall commentary on the family, characters, and the solidification of relationships, and as a way to deliver various pedagogical and political arguments about Japanese American incarceration and 1940s labor practices. Ultimately, then, despite the fact that she is a mixed race figure and plays a prominent role in the narrative, the film forgoes the development of Mini and the role of mixed race as an important part of her identity in favor of the visualization of her body for a variety of other narrative purposes.

While Jack McGurn (Dennis Quaid) is the primary character in the film, and Lily (Tamlyn Tomita) is a close secondary one, Mini (Elizabeth Gilliam, Shyree Mezick, and Caroline Junko King), though the actors who play her appear much farther down in the film credits, is also very important, even critical, to the film. After all, because she ages from the beginning to the end of the film, to capture her body's growth, and to imply three different structural and historical parts of the narrative, three different actors play her. It is important to say that the third Mini exists only in the film's present, as the film is told primarily as a series of extended flashbacks, structured by and interspersed with a dialogue between Mini and Lily as they approach, and then wait at, a train station for Jack to return to them from the war, which is matched with scenes interrupted by and layered with (primarily) Lily's voice-over narration atop the flashback scenes. The film begins with a long take, followed by mostly shorter takes, of a conversation between Mini and Lily as they walk toward the camera. The vast majority of the film is an extended flashback sandwiched between this initial scene with Mini and Lily and a penultimate scene with Mini and Lily reuniting with Jack. The film returns intermittently to the present, with Mini and Lily farther along their film-length journey to the train station to meet Jack. Mini and Lily's conversation, which covers events from before 1937 to the end of World War II, the film's present, largely recounts for Mini and spectators what happened in the past and serves to construct an "objective" narration of the historical.[7]

Mini, as she listens to her mother tell the story, serves as a vehicle for delivering important information about the film's "message," as much of the film is pedagogical, arguably didactic, in style, foregrounding information to help spectators understand and have opinions about Japanese

American incarceration and World War II era U.S. labor practices and labor unions. Additionally, in the flashbacks, Mini's character helps develop individual characters as well as relational dyads in terms of racial identity, thus defining race relations in the film.[8] In the sections that follow, with section headings titled in such a way (some might argue, too literally) as to demonstrate how the character of Mini facilitates the narrative construction of other characters and their relationships, first I discuss the way Mini is used to develop Jack's character, in particular. Then, I examine the role her character plays in the development of three relational dyads: Jack and Lily; Lily's mother, Mrs. Kawamura, and Lily; and finally Lily's father, Mr. Kawamura, and Lily. In each instance, Mini functions largely as a prop; she is useful only insofar as she helps facilitate the development of another character, or two characters' relationship, as well as the film's overarching political position. Before concluding, I offer a section that reflects on how attention to Mini's mixed race identity is a structured absence in the film.

## Mini and the Development of Jack's Character

While there are many moments in the film when Mini helps us learn about Jack, one that stands out is when Jack takes Mini to see Santa at a local store. Jack has just returned to the family after being arrested for participating in a labor protest.[9] The scene initially emphasizes Mini's point of view, with the camera inside the store showing her on the other side of the window; Mini is holding Jack's hand and looking through the window slightly left of camera. "Hark the Herald Angels Sing" plays on the sound track, signaling a Christmas time frame. However, Jack's point of view is ultimately centered within the scene. Jack takes Mini inside to sit on Santa's lap, but as soon as Mini turns to look at Santa, he recognizes her as Japanese and says to Jack, "Scoot, pal. I ain't sitting no Japanese kid on my lap. For Christ's sakes." Jack intervenes and insists that they were next in line. When Santa again refuses, Jack removes Mini from the action that is about to happen and in essence decenters her. He lifts her off of Santa's lap and sets her down a few feet away from where Santa is sitting, then grabs Santa's beard threateningly and says, "Now either you're gonna sit her on your lap and let her tell you what she wants for Christmas . . . or I'm gonna stuff this fuckin' beard down your fuckin' throat." Santa calls to another man, who then rushes down the stairs before escorting Jack and Mini out of the store. In the process, the man asks Jack if he is from an orphanage, and Jack says, "No, I'm not from an orphanage. She's an American, and I'm her father." Jack then turns before leaving the store as if speaking directly to Santa from a distance, "She's an American. Merry Christmas."

While initially we might have understood the scene to be about Mini, eventually we come to understand that Mini is simply the reason for the confrontation. She helps us learn more about Jack's politics, his persistent and everyday struggles against oppression, and the public stance he is willing and able to take as a resister and challenger of racial discrimination. The film here is pedagogical, as if educating the ignorant, undereducated, or unaware about the history of racism against Japanese Americans, a racism made unequivocally egregious because it is practiced against a child at Christmastime, yet palatable for the spectator given that Mini, the actual victim of racism, remains seemingly impassive during the action. In the scene, Jack takes a political stance even before the racism becomes apparent. Before Mini approaches Santa, Jack gives Mini information about Christmas and says, "Now what you do is you tell him who you are and then you tell him you've been the goodest girl in America. And then you just sort of slip in about what you want for Christmas. Okay? And then he's gonna tell his elves. And his elves, they work for him. They work overtime for no pay." In this context, Mini serves as a vessel to be filled with information about Jack's interpretation of the mythology of Santa Claus as a labor narrative, a narrative in which grand Santa, the boss, benefits from the slave labor of his elves, who really make the presents (and ostensibly should receive the credit and monetary compensation for having made the gifts). Moreover, when Jack then confronts Santa, he stands up for Mini's right not to be discriminated against because of her race and (assumed) religion: Buddhism. As he does this, she silently watches. Thus, not only does she not speak, but Jack speaks for her, defining her identity as not Buddhist but Christian, as not "a Jap" but a U.S. citizen, and as not an orphan but his daughter. On the way out the door, he denies she is Buddhist, thus implying she is Christian (like him?), hence righting Santa's misinformation, misinformation Santa articulates as part of his justification for denying her a seat on his lap. Jack also nationalizes her, stating she is an American, and hence has rights that go along with being a U.S. citizen and should be treated like other children, equally and fairly.

In the scene, Jack defines and defends Mini's identity. Perhaps she is too young to do so, but she never says one way or another whether or not she identifies as Christian, Buddhist, or some other religion. That her mother and mother's family may or may not identify with Christianity is an important question to ask in relation to the history of Japanese America, but the film does not explore this question. It also does not take the opportunity to represent a mixed race perspective in a complex way, one, for instance, in which Mini identifies with and practices more than one religion. In essence, Mini exists in this scene so that we might learn more about Jack, Jack's beliefs about Christianity, citizenship, and equality, and his strong feelings and willingness to take unpopular and sometimes offensive stances against acts of injustice and oppression. Furthermore, Mini's mixed race identity is both necessary and irrelevant within the scene. It is necessary in the sense that for Santa to read her as Japanese, we witness him observing phenotypical markers that racialize Mini as Japanese. Simultaneously, however, for her father to claim her Americanness (also read: whiteness), she must not be an "alien" or "enemy" Japanese; she must be Jack's biological (explicitly not adopted or orphaned) daughter. Thus, her mixed racial identity allows Jack to argue for her racial exceptionalism in the context of both nation and religion in order to counter Santa's claim of her Buddhist, Japanese identity. Moreover, had he been defending first-generation Buddhist Issei, he would not have been able to make the argument for exceptionalism based on citizenship by birthright and Christianity. Mini's mixed race identity is also immaterial, since the scene does not explore her perspective on the battle between Santa and her father, between racial exclusion and racial inclusion, or between the assumption of interracial adoption and the reality of interracial marriage and procreation.

## Mini and the Development of Jack and Lily's Relationship

At times, Mini appears as a narrative afterthought, such as in a scene in Lily, Jack, and Mini's apartment that helps us understand Lily and Jack's relationship. Although Jack has promised not to become involved further in labor organizing activities, he tells Lily of his intention to protest unfair labor practices at the fish cannery where he works. In this scene, we learn that, unlike Lily, Jack is willing to take a bold stand against oppression. However, in order to follow his personal convictions, he also willfully goes against Lily's wishes. In the argument, after Lily tells him, "We're happy, Jack!" he responds,

Happy? What in the hell does happy have to do with any of this? You're happy. Maybe I'm not so happy. Lily, it's not you. I swear to God, it's not you. It's just that maybe things bother me that you don't know about. Maybe things bother me so much that I can't speak sometimes, I get so choked up with rage and I. . . . I agreed to hand out a bundle of leaflets on a street corner and you act as if I'm going out to kill someone.

We learn from this that Jack sees himself as willing to stand up against oppression in a way in which Lily cannot, that his sense of being American that requires standing up boldly against oppression differs from hers, and thus that he is in a better position to challenge the incarceration of Japanese Americans.

Not only is Jack able to recite the letter of labor laws, and hence access the language of the institutional power, but he gets to argue on behalf of Japanese Americans over and over to those responsible for their oppression, including chasing white boy vandals away from the home of the Kawamuras (who have already been taken to camp) and stopping them from smashing wooden boxes containing the Kawamuras' chickens. He tells Santa and an authoritative store attendant Mini is not Buddhist but a Christian American and his daughter. He tells a government agent he opposes the incarceration and is pro-Japanese; he "married one."[10] His ability and willingness to fight against injustice are further distinct from Lily's inability to do so because he goes outside the domestic space of their home to protest and later crisscrosses the barbed wire fence of the camp repeatedly, while Japanese Americans, including Lily, remain constrained within it. He is the "public man" exerting masculine agency, able to cross even barbed wire, while feminized Japanese Americans, like Lily, must remain behind in their homes, prison, or both.

Mini is merely an onlooker in the scene that highlights the contrast between Jack as a liberal Irish American Christian and Lily as a Japanese American soon to be incarcerated. Jack and Lily are in the kitchen, while Mini is in a bedroom just off of the kitchen. We see her watch Lily and Jack argue from her bed. In the next scene, after Jack does not come home to eat the dinner Lily has carefully prepared for him (Lily does not know that he has been kicked in the arm by a police horse while protesting and has been taken to jail in a police van), we see Mini in bed open her eyes briefly before her mother blows out the candlelight dinner candle. While Mini might imagine her father is missing, and while her realization of his absence may worry her and be the reason for her waking briefly in this scene, the film shows no meaningful concern, distinct from Lily's, by Mini about Jack's whereabouts. Moreover, the film's comparison of Irish American radicalism and Japanese American docility relies on a false assumption that Japanese Americans are treated unfairly as an ethnic, not a racial, group.[11] How Mini understands both her Irish American and Japanese American ethnic/racial self, and how she makes sense of Jack's false conflation of his experiences and Lily's are not explored. Here, as in the Santa scene, Mini is an onlooker onto events that structure her very existence—indeed, are core to it—but about which she neither comments nor is endowed with the ability to explain how they affect who she is. Thus, the film uses the existence of a mixed race identity to explore monoracial experiences and relations.

Since romance is so central to the film, it is also central to Mini. It is her parents, after all, who are engaged in the cross-racial romance, temporarily waylaid in this pivotal scene, which Mini witnesses. Since the story is told after the fact, Mini's own existence, therefore, depends on at least the initial romantic relationship having happened. What child would not want this relationship to work out? What child would not want her parents to be in love? Thus, while the film does not depict her as thinking about it, Mini, more than any other character, is positioned as a figure who would want her parents to get along, and, by extension, for white people and Japanese American people to make nice. Thus, simply by witnessing Jack and Lily's relationship, as a mixed race child Mini represents the desire for racial harmony. Any specific perspective her character might have on the situation is beside the point. It is her optimal position as a child caught between, and as part of both, warring races that creates the exigence for a loving resolution.

## Mini and the Development of Japanese American Family Relationships

Mini also provides the context for Japanese American characters to establish stronger relationships with one another. In two primary scenes, Mini's appearance creates the salve to heal the wounds of family division. The first occurs after Lily and Mini leave Jack. The music, sung in Japanese, begins as Lily and Mini walk through Little Tokyo to get to Lily's parents' home. Once, there, Lily witnesses FBI agents carrying her parents' belongings out of the house. Her brother informs her that their father has been arrested. She climbs the stairs alone and finds her mother sitting down, facing a wall. Lily bends down and begins talking to her. She says she forgives her mother

*A somber portrait of Mini and her mother, in* Come See the Paradise.

for not answering all her letters and says she understands her father would not let her respond. Her mother, whose body is turned toward a small altar where she has been praying, remains stoic, even as Lily's pleas for recognition become more and more insistent.[12] When Mini enters the room, however, Mrs. Kawamura's icy stoicism begins to melt away. Mini, waiting by the door, says simply, "Mama?" The camera cuts from a tight shot of Lily to that of Mini, both from the grandmother's point of view. The grandmother says "Mini-Chan" and gestures for Mini to come to her. It is not because of anything Mini does, says, or thinks, in particular, but because of Mini's presence alone, her very existence, that generational wounds heal. And although Mini is mixed race, in this scene she is welcomed as a granddaughter in a Japanese American family, a full member of the family who is important enough to bring her mother and grandmother back together. While the scenes with Santa and in the apartment kitchen acknowledge Mini's mixed race identity but leave a mixed race perspective undeveloped, here Mini's mixed race identity is irrelevant, indeed disavowed.

The same is the case in the third important scene in which Mini arbitrates familial relationships. The entire family (except Mr. Kawamura and Jack) is now in the concentration camp, and Charlie and Harry, as the two eldest sons, argue and denigrate their mother in the process, suggesting the lack of parental authority has created a child empire society,[13] until in walks their father, finally released from custody and allowed to rejoin his family in their camp/prison. While the rest of the family goes to his side, Lily, carrying Mini, waits behind. Having married Jack against her father's will and having jilted the suitor chosen for her by her father, Lily stays back with her daughter, the product of the forbidden relationship. However, when her father sees them (both?), he smiles, and Lily goes to his side with Mini. When he sees Mini, he too utters, "Mini-chan." When they come to his side, he immediately looks to Mini and hugs her. This scene thus parallel's the healing scene between Lily and her mother; Mini's presence has now brought the entire Japanese American family back together.

Once this bond is established between Mini and her grandfather and once that bond serves to heal Japanese American familial wounds, it goes on to resolve interracial familial tensions. Later in the film, when Mr. Kawamura's health has begun to deteriorate, Mini, with the camera depicting her point of view alone, goes to his bedside to comfort him. Then, after he has built himself a chair, and the narrator informs us of his demise, she sits in his lap reading. Finally, when he is lying on his bed, ill, it is she, Middle Mini now, who recognizes he is feeling poorly. Mini's knowledge then signals to Jack that even though he has arrived for a visit after being away from Lily for a very long time, Lily has to leave while Jack gains Mr. Kawamura's affection. Thus, in addition to serving as a positive mediator between Lily and both her mother and her father, Mini's presence and point of view structure the healing relations between the races. With Mini as a justification, the adults set aside their (represented now as) silly differences to recognize what is common across racial boundaries—familial love.

### (The Absence of) Mini as Mixed Race

Given the film's construction of Mini's mixed race identity as simultaneously necessary to the narrative progression and yet irrelevant as a concern of the film, I turn now to a discussion of the implications of this type of representation of mixed race. Representations of mixed race Asian

Americans have, like the histories of other racial stereotypes, been told as a history of desire and loathing, in some instances reflecting an "American love/hate relationship with Asia."[14] On the one hand, mixed race Asian Americans have been depicted negatively as products of tragedy, prone to congenital inferiority and later psychological maladaption.[15] On the other hand, they have been depicted "positively" in equally problematic ways as emblems of melting pot and multicultural America and figures who can lead America into a racially progressive future.[16] The promise of mixed race Asian Americans as magically, by their very existence, solving racial divisions is a commonplace and deeply problematic representation in popular culture. In *Come See the Paradise*, Mini is not the tragic figure of the early twentieth-century United States; she represents the more contemporary model minoritarian representation of mixed race Asian Americans—the hope and promise of the future, a future where Japanese

*A romantic embrace between Lily Kawamura and Jack McGurn, in* Come See the Paradise.

Americans and whites get along and in which Japanese American family estrangement resulting from the incarceration era is healed. Family members almost instantaneously overlook hurt, anger, resentment, distrust, and political and ideological difference simply at the sight of Mini.

It is ironic that Mini plays such a significant role in helping to heal the wounds caused by destruction of the Japanese American family during wartime and creating stronger relationships within the Japanese American family, because Mini is not "only" Japanese American. Hence, the Japanese American family is reunited upon envisioning the mixed racial family member, someone who is both Irish American and Japanese American and who also is syncretically a member of an additional racial/ethnic class altogether, that of mixed race people. Unlike the Japanese American community members who became anxious about the appearance of a significant number of mixed race Nisei Week beauty pageant participants,[17] for example, the film pays no apparent attention to the mixed race composition of the future of Japanese America. The film contends instead that the Japanese American family will survive and continue, in part because Mini helps bring people together. The mixed race figure, then, serves as a narrative tool to assure the audience that the Japanese American family of the film's future (and spectator's present) continues to exist, is happy and harmonious, and harbors no continuing ill will toward white North America. In fact (through the figure of mixed race Mini), it absorbs whiteness with no apparent discomfort.

In addition to being the salve that heals the family wounds and brings family members together, Mini stands in for the third Japanese American generation, the Sansei, and is the convenient receptacle for what the Nisei—here, specifically, Lily—have to teach her about the incarceration. In Mini's first appearance in the film, she is singing a Japanese song in Japanese. Moreover, in her conversation with her mother on her trip to the train station, she goes back and forth between speaking English and Japanese fluidly. Thus, Mini is ideally suited to the task of archivist of Japanese American historical events and presumably is prepared to receive and protect the Japanese American memories her mother will give her.[18]

In the film, Mini's own, local memories, or what Maurice Halbwachs would call autobiographical memories,[19] those that she experiences firsthand, are subordinated to a much larger set of memories conveyed through Lily's flashback. Mini's first memory takes place after Pearl Harbor, when Lily and other parents arrive at her school and interrupt her class's rendition of "Twinkle Twinkle, Little Star." Indeed, when we see

Mini for the first time within the flashback, fifty-one minutes into the film, it is after the third Mini of the present asks, wishing to hear about her birth, "What about me?" We see the first Mini, already able to walk, wearing a long coat and donning a bowl haircut.[20] In this instance, what Halbwachs calls collective memory, her mother's story, takes precedence over Mini's own autobiographical memories. That the film text is invested in a collective memory that is largely dissociated from Mini's own experiences and autobiographical memory; that Mini asks about her birth, yet the image matched to her mother's story of Mini's birth is of her as a (mature) toddler; and that the third Mini appears to have little knowledge of events Lily describes with the first and second Mini in them suggests Mini's knowledge derived from experience is inconsequential.

Mini is a convenient figure, for while she stands in for the Sansei generation, she also expands and broadens the spectatorial address of the film, standing in for any audience member, including white and white-identified spectators, who must hear Lily's story from beginning to end in order to understand the incarceration. In this way, Mini functions as what Angharad Valdivia suggests is an efficient, ambiguous strategy for the representation of racial hybridity, a way to appeal to multiple audiences through just one figure whose unclear racialization allows her to signify across multiple racial groups, thus minimizing the need to have several separate representatives from all represented racial groups.[21] In *Come See the Paradise*, Mini is at once a morphing, a representation of the physiological combination of Lily and Jack—not unlike the image of the future "Eve," a computer-generated composite image produced from images of multiple women, on the cover of the fall 1993 special issue on "Rebirthing America" of *Time* magazine[22]—and she is also what Valdivia calls "ambiguous," politically representing multiple groups, hence "undifferentiated" (312–13). I would add that in her own identity she is inconsequential; as a hybrid figure she is emptied of identity in order to serve the purpose of all but herself.

In this way, Mini also mediates the future. In her study of Amerasian progeny in Vietnam War films, Velina Hasu Houston suggests the mixed race figure is a symbol or emblem that helps recuperate "victory by reclaiming the children as imperial product, as figures of innocence who can be liberated only by deliverance into Western beneficence."[23] Thus, the mixed race figure is used as an aid in Vietnam War revisionism, allowing a narrative of the "good" West to be recaptured. Like Mini in *Come See the Paradise*, in *Indochine*, for example, the mixed race figure "is not a person, but a tool for recuperation of the West" (73). Mini is a vehicle that helps make possible the lengthy narration of a story in which Jack emerges as a white hero. This then renders *Come See the Paradise* a revisionist history of how whiteness as a historical power bloc derogated and imprisoned Japanese Americans during World War II.[24] Mini is also a vessel of Japanese American ideology. In *Come See the Paradise*, miscegenation wins out, and Mini becomes the receptacle for a newly formed Japanese American perspective that sees history as friend and Japanese Americans as recipients of the positive legacy that history, as presented on film, portends. Thus, the film is invested in foregrounding both white heroism and the Japanese American experience of incarceration, one that acknowledges the injustice but is then able to move on from it.

## Conclusion

Even as Mini's role in the film renders her an important figure to discuss, as I have suggested throughout this chapter, the film neither takes seriously nor complicates the representation or discourse about mixed race. As a Hollywood film, *Come See the Paradise* becomes an active agent in the telling of history, one with a particular message about incarceration and the role mixed race Japanese Americans can play in the future. Not unlike its more recent Hollywood counterpart, *Snow Falling on Cedars* (1999), *Come See the Paradise* tells the story of the Japanese American incarceration as a history of benevolent white antiracism and does so through the generic framework of the heterosexual romantic narrative. In this context, Mini is a narrative tool, a tool about which very little information is needed and one whose own perspective on events—and own (mixed race) identity—is beside the point.

*Come See the Paradise* constructs the memory of the incarceration through mixed race, childish (passive) Japanese American eyes. Mini, both literally (her body) and figuratively (as a stand-in for the generic spectator) marks the possibility of a "progressive" racial future. Thus, just at the moment of redress in the early 1990s, this film emerges and acknowledges the history of Japanese American incarceration through Mini's existence and role as onlooker onto that history, without having to address the very struggle for redress and the suffering that ultimately led to a federal apology for the wartime imprisonment. Both nation and Hollywood—and by extension the mixed race future—have accepted as fact what happened in the past; both assume redress has been made or seek to make redress. Mini's availability as recipient of this narrative is the vehicle for its "progressive" message, for its critique of past racism, and for its avoidance of continuing white structural and institutionalized racism. It is not particularly surprising that Hollywood turns to individualized romance to tell this story. The irony is that Lily's personal odyssey, and her expression of personal strength in challenging her parents so she can marry Jack, is central to the story of Japanese American racial oppression. And—specifically because her mixed race identity is present but undeveloped (i.e., absent)—Mini stands in for the generic spectator of the future who can comfortably take all this in from a position of liberal postracism, a position that angles away from questions about contemporary racial oppression, questions that ultimately might lead to answers that challenge the political and racial logic of the film.

NOTES

1. The relevant films *Little Tokyo, U.S.A.* (1942), *Go for Broke* (1951), and *Japanese War Bride* (1952) appeared before *Bad Day at Black Rock* (1955). *G. Men vs. the Black Dragon* (1943) also appeared before *Bad Day at Black Rock* but is less relevant because it depicts the post–Pearl Harbor hysteria and figures Japanese as yellow peril but does not address the incarceration of Japanese Americans. Other films, such as *Sayonara* (1957) and *Bridge to the Sun* (1961), take place during the time period, but incarceration does not figure prominently. John Streamas points out that Komoko died before the camps began and writes, "One of the story's ironies is of course that Komoko never lived long enough to be incarcerated. In fact, the film's only direct reference to the camps is Smith's lie to Macreedy in claiming that Komoko went to a 'relocation center.'" John Streamas, "'Patriotic Drunk': To Be Yellow, Brave, and Disappeared in *Bad Day at Black Rock*," *American Studies* 44, 1–2 (Spring/Summer 2003): 99–119.

2. It is beyond the scope of this project, and would do a disservice to those who have conducted research, to attempt to enumerate (even summarily) the scholarship that has been conducted on the subject of World War II Japanese American incarceration. I hesitate to mention any works at all because I do not wish to draw attention away from key scholarship, but because I also do want readers to be able to read further on the subject, I will mention two as starting points: Michi Weglyn's *Years of Infamy: The Untold Story of America's Concentration Camps* (Seattle: University of Washington Press, 1996); and Roger Daniels's *Concentration Camps USA: Japanese Americans and World War II* (Hinsdale, IL: Dryden Press, 1971).

3. Rea Tajiri notes this absence in her film *History and Memory* (1990) 32 min.

4. While true in the 1950s and 1960s (the obvious example being *To Kill A Mockingbird*, from 1962), more contemporary examples include another of Parker's films, *Mississippi Burning*; Steven Spielberg's *Schindler's List*; *A Time to Kill*; and *Dangerous Minds*.

5. Mixed race Japanese Americans are implicitly referenced whenever there is mention of the famous statistic that even those who were one-sixteenth Japanese American were incarcerated. Still, even in literature on the incarceration, there is no study to my knowledge specifically focusing on incarcerated mixed race Japanese Americans. Incarceration is mentioned in, although it is not a primary focal point of, the video *Doubles*. For a critical analysis of mixed race Asian Americans and *Doubles*, see my article on the subject: Kent A. Ono, "Communicating Prejudice in the Media: Upending Racial Categories in *Doubles*," in *Communicating Prejudice*, ed. Michael L. Hecht (Thousand Oaks, CA: Sage, 1998), 206-20.

6. By coining the concept "model minoritarian," I wish to signal the degree to which racial exceptionalism can be constructed differently across different social contexts and thus to suggest that there are many ways model minority representations are configured, such as in this case of a mixed race Asian American construction of the model minority stereotype.

7. Many of the flashback scenes contain information neither Lily nor Mini personally experienced, although admittedly this information could have been relayed to them off screen by others, such as Jack.

8. While Mini helps the film develop Lily's and her father's characters, in order to offer a more thorough analysis and because of space constraints, I limit my discussion to the way Mini helps develop Jack's character.

9. This scene follows a scene in which, upon Jack's return from jail, Jack and Lily have sex in a back room where Lily works. Throughout the film, there are other scenes in which Jack and Lily having sex is followed by shots and scenes of Mini. The rather literal figuring of her as their mixed race offspring lacks subtlety.

10. Here, Jack misidentifies Lily as Japanese, not Japanese American, and hence facilitates the agent's misrecognition of the difference between friends and enemies, citizens and aliens.

11. See Michael Omi and Howard Winant, *Racial Formation in the United States: From the 1960s to the 1980s* (1986; New York: Routledge, 1989), which draws a distinction between ethnicity and race paradigms. Within the ethnicity paradigm, they argue, all nonwhite racial groups are simply parallel instances of ethnic white immigrants, in this case, Irish Americans. The argument becomes: immigration causes discrimination, prejudice, and subjugation, not culture and biological phenotype.

12. This setting seems to confirm that Lily's mother is Buddhist. How she or Lily might respond to Jack's coding Mini as Christian also goes unexplored in the film.

13. Prior to being incarcerated, the father is positioned as the unassailable patriarch, forbidding Lily and Jack's relationship, firing Jack, gambling despite Lily's protestations, and insisting on an arranged marriage for Lily with Mr. Fujioka.

14. Cynthia L. Nakashima, "Servants of Culture: The Symbolic Role of Mixed-Race Asians in American Discourse," in *The Sum of Our Parts: Mixed-Heritage Asian Americans*, ed. Teresa Williams-Leon and Cynthia L. Nakashima (Philadelphia: Temple University Press, 2001), 41.

15. See, for instance, Helena Grice, "Face-Ing/De-Face-Ing Racism: Physiognomy as Ethnic Marker in Early Eurasian/Amerasian Women's Texts," in *Re/Collecting Early Asian America: Essays in Cultural History*, ed. Josephine Lee, Imogene L. Lim, and Yuko Matsukawa (Philadelphia: Temple University Press, 2002), 255-70. See also Cynthia L. Nakashima, "An Invisible Monster: The Creation and Denial of Mixed-Race People in America," in *Racially Mixed People in America*, ed. Maria P. P. Root (Newbury Park, CA: Sage, 1992), 162-80. See also Cynthia L. Nakashima, "Asian American Studies through (Somewhat) Asian Eyes: Integrating 'Mixed Race' into the Asian American Discourse," in *Asian American Studies after Critical Mass*, ed. Kent A. Ono (Malden, MA: Blackwell, 2005), 111-20.

16. See, for instance, Nakashima, "Servants of Culture." See also John Chock Rosa, "'The Coming of the Neo-Hawaiian American Race': Nationalism and Metaphors of the Melting Pot in Popular Accounts of Mixed-Race Individuals," in Williams-Leon and Nakashima, *The Sum of Our Parts*, 49-56. See also Ono, "Communicating Prejudice in the Media." See also Henry Yu, "How Tiger Lost His Stripes: Post-nationalist American Studies as a History of Race, Migration, and the Commodification of Culture," in *Popular Culture: A Reader*, ed. Raiford Guins and Omayra Zaragoza Cruz (Thousand Oaks, CA: Sage, 2000), 168-209. See also Hiram Perez, "How to Rehabilitate a Mulatto: The Iconography of Tiger Woods," *East Main Street: Asian American Popular Culture*, ed. LeiLani Nishime, Shilpa Dave, and Tasha Oren (New York: NYU Press, 2005), 222-45.

17. Rebecca Chiyoko King-O'Riain, *Pure Beauty: Judging Race in Japanese American Beauty Pageants* (Minneapolis: University of Minnesota Press, 2006), 69–70. "Issei" refers to first-generation Japanese Americans, migrants from Japan who permanently settled in the United States. "Nisei" refers to the Issei's children, the second generation. "Sansei" refers to third-generation Japanese Americans.

18. Mini may even be constructed as a more suitable locus for Japanese American memories than her mother, Lily. Lily says early in the film that she speaks Japanese only at the dinner table (even though we see her speak it outside of that context throughout the film).

19. Maurice Halbwachs, "Individual Memory and Collective Memory," in *The Collective Memory*, trans. Francis J. Ditter Jr. and Vida Yazdi Ditter (1950; New York: Harper and Row, 1980), 22–49.

20. Intertitles tell us the film starts in 1936, and Lily tells Mini she was born Christmas Day, 1937.

21. Angharad Valdivia, "Geographies of Latinidad: Constructing Identity in the Face of Radical Hybridity," in *Race, Identity, and Representation in Education,* ed. W. Critchlow, G. Dimitriadis, N. Dolby, and C. McCarthy (New York: Routledge, 2005), 307-17. Valdivia examines representations of racial hybridity in contemporary popular culture and describes four strategies—morphing, visual shattering, palette, and ambiguity—for representing hybridity.

22. As James R. Gaines, the managing editor, writes about the image, "When the editors were looking for a way to dramatize the impact of interethnic marriage, which has increased dramatically in the U.S. during the latest wave of immigration, they turned to morphing to create the kind of offspring that might result from seven men and seven women of various ethnic and racial backgrounds." James R. Gaines, "From the Managing Editor," *Time*, December 2, 1993.

23. Velina Hasu Houston, "To the Colonizer Goes the Spoils: American Progeny in Vietnam War Films and Owning Up to the Gaze," *Amerasia Journal* 23, no. 1(1997): 70.

24. After all, at the end of the film, in a shot of her walking off down the tracks away from the Florin train station, she is holding the hands of her Japanese American mother and white father. That she is in the middle and is the product of their heterosexual romantic affections and biological sex serves to erase, or in large measure reduce, animosity between Japanese Americans and whites.

# Part III

# Genre, Mixed Race, and Evolving Racial Identities

# 7

||||||||||||||||||||||||||||||||||||||||||||||||||||||

# Race Mixing and the Fantastic

## Lineages of Identity and Genre in Contemporary Hollywood

## Adam Knee

Genres of the fantastic (and, in recent years, horror in particular) have functioned as a particularly significant popular means of working out cultural
tensions, anxieties, and potentialities regarding racial and ethnic mixing,
given the singular latitude their narratives offer for dramatizing interactions
and amalgamations among all manner of beings. This chapter proposes to
offer a comparative analysis of the way issues of racial, ethnic, and cultural
mixing have been articulated within three recent highly popular Hollywood
films in the realm of the fantastic—two horror films (*Jeepers Creepers*, 2001;
*Underworld*, 2003) and a romantic comedy containing fantastic elements
(*Bewitched*, 2005)—with an aim to adumbrate certain salient popular culture discourses about racial mixing and to detail the operations of genre
with respect to these discourses. More specifically, I will argue that *Jeepers Creepers*, *Underworld*, and *Bewitched* can be seen as a popular generic
response, over a five-year period, to the emergence of a new awareness of
American racial identity as inherently complex and hybrid, as not reducible
to the long-standing, discrete, and ideologically loaded categories (such as
white, black, Asian, Latino) that still make up the lexicon of American racial
discourse. This new social perception, which perhaps reached a temporary
peak in the late 1990s at the time of a number of popular newsmagazine
articles on the changing racial makeup of the United States (and the addition of new options for self-identification as multiracial on the 2000 U.S.
census) can be seen in some sense as playing itself out through the generic
forms of these films (and in the process altering said forms).[1]

Pertinent to this analysis are some of George Lipsitz's observations about interrelationships among popular genre film, race, and ideology. While Lipsitz sees such popular entertainments, in their inherently formulaic nature, as tending toward a social conservatism,[2] he offers that they can in certain contexts provide a forum for addressing or working through social or cultural shifts. He argues that such potentially progressive or subversive strains are mostly likely to surface at moments of social crisis, and register at the level of popular representation in the form of tension and/or innovation within generic form—what he terms "genre anxiety." Lipsitz examines the specific instance of such anxiety operating in a number of 1970s genre films in the wake of a range of historical tensions regarding the status of blacks in American society.

I will argue that a parallel kind of phenomenon can be observed in the films to be analyzed here—that potentially anxiety-inducing perceptions of fundamental shifts in the nature of the American racial landscape at the start of the new millennium (such as a change in the country's racial demographics, the end of a white majority in some regions, and the increasing prevalence of racial intermixing of all kinds) have their corollary in new tendencies within genres of the fantastic, in particular the presence of texts wherein the uneasy coexistence and potentially violent interaction of differing blood lineages take on a new narrative and aesthetic prominence. But where the "genre anxiety" Lipsitz identifies arises largely through "adding unconventional racial elements to conventional genre films," the "genre anxiety" in the films to be discussed here is also and just as significantly evinced through mixing a range of generic elements traditionally considered alien to one another.[3] More concretely, it will be argued here that the sense of social tension and change registered in *Jeepers Creepers*, *Underworld*, and *Bewitched* is manifested not only through a thematics of the interaction of once discrete blood lineages, but also, and in tandem, at the level of generic discourse, through a novel and sometimes uneasy negotiation of disparate generic lineages. Or, to put it more succinctly, these analyses will work to highlight an anxiety not only *in* genre but *of* genre.

I would also contend that it is not mere coincidence that prominent among the examples Lipsitz chooses to document his case about popular genres are horror films. More than a few writers have noted the centrality of issues of difference (or otherness) to fantastic genres (horror and science fiction in particular), and some among these have analyzed the particular affinity of these forms to issues of racial difference. As Ed Guerrero explains it:

The social construction and representation of race, *otherness*, and non-whiteness is an on-going process, working itself out in many symbolic, cinematic forms of expression, but particularly in the abundant racialized metaphors and allegories of the fantasy, sci-fi, and horror genres. This practice can be explained by several mutually reinforcing factors including these genres' dependence on *difference* or *otherness* in the form of the monster in order to drive or energize their narratives; the now vast technological possibilities of imagining and rendering of all kinds of simulacra for aliens, monsters, mutant outcasts, and the like, and the infinite, fantastic narrative horizons and story worlds possible in these productions. Taken together, these themes and techniques give free associative range and symbolic play to the pent-up energies of society's repressed racial discourse. Because the representational and narrative conventions of sci-fi, fantasy, and horror films almost always defy or transcend dominant cinema's illusionist, linear style of depicting a naturalized "realism," the genre is open to subversive politics.[4]

Of particular relevance for the analysis to be offered in the present chapter is Guerrero's emphasis here on the freedom and fluidity of fantastic forms. On the one hand, these generically specific qualities help account for the presence of ideologically oppositional currents (of the kind Lipsitz also identifies) within these putatively mainstream films, a point Guerrero indeed goes on to make explicitly (as he notes that many of the films in these genres "offer quite sharp countercultural critiques"). On the other hand, the broad-ranging fluidity of these films (in many respects) not only allows them to "hold great possibility for imagining *difference*" (as Guerrero explains), but likewise for imagining *mixing* or *hybridity*, for imagining new kinds of racial or ethnic (or, for that matter, species) merging that dominant paradigms do not as yet encompass.

The horror film in particular, it can be argued, is well suited to the representation of novel kinds of merging, the transgression of boundaries formerly assumed sacrosanct or impermeable. A number of cultural theorists have argued in differing ways the centrality of such transgression to the horror genre—for example, in a fairly literal sense in narratives of home, national, or planetary intrusion (often resulting in bodily intrusion as well); or, as Noel Carroll has asserted, in the very nature of the monster itself. For Carroll, the horror genre is predicated upon the presence of a monster that invokes fear and disgust, the latter emotion precipitated by the "impure" nature of the monster. Drawing upon the work of anthropologist Mary Douglas, Carroll contends this sense of impurity arises from "interstitiality and categorical contradictoriness," and further elaborates that "impurity involves a conflict between two or more standing cultural categories."[5]

Carroll goes on to specify mechanisms by which horror's monstrous and impure entities are constructed, chief among them what he calls fusion and fission. "In fusion," he explains, "categorically contradictory elements are fused or condensed or superimposed in one unified spatiotemporal being whose identity is homogeneous." A classic example of this would be the pieced-together nature of Dr. Frankenstein's monstrous creation. In Carroll's fission, on the other hand, "the contradictory elements are, so to speak, distributed over *different*, though metaphysically related, entities"—for example, the distinct human and wolf forms of the werewolf.[6]

While, in developing this kind of broad theoretical account of the nature of horror, Carroll's particular aim is not to illustrate the specific political or ideological resonances of such mechanisms, his discussion does allude to the genre's propensity to articulate affronts to culture's dominant conceptual schemes on a range of levels:

> In the most fundamental sense of fusion and fission, these structures are meant to apply to the organization of opposed cultural categories, generally of a deep biological or ontological sort: human/reptile, living/ dead, etc. But it is also true that in much horror, especially that which is considered to be classic, the opposition of such cultural categories in the biology of the horrific creatures portend [sic] further oppositions, oppositions that might be thought of in terms of thematic conflicts or antimonies which, in turn, are generally deep-seated in the culture in which the fiction has been produced.[7]

As Carroll a bit later more directly articulates the implications of this, "It is frequently the case that the oppositional biologies of fantastic beings correlate to an oppositional thematics."[8]

Such accounts of the oppositional potentials of fantastic genres, particularly with respect to dominant conceptualizations of social categories, will be germane to the analyses offered here. This chapter will not be making the claim that such genres of necessity articulate ideologically subversive or progressive views (nor, in fact, do the accounts cited earlier), which would indeed fly in the face of much sound criticism of ideologically regressive dimensions of horror, for example. But this analysis will highlight the way that fantastic genres *can* allow for the articulation of oppositional perspectives (whether presented in positive or negative terms), in particular as regards threats to and/or disruptions or amalgamations of dominant social categories—including those of race, class, nation, and sexuality. That the three key examples to be discussed, from over a five-year period, exhibit overlapping preoccupations related to such disruptions suggests they are symptomatic of a distinctive social concern regarding changing perceptions of race in particular. In all three productions, tensions over changing social conceptions of categories of identity resonate with category crises on a range of other levels, including that of generic form and generic categorization itself.

To address the first (and historically earliest) example for this chapter, *Jeepers Creepers* foregrounds these issues of generic uncertainty by having them as the driving motivation for much of the plot: a brother and sister (Darry and Trish) returning home from college are terrorized by an antagonist the nature of which they cannot divine, as increasingly inexplicable and horrific events unfold. As the siblings receive new clues about the entity that terrorizes them, audience members, too, gain more generic clues upon which to base an interpretation of events—but the film continues to mix subgeneric categories in an uneasy way. Trish and Darry's pursuit, along rural roads, by a mysterious figure driving an aging, rusting truck, brings to mind a range of films focusing on rural psychopaths and/or feral families, most famously *The Texas Chainsaw Massacre*; the brother's only partially tongue-in-cheek assertion that this figure must be the result of inbreeding and our discovery that he inhabits an old, isolated dwelling serve to further support this initial reading of the film as fitting into this nonsupernatural horror subgenre. But then some of the subsequent clues appear to engage the conventions of the stalker or slasher subgenre: We hear of a teenage couple that has disappeared on a prom night (recalling the *Prom Night* slasher film series), and soon Darry discovers their embalmed (and stitched-together) corpses in the basement of the aforementioned isolated dwelling, along with those of many others. It then becomes clearer that the siblings are being pursued by a powerful, elusive, and murderous antagonist of large build and almost supernatural prowess (referred to in the credits as the Creeper)—which brings to mind the recurrent antagonists and plots of the *Halloween* and *Friday the 13th* series. The fact that Trish eventually emerges as the stronger of the two siblings, indeed protecting her brother when she can and proving to be one of the only characters able to survive an encounter with the Creeper, links her to the slasher film's figure of the "final girl." The film's self-consciousness in its subgeneric indeterminacy and play is alluded to in a number of humorously reflexive lines of dialogue, as when the sister tells her brother, as he daringly prepares to seek possible victims of the Creeper at the end of a drainpipe, "You know the part in scary movies where somebody does something really stupid and everyone hates them for it? This is it." Later still, when she has run the Creeper over with her car and her brother asks whether she thinks he's dead, her response is a generically savvy, "They never are."

As the Creeper's supernatural powers and ability to avoid death become ever more evident, we are invited to make comparison to such more supernatural models as *The Nightmare on Elm Street*'s Freddy, to whom the Creeper, in some scenes, does bear a passing resemblance; but evidence of still greater supernatural powers and idiosyncratic physical traits (such as a large pair of wings) and behaviors frustrates efforts to fit him to any antagonist template. Indeed, the siblings seem a proxy for the audience's own interpretive frustration and revulsion at the being's proclivities when, while watching the Creeper sniff a policeman's freshly detached head and then proceed to eat the tongue out of his mouth, the brother asks, "What is that?" and the sister adds, "I'm not seeing this. . . . What is

*Darry and Trish are aided by Jezelle in their efforts to escape the Creeper in* Jeepers Creepers.

*Darry is confronted by the grotesque Creeper in* Jeepers Creepers.

he doing?" Even Jezelle, a local psychic with some insight into the nature of the Creeper who tries to aid the siblings, is at a loss for a precise explanation of its identity, telling Darry, "I don't know if it's a demon or a devil or just some hungry thing from some dark place and time."

Darry's query of "What is that?" can arguably serve as a watchword for the film: a crisis of categorization resonates on a number of levels here. There is a lack of clarity about the generic allegiance of events, in conjunction with a lack of clarity regarding the basic constitution and even the ontological status of the antagonist. Indeed, the narrative of *Jeepers Creepers* in effect hinges upon tandem enigmas of generic identity and genetic identity, a concern with ascertaining the "nature of the beast" in both textual and biological terms. The Creeper frustrates efforts at such identification owing to its strangeness and the seeming multiplicity and incongruity of its traits; and as the plot develops, it becomes evident not only that the grotesque multiplicity and strange indeterminacy of the Creeper exist on several levels, but that they arise in relation to an actual amassing of traits from various biological lineages (as shall be explained further later) and therefore invites a reading as a monstrous metaphor for racial mixing.

Apropos to the construction of such a metaphor is the film's tendency to "make strange," to defamiliarize processes of human sexual reproduction and genetic inheritance. It is pertinent, for example, that the creature's strangeness and indeterminacy, indeed its "queerness" in several respects, even extends to its gender and sexuality. The Creeper is (from its size and build and attire) masculine in appearance, but it (or, perhaps, he) also repeatedly seems to evince desire for other males. For example, when it is in pursuit of Trish and Darry, it is spotted by patrons of a diner in the act of sniffing Darry's dirty laundry, and, as a waitress notes with visceral disgust, "it looked like he was liking it too." This hint of a queer desire subtly resonates with the earlier images of the first Creeper victim Darry encounters (at the end of that drainpipe)—a sweet-faced, mute young man who gestures to Darry to pull the sheet off his bound, bare, and largely hairless torso before trying to whisper into his ear—and is then seemingly reaffirmed in the previously mentioned tongue-eating scene: Trish's response of confusion, disgust, and disbelief during that latter scene evidently arises *both* from the Creeper's appearance of wanting to make out with the detached head of a policeman previously designated as a sex object (Trish had joked about his "strip-a-gram cop" appearance) and from its activity of ingesting the policeman's tongue. When we eventually learn more about the true nature of the Creeper, it turns out that its sexuality is more genuinely "queer" than might have been generically anticipated: it is suggested that the Creeper is an entity who propagates its existence by consuming the body parts of others that it feels it needs. Moreover, while its reproductive sexuality is consummated by literal consumption, it is aroused, it seems, by smell: Jezelle tells the siblings that the reason it scares people is so it can smell them better. The fact that (again, according to what Jezelle perceives with her psychic abilities) the Creeper's self-regenerative activities of feeding take place not on an ongoing basis but cyclically—once every twenty-three years—again points to them as characteristic not of typical monster or stalker mayhem but of a clearly defined (and "queer," not entirely human) reproductive cycle.

Nor is this sense of "queerness" and fluidity in terms of sexuality limited solely to the Creeper. Darry's positioning as an object of male desire, for example, is anticipated by his "misreading" of a license plate in a road game he plays with his sister at the film's opening as saying "gay fever." (This goes hand in hand with the film's running joke about his having pink [read feminized] underwear as a result of a college prank; Trish's comment to Darry about the pranksters is that "maybe they know something about you that you don't.") His sister, in opposition, assumes the masculinized position of the strong, heroic "final girl"; she goes so far in this role as to tell the Creeper it ought to take her own body part rather than her brother's, with the reasoning that she "has everything the same inside." This sense of fleshly identity and intimacy between brother and sister reverberates with another kind of "queer" sexuality repeatedly alluded to in the text, that of incest, as when, humorously, Darry and Trish tease one another with the epithets "Daddy's whore" and "Momma's boy"—and it is significant in this respect that we are led to believe when we first see Trish and Darry driving together that they are a couple, until dialogue cues reposition them as siblings.[9] Again, Darry's own initial comment about the Creeper is that it is the issue of "in-breeding," and he later goes on to describe his rural environs as "the incest capital of the world."[10]

On the whole, then, the film tends to characterize sexuality (in particular, but not only, as embodied through the Creeper) as messy and strange, fleshy and odoriferous, polymorphous and boundary breaking, hurtful and revolting. More specifically, the Creeper's activities and its own nature, its own makeup, appear to allegorize and defamiliarize human processes of sexual reproduction in a grotesque fashion. Its goal is to propagate itself—just as the human reproductive goal is also, in large measure, self-replication (a point emphasized through sibling protagonists with "everything the same inside"). It achieves this goal through a messy, painful intimacy with those ontologically different from itself, the end result being a partially new entity amalgamating some of its own earlier characteristics and characteristics of those with whom it has been "intimate." That this echoes and mocks (earthly) sexed, genetic reproduction—and human reproduction in particular—is perhaps allegorized most grotesquely in the specter of the Creeper's prom night victims that Darry comes across: the boy and girl are stitched together in one single fleshy mass but with their original likenesses apparently chemically preserved, just as the offspring of human sexual unions bypass the physical differences of the two partners through genetic combination in a single body that preserves the likenesses of the original parents. Even the pain and violence involved both in this singular instance of the Creeper's corporeal sculpture and in its interactions with human victims in general can be seen, the film suggests, to have their correspondence to dimensions of "normal" human sexual relations. The opening conversation between brother and sister, for example, intimates that Trish has just gone through a messy, painful breakup. Darry tries to make light of the situation by singing an impromptu country song with the lyric, "You broke my heart in two, now I can't find the duct tape to put it together," anticipating the particular kinds of bodily violence and recombination the Creeper literalizes later on. Seeing his sister's glum mood, Darry goes on to ask if the boyfriend was "beating you"—and at that moment it occurs to him that the license plate on the Creeper's truck, "BEATNGU," can be read as "beating you." (It is only subsequently that he divines a related, but more grotesque and germane reading: "Be eating you.") The siblings' conversation suggests that their mother, too, is unhappy in her domestic situation, though details on this point are not developed.

But while *Jeepers Creepers* figures human biology as inherently grotesque, as involving messy propagation through amalgamation, it should again be noted that the film's reproductive allegory is conjoined in particular with an anxiety over racial mixing. The Creeper propagates itself not through intimacy with its own kind but with those who are essentially other—humans—and its own physical appearance (as an emblem of category transgression, a figure of fusion) is by turns obscure, motley, and hideous. It is assumed to be human at first, but as its physical properties are unveiled, it becomes clear it was only passing as such: its facial features are exaggerated (much in the manner of racial caricatures of various types), it has appendages on its face and back (confirming, as it were, the assumption of essential physical difference at the base of various racial myths), and it exhibits superhuman strength (also part of certain racial myths). Yet at the same time that it seems it must be categorized as nothuman, even originating in an entirely different realm, it is also made clear that it is composed, at least in part, *of* humans, has propagated itself by absorbing human parts and making them its own. And this mixed lineage, this monstrous multiplicity, this straddling of categories human and not human, expresses itself in the creature's revolting appearance and fearful behavior.

The attendant sense of anxiety and revulsion over racial mixing suggested here furthermore clearly resonates with the film's rural American setting—a setting that, though not precisely specified, looks somewhat like the South (given the abundance of creeping moss on trees and buildings) and that has, both in history and in previous film representations, often been associated with racial intolerance. (The film was in fact shot in Florida, with the filmmakers hoping it could stand for a "rural heartland.")[11] It is thus quite striking that, at the back-road gas station café where Trish and Darry seek help in their flight from the Creeper, black and white diners are seen contentedly sharing tables with one another, constituting a utopian image of an integrated America in the heart of the rural South. This sense of a racial utopianism continues in the representation of the police officers who respond to the call for help from the diner—a white man and a black woman who, during their brief appearance in the film (before being dispatched by the Creeper), exhibit an evident ease and camaraderie with one another rarely seen in such cinematic cross-racial, cross-gender partnering.

Perhaps even more significant than the foregrounding of race through the striking utopianism of the café scene is the casting choice made for Jezelle, the one human who appears to have the most profound insight into (and hence is by association most directly linked to) the Creeper. Jezelle is introduced (although her image remains withheld) in that same racially mixed café scene, as she telephones the establishment to warn Darry of the dangers in store for him. When she finally does appear, in a scene toward the close of the film when the siblings seek assistance at a police station, it is evident that she is likely of African descent—and also evident that she has a relatively fair complexion, a lighter skin tone than the other African Americans shown in the film. Jezelle herself is thus presumably someone whose racial inheritance comes (at some point in the past) from multiple lineages, and her narrative linkage to the Creeper thereby further endorses a reading of it as an embodiment of anxieties over racial mixing. Relevant in this regard is the fact that, while plainly not responsible for the Creeper's pursuit of Darry, Jezelle nevertheless comes under fire from those she tries to help for her lack of sufficiently clear knowledge about the Creeper and what it will do (her information comes only from vague dreams and visions she has)—in effect she does end up receiving some of the blame for events if only because of her superior knowledge, becoming damned by association. Indeed, for someone who puts herself in danger to help others, she is accorded surprisingly little respect by either the siblings or the staff at the police station (who seem to be familiar with her as a local "character"). At the close of the film Jezelle even ends up deflating her own authority, though evidently as a means of trying to soften the blow to Trish, who has now lost her brother to the Creeper; "I'm just a crazy old woman," she tells the sister. It is quite clear, however, that Jezelle does not believe this, that indeed the supernatural danger she has warned of is quite real, just as is the history of racial mixing she also brings to mind, further embodied in a creature that makes clear that *all* human reproduction involves such category collapse by its very nature.

To summarize some of the key claims being made about the film here: *Jeepers Creepers* projects a sense of unease and horror in large measure through its representation of a monstrous protagonist that frustrates and mixes socially understood norms of categorization (including, at a metatextual level, those of subgeneric classification). Moreover, this representation, in conjunction with a range of images and motifs throughout the text, works to defamiliarize human processes of sexual reproduction and genetic mixing and inheritance, rendering them seemingly grotesque in themselves. These tendencies in the aggregate (along with such cues as the film's multiracial casting) work to suggest that one particularly significant preoccupation of the film is a tension or anxiety with regard to racial mixing and its attendant frustration of older received norms of identity categorization. *Jeepers Creepers* thus offers an apt illustration of the potentials fantastic genres (and the fantastic beings they accommodate) hold for evoking contemporary discourses and tensions regarding human identity.

With regard to this, it is interesting also to note that one further kind of identity category transgression the film alludes to in passing is that of national identity: opening and closing credits indicate (by reference to German production companies) that the film is an international coproduction. Thus, while *Jeepers Creepers* focuses on the problematization of a raced identity in the American heartland, the larger, real-world globalized production context suggests just how much such issues are in play at a macro level as well. Indeed, in *Underworld*, the next film to be examined here, such issues of national mixing come much more strongly and self-consciously to the fore, most literally in a final onscreen credit that reads, "A British-German-Hungarian-United States Co-production," but also, from early on, in the fact that we are presented with a distinctly Old World, Eastern European setting that is never precisely specified (many of the exteriors were filmed in Budapest) and in which English is spoken with a wide range of accents, both American and European. This motif of transnational interaction and mixing is immediately posited as germane, moreover, in that the opening voice-over, from vampire protagonist Selene, establishes a narrative context of war between people from two different "nations" or lineages—specifically, the vampires and the lycanths (or werewolves). Here, then, the horror genre once again provides a context that allows for the playing out of a drama concerned with the mixing of differing categories of identity or lineage; and also once again, the encounter among these categories is played out as a mixing and melding of subgeneric categories—most immediately, those of the vampire film and the werewolf film—and in a globalized production context that itself requires international exchange and interactivity.[12]

*Underworld* provides strong cues to allow its drama of intergroup conflict to be read on a variety of metaphoric levels. In the most general terms, the film can be read as a comment on the senselessness and brutality of war, given the pointed reference to the torture and violence inflicted by both sides, as well as the fact that the historical motivating factor for the conflict, the purported event that initiated it, is revealed to have been a fiction. Given the evidently Eastern European setting, the representation of intense animosity among people of differing bloodlines who inhabit the same city, and each side's professed goals of extermination of the other, an additional and more specific allusion would appear to be to the Balkan conflict (among Serbians, Croatians, and Muslims) of 1992–95, which took place just over the national border from the Hungarian shooting location and has in subsequent years become notorious not only because of the intensity of interethnic hatred it represented but because of evident efforts at genocide (just as in the film) that were a part of it. Even the film's central romantic subplot, in which Selene starts to fall in love with a man from the other "tribe," to the dismay and anger of her fellow vampires, recalls a number of "tragic romances" between people from different ethnic groups reported by the media during the conflict. The reference to race hatred and interethnic extermination in a historic European context could also be interpreted as referencing Nazi policies toward "lesser" races—in particular in light of the imagery of genetically related medical experiments performed upon racial enemies by an Austrian-accented scientist.

But no matter which specific reference or references one reads here, there is clearly a broader allegory at work involving issues of racial hatred and racial mixing—and *Underworld*, like *Jeepers Creepers*, makes use of the potentialities generated by horror's fantastic biologies to highlight such issues.[13] The feud between the vampires and lycans, we learn, goes back to some affront generations in the past, but that history has become hazy, and it is forbidden to revisit it: it is simply a given that the other group, the other bloodline, is the enemy and must be eliminated. In an echo of real-world racial tensions, the film also suggests historically based class dimensions to this racial feud: the vampires clearly look down upon the lycans, whom they refer to as animals and whom they assume are incapable of higher kinds of intellectual activity; even the lycan leader himself warns his fellow werewolves that they will not defeat the vampires if they behave "like a pack of rabid dogs." While the rough-looking lycans appear to dwell in various squalid urban hiding places, the stylishly accoutred vampires enjoy the luxury of a posh, aristocratic mansion on the outskirts of town. And when the "backstory" of the present-day conflict is finally revealed, we learn that the classed dimensions of this conflict have deep historic roots: in ancient history, the lycans had been the slaves of the vampires, protecting them during the daylight hours.

On some levels, it can be argued that *Underworld* panders to a number of regressive stereotypes about race and racial difference. By having lycans stand in as one of the races in this conflict, it is able to literalize the notions of the socially disempowered race as being animalistic—and as though to play at the edges of stereotypes about blackness, the first lycan we see transforming from human to animal form (and someone who clearly has authority among the lycans) is black, whereas the first vampire we see (Selene) is white. The aforementioned black lycan's unusual name, "Raze," in its very sound seems to allude to issues of race and (by association with the character) to link blackness to these issues (and thus to contribute to the naturalization of whiteness by contrast). The film does set aside this initial allusion, however, by then showing both groups as appearing (in their more human forms) as multiracial—evidently a mix of black, white, and Asian. This is not as illogical as it might at first sound, since induction into one of these two groups, with specific physical properties and a specific blood type, can come as a result of being bitten by a member of the group; race is herein figured as viral. Once one is a lycan or vampire, moreover, one not only shares some of the (transformative) physical attributes of that group but also partakes of some of its thoughts and memories, no matter what one's own history is; thus, everyone of a given clan or race automatically shares a certain dimension of consciousness and cannot escape a certain race memory.

But while the film does on occasion indulge certain fictions about the nature of race, it also uses its fantastic racial allegory to imagine possibilities of racial mixing and the overcoming of seemingly intransigent racial or ethnic conflicts. In this regard, it is pertinent that whereas in *Jeepers Creepers*, the figure most closely associated with category mixing (and, by association, race mixing), the Creeper, elicits revulsion, in *Underworld*, the one figure who comes closest to embodying such notions is much more positive, ultimately emerging as both romantic lead and hero. This figure is Michael, who starts the film as a human but soon transitions to lycan owing to lycan blood that is introduced into his system. But while he does become a member of one of the races, of necessity sharing its members' attributes and memories, he also retains his previous (human) consciousness and personality, allowing him to bring a reasoned outsider perspective to the irrationality of the long-running blood feud. ("Why do you hate them so much?" he asks Selene, to which the only response she can offer is, "We're at war.") Michael later gets a dose of vampire blood as well, and while the transformation he undergoes is fleetingly grotesque, the end result is that he is evidently both more resilient than either a vampire or a lycan and uniquely attuned to both sides.

Michael's advocating of peace between the two sides, and his successful embodiment of the mixing of bloodlines, stands in sharply positive contrast to the clearly racist chauvinism of vampire elder Viktor, who exhibits not only a visceral revulsion toward lycans but a stronger disgust still at the idea of lycan-vampire miscegenation. When he learns of Selene's romantic interest in Michael, he describes her as having been "tainted by an animal" and hence no longer trustworthy. It is eventually revealed that the start of the current feud in fact occurred (in a past historical era) when Viktor discovered that his daughter was in love with and pregnant by one of their lycan slaves—the present-day lycan leader Lucian. His response was to kill his daughter; as he now tries to justify it to Selene, "I loved my daughter, but the abomination growing inside her womb was a betrayal of me and the coven. I was forced to protect the species." (The elder vampire also uses the term "abomination" when he hears of a lycan plan to mix the two bloodlines.) Viktor cites this same concern with species survival when (earlier) explaining his chastising of Selene for consorting with a lycan: "These rules are in place for a good reason, and they are the only reason we have survived this long."

Viktor's conceptualization of miscegenation as a threat to his kind clearly resonates with a range of long-standing racial separatist discourses in both America and Europe, and, in the film's terms, puts Viktor (whom screenwriter Danny McBride describes as the "plantation owner" on the DVD commentary) morally in the wrong.[14] Viktor's emergence as one of the clear villains of the piece, moreover, coincides with the revelation of his efforts to falsify history—effacing vampire oppression of lycans and wrongly attributing to them blame for the start of the war. Such a conflict over histories of course also has its corollary in real-world racial struggles—the call for acknowledgment of and reparations for the historical enslavement of blacks in the United States and a range of controversies over Nazi Holocaust denial worldwide being the two most prominent examples.

It is completely in line with a classical narrative economy that, as Michael emerges a heroic and morally righteous figure, Selene's primary emotional attachment shifts from Viktor (whom she had wrongly perceived as an appropriate ally and protector) to him, as a new romantic interest. Possible interracial futures are suggested here both through Michael's newly multiracial identity (lycan, vampire—and human as well) and through his love relationship with a partial species-other, the vampire Selene (a relationship that showed its first sparks before Michael had any vampire in his own makeup). Indeed, it is in no small measure because of her love for Michael that Selene is able to set aside some of the hatred for lycans that had previously been bred into her, to work to achieve (at least temporarily) a lull in the conflict between lycan and vampire.

Yet while interracial love and multiracial identity are thus posited as possible palliatives for interhuman conflict of various kinds, the film also chooses in some sense to hygenicize its images of interraciality (in stark contrast to the messy amalgamations of *Jeepers Creepers*): the lycans and the vampires both are monsters that embody Carroll's principle of fission, each existing alternately in a human-appearing form and a nonhuman form (indeed, the film's vampires undergo fairly stark physical (especially facial) transformation in shifting to nonhuman form, more so than in most traditional vampire representations), but choosing for the most part to "pass" as human, their "raced" identity kept covert. Even Michael, who ends up embodying both of the combinatory mechanisms Carroll describes, as a fusion of two different fission figures, ultimately shifts back to a human appearance, as noted. Thus, the romantic resolution of lycan-vampire and vampire can be figured as the pairing of two humans who are as attractive as movie stars.

In order to achieve its harmonious merging of contradictory categories, the film must not only dramatize romantic closure (achieved, in part, through the downplaying of physical alterity), but also negotiate the subgeneric disjuncture noted earlier, the gap between the realm of werewolves and that of vampires; any sense of mixed-generic "abomination" needs to be effaced.[15] Although combined werewolf-vampire narratives are certainly not without precedent in horror genre history, they have tended to occur either in less prestigious or more industrially marginal examples of the genre (e.g., the films of cult horror star Paul Naschy), or in films made at times when the horror cycle is in a period of exhaustion (e.g., *House of Frankenstein*, 1944; *House of Dracula*, 1945) or in parodies. *Underworld* in effect sidesteps some of the difficulties that obtain with subgeneric mixing by placing vampire and werewolf conventions within another generic framework altogether—that of the action film. This is not to say that *Underworld* does not also engage the conventions of the horror genre—but its generic dominant is arguably that of the action film. This is evidenced, for example, by a narrative emphasis on a war between two clans, as well as by a formal emphasis on scenes of direct combat featuring extensive martial arts action, elaborate fight choreography and stunts (often in slow motion), and novel and intricately designed weaponry. In conjunction with these emphases, the supernatural dimensions of werewolf and vampire conventions are set aside in favor of "scientific" explanations of these phenomena: lycanthropy and vampirism are rendered as diseases of the blood, a maneuver that makes them generically more compatible both with one another and with the larger action film context. The werewolves and vampires of *Underworld* are thus not supernatural monsters so much as they are fantastic beings with various extrahuman qualities and skills that they regularly use in battle with one another; and in this they are entirely consonant with the superheroes and supervillains of various contemporaneous comic book–based action films.

In some sense, *Bewitched* focuses still more centrally than the earlier two films analyzed here on the social tensions that obtain with interlineage romance but moves these to the far less angst-ridden genre of the romantic comedy, albeit with a fantastic plot twist (hence, at the same time, with a generic tension)—that the female protagonist is a witch. That the film concerns an outsider trying to mainstream herself—trying to bridge social categories—is established as the central dramatic premise from the very opening: while the credits are still rolling, we are presented with protagonist Isabelle's goals and active efforts to leave the world of witches and establish herself as a human, acquiring a suburban home in "the Valley" and swearing off witchcraft. A conversation with her warlock father as she shops in her local Bed, Bath, and Beyond for the accoutrements of the Southern California lifestyle makes clear that part of what she perceives as central to becoming "normal" (as she terms it) is to become part of a human couple: "I'm through with warlocks," she asserts. Thus, this romantic comedy is immediately positioned as a drama about a desire to "pass" in a human society and to intermarry, by way of the addition of fantastic elements (relating to character identity) to a genre not ordinarily aligned with the fantastic.[16]

Isabelle is able to quickly move toward having several of her dreams realized through a chance meeting with Jack, an actor with a faltering career who is in search of a neophyte actress appropriate for the part of the female lead Samantha in a remake of the classic 1960s television series *Bewitched* (a series that is plainly the film's key intertextual reference and inspiration and that itself, significantly, often alludes to issues of intermarriage and assimilation, as Walter Metz has recently highlighted).[17] Isabelle accepts the lead role not, it seems clear, out of a desire for fame and fortune (when Jack asks if she wants to be rich and famous, she responds honestly that she just wants to be normal), but rather out of a desire to aid and accommodate Jack, whose helplessness and need for her she finds endearing; it is clear she agrees as well in hopes that his human emotions for her will eventually grow stronger.

The identity problems Isabelle must subsequently face in making the transition to a human career are humorously played out in terms reminiscent of various dramas of racial passing and/or intermarriage. For example, her father, upon learning of her new employment, calls the original television series "an insult to our way of life" and goes on to declare accusingly, "You've turned your back on your own kind, and now you live down the street from a Denny's." At a number of points in the film he reminds her that she can't stop being what she is. As in other narratives of passing or intermarriage, some of the dramatic tension (here played out in comic terms) arises with the unexpected or unwelcome appearance of her relatives, with their possibility of revealing the true nature of her identity. Given the relatives' supernatural prowess, these appearances are often quite literally just that, as when Isabelle's father manages to materialize in her foyer without having to use the front door (or manages to emerge from a painted backdrop at the *Bewitched* soundstage), or when Aunt Clara enters her home by way of the chimney. Both of these elderly relatives, representing the traditions of Isabelle's people, have to be cautioned not to reveal her true identity to her friends—and both are quite disinclined to cooperate.

A romance does eventually emerge between Isabelle and Jack once she is able to get him to move beyond some of his self-centered tendencies and to appreciate her more—and this naturally leads to a more serious dramatic tension over her hidden identity. Isabelle feels it is her obligation to reveal her identity to her mate, especially after he toasts her as "a woman who would never trick me into thinking she was something she wasn't" —but when she does reveal this identity (and finally convinces him of it), his reaction is one of fear and revulsion. The ensuing sequence shows each of the two heartbroken until Jack, upon realizing how much

Isabelle means to him, pursues her as she prepares to return to the world of witches and convinces her to resume their relationship; a brief epilogue then shows the two as happy newlyweds.

The fact that what should be the key dramatic culmination of the film is reached with such little hindrance—and indeed seems something of an anticlimax—points to what is arguably a contradiction in the dramatic framework of the film: while the key dramatic issue is that of the difference that witches represent, such difference is not, in point of fact, figured in very stark or extreme terms here. Isabelle is able to pass so readily because neither she nor her forebears are members of a "visibly recognizable minority," evidently possessing no physical difference from humans. Rather, the difference is figured as one of inherent skill (possessing magical powers) and of lifestyle—and in the latter area, Isabelle is eminently assimilable, as is evidenced by the relish with which she patronizes the supermarkets, chain stores, and chain restaurants that provide the cornerstone of SoCal living.

One possible determinant of this de-emphasis on physical otherness, in allegorical terms, may be that this is a film about interracial negotiations within a relatively integrated and politically liberal milieu: *Bewitched* is set firmly in the upper-middle-class to upper-class world of Southern California and its film industry, a fact emphasized in the extensive sweeping helicopter shots of the general setting that open the film. It is thus a milieu that in racial and political terms is worlds away from the rural South of *Jeepers Creepers* or the Eastern European metropolis of *Underworld*. Still another possible (and not mutually exclusive) allegorical reading suggested here would pertain to Jewish-gentile relations (all the more so given the film's setting in a city with a substantial Jewish population and an industry that historically has had many significant Jewish figures); the film represents a "white-on-white" racial intermixing, in which the witch's (read Jew's) family members chastise her for wanting to get away from her own people and intermarry with people who are different in essence even if similar in appearance, and warn her that she can never change who she is. Indeed, Isabelle's particular process of assimilation to human society here could be said to parallel that undergone by Jews at a time in U.S. history (the postwar era) when they were being repositioned as white Americans (rather than not-quite-white immigrants): she moves to the suburbs and achieves economic mobility (and humanness/whiteness) through employment in one of the few major industries that had (during that historical period of assimilation) been open to Jews.[18] In relation to this allegory, it is also relevant that the witch's mark of difference, that which attracts Jack's attention to her to begin with, is her nose—the same body part conventionally often associated with notions of Jewish physical difference: Isabelle is initially of interest to Jack only when he notices she has the same nose as Samantha from the television series.[19]

As in *Underworld*, it is again suggested that love is a key force in overcoming barriers (much milder here than in the earlier film) to interracial relationships; and in its power to effect such bridging or transcendence, the film aligns love with both magic and, interestingly, the work of mediamaking. Although desiring to forswear magic in her transition to "normal" existence, Isabelle does hesitantly agree to utilizing magic as a means to attract Jack's romantic interest earlier on; but when this backfires, she chooses to set such spells aside and simply express her own frustrations with Jack frankly (in normal, if assertive, human fashion). This new assertion of her own agency (in nonsupernatural form) garners sufficient interest from Jack that a romance in any event does blossom, upon which Isabelle comments (to her cat) in surprise, "Something magical happened all by itself." Significantly, however, this "magic" has the chance to occur only by way of the medium of the media industry: the couple only meets because of the failing movie actor Jack's need for a female lead for his new television series, the two become further acquainted with each other (at least initially) only by way of their work together on the show, and their first serious romantic scene together (save for those brought on by a spell, later reversed) takes place as they dance together on the soundstage for the show (recalling Gene Kelly and Debbie Reynolds's soundstage musical courtship in *Singin' in the Rain*, 1952). When the couple has a falling-out over Isabelle's identity, it is Jack's conversation with an apparently fictive media character—Samantha's Uncle Arthur from the original *Bewitched* series—that brings him to the realization of his need for Isabelle; he runs to find her and reconcile with her at the show's studio soundstage once again, as she sits in front of the simulated housefront for the series.[20] Lest the connection being made here between media constructions of domesticity and the conduct of real-world relationships be lost, the film fades directly from this housefront to the identical housefront of the couple's new real-life abode, six months later and, it turns out, after their marriage.[21]

Love may be the key to interracial conciliation and an interracial future, then, but there is clearly also the suggestion that the imaginative potentials of the mass media play a significant role in helping us reconceptualize and reenvision the racial terms of our existences and thereby help us move toward a multiraciality that may not as yet be the reality of contemporary existence. While such an envisioning of a new (mildly) interracial domesticity can be seen as having an ideologically progressive leaning—as a revision of a social status quo—it is also only a partial revision, leaving other ideologically conservative strains intact. The classic upper-middle-class American suburban home and lifestyle Jack and Isabelle dream of and finally achieve, the classic heterosexual monogamy it is designed to contain (while also being policed, we see, by nosy neighbors across the way), hardly seem to suggest in the aggregate much of a revised (and certainly not a radical) conceptualization of social existence. Isabelle's final gesture in the film of using magic to produce a flowering tree in her new front yard seems to embody just these contradictions: on the one hand, it marks a traditional (and in some ways conventionally "feminine") impulse to beautify her home, and with an object that bespeaks feminine fertility (for her new "nest"); but on the other hand, the gesture is simultaneously a reassertion of her essential racial difference (in its employment of her nonhuman powers), an affront to the ontological and epistemological suppositions of her neighbors (so much so that the one who witnesses the gesture is overwhelmed and immediately faints), and a direct disobeying of the express wishes of her new husband, with whom she has been engaged in a power struggle of sorts throughout the film.

That this film ends on a gesture of female will and power is clearly apropos to the narrative focus of romantic comedy—and in fact the expressed thematic interest of the film's director and cowriter.[22] This chapter's particular emphasis has been more centrally on the dynamics of racial interaction and mixing in this and the two earlier films, but the issue of gender is in fact very directly linked to that of racial mixing in all these films, in particular because heterosexual love and union are the key vehicle for such mixing. Thus a refiguring of racial relations in these instances logically involves a refiguring of gender relations as well. Moreover, because the dynamic of this refiguring involves the breakdown, mixing, and reconstitution of social categories, it is germane, then, that a strong female protagonist, who either partially or fully takes the place of the traditional male protagonist, emerges in each of the films discussed here, in contradiction to traditional generic norms: Trish, in *Jeepers Creepers*, develops into a distinct variation on the strong "final girl" protagonist of much contemporary horror; Selene, in *Underworld*, though initially supportive of an unjust and brutal battle, proves herself to be a skillful, strong, charismatic, and ultimately moral figure, and therefore able to take the majority (though not all) of the hero function over from her male love interest; and Isabelle is clearly the center of *Bewitched*'s focalization from the very opening of that film, her transracial aspirations constituting the chief impetus for the narrative line.

This discussion has endeavored both to trace out certain discourses of interraciality in contemporary Hollywood cinema and to show how genre dynamics (in particular the interaction of disparate generic elements) can inform these discourses. I have been further interested in suggesting the potentials that fantastic genres offer for reimagining multiracial contexts and identities in the popular media. But while I have tried to demonstrate certain *tendencies* and *possibilities* here, I do not want to formulate or imply any all-encompassing generalizations about how horror films, or fantastic films more broadly, or multiple-genre films operate in relation to racial ideologies. To the contrary, by showing that these films offer a wide range of divergent messages about race and racial mixing (sometimes even within a single text), I hope to have demonstrated the need for rigorous, concrete textual analysis in any given instance, and to have indicated in practical terms a particular set of tools for carrying out such analysis.

### NOTES

1. See Jack E. White, "I'm Just Who I Am," *Time*, May 5, 1997, 32+; and Jon Meacham, "The New Face of Race," *Newsweek*, September 18, 2000, 38, which introduces a "Special Report" composed of eight additional articles on the country's changing racial makeup.

2. As Lipsitz summarizes it, "Generic codes often connect activity to identity, reserving clearly defined roles for distinctly gendered, classed, and raced characters." George Lipsitz, "Genre Anxiety and Racial Representation in 1970s Cinema," in *Refiguring American Film Genres*, ed. Nick Browne (Berkeley: University of California Press, 1998), 209.

3. Ibid.

4. Ed Guerrero, *Framing Blackness: The African American Image in Film* (Philadelphia: Temple University Press, 1993), 57.

5. Noel Carroll, *The Philosophy of Horror* (New York: Routledge, 1990), 43. See also Mary Douglas, *Purity and Danger: An Analysis of Concepts of Pollution and Taboo* (New York: Praeger, 1966), especially chaps. 2 and 3.

6. Carroll, *The Philosophy of Horror*, 46.

7. Ibid., 48.

8. Ibid. Although Guerrero's and Carroll's arguments on the oppositional

potentials of the fantastic are in large measure conceptually related to one another and compatible, I do not mean to suggest they are one and the same: Guerrero puts more of an emphasis on the genres' various affronts to the realist codes
of the dominant commercial narrative cinema, while Carroll focuses more specifically on the challenge posed by the categorical transgressions that constitute
monstrosity.

9. Interesting with regard to this is a claim on a number of Web sites (including the Internet Movie Database) that in a discarded ending to the film it
is revealed that the whole tale was being told by a young man to his girlfriend,
played by the same actors who play Darry and Trish, respectively. That this is
much different from the alternate ending to be found on the DVD (and that I
have seen no authoritative claims to this effect) suggests this is in all probability
untrue—but the fact that the story is circulating in the discourse about the film in
itself points to a level of slippage present in the film between siblings and lovers.
Internet Movie Database, "Alternate Versions for Jeepers Creepers," http://imdb.
com/title/tt0263488/alternateversions/.

10. Darry also refers to local law enforcement personnel as "bum-fuck police,"
thus positing the setting of the narrative as characterized by two forms of non-
normative sexuality: incest and anal intercourse.

11. Victor Salva, "Commentary," *Jeepers Creepers*, special edition DVD, directed by Victor Salva (Santa Monica, CA: MGM Home Entertainment, 2002).

12. It could also be noted that themes pertaining to racial or ethnic identity
arguably already inhere in the vampire subgenre in itself: a number of scholars
have demonstrated how, for example, earlier vampire narratives in literature have
engaged discourses of anti-Semitism or have articulated anxieties engendered
by transnational encounters. See, for example, Ken Gelder, *Reading the Vampire*
(London: Routledge, 1994), especially chap. 1; Judith Halberstam, *Skin Shows:
Gothic Horror and the Technology of Monsters* (Durham, NC: Duke University
Press, 1995), chap. 4; H. L. Malchow, *Gothic Images of Race in Nineteenth-Century
Britain* (Stanford, CA: Stanford University Press, 1996), 148-66; and Teri Ann
Doerksen, "Deadly Kisses: Vampirism, Colonialism, and the Gendering of Hor-
ror," in *The Fantastic Vampire: Studies in the Children of the Night*, ed. James Craig
Holte (Westport, CT: Greenwood Press, 2002), 137-44.

13. On the commentary track provided on the DVD, it is clear that the filmmakers themselves conceptualized the film in terms of a black-white racial allegory. Their professed aims do not in themselves confirm that the black-white
reading is *the* "correct" one—other meanings, other discourses may certainly
also be present in the text, which, like any such text, came into being in relation to culture and society through a complex variety of mechanisms—but they
*do* point to black-white racial tensions as one particularly relevant discourse. To
quote Kevin Grevioux, an African American actor who plays a lycan named Raze
and who also has associate producer and co-story writer credits: "The interesting

thing about what's going on here between the vampires and the werewolves was, allegorically speaking, what we tried to do was create a race war, you know, much like black versus white, and a story about interracial couples, and looking at the story you can kind of tell what's going on, that it is about the problems that two races have with each other just because of their existence, and how silly that really is." Kevin Grevioux, Danny McBride, and Len Wiseman, "Commentaries," *Underworld*, widescreen special edition DVD, directed by Len Wiseman (Culver City, CA: Sony Pictures, 2004).

14. Ibid.

15. For more on the mechanisms by which multiple generic affinities are merged in Hollywood film, see Adam Knee, "The Compound Genre Film: *Billy the Kid versus Dracula* Meets *The Harvey Girls*," in *Intertextuality in Literature and Film*, ed. Elaine D. Cancalon and Antoine Spacagna (Gainesville: University Press of Florida, 1994), 141-56.

16. It should be noted, however, that the two decades prior to the production of this film saw increasing numbers of fantasy/romance hybrids (some involving witchcraft)—part of a trend of adding a "high-concept hook" as a "means of repackaging the attractions of romantic comedy for a broad-based mainstream audience." Frank Krutnik, "Conforming Passions? Contemporary Romantic Comedy," in *Genre and Contemporary Hollywood*, ed. Steve Neale (London: British Film Institute, 2002), 135. These films do have a few well-known classical-era predecessors, though they are noted as unusual for their fantastic elements—for example, the ghost-themed *Topper* (1937) and its sequels, and the witch romances *I Married a Witch* (1942) and *Bell Book and Candle* (1958); a street-lamp-extinguishing prank performed by Jack Lemmon in the latter witch film is arguably referenced in the new *Bewitched* in a comment a witch character makes about having performed a similar feat.

17. Walter Metz, *Bewitched* (Detroit: Wayne State University Press, 2007); see, for example, 25-26, 40-41, and 77-81.

18. See Karen Brodkin, *How Jews Became White Folks and What That Says about Race in America* (New Brunswick, NJ: Rutgers University Press, 1998), chaps. 1 and 5; and Eric L. Goldstein, *The Price of Whiteness: Jews, Race, and American Identity* (Princeton, NJ: Princeton University Press, 2006), chap. 8.

19. To quote Sander Gilman, "The Jew's nose makes the Jewish face visible in the Western Diaspora." Sander L. Gilman, "The Jew's Body: Thoughts on Jewish Physical Difference," in *Too Jewish? Challenging Traditional Identities*, ed. Norman L. Kleeblatt (New York: The Jewish Museum; New Brunswick, NJ: Rutgers University Press, 1996), 61.

20. The development of romance through self-conscious reference to a past, nostalgically remembered televisual representation of love here is in keeping with a tendency Frank Krutnik identifies as central to the contemporary romantic comedy: "The present cycle [of films] persistently remobilises the signifiers of

old-fashioned romance, with many comedies invoking keynote romantic texts of the past." Krutnik, "Conforming Passions?" 139.

21. Media, magic, and real-world romance also coincide in the comic gag of having a video rewind icon appear on the screen when love (or other) spells are undone, as people walk backward through their earlier actions.

22. To quote director and cowriter Nora Ephron's remarks on the close of the film from the commentary track of the DVD, "Unlike in the old *Bewitched* where she constantly chose not to be a witch, what she is left with at the end of this movie is that you don't have to choose, that you can be both things—which is a thing that makes it contemporary as opposed to then: You can be powerful and be in love if you are a woman." These remarks extend others made earlier on the track that interestingly both set up the director's focus on female power within heterosexual relationships and indicate an awareness that indeed she is *not* emphasizing mixed race issues: "People look at [the series] *Bewitched* in a kind of very Rorschach-y way. You know it really tells who you are. I have a friend who thinks it's about mixed marriages. I don't happen to think it's about mixed marriages, but she does, and there are people who will tell you that it was an important feminist television show because of a woman who used her powers. I happen to think it wasn't really, because she always had to pretend she didn't want to use them, and she was mostly using them for things that seemed domestic to put it mildly, but nonetheless, that question of how powerful you can be in a relationship with a man and not lose his love is something that I think women always struggle with." Nora Ephron, "Commentary," *Bewitched*, DVD, directed by Nora Ephron (Culver City, CA: Sony Pictures, 2005).

|||||||||||||||||||||||||||||||||||||||||||||||||||||||||

# 8

# Virtual Race

## *The Racially Ambiguous Action Hero in* The Matrix *and* Pitch Black

### *Jane Park*

In "Racial Actors, Liberal Myths," Josephine Lee considers the ideological implications of the two dominant progressive approaches that have been used to represent nonwhite bodies in contemporary U.S. theater: the "color-blind" integrationist approach, which assigns roles to actors regardless of their racial background, and the more color-aware, cultural nationalist approach, which assigns roles to actors that explicitly politicize their nonwhite identities. Lee points out that the shared trope of racial difference as "mask" connects these two seemingly opposite approaches, an idea she sums up as follows: "If liberal integrationism felt that race was a false 'mask' over the deracinated real self, cultural nationalism insisted on the importance of the racial 'mask' as a ritualized enactment that would bring forth the 'true self.'"[1] She concludes by positing an alternative trope—the "racial mask" as inseparable from the face it covers or exposes—drawing on a lively listerv discussion that reveals the unstable status of mixed race actor Keanu Reeves's "Asian American" identity. According to Lee, the Internet discussants' opinions ranged from the integrationist position, which insisted that Reeves's racial background simply did not matter, to the cultural nationalist one, which rejected him as Asian American due not to his phenotype but, rather, to his lack of political affiliation with that community.

Significantly, the actor's racial ambiguity had opened up a space for these viewers to reinterrogate Asian American identity vis-à-vis whiteness. Taking that ambiguity into account, Lee suggests a separate category for Reeves "as a third type of racial actor: the body that is racially identifiable, but whose race is neither a stereotype, a burden, nor a false mask."[2] Put another way, the general response to his mixed race background by the members of this online community gestures toward a way of acknowledging racial difference that does not privilege whiteness as the signifier of unspoken authentic subjectivity against which nonwhiteness functions as an objectified "mask." Reeves was "outed" as nonwhite in the listserv, but the Asiatic part of his racial background was not treated as a "burden" to be relegated to the margins and ignored (as in the color-blind approach) or, conversely, thrust into the foreground and highlighted in a "positive" way (as in the cultural nationalist one).

With Lee's evocative reading in mind, this chapter examines the role of the racially ambiguous heroes in two science fiction action films released at the turn of the millennium: *The Matrix* (1999) and *Pitch Black* (2000).[3] It identifies some of the social, political, and industrial factors that led to the emergence and popularity of these characters and in its analysis of the two films illustrates how recent forms of multiracial representation offer new ways of thinking about racial identity, difference, and discrimination.

### "Multiracial Chic" and Virtual Race

As noted in this volume's introduction, the number of multiracial people in the United States has grown substantially since *Loving v. Virginia* struck down antimiscegenation laws nationally in 1967. Hollywood, meanwhile, has undergone a revolution of its own. Nonwhite and mixed race actors who could not pass gained more presence in film and television in the 1970s and 1980s as a consequence of social movements, including the civil rights and Black Power movements and similar movements they inspired among the Chicano, American Indian, and Asian American communities. Many filmmakers of color such as Gordon Parks, Wayne Wang, and Gregory Nava gained experience in media production by working on documentaries and short films within these movements broadly. Also, thanks to affirmative action initiatives, more people of color matriculated into film programs in this period, resulting in the emergence of the Los Angeles school and the blossoming of low-budget documentaries and feature films about racial minorities. Many of these politicized filmmakers, actors and actresses, producers, and writers of color eventually entered the commercial film industry and contributed to the growing visibility of non-Western bodies and cultures both behind and in front of the camera. Their presence, along with the commercial popularity of Blaxploitation and martial arts films in the 1970s, led to the emergence of more non-white imagery on the big screen in the following decade, which found expression in a multicultural mise-en-scène and racially diverse casting. This imagery appeared primarily in action genre films such as *Escape from New York* (1981), *Blade Runner* (1982), and *Repo Man* (1984), and biracial buddy films such as *The Lethal Weapon* series (1987, 1989, 1992, 1998) and the *48 Hours* series (1982, 1990).

The increased visibility of racial difference in eighties Hollywood was followed by the "multiracial chic" of the nineties. During this period mixed race people became more visible, socially and politically, in the United States, as epitomized by the cover models of *Time* in November 1993 and *Mirabella* in September 1994, which were digital pastiches of individuals of various racial and ethnic backgrounds.[4] Hollywood in turn seemed to be reflecting and catering to this demographic trend. A *New York Times* article in summer 2002 announced the birth of a new kind of action hero following the success of *The Matrix*. According to the industry players interviewed, *The Matrix*, which starred the enigmatic Reeves, demonstrated that with the liberal use of special effects in action sequences, actors with body types and temperaments not typically associated with the genre could still be cast as protagonists.[5] The article lists as examples of the "new action hero" white actors such as Matt Damon, Heath Ledger, Owen Wilson, and Toby McGuire. However, it ends with two actors whose muscular physicality and "meathead" roles contrast sharply with the leaner physiques and more cerebral characters of their white counterparts and seem to hark back to more traditional action heroes: the racially ambiguous former bouncer, Vin Diesel of *The Fast and the Furious* (2001) and *XXX* (2002) and Afro-Asian Dwayne "The Rock" Johnson, a wrestling star who crossed over into film with his lead role in *The Scorpion King* (2002).[6] Diesel and Johnson are positioned rhetorically at the pinnacle of the action genre's explicitly digital and implicitly racial "evolution" and touted as representatives of an increasingly racially diverse nation. How do we explain this celebratory attitude toward mixed race actors such as Johnson and Diesel, and what does this new attitude suggest with regard to changing definitions of race in this country?

Scholars in a variety of disciplines have begun to take up this question. In particular, sociologists have begun to consider the kind of racial shifts that might accompany the realization of the nonwhite and mixed race "global" future depicted in these films. F. James Davis, for example, predicts optimistically that the United States will follow the "egalitarian pluralist" model of Hawai'i, where race supposedly is subsumed by class, racism is frowned upon, and ethnic diversity is celebrated.[7] Similar to Robert Fox's provocative idea of a "post-white" future, Davis's scenario associates the growth of the multiracial population with the destabilization and ultimate eradication of white privilege and the racial hierarchy that maintains it.[8] In contrast, Eduardo Bonilla-Silva and David Embrick predict that the growing numbers of mixed race Americans will lead to the pigmentocratic model of racial hierarchy that characterizes most Latin American countries, "a loose triracial stratification system with whites at the top, an intermediary group of honorary whites, and a nonwhite group, or the collective black, at the bottom."[9] Like many other critical race theorists, Bonilla-Silva and Embrick argue that what may look like the "end of race" as more people of color gain political, social, and cultural visibility actually veils a redistribution of power along the axes of race, class, gender, and sexuality that continues to privilege whites.[10]

Bonilla-Silva and Embrick elaborate that a more egalitarian model might emerge if the members of the "collective black" are able to politicize the breakdown of the black/white binary. If so, the resulting scenario could reflect the descriptive framework for multiracial subjectivity proposed by Gloria Anzaldúa in *Borderlands/La Frontera*. Anzaldúa's idea of a "Mestiza consciousness" draws on her own experiences as a biracial Chicana lesbian feminist to reclaim the liminal status of the mixed race subject, whose phenotypical and cultural ambiguities present a mass of contradictions to the monoracially framed world. Born of the attempt to synthesize these contradictions, this consciousness critiques the monoracial worldview in which non-Western racial and cultural differences have been rendered abject or invisible.[11]

Almost twenty years later, a highly commodified form of mestiza consciousness appears to have replaced this worldview: in contemporary popular media, racial difference, properly contained and sanitized through class and/or cultural capital, is neither ignored nor reviled but, rather, actively celebrated and portrayed as desirable. W. E. B. Du Bois's still relevant question for many members of poor and working-class minority groups, namely, "How does it feel to be a problem?" does not seem as relevant for those of nonwhite and mixed race groups who have come to embody and endorse this liberal middle-class multiculturalism.[12] Instead, a modified version of Du Bois's question might be asked of these groups, something along the lines of "How does it feel to be a trend?" In her seminal essay, "Eating the Other," bell hooks explains the popular appeal of racial and ethnic otherness for members of dominant culture thus:

> Within current debates about race and difference, mass culture is the contemporary location that both publicly declares and perpetuates the idea that there is pleasure to be found in the acknowledgment and enjoyment of racial difference. The commodification of Otherness has been so successful because it is offered as a new delight, more intense, more satisfying than normal ways of doing and feeling. Within commodity culture, ethnicity becomes spice, seasoning that can liven up the dull dish that is mainstream white culture.[13]

Racially ambiguous characters in science fiction action films complicate the white appropriation of racial difference that hooks critiques by performing, in deliberate and nondeliberate ways, what I call *virtual race*, or the idea of racial and ethnic identity as an ornamental product that can be marketed and consumed, put on and taken off. I argue that this dismantling of traditional racial and ethnic identities and affiliations neither signals the happy eradication of racism nor is a simple reiteration of white privilege. Instead, the current situation is much more complex, with mixed-race bodies blurring the boundaries between whiteness and nonwhiteness even as they receive certain privileges that historically have been conferred upon those with white bodies. It is important to note here that the concentration of nonwhite characters and motifs in recent years has occurred in various hybrid action genres—horror, thriller, and urban action as well as science fiction—which, with their emphasis on the visual and the visceral, fit the requirements of the high-concept blockbuster film. What Yvonne Tasker observed of Hollywood action films in the early 1990s continues to hold, with the modification that nonwhite, nonblack performers, namely, those of Asian, Latino/a, and mixed race descent, have begun to appear as protagonists:

> Action heroes and heroines are cinematically constructed almost exclusively through their physicality, and the display of the body forms a key part of the visual excess that is offered in the muscular action cinema. Such an emphasis on physicality has . . . opened up a space in the action cinema for black performers who have been almost totally excluded from other Hollywood genres.[14]

The science fiction action film, which became a generic staple in the blockbuster era with hits like *Star Wars* (1977), *Alien* (1979), and *The Terminator* (1984), draws on the spectacle of special effects and, increasingly, of racial and cultural difference to dramatize the conflict between self and other, human and alien (in the form of extraterrestrials or technology) so central to the genre. As our relationship to technology has become more ambivalent, so has our relationship to the "other" in science fiction cinema as Vivian Sobchack, Scott Bukatman, and others have discussed.[15] Also, the body functions as the primary site upon which the instability of the self/other boundary plays out, from early films such as *The Invasion of the Body Snatchers* (1956) to later ones such as *RoboCop* (1987) and *eXistenZ* (1999). That the bodies of the key characters in a number of contemporary science fiction action films are racially ambiguous is particularly significant within this generic context.

These characters literally embody the racial and ethnic diversity of the mise-en-scène and supporting characters in the films in which they star, appearing to signify the end of racial boundaries. Not surprisingly, as nonwhite, racially ambiguous, and mixed race characters have become more visible and have been developed further on the big screen, whiteness seems to have lost much of its former social and cultural cachet. As Mary Beltrán points out in "The New Hollywood Racelessness," urban action films such as *Romeo Must Die* (2000) and *The Fast and the Furious* feature mostly nonwhite casts situated in hyper-multicultural milieus in which whiteness, on a superficial level, is marginalized, ridiculed, and demonized. For instance, the chief villain in *Romeo Must Die*, a cowardly white snob, pits the black and Chinese gang families against each other through the colonialist "divide-and-conquer" strategy—a move that the film clearly critiques. Likewise, Brian (Paul Walker), the undercover white male protagonist of *The Fast and the Furious*, must work hard to earn the "respect" of the predominantly nonwhite street racers led by racially ambiguous Dom (Vin Diesel).[16] According to Beltrán, characters like Dom exhibit a new kind of "cultural competence," which "holds . . . more credence and power in the polyglot millennial environment."[17]

My idea of mixed race and/or racially ambiguous characters as virtually raced pivots crucially on this issue of "cultural competence," which draws on a character's embodiment and/or knowledge of nonwhite cultures. While Hollywood narratives continue to feature white male characters who gain valuable "cultural competence" through their relationships with nonwhite characters, more and more, at least in the action genre, this competence is being exhibited by racially ambiguous, often mixed race actors and actresses who are coded white narratively yet exhibit traces of racial difference through their appearance and performance. Their characters thus render visible certain elements of non-Western cultures; however, this visibility is limited insofar as those cultures are decontextualized historically, socially, and politically to appeal to mass audiences. A critical consideration, then, of how mixed race and racially ambiguous performers appear onscreen could provide new ways to understand the complex ways in which certain raced bodies are becoming cultural sites for redefining notions of "whiteness" and, subsequently, "race." The following brief readings of *The Matrix* and *Pitch Black* attempt to outline the contours of this kind of analysis.

### Neo as Techno-Oriental Savior

*The Matrix*, the science fiction sleeper hit of 1999, and its sequels, *The Matrix: Reloaded* (2003) and *The Matrix: Revolutions* (2003), display an image of the future quite different than those in previous science fiction films, as a number of scholars have noted.[18] Whereas in movies such as *Escape from New York* and *Blade Runner*, nonwhite bodies function as objects in the background or as villains who have overstepped social and legal boundaries, here they take center stage, coming to stand for the whole of a beleaguered humanity fighting the planetary domination of sterile, sentient, and homogeneously "white" machines. Yet this interpretation of the film as embracing a "postwhite" future is complicated by the fact that its protagonist is played by a mixed race actor who is considered white by dominant audiences.[19] While Keanu Reeves is "hapa," the Hawaiian term for mixed race, he has never identified culturally or politically with the Asian American or Pacific Islander communities, nor has he been cast as a person of Asian descent, with the exception of Bernardo Bertolucci's *Little Buddha* (1993), for which he transformed himself into an exquisitely emaciated Siddhartha Gautama. Put another way, Reeves and the characters he plays are white by default, passing "passively," the turn of phrase used by Teresa Kay Williams to describe the commonly assumed whiteness of such Eurasian actors as Kristin Kreuk, Dean Cain, and Jennifer Tilly.[20]

At the same time, subtle acknowledgment of Reeves's Asiatic roots often underscores assessment of his on-screen and offscreen personae. Many critics and fans attribute an appealing quality of otherness in the star that finds expression not only in sexual terms, as Michael DeAngelis discusses in *Gay Fandom and Crossover Stardom*, but also in racial ones, as made apparent in the consistent use of distinctly East Asian signifiers to describe the versatile, minimalist actor: his "almond shaped eyes," his "exotic" Hawaiian name, and his inscrutable, "enigmatic" persona.[21] Likewise, Reeves's racial ambiguity shapes Neo, the character he plays in *The Matrix* narrative. As I discuss in more detail elsewhere, Neo must suffer a choice between two racial and ontological worldviews and identities: that of the "real world," "old" technology, and political resistance, represented by his black mentor, Morpheus (Laurence Fishburne), and that of the Matrix, "new" technology, and social conformity, represented by his white nemesis, Agent Smith (Hugo Weaving).[22] This tenuous position of racial and ideological middleman is one that Asian Americans historically have occupied.

In addition, Neo embodies and performs a softer, somewhat "effeminized" masculinity that has been associated with men of East Asian descent in the U.S. imaginary.[23] Throughout most of *The Matrix*, Neo does not exhibit the recognizable machismo traits of the traditional Hollywood male action star. Instead, Neo's character, played with Reeves's characteristic minimalism, strongly resembles the male protagonists of anime, which Mary Kittleson describes in the following way:

> Heroism in most manga and anime is internal: heroes must be sincere and they must be selfless, at least at the moment of heroism. It is not necessary for a manga or anime hero to be an [sic] saint, to fight for the right side, or even to be successful. Anyone who sincerely gives his or her best efforts to almost any task can be a hero.[24]

When we are introduced to Neo, he reflects the passivity, ennui, and confusion of these youth; a computer programmer by day and a hacker by night, Thomas Anderson/Neo leads a somnolent existence with no apparent meaning or larger purpose. When his abilities initially are tested, he demonstrates the mixed emotions and actions of most anime heroes. Too scared to follow Morpheus's phone orders to escape using the highrise scaffold, Neo is captured by the agents while Trinity watches from her motorcycle mirror. Later in the Construct, Neo fails again when he is unable to jump from one roof to another, disappointing the crew and questioning their faith in him as a potential savior. It is only at the end of the film, when Neo acts out of altruistic love for his mentor, friend, and surrogate father, that he proves himself to be a "hero." Even then, his heroism contains a certain kind of receptive humility. As DeAngelis notes, Reeves's softer, pansexual appeal differs noticeably from that of the "hard bodies" and hard actions that characterize Hollywood male heroes in the 1980s.[25]

Along with his passive masculinity, Neo's ability to defeat the machines by thinking and acting like them recalls techno-orientalist stereotypes of Asians and Asian Americans that conflate them with dangerous new technologies.[26] Historically used to reinforce Yellow Peril sentiments toward Asians and Asian Americans, as in the passage of the Chinese Exclusion Acts and the internment of Japanese Americans in World War II, these stereotypes function somewhat differently here. Like earlier Hollywood representations of Chinese coolies and Japanese kamikaze pilots, Neo is a hybrid of human and machine. Existing initially as "food" for the machines, he is linked inextricably to them, through the plugs that remain in the back of his head, his extraordinary hacker skills, and his doubling with Agent Smith, which plays out further in the sequels. However, unlike past techno-orientalist representations of Asian American masculinity, Neo comes to stand in for the very figure of the human, in large part due to—rather than despite—his racially (symbolically both black and white) and ontologically (both human and machine) hybrid status. To be more specific, what distinguishes Neo from Morpheus and the other rebels, and ultimately convinces everyone that he is the One, is his ability to see the world of the Matrix for what it is, namely, the virtual architecture of fantasy embedded in computer code.

This requires an ability to mimic and pass as the enemy other, a character trait central to many racial stereotypes specific to Asian Americans. Once he is able to experience the code as mere data, Neo, the consummate hacker, can control and contain his enemies effortlessly—a position of power usually given to white male protagonists. In other words, according to the film, it is precisely the trait of mutability, the ability to move across racial, social, and ontological boundaries via the conditional status of the racially ambiguous model minority, that will save the human race.

Key to my reading of Neo's fluid racial and to some extent sexual identity in *The Matrix* is Reeves's relationship to Richard Dyer's figure of the "dark white man." In *White*, Dyer states that the universal appeal of that figure, epitomized by all-American actor Harrison Ford, lies in the tinge of moral, ethical, and/or physical "darkness" in and on his person. This darkness represents the sexualized racial other that threatens to overwhelm the hero; his conflict with and ultimate subjugation of this other is precisely what gives him his masculine power and charisma.[27] In *The Matrix* the assumption behind the trope of the "dark white man"—that is, that the hero is white—is unsettled by the racial ambiguity of Reeves playing Neo, namely, the phenomenon of a passively passing Eurasian actor in the role of an orientalized white hero paying homage to black style. Rather than simply dismiss Neo as another version of the "dark white man," however, which is precisely what happens in the previously mentioned *New York Times* article, I propose that Reeves's distinctive phenotype at least extends this category if we read the actor as white and at most potentially inverts it to that of the "white dark man" if we read him as mixed race.

## Riddick as "Hip-Hop Thug"

That said, how are we to interpret the character of Richard Riddick, played by similarly racially ambiguous Vin Diesel, who, with his dark skin, slightly kinky dark hair (when his head is not wholly shaved), and incredibly cut body, would seem to lie at the opposite end of the passing spectrum? Inasmuch as Neo codes symbolically as Asian American in *The Matrix*, Riddick codes symbolically as African American in *Pitch Black*. Even more so than Reeves, Diesel has remained notoriously enigmatic about his racial background, resulting in the mainstream perception that he is white with vaguely ethnic roots. Note, for instance, the following description of Diesel as Riddick in William Holden's review of *Pitch Black* in the *New York Times*:

> In the movie's opening scenes, in which Riddick tears off his manacles, he suggests a bone-crushing hybrid of Hannibal Lecter, Harry Houdini and Hulk Hogan stomping out of a leather fetishist's private dungeon. . . . As styles of macho, shaved-head antihero go, he is a new variation on something familiar. Think of Telly Savalas as a hip-hop thug, and you'll get the idea.[28]

Riddick provides a darker version of the "white dark male" than Neo, since Diesel is even less able than Reeves to pass, passively or actively, as a white Anglo-Saxon Protestant male. Instead he generally codes as "off-white," a term coined by Diane Negra to describe ethnic whites in Hollywood, as we see in the preceding passage in which Holden compares

Diesel to Greek American actor Telly Savalas.[29] Along these lines, Diesel could be said to exemplify the extreme of Dyer's "dark white man": his masculinity is commensurate not only with the amount of "darkness" (i.e., ethnic otherness) visible on his body but also the extent to which the assumed whiteness of his characters is able to contain that otherness. This assumption that Diesel and the characters he plays are ethnic white would seem to be validated by the actor's first film role as an Italian American army private in *Saving Private Ryan* (1998).

Unbeknownst to most of the general public, however, is what landed Diesel this important part, namely, a short film written, directed, and produced by the then-unknown actor that happened to catch Steven Spielberg's eye at the Cannes film festival in 1995.[30] Produced as a promotional piece to showcase Diesel's acting skills and told in a seemingly autobiographical style, *Multi-Facial* addresses the challenges that Mike, a struggling biracial actor in New York, faces in finding employment within a media industry that reinforces rigid racial and ethnic boundaries in its casting practices. Diesel plays Mike, virtuosically performing a succession of different ethnicities—Italian, Latino, black—for the casting judges and the camera. The film ends with a poignant monologue in which Mike plays a biracial character with a white mother and a black father. After describing his admiration for his father, Mike (in character) says he was "never black enough" to become what he always thought his father wanted him to be: a "great black actor." The monologue ends with Mike's realization that his father's wish was for him "to go one step further . . . to be an actor. Just an actor." It is more than a little tempting to read this final statement in the monologue as advocating a liberal color blindness in which "just an actor" becomes synonymous with "white actor." Yet to resort automatically to such a reading is, in some ways, to refuse to recognize the option of the "third racial category" Lee posits—that is, mixed race as a category that is white and nonwhite and, at the same time, neither. In any case, *Multi-Facial* suggests the possibility that Diesel playing Mike playing the biracial actor might himself be part black. As when we acknowledge Reeves's hapa identity, considering this possibility inverts the terms of the model of the "dark white man" to those of the "white dark man."

This comparison takes us back to the assertion I made earlier, that while both science fiction protagonists Neo and Riddick are racially ambiguous and possibly mixed race, they also exhibit representational traits that have been connected with Asian American and African American men, respectively, in U.S. popular culture. More specifically, Neo exemplifies stereotypes of Asian American men with his technological expertise and passive asexuality, whereas, in contrast, Riddick exemplifies those of African American men with his proximity to the natural (whether the organic environment or body) and his hypersexualized masculinity. As noted earlier, these characters appear in a film genre known for style and spectacle rather than complex narratives or deep character development—traits that translate profitably into the video game medium. For instance, *The Chronicles of Riddick* (2004), the sequel to *Pitch Black*, performed poorly at the box office but managed to recoup a good portion of its high production costs through the success of its ancillary video game, which drew on and expanded the film's many digitally enhanced action sequences.[31] Within this convergent space, the "virtual race" of these characters takes on another level of meaning. If Neo projects a "cool" hacker with whom technologically savvy youth might identify, Riddick embodies a supermuscular, testosterone-driven avatar that these youth might "play."

That image is sustained throughout *Pitch Black*, directed by David Twohy, best known for other science fiction films such as *Grand Tour* (1992) and *The Arrival* (1996). A spaceship carrying a motley crew including Riddick, a psychotic convict, experiences a malfunction and is forced to land on an eerie, desertlike planet. The planet shows no signs of life until an eclipse of its three suns occurs, at which point the crew encounters its dangerous inhabitants, weird flying creatures that come out only in the dark and track their prey kinesthetically. Thanks to his almost supernatural abilities to understand and deflect these creatures, Riddick assumes leadership of the crew and is able to get what remains of it back to the spaceship and off the planet. The subplot revolves around the sexual tension between Riddick and Carolyn Fry (Radha Mitchell), the ship's blond white female pilot, who, like Riddick, is portrayed as a morally ambivalent character. While the audience, Riddick's captor William Johns, and later Riddick himself learn that Carolyn willingly tried to sacrifice the crew to save herself, that knowledge is kept secret from the other characters, and so she remains a heroic figure in their eyes. Conversely, Riddick immediately becomes the prime suspect when members of the crew start to die, and he continues to be marginalized throughout the narrative due to his criminal past and persona, which are associated with the rebellious black masculinity epitomized in the image of the "hip-hop thug" referenced earlier by Holden. Even as this racialized criminality makes the other characters and the audience uneasy, it is also what gives Riddick his sexual appeal and "cultural competence," that is, the mental and physical skills to outwit the alien creatures, which will be discussed in more detail shortly.[32]

The film opens, appropriately, in "pitch black" with Riddick's low, growling voice describing "cryo-sleep" as a state of deep slumber in space travel in which "the only part of your brain that doesn't turn off is the primitive side, the animal side."[33] Even in this somewhat comatose state, he is able to sense the presence of other bodies on the spaceship: a "hoodoo holy man," a "woman," and a "blue-eyed devil."[34] These three characters, Abu "Imam" al-Walid (Keith David), Carolyn, and Johns (Cole Hauser), respectively, function as distinct racial and cultural (and, in Carolyn's case, gender) foils for Riddick. While his voice-over continues, the scene opens to a medium close-up of Riddick sitting mostly in shadow, blindfolded and chained, a pose that strongly suggests the plight of enslaved black people in the Middle Passage. The allusion to slavery is made explicit toward the second act of the film when Johns "frees" Riddick on the condition that he help the crew. He accuses Riddick of murdering Zeke, one of the nonwhite secondary characters, an accusation Riddick denies, underscoring that Zeke was "the wrong color." This comment aligns Riddick with people of color against the white establishment that Johns represents. It is worth noting here that of the handful of nonwhite crew members, Zeke is the most westernized: he looks to be of South Asian or Middle Eastern descent and speaks with an Australian accent. The others—two young Middle Eastern boys and their teacher Abu, the imam—are devoutly Muslim, speak with Arabic accents, and are conflated consistently with the desert landscape, narratively and visually. Abu, the darkest of this group and the only explicitly black character in the film, comes to lead the crew spiritually, complementing Riddick's physical leadership. He is also the only character besides Riddick who adjusts quickly to the harsh environment of the alien planet and possesses the skills and intelligence to find water and predict the eclipse. Much like Morpheus in *The Matrix*, Abu, with his calm and controlled masculinity, acts as a spiritual and moral mentor to Riddick and, by extension, the crew and the film audience. Though Riddick seems to reject his advice, he listens to and clearly respects Abu.

In contrast, he neither listens to nor respects Johns, the primary white male character of the film, who initially seems to embody the authority of the law. With his blond hair, blue eyes, and southern drawl, Johns presents an instantly familiar Hollywood caricature of the overtly racist white man, which has become the new "other" in the commercially multicultural media. Eventually we learn that Johns is weak and corrupt; he is addicted to morphine and as a bounty hunter represents not the law but his

*In* Pitch Black *(2000) Riddick (Vin Diesel) uses his surgically enhanced, artificial eyes— emblems of time served in prison and his alienation in dominant culture—as a weapon against the alien creatures. Photo courtesy of Movie Market, Ltd.*

own selfish interests. In a standoff moment when the two vie for control of the leadership, Riddick puts a knife to Johns's crotch and mocks his masculinity, calling him "seventy-nine kilos of gutless white meat."[35] Soon thereafter the alien creatures complete the castration motif when they decapitate Johns. The only other white male character in the film, Paris Ogilvie (Lewis Fitz-Gerald), a pretentious, high-strung antiques dealer, is even less effectual than Johns, and the audience is likely to care little when the creatures kill him as well.

Unlike these white male characters, Riddick possesses certain forms of "cultural competence," as mentioned earlier, which make him the natural leader on this dark planet. Unlike the other characters, he is able to comprehend and therefore effectively control its hostile terrain. The film thus depicts Riddick's "primitive" physical traits as the most valuable and desirable on the alien planet. While such a representation obviously draws on the dominant stereotype of black people as being defined principally by their bodies, it does not wholly reduce Riddick to his body. Rather, the character's expert ability to control and manipulate his body becomes integral to the survival of the crew. He is in top physical shape, with much sharper senses than those of the other crew members and, by extension, other average human beings. Further, he is extremely strong and quick and acts on his well-honed instincts without hesitation. As such, our protagonist resembles a rather dangerous and sexy predatory animal. At the same time, the naturalistic imagery used to define Riddick is undercut by the fact that his eyes—his most important assets in the film, since they allow him to spot the aliens in the dark—are artificial.

When Jack, a young girl passing as a boy (whose real gender is revealed later by Riddick's highly developed sense of smell), admires his eyes and asks him where he got them, he tells her they are "surgical enhancements, shine job. . . . You gotta kill a few people and get in the slammer where they tell you you'll never see light again."[36] Even as Riddick uses his eyes as a weapon against the alien creatures, they also connect him with these nonhuman enemies, a connection reinforced by the ways in which the camera represents his point of vision and that of the creatures. Objects and figures appear as lines in the creatures' point of view and as dark masses framed by an orange halo in Riddick's—the latter recalling the point of view of the alien in *Predator* (1987).

Riddick is comfortable on the hellish planet because it resembles his formative experience in prison, which gave him certain survival skills as well as an oppositional stance toward dominant culture expressed in his eager association with and embrace of imagery commonly coded as sinister. For instance, he has no fear of the dark (of "pitch blackness") and describes a swarm of bats his crew members find dangerous and repulsive as "beautiful." He shaves his head with a machete, linking him not only to Hannibal in *Silence of the Lambs* (1991) but also to Kurtz in *Apocalypse Now* (1979), both highly intelligent and insane bald men. Finally, he appears to care for no one but himself. Indeed, the tagline, "Fight evil with evil," directly associates him with evil. At the same time, Riddick's obvious ressentiment makes him a sympathetic character. He constantly refers to his marginal status with a certain sense of pride, playing off the hatred, suspicion, and resentment that others direct at him, questioning the superficial criteria used to determine what is true and good over what is false and bad. In this sense, his racial ambiguity, like that of Neo, underscores and enhances the mediating role that he plays between the human/self and the nonhuman/other. Embodying such contradictions, Riddick is a thoroughly ambivalent antihero, and the excessive way that Diesel performs those contradictions keeps the audience from identifying with Riddick in any complete or consistent fashion.

Yet this antiestablishment antihero role appeals strongly to one of the youngest crew members—the female "tween" who gender-passes for much of the movie. In her hero worship of Riddick, Jack goes so far as to imitate him, shaving her head and wearing the same kind of oversized gogglelike sunglasses. This comic doubling reinforces Riddick's hypermasculine appeal but on a queer register: "queer" because his admirer at first glance codes as a young boy; "queer" even after we discover Jack is a girl because she is not yet suitable socially to be his romantic partner; and finally, "queer" because, in both cases, Riddick's hypermasculinity via Jack's playful imitation also is exposed as a kind of play, a spectacular performance of racialized masculinity that is not contained by the heteronormative closure typical of most Hollywood action movies. More to the point, Carolyn, the white female love interest, dies orgasmically after embracing Riddick in the final scene. It is only when the camera pans out that we see she has been killed by one of the creatures and not by Riddick. The only surviving members of the crew are Riddick, Jack, and Abu. The fact that the racially ambiguous protagonist remains single at the end of the movie, jetting off into the inevitable sequel with a black spiritual leader and a gender-confused white girl, seems to fly against many of the conventions of the Hollywood blockbuster film.

## Conclusion

In *The Matrix* and *Pitch Black*, racially ambiguous protagonists draw on stereotypes and codified representations of nonwhite groups to delineate "new" modes of heroism without calling attention to the social, historical, and political contexts of these groups in the United States. This trend consistently appears in other contemporary science fiction films and television shows such as *The Cell* (2000), *Final Fantasy: The Spirits Within* (2001), *Firefly* (2002), *Serenity* (2005), and *Battlestar Galactica* (2004–present), and reflects a larger cultural phenomenon in which many multiracial actors and actresses such as Vin Diesel, Jessica Alba, and others downplay their specific nonwhite ethnic roots, referring to themselves more generally and generically as "people of color." Outside Asian American circles, for instance, the question of nonwhite ethnicity hardly comes up, if at all, around the Eurasian actors mentioned earlier. And a similar pattern can be discerned in the critical reception of Latina/o actors such as Cameron Diaz, Raquel Welch, Martin Sheen, and Anthony Quinn.

With regard to narrative structure, the racially ambiguous protagonists in *The Matrix* and *Pitch Black* lead racially diverse crews and are associated closely with primary black characters while other nonwhite and off-white characters serve as backdrop. Principal white characters are vilified if male (Agent Smith in *The Matrix*, Johns in *Pitch Black*) and paired romantically with the protagonist if female (Trinity in *The Matrix*, Carolyn in *Pitch Black*). In both cases, the protagonists are superhuman physically and/or mentally but ethically ambivalent or otherwise compromised. As a result, the audience does not identify with them consistently, if at all. The mise-en-scène is not only multicultural but also heavily technologized, and this, along with the emphasis on action sequences, gives the films a distinctly virtual, video game feel. Finally, the protagonists metaphorically reference nonwhite forms of masculinity (Asian American and African American in *The Matrix* and black and Arab identities in *Pitch Black*) to present alternative depictions of virility and heroism.

On this last point, it is worth noting that the boundary crossings between whiteness and nonwhiteness, which occur actively and/or passively in these racial performances of (hetero) masculinity, parallel the gender and sexual crossings associated with the now rather nebulous term "queer." More specifically, Neo represents a passive sexuality that has been associated with Asian and Asian American men, whereas Riddick represents its hypersexual counterpart, which has been associated with African American men. Both representations of racialized masculinity trouble the white, heterosexual masculine norm that Hollywood action stars have embodied traditionally. Reflecting tendencies of the postmodern project, multiracial and multisexual movements radically stretch and, at times, seem to erase the boundaries that have separated and thus defined traditional identity categories. Racially and sexually ambiguous people who are able to move fluidly across, into, and out of various groups are threatening because they embody the potential for a future where present categories of difference have ceased to matter. Such potential is threatening not only for all manner of racists, sexists, and homophobes but also for those who perceive themselves to be antiracist, feminist, and "queer friendly." It is difficult to imagine a world in which now important criteria that define who we are—how we see ourselves and how others see us—do not exist. Yet it is precisely this near-utopic state that we are being shown, not only as the future but also as the present, in mass media narratives.

Does this striking development in the mediascape signal the disappearance of racial discrimination and perhaps of "race" itself as a sociopolitical category in the United States? Along with various scholars and pundits, journalist Leon Wynter seems to think so, as encapsulated in the following passage from his book *American Skin: Pop Culture, Big Business, and the End of White America*:

> The much maligned melting pot, into which generations of European American identities are said to have dissolved is bubbling again, but on a higher flame; this time whiteness itself is finally being dissolved into a larger identity that includes blacks, Hispanics, and Asians. . . . The transracial vision has acquired an aspirational value in the broad market not because it's politically correct but because it's how America wants to see itself: as a unified multiracial society.[37]

Wynter argues that historical definitions of whiteness are being absorbed into a "transracial" order, linking this futuristic vision of a mixed race nation to the consumerist desires of American people who "want to see [themselves] . . . as [members of] a unified multiracial society."

While his words may seem to document what is happening on a superficial level as mixed race and racially ambiguous bodies become more visible in popular culture, we need to question rigorously the terms and conditions of that visibility. A kind of unconscious privileging of whiteness continues to be evident in the current popularity of multiracial and racially ambiguous faces and bodies in U.S. dominant culture. More easily than monoracial people of color, multiracial folks can be regarded as symbolically white because they already contain visible traces of whiteness, which hint at the invisible, historically fetishized biological property of white blood. As such, multiracial bodies can be appropriated easily by both the Right and the Left to reflect a near future society in which Other and Self have merged without conflict, that is, without disrupting or displacing current hierarchies of power. If the tragic mulatto of the past reinforced the incompatibility of two distinct races, the racially ambiguous star of the present epitomizes the desirable compatibility of many races and ethnicities. To what extent this reproduces existing racial hierarchies and to what extent it significantly reworks what it means to be white and nonwhite remain to be seen as popular multiculturalism and, now, popular multiracialism become the racial standard for future generations.

NOTES

1. Josephine Lee, "Racial Actors, Liberal Myths," *Xcp: Cross-Cultural Poetics* 13 (2003): 105.

2. Ibid., 107.

3. Many thanks to Doug Norman, Catherine John, Anne Soon Choi, and Julia Ehrhardt, as well as to coeditors Mary Beltrán and Camilla Fojas, for their insightful comments on various drafts of this chapter, the first of which I presented at the annual International Communication Association conference in Dresden, Germany, on June 20, 2006.

4. See Lauren Berlant, *The Queen of America Goes to Washington City: Essays on Sex and Citizenship* (Durham, NC: Duke University Press, 1997); and Donna Haraway, *Modest_Witness@SecondMillennium.FemaleMan-Meets-OncoMouse: Feminism and Technoscience* (New York: Routledge, 1997).

5. Rick Lyman, "Job Openings in Hollywood: Heroes Wanted," *New York Times*, August 4, 2002, LexisNexis Academic, December 5, 2002, http://80web.lexisnexis.com.content.lib.utexas.edu.

6. Ibid.

7. F. James Davis, "Defining Race: Comparative Perspectives," in *Mixed Messages: Multiracial Identities in the "Color-Blind" Era*, ed. David L. Brunsma (Boulder, CO: Lynne Rienner, 2006), 20–27.

8. Robert Elliot Fox, "Becoming Post-White," in *MultiAmerica: Essays on Cultural Wars and Cultural Peace*, ed. Ishmael Reed (New York: Viking, 1997), 6–17.

9. Eduardo Bonilla-Silva and David Embrick, "Black, Honorary White, White: The Future of Race in the United States?" in Brunsma, *Mixed Messages*, 33–34.

10. See Iris Marion Young, *Justice and the Politics of Difference* (Princeton, NJ: Princeton University Press, 1990); Howard Winant, *The New Politics of Race: Globalism, Difference, Justice* (Minneapolis: University of Minnesota Press, 2004); and David Theo Goldberg, *The Racial State* (Walden, MA: Blackwell, 2002).

11. Gloria Anzaldúa, *Borderlands/La Frontera*, 2nd ed. (San Francisco: Aunt Lute Books, 1999), 79–80.

12. W. E. B. Du Bois, *The Souls of Black Folk* (New York: Penguin, 1969), 43.

13. bell hooks, *Black Looks: Race and Representation* (Boston: South End Press, 1992), 21.

14. Yvonne Tasker, *Spectacular Bodies: Gender, Genre, and the Action Cinema* (New York: Routledge, 1993), 35.

15. Vivian Sobchack, *Screening Space: The American Science Fiction Film*, 2nd ed. (New Brunswick, NJ: Rutgers University Press, 2001); and Scott Bukatman, *Terminal Identity: The Virtual Subject in Postmodern Science Fiction* (Durham, NC: Duke University Press, 1993).

16. Beltrán, The New Hollywood Racelessness," 57–63.

17. Ibid., 54.

18. See, for instance, Lisa Nakamura, *Cybertypes: Race, Ethnicity, and Identity on the Internet* (New York: Routledge, 2002), 61–86; William Irwin, ed., *The Matrix and Philosophy: Welcome to the Desert of the Real* (Chicago: Open Court, 2002); Pat Mellencamp, "The Zen of Masculinity—Rituals of Heroism in *The Matrix*," in *The End of Cinema as We Know It*, ed. Jon Lewis (New York: NYU Press, 2001), 83–94; Peter Feng, "False and Double Consciousness: Race, Virtual Reality and the Assimilation of Hong Kong Action Cinema in *The Matrix*," in *Aliens R Us: The Other in Science Fiction Cinema*, ed. Ziauddin Sardar and Sean Cubitt (London: Pluto Press, 2002), 149–63; and Kim Hester-Williams, "NeoSlaves: Slavery, Freedom, and African American Apotheosis in *Candyman*, *The Matrix*, and *The Green Mile*," *Genders* 40 (2004), www.genders.org/g40/g40_williams.html.

19. LeiLani Nishime, "Is Keanu Reeves a Cyborg? APAs at the Century's End" (paper presented at the annual conference of the Society for Cinema Studies, Minneapolis, Minnesota, March 2003); and William Wu, *Yellow: Race in America beyond Black and White* (New York: Basic Books, 2002), 296.

20. Teresa Kay Williams, "The Theater of Identity: (Multi-)Race and Representation of Eurasians and Afroasians," in *American Mixed Race: The Culture of Microdiversity*, ed. Naomi Zack (Lanham, MD: Rowman and Littlefield, 1995), 86.

21. David Ansen, "Goodbye, Airhead," *Newsweek*, June 13, 1994, 52; Geoff Pevere, "Whoa! Betide Us," *Toronto Star*, February 18, 2005, D1; Jamie Portman, "Enigma: Superstar Whose Remoteness Tantalizes," *Windsor Star*, February 18, 2005, C3; Michael DeAngelis, *Gay Fandom and Crossover Stardom: James Dean, Mel Gibson, and Keanu Reeves* (Durham, NC: Duke University Press, 2001).

22. Jane Park, *Yellow Future: Oriental Style in Contemporary Hollywood Cinema* (Minneapolis: University of Minnesota Press, forthcoming).

23. See Richard Fung, "Looking for My Penis: The Eroticized Asian in Gay Video Porn," in *Bad Object-Choices*, ed., *How Do I Look: Queer Film and Video* (Seattle, WA: Bay Press, 1991), 145–68; David L. Eng, *Racial Castration: Managing Masculinity in Asian America* (Durham, NC: Duke University Press, 2001); and Daniel Kim, *Writing Manhood in Black and Yellow: Ralph Ellison, Frank Chin, and the Literary Politics of Identity* (Stanford, CA: Stanford University Press, 2005).

24. Mary Kittleson, "The New American Hero: Made in Japan," in *The Soul of Popular Culture: Looking at Contemporary Heroes, Myths, and Monsters*, ed. Mary Kittleson (Chicago: Open Court, 1998), 72.

25. DeAngelis, *Gay Fandom*. For analyses of masculinity in 1980s Hollywood, see Tasker, *Spectacular Bodies*; and Susan Jeffords, *Hard Bodies: Hollywood Masculinity in the Reagan Era* (New Brunswick, NJ: Rutgers University Press, 1994).

26. David Morley and Kevin Robins, *Spaces of Identity: Global Media, Electronic Landscapes and Cultural Boundaries* (London: Routledge, 1995), 169.

27. Richard Dyer, *White* (New York: Routledge, 1997), 28.

28. Steven Holden, "Dark and Dismal Doings on a Planet with 3 Suns," *New York Times*, February 18, 2000, sec. E, pt. 1, p. 12.

29. Diane Negra, *Off-White Hollywood: American Culture and Ethnic Female Stardom* (London: Routledge, 2001), 1–24.

30. Sarah Caden, "A Mass of Pure Muscle with a Soft Centre," *Sunday Independent,* July 17, 2005.

31. Stuart Andrews, "Games," *Sunday Times*, January 9, 2005, 32.

32. See Herman Beavers, "'The Cool Pose': Intersectionality, Masculinity, and Quiescence in the Comedy and Films of Richard Pryor and Eddie Murphy," in *Race and the Subject of Masculinities*, ed. Harry Stecopoulos and Michael Uebel (Durham, NC: Duke University Press, 1997), 253–85; and Patricia Williams, *Black Sexual Politics* (New York: Routledge, 2004), 149–80.

33. *Pitch Black* (David Twohy, 2000).

34. Ibid.

35. Ibid.

36. Ibid.

37. Leon Wynter, *American Skin: Pop Culture, Big Business, and the End of White America* (New York: Crown, 2002), 5.

# From Blaxploitation to Mixploitation
## Male Leads and Changing Mixed Race Identities

### Gregory T. Carter

Typecast as a pimp, O'Neal also had to battle another dilemma: light skin and straight hair. "People would tell him, Sorry, you don't look black enough for this role,'" said Audrey O'Neal. "He couldn't understand how people could think that way. He believed that art transcended color and race."[1]

While black filmgoers consider Vin one of our own, what's surprising is that white audiences have claimed him as well. So which side is right? Is he African American, Italian, Jewish or perhaps Hispanic? It's really an absurd question, but it is nevertheless relevant in light of the world we live in.[2]

Like Vin Diesel, The Rock's ambiguous features allow audiences to attach whatever label they like. However, unlike Diesel, The Rock has shown up at the NAACP Image Awards with his equally Brown wife and told JET about his Black and Hawaiian heritage—facts that, at least for Black folks, make him an honorary Negro.[3]

These quotations bring together three male action leads from the past thirty years. The last two, Vin Diesel and The Rock (Dwayne Johnson), rose to fame in the late 1990s as stars in movies such as *Pitch Black* (2000) and *The Mummy Returns* (2001), respectively. An important contributor to their fame is their mixed racial backgrounds; Diesel is black and Italian American, and The Rock is black and Samoan. The matter of their racial makeup is as central to their public image as the roles they take. The third, Ron O'Neal, played the lead in the Blaxploitation classic *Super Fly* (1972). Appropriate to the times, his racial makeup was never an issue; he was merely black. However, the preceding statement by his widow, Audrey O'Neal, reveals that his physical appearance ("light skin and straight hair") and, thus, his racial makeup, did influence his career. Information on his parentage is hard to come by, but the legacy of racial mixing is something that many African Americans face. Regardless of complexion, many blacks have known that they have a white forebear, perhaps in recent generations or perhaps farther back.[4] Light-skinned blacks with white ancestry may consider themselves black, but they often face a paradox of both acceptance and scrutiny by fellow blacks. However, O'Neal experienced this paradox outside the black community, where casting directors often considered him, as a light-skinned black, unable to portray a black person on screen. Though these dynamics still exist to this day, Vin Diesel and The Rock have been able to identify in a number of ways, and the mainstream and African American presses have deployed them accordingly, while in earlier decades Ron O'Neal was simply a black actor who had a hard time getting work.

A sea change has taken place between the early 1970s and the late 1990s in regard to mixed race identity. As a result of legislative gains for civil rights, changes in immigration laws, and the striking down of antimiscegenation laws, mixed race Americans gained a visibility that exceeded that during any other period in United States history, both statistically and via media representations.[5] These changes created more latitude regarding self-identification for a mixed race, public figure. A language for describing mixed race identity also developed, bringing terms such as "biracial," "multiracial," "MATA" (mark all that apply), "Cablinasian," "hapa," and so on, into the vernacular. Such discourse allows for the description and creation of identities appreciating multiplicity, in contrast to past decades, which operated on much more of an either-or basis.

What follows is an exploration of the public, racial identities of Ron O'Neal, Vin Diesel, and The Rock. What kinds of racial labels have the media placed on these stars? What identities have they created for themselves? Have they eschewed all racial markers? This chapter aims to explore these questions, using these three personalities as starting points. In the end, I argue that they have made choices that complicate the idea that they are part of a move toward "racelessness." According to philosopher Naomi Zack, mixed race Americans are by definition raceless: "Perhaps it is the very racelessness of being of mixed race in a biracial system that makes the possibility of such an identity valuable." [6] While some aspects of Vin Diesel's and Dwayne Johnson's careers comply with this dynamic, closer examination points to how contemporary mixed race film stars are not wholly part of a movement that aims to abandon old ways of racial thinking in the hopes of creating what Zack calls "the complete dissolution of the American concept of race." [7]

Opponents of this perspective on mixed race point out two flaws in its reasoning. First, mixed race does exist as a social reality in the United States. Rather than being able to choose affiliations independent of one's parent groups, mixed race people actually have doubly as much race, and possibly multiple connections to traditional racial groups. [8] Second, mixed race people do not dissolve race by their mere presence. [9]

The current popularity of Vin Diesel and Dwayne Johnson motivated this chapter's conception, leading to an inquiry into mixed identities of the past, hoping to gain insight into whether this phenomenon is more prevalent now than a generation ago. Reading press releases around Ron O'Neal's January 2004 death brought the last few decades into conversation, spotlighting a set of mixed, black male leads in action movies. In this exploration I avoid conflating O'Neal's, Diesel's, and Johnson's roles with their personal identities, analyzing their public statements and career paths more so than the content of their movies. I also accept that Vin Diesel and The Rock are racially mixed in ways much different than Ron O'Neal was, acknowledging that most around him would never have considered him biracial, multiracial, or any such label. However, statements about his physical features and racial challenges after *Super Fly* indicate that his white heritage influenced his life, no matter how distant. Similarly, I want to avoid suggesting that trends in racial identity have followed a linear, progressive vector since the 1970s, preventing racially mixed people from constructing other identities throughout the past. [10] Rather, in hopes of complicating the indictment of mixed race celebrities (and common folk) for abandoning race, this chapter focuses on the interplay of discourse, identity, and celebrity.

All three actors have had a presence in action films, although in different incarnations of the genre. Ron O'Neal starred in a seminal Blaxploitation movie, and the other two appear in what I call "Mixploitation" movies. Blaxploitation movies began with *Sweet Sweetback's Baadasssss*

*Song* (1971), written, directed, and produced by Melvin Van Peebles and initiating an ethic of creating film by, for, and about black people. Van Peebles's work follows the adventures of a hustler, sexual stud, and revolutionary on the run for having killed a cop in self-defense. The story appealed to urban black audiences at a time when dissatisfaction with the civil rights movement had progressed toward an embrace of black power. Black youth, in particular, eschewed the respectable gradualism of the prior generation for a viewpoint that threatened violence to attain racial justice and encouraged cultural nationalism to promote racial pride. A figure like Sweet Sweetback appealed to these trends, and the film became a success in independent black theaters. Eager to replicate Van Peebles's profits, Hollywood studios started to produce their own urban movies, such as *Shaft* (1971), *Super Fly* (1972), and *The Mack* (1973). These followed traditional genre formulas but put rebellious, black leads at the forefront. Even though they incorporated elements of ghetto life, racial pride, and black power to flesh out their black, urban aesthetic, they were mostly the products of white filmmakers, cheaply made to garner maximum profits. The formula proved very successful for the studios, staving off the effects of white flight from urban markets, satisfying the needs of African American filmgoers, and spreading the work of many black actors, directors, writers, and musicians. However, with their antiestablishment plots and rebellious antiheroes, Blaxploitation movies met with opposition from blacks and whites because of their "negative images" glorifying crime, drugs, and sex. Still, Blaxploitation exerted a stylistic influence on many later works, marking a shift in genres from niche products to the blockbusters in which Vin Diesel and The Rock would later star.[11]

"Mixploitation" is my own coinage to describe a set of contemporary movies that forefront mixed race movie stars. They often self-consciously present diverse, conventionally attractive casts, making the exotic looks of the mixed race stars a marketing point. These products cross genres but include movies such as *Honey* (2003, starring Jessica Alba), the *Matrix* trilogy (1999–2003, starring Keanu Reeves), *D.E.B.S.* (2003, 2004, Devon Aoki), and *Sin City* (2005, with Jessica Alba, Rosario Dawson, and Devon Aoki). Television shows like *Dark Angel* (2000–2002, Jessica Alba), *Half and Half*, and *Feast of All Saints* (2001) (both with Nicole Lyn) also fit this set. However, the action movies of Vin Diesel and Dwayne Johnson, including *The Fast and the Furious* (2001), *XXX* (2002), and *The Scorpion King* (2002), are most relevant because they share the action genre with Blaxploitation movies of the 1970s.[12] They feature superhuman male leads who are stronger, smarter, braver, and more charismatic than anyone else around them. They present a vision of diversity reflecting their times. Just as O'Neal and others worked within the imaginary ghettos, styles, and power dynamics of Blaxploitation movies, decades later Diesel and The Rock work within the aesthetics of contemporary, supposedly color-blind cityscapes. While the Blaxploitation ghetto was usually dystopic, contemporary milieus are often utopic to a fault. Beyond the appearances of multiculturalism they provide, the realities of our multicultural society—whether inequality, segregation, or prejudice—remain out of sight for the coalitions of racial and ethnic types who inhabit them.[13]

The greatest commonality between Blaxploitation and Mixploitation, however, is that the racial identities of the leads are the commodity the producers use to tap into young, diverse markets. Just as Blaxploitation leads conformed to a static, Afrocentric idea of blackness to gain ticket revenues from African Americans of the 1970s, Mixploitation's leads are racially ambiguous—sometimes seen as mixed race, sometimes black, sometimes white, sometimes Latino, depending on viewer knowledge—to gain the patronage of many, newly appreciated, racial markets of the 1990s. As Santiago Pozo, founder and president of Arenas Group and marketing consultant to Universal Pictures for *The Scorpion King* and *The Fast and the Furious*, says, "What we're seeing is the browning of America. So young moviegoers want black and brown heroes. When they see The Rock or Vin Diesel, they recognize themselves." Pozo made sure that the promotion of these movies targeted clubs and concerts with "street teams" resembling the movies' diverse casts.[14]

### *"Answer Me, You White-Lookin—": Ron O'Neal, the Link between Two Genres*

Ron O'Neal was born in Utica, New York, in 1937 and began acting as part of the interracial Karamu House theater in Cleveland, Ohio. He played lead roles in *Kiss Me, Kate* and *A Streetcar Named Desire* while supporting himself as a house painter, then moved to New York City in 1970, taught drama in Harlem, and starred in the Pulitzer Prize–winning play *No Place to Be Somebody* at the Joseph Papp Public Theatre. His performance attracted rave reviews and garnered the Drama Desk, Clarence Derwent, and Theatre World awards, as well as an Obie, the highest prize for an off-Broadway performance. In hopes of duplicating MGM's success with *Shaft*, which grossed $12.1 million in 1971, Warner Brothers distributed *Super Fly*, which Gordon Parks Jr. (who had helped his father with *Shaft*) directed with the help of independent funding from Sig Shore and a group of black businessmen. O'Neal's performance at the Public Theatre made him the preferred choice for the lead.[15]

In addition to his stage acting credits, O'Neal stands out from his fellow Blaxploitation leads through his physical appearance, namely, his light skin and straight hair. However, he identified as black. Evidently he hoped *Super Fly* would bring "hope" and "pride" to the black community. "My success is indeed a success for my people," he is quoted as saying.[16]

Donald Bogle praises O'Neal as more at ease in front of the camera than fellow Blaxploitation actors Richard Roundtree and more introspective than Jim Brown. Bogle characterizes O'Neal's Youngblood Priest in terms that also apply to the ornery tragic mulatto type.[17] In his restlessness, dissatisfaction, and brooding, Priest is like many tragic mulattoes.[18] However, *Super Fly* offers an intervention on the antebellum trope: whereas white audiences sympathized with the characteristics that came from the "white" part of the mulatto's parentage, including intelligence, fine features, and a love of freedom, within the Blaxploitation genre, black audiences got to appreciate him for his so-called black traits, including style, rhythm, and an easy physicality. At the end of *Super Fly*, Priest makes his money, beats the mobsters, and escapes the reach of the law.

While the film's success was exciting for O'Neal, ultimately his experience with *Super Fly* left him with misgivings. The movie also drew criticism from a coalition of African American organizations and concerned parents because of its supposed glamorization of crime and drug use. Meanwhile, according to his widow, O'Neal defended it as "a story about a man who wants to legitimize himself," to escape a lifestyle he ended up in for reasons beyond his own choices.[19] He directed the film's sequel, *Super Fly T.N.T.*, which he hoped others would see as more "positive," but it was a failure. Ultimately, O'Neal became bitter about the movie's negative reception, claiming in 2002, "There's nothing left to say about me or *Super Fly*."[20]

This disillusionment also stems from the typecasting he met after the 1972 film's success, which hampered his acting career for a number of years. Not only did he have a hard time getting roles because of the preeminence of his Youngblood Priest, but perceptions of his physical appearance also hampered his opportunities. Reuben Silver, who directed O'Neal in the Karamu House production of *A Streetcar Named Desire*, characterized him as an actor who resisted typecasting: "He was an actor of enormous talent and depth. He could play any character. But because he was African-American, he ran into trouble."[21] Writing for Black Entertainment Television (BET), Esther Iverem expands on this idea:

> While O'Neal enjoyed the celebrity that comes with such a starring role, his straight hair did not make him a ready heartthrob during an era of globular afros. . . . When he tried to get other roles after *Super Fly*, he was often told that he just didn't look Black enough. Most of the roles offered were more of the pusher and pimp variety, and he didn't want to do those anyway.[22]

Even though he believed that acting could transcend race, racial identities of the time bounded him.

Regarding the decades following *Super Fly*, O'Neal has said, "I didn't work. I would go two or three years without working at all. It was a little crazy for me. I was divorced during that period—I think it probably helped break up my marriage."[23] Of the supporting roles he did garner, he has said, "Frankly, I've not been pleased with most of what I've had to do. I have a considerable amount of experience, and what they've asked me to do has not demanded that much of me."[24] The more notable of his post–*Super Fly* roles include the television show *The Equalizer*, the cold war era fantasy *Red Dawn* (1984), and the Blaxploitation reunion vehicle *Original Gangstas* (1996), which also featured Fred Williamson, Jim Brown, Pam Grier, and Richard Roundtree. Then, in the middle and late 1980s, he began to be cast in a variety of ethnic roles other than African American, ones that were Malaysian, Arabic, and Mexican.[25] This is a pattern Vin Diesel would follow later, apparently with the same belief that art transcends color and race. However, Diesel would embrace racial ambiguity above all other labels. He would also find it easier to play various ethnicities, so much so that it has become his trademark.

### "My Drawback Is Now My Biggest Selling Feature": Vin Diesel, the Every-Man[26]

In *Saving Private Ryan* (1998), Vin Diesel played Italian American army private Adrian Caparzo. His character in *The Fast and the Furious* had an Italian surname (Toretto), but some writers described him as Cuban American.[27] In *Knockaround Guys* (2001), he played a Jewish mob strong arm. His other notable roles, including characters in *Pitch Black, XXX*, and

*The Pacifier* (2005), have Anglo-American names that may connote African American, but the films provide no other clues to their racial identity. In each, Vin Diesel looks exactly the same—shaved head, muscle-T, and bouncer's scowl. His grumbling, New York City accent serves them all, regardless of the racial or ethnic signifiers the roles apply to him. The constancy of Diesel's appearance and performances foregrounds the fact that these movies are built around his ambiguous physical appearance and his urbane, muscular qualities.

Meanwhile, the press has called him a "New American," and "Hollywood's first bona fide action star of the new millennium."[28] The studios certainly profit from marketing Vin Diesel, and he has reaped benefits from his films' successes. The entertainment industry's exploitation of his exotic looks has opened up spaces for new modes of identification that Ron O'Neal could not explore in the 1970s. The changes in society and the recently acknowledged marketability of racially ambiguous celebrities removed him from the experiences he portrays in *Multi-Facial*, but this does not mean that racialization has ended. As Rob Cohen, his director in *The Fast and the Furious* and *XXX*, says, "He's a new American. You don't know what he is, and it doesn't even matter, because he's everybody. Everybody looks at Vin and goes, 'I see myself.'"[29] Cohen's statement taps into a wish for the irrelevancy of racial categories, as well as the idea that the actor is a blank racial slate onto which any identity can be applied.

Born in 1967, the year that the Supreme Court invalidated the nation's remaining antimiscegenation laws, Vin Diesel (born Mark Vincent) grew up in Maspeth, a subsidized artists' community in New York City. His mother is Italian American, and his father was probably African American. What complicates Diesel's background is that he does not know for sure (or chooses not to say). Diesel has admitted, "I don't know what I am. . . . I'm a combination of many things."[30] He elaborated, "I never knew my biological father. I've always had less information that [*sic*] I would have liked to have had. All I know from my mother is that I have connections to many different cultures."[31] However, his stepfather is African American, and Diesel credits him with shaping his upbringing: "The man who raised me is black. Culturally he made me who I am. He was a theatre director so he also guided me artistically."[32] Even if Diesel chooses to shape his public image in some way divergent from the one-drop rule, his biological father, his adoptive father, and his upbringing make his minority, racialized background a reality for him in private and public, especially with those who possess knowledge of his mixed background.

We can find a more intimate view of Diesel's identification in his own film, *Multi-Facial* (1995). This twenty-minute short follows Mike, a young, mixed race actor, during a day of auditioning in New York City. Mike moves from casting call to casting call, trying out for roles that are Italian American, Latino, and African American. He never claims to be any of these ethnicities himself, but others assume he is. However, he constantly runs into snags: his performance of an Italian "guido" comes across more homophobic than he would like; an actress slips into Spanish, which he cannot speak, during their dialogue; a casting director tells him he's too light-skinned, and so on. At his last audition for the day, he performs a monologue reflecting on seeing his father act, a childhood experience that inspired him to be an actor. Mike offers a commentary on his performances in the other scenes, suggesting that he wants to become "just an actor." In the closing shots, Mike overhears a young actress at a diner lament about appearing "too blond" and seems to appreciate that everyone has challenges. The film features some rich exchanges between characters concerning acting and racial identity without patronizing the viewer with an explanation of its main theme: racially mixed actors can qualify for a variety of roles, but society's racial preconceptions can stop them from actually landing them. Diesel has stated that *Multi-Facial* is an autobiographical work and that the challenges facing Mike were his own.[33] They were also Ron O'Neal's through the 1970s and 1980s, showing that change in the industry—as in the outside world—is slow and fitful. For actors like O'Neal and Diesel (and his fictional counterpart), race persists, as casting directors, fans, and journalists insist on categorizing them.

However, Diesel's break came after Steven Spielberg saw the short film at Cannes and cast him in *Saving Private Ryan*, allowing Diesel to fulfill Mike's goal: to take on whatever roles (and ethnicities) he could. Regarding the shift in his acting career, Diesel has said, "Whereas that ambiguity might have been a curse to me earlier, it's actually a blessing now. . . . Since *Private Ryan*, I've been feeling some heat around me as an actor and acting is the one time I am sure about my identity. It's very therapeutic because it's there on paper who I am."[34] Diesel has made a policy of refusing to state his racial makeup. When required to describe himself racially, he calls himself "multicultural," an indication that he equates *multicultural* with *mixed race* (or *multiracial*). In interviews, conversations about his racial makeup usually end at his prompting, when he says something like, "Race shouldn't matter. I just want you to come see my movies," or "I want to keep my mystery. It's not that I'm hiding anything. It's just that I would rather spend time talking about more productive things."[35] Here we have an admission that he is being enigmatic, an allusion to the fact that he does not know or does not wish to share his exact racial makeup, and a maneuver to guide the conversation back to promoting the movies he stars in. Through his secrecy and his dismissal of race, Diesel is protecting a central ingredient in the Mixploitation formula, his own racial makeup. To be more forthcoming would make his ambiguity less profitable.[36]

Ironically, this tactic has narrowed the space in which he can display what sociologist Kerry Rockquemore calls "protean identity," or the "capacity to move between and among several racial identities that are interchangeable. Individuals may move fluidly among black, white, and/or multiracial identities, using whichever identity may be situationally appropriate for a specific interactional context."[37] In regard to Vin Diesel, he portrays a wide number of ethnicities in his roles, resulting in a screen image that is consistently ambiguous. However, by reining in the conversation on his racial background, he has limited the breadth of identities he can assume. His nearly identical performances contribute to this, as do the constant physical appearance and demeanor I mentioned earlier. Beyond his screen appearances, the public image he creates in interviews also limits him. Rarely does he attribute some fact about his background to his present life, nor can he speak about synthesizing various parts of his racial identity. The only identity he can claim is—"my secret." In the end, Vin Diesel may have "connections to many cultures," but there is no telling if he can identify with any of them in public.

### *"I Can Do Anything But Make a White Baby, and Even That Maybe I Could": The Rock*[38]

In contrast to Vin Diesel, Dwayne Johnson, aka The Rock, has met with wide praise from the black press, namely, *Ebony* and *Jet* magazines, and BET. This is because of his clear embrace of blackness in his public image, accepting the same things those who promote racelessness eschew. Born in 1972 to an African American father and a Samoan American mother, Dwayne Johnson was raised in a family of professional wrestlers, including his father, Rocky Johnson, and his maternal grandfather, Pete "High Chief" Maivia. As he says, "I've never been anything but open about my family and where I come from, and I don't think it has really ever been an issue for me."[39] After growing up in Hawai'i and other places, Johnson entered the University of Miami as a starting defensive end. Injuries ended his college football career, and he turned to professional wrestling, rising in the World Wrestling Federation as The Rock, "the people's champion." As a charismatic and comedic performer, The Rock guest hosted a top-rated episode of *Saturday Night Live*, then appeared in *The Mummy Returns* (2001), which parlayed into a spin-off, *The Scorpion King* (2002), and leads in *The Rundown* (2003) and *Walking Tall* (2004).

While Vin Diesel's reticence toward his racial identity has led to less coverage from the black press, Johnson has received more attention from these stalwarts. For example, in a cover story in *Ebony* he is praised for appreciating and representing the black race, marrying an "equally brown" wife, and respecting his parents. Likewise, BET.com has expressed admiration for his going to black-themed award ceremonies and explaining his racial makeup in clear, blood-quantum terms—things Vin Diesel abstains from.

Whereas Diesel's enigmatic stance has allowed him to take on a variety of roles and thus explore a variety of identities, Johnson's traditional position has made him a more accessible celebrity. Publications have described him as "pretty humble, and mellow, and thoughtful," "affable and animated, a gentleman in the classic manners sense," and "an exuberant player, full of laughter and motion."[40] Some writers and spectators have wondered about his racial makeup. However, Johnson is happy to explain it, stating in a 2003 cover article for *GQ*, "I am very proud of my Samoan/ Black Heritage, so *mahalo* for helping me share it with the world!"[41] In fact, Andrew Corsello, the article's author, admires Johnson's approach, commenting, "There is nothing about his public image that you are not meant to understand. . . . Mysteriousness is anathema to all that is The Rock. His stardom survives on transparency,"[42] in direct opposition to Diesel's inscrutability.

Likewise, while Diesel's autobiographical statement, *Multi-Facial*, explores the everyday challenges and nuances of being mixed race, Johnson's autobiography, *The Rock Says . . .* (2000) sets forth a straightforward history of his life. He states that he is proud of his roots and has deep respect for both his black parent and his Samoan parent. He describes his girlfriend's Cuban American family, who wanted her to date white, as "a bit less enthusiastic" about him than his would be about her. Johnson was hurt over this brush with prejudice because it was an insult to his family, but was happy that the ice thawed a bit after he and Dany married. Later, he joined a wrestling team called the Nation of Domination, which he describes as "almost like the Black Panthers in terms of ideology, or at least in terms of its dislike of white America . . . a hard-core, militant, black group."[43] Fans, however, describe the crew as "a parody of Louis Farrakhan's Nation of Islam."[44] In any case, the former World Wrestling Federation star was able to transform his reputation from "babyface" to "heel" through his membership in the troupe, and this transformation now serves as part of The Rock's backstory.[45]

Regardless of appearing at both the Democratic and Republican national conventions in 2000 as part of the World Wrestling Federation's Smackdown Your Vote! drive and joking that he could become president one day (a subtly nativist statement promising to surpass Arnold Schwarzenegger's gubernatorial victory), whether Johnson has a political framework to his mixed identity is a mystery. Like any shrewd celebrity, he has kept his politics a blank. In fact, any beliefs he may have regarding being a minority in America are unknown. What does come through, especially in black publications, is the fans' hope that he will break down racial barriers and become "the first big box-office action hero who is a man of color."[46] People like his "positive image" and his candor regarding his racial makeup. If his public statements indicate a constellation of beliefs, then most what comes through are hard work, good humor, and normative family relationships, values fans and writers find very acceptable.

These themes continue in *Walking Tall* (2004), in which Johnson plays Chris Vaughn, a Special Forces soldier who returns to his hometown in Washington State with the aspiration to work at the local sawmill. After discovering the closure of the plant, he also learns of the prostitution, unemployment, and gambling that have taken over the town. The locus of these iniquities is the nightclub owned by a former high school classmate (also the inheritor and closer of the mill). Moral outrage over teen drug use leads Vaughn to ransack the business, attacking both employees and property with a two-by-four. At his trial, he chooses to defend himself, promises to clean up the town, and gains an acquittal. With a piece of lumber in hand, Vaughn becomes sheriff and purges the town of its corruptors. All the while, the character's easygoing style (along with his chiseled features and impressive muscles) make the individualism, vigilantism, and breakdown of due process palatable.[47]

Also notable in *Walking Tall* is how at ease Vaughn is in the predominantly white town. High school friends value his football skills, and others respect his military service. His problems are villainous individuals, not institutional racism or petty prejudice. In the grand scheme, this feeds the contemporary wish to move beyond race as a relevant topic, focusing on individual success (or villainy) rather than group inequities. But on the interpersonal level, Vaughn is racially marked via his interracial family. His white mother and black father stick together and support their son through his encounters. He also has a sister and a nephew who resemble the others in the family. Their presence gives the movie's hero a history; while his family members are the only racial minorities in town, this is plausible in many American locales. *Walking Tall* builds a vision of diversity around Dwayne Johnson, whether viewers notice it or not. This milieu is much different than those featuring Vin Diesel, which take place on the streets of Los Angeles, in underground nightclubs, and stranded in outer space, but it is an idealized multicultural aesthetic, nonetheless.

### "Forget Black, Forget White. The Future Is Generation E(thnically) A(mbiguous)."[48] Or Is It?

The preceding quotation comes from one of several recent feature articles that explicitly addressed what some have known for years: Americans are fascinated with racially mixed people, and marketing firms are using this to sell movies, fashion, and print media itself.[49] These writers often place stars like Diesel and Johnson, featured in contemporary Mixploitation films, at the forefront of a trend toward the end of race as a meaningful descriptor. Even Jon Stewart has joked that "with an increasingly diverse population and an evolutionary process creating larger, hairless Homo Sapiens with gigantic craniums," the American of the future will look like Vin Diesel.[50] However, exploring the public, racial identities of Vin Diesel and Dwayne Johnson, along with Ron O'Neal, star of *Super Fly* (1972), reveals more about the identities the media place on racially ambiguous stars, the identities they create for themselves, and the identities they cannot escape. O'Neal's physical features put him at the middle of a paradox many African Americans face. His light skin and straight hair belied racial mixing in his background, even if his parents were not of two different racial groups. In the 1970s, this made him black, even if Hollywood did not consider him "black enough" to play the roles available to African Americans at the time. For much of his career after *Super Fly*, he was unable to get roles beyond his signature performance in that Blaxploitation classic.

O'Neal's challenges were faced by other racially ambiguous actors well into the 1990s, as Vin Diesel's autobiographical film, *Multi-Facial*, attests.

However, by the mid-1990s, both Hollywood and Madison Avenue realized the utility of racially ambiguous stars in selling movies, fashion, and advertising. A prominent role in Steven Spielberg's *Saving Private Ryan* helped Diesel's career, and now he performs a variety of ethnicities. He conceals his racial makeup more than most racially mixed actors, which protects it as a commodity but also limits the modes of identity he can take in his public life. For some fans, this may be irrelevant. For movie producers, this helps promote what Mary Beltrán calls "the new Hollywood racelessness." While fans may know he is mixed, or at least some sort of minority, the racialization of his public image continues, regardless. Even as enigmas, race and mixed race have been lived realities in Vin Diesel's career.

The Rock, who stars in a number of Mixploitation action movies contemporaneous with Diesel's, takes a more conventional approach toward his background, sharing his racial makeup with the public. This has led to an embrace by the African American press, as well as a characterization antithetical to Diesel's inscrutability. Both are equally popular, starring in movies that market their mixed looks to the public. However, The Rock's openness has contributed to a much different kind of public persona, both traditional and modern at the same time. The 2005 remake of *Walking Tall* reflects this, placing Mixploitation elements in a rural setting and providing the lead with a mixed family, rather than suggesting he appeared, autochthonous and ready to lead a coalition of attractive, diverse youth down the speedway, onto the dance floor, or across the desert. *Walking Tall's* deployment of a mixed race movie star results in an innovative, yet idealized, vision of diversity in middle America.

These developments are unfolding at this very moment. Vin Diesel's and The Rock's careers are still developing, and if Arnold Schwarzenegger's career serves as a model for male action-movie stars, they may be around for a long time, changing movie genres and public images as the governor of California has done. At the same time, our understanding of Blaxploitation, its stars, and the period that spawned them changes as scholars, fans, and producers continue to evoke them. The hopes of this chapter have been to shed light on the current moment, as well on racial identities in the early 1970s. By putting Ron O'Neal, Vin Diesel, and The Rock in conversation with each other, this chapter shows how the racelessness ideal is an effort some participate in more than others. Most important, exploring three racially ambiguous male leads guides us in understanding how, every day, mixed race Americans negotiate the discourse of racial identity in public life.

NOTES

1. John Petkovic, "Ron O'Neal, Star of Film 'Superfly,' Dies; Acting Career Began on Cleveland Stage," *Plain Dealer*, January 16, 2004.

2. Gil Robertson, "The Robertson Treatment: Vin Diesel—to Thy Own Self Be True," *Sentinel*, August 28, 2002.

3. James Hill, *Bet.Com—the Rock Rules "the Rundown,"* BET.com, September 26, 2003, www.bet.com/articles/1,c5gb7535-8359,00.html (accessed May 12, 2004).

4. The experiences of Malcolm X, Charles Mingus, and Billie Holiday reflect this. Within my own family history, those of my grandparents' generation knew they had a white parent or grandparent but rarely spoke about it. Billie Holiday, *Lady Sings the Blues* (Garden City, NY: Doubleday, 1956); Charles Mingus, *Beneath the Underdog; His World as Composed by Mingus* (New York: Knopf, 1971); Malcolm X and Alex Haley, *The Autobiography of Malcolm X* (New York: Grove Press, 1965).

5. In addition to the social changes that precipitated from the 1960s legislation, three other occasions marked shifts in public opinion on mixed race. First, *Time* magazine's New Face of America issue, with its computer-generated cover star, which made racial mixing safe to talk about; second, Tiger Woods's Masters victory in 1997 and his coinage of "Cablinasian" on *The Oprah Show*; and, third, the debates around the inclusion of a "Multiracial" category on the 2000 census. "The New Face of America," *Time*, April 2001.

6. Naomi Zack, *American Mixed Race: The Culture of Microdiversity* (Lanham, MD: Rowman and Littlefield, 1995), x.

7. Naomi Zack, *Race and Mixed Race* (Philadelphia: Temple University Press, 1993), 163-64.

8. Ronald R. Sundstrom, "Being and Being Mixed Race," *Social Theory and Practice* 27, no. 2 (2001): 285–307.

9. George G. Sanchez, "Y Tu Que? (Y2k): Latino History in the New Millennium," in *Latinos: Remaking America*, ed. M. M. Suarez-Orozco and M. M. Paez (Berkeley: University of California Press, 2002); Paul R. Spickard, "Does Multiraciality Lighten? Me-Too Ethnicity and the Whiteness Trap," in *Crossing Lines: Race and Mixed Race across the Geohistorical Divide*, ed. Marc Coronado, Rudy P. Guevarra Jr., Jeffrey Moniz, and Laura Furlan Szanto (Santa Barbara, CA: Multi-Ethnic Student Outreach, 2003).

10. For example, the Harlem Renaissance writer Jean Toomer, who descended from New Orleans and Washington, D.C., "mulatto elite," formed an identity that encompassed *all* of the above, not *none* of the above, or *one* of the above. Langston Hughes acknowledged his white parentage but strongly identified as black. On the other hand, writer and book critic Anatole Broyard racially passed for white until his death in 1990. Henry Louis Gates, "The Passing of Anatole Broyard," in *Thirteen Ways of Looking at a Black Man*, ed. Henry Louis Gates (New York: Random House, 1997); Arnold Rampersad, *The Life of Langston Hughes*, 2nd ed., 2 vols. (Oxford:

Oxford University Press, 2002); Jean Toomer and Frederik L. Rusch, *A Jean Toomer Reader: Selected Unpublished Writings* (New York: Oxford University Press, 1993).

11. Harry M. Benshoff and Sean Griffin, *America on Film: Representing Race, Class, Gender, and Sexuality at the Movies* (Malden, MA: Blackwell, 2004), 85-88; Donald Bogle, *Toms, Coons, Mulattoes, Mammies, and Bucks: An Interpretive History of Blacks in American Films*, 4th ed. (New York: Continuum, 2001), 234-42; Ed Guerrero, *Framing Blackness: The African American Image in Film, Culture and the Moving Image* (Philadelphia: Temple University Press, 1993), 85-111.

12. In *Pitch Black*, Riddick (Diesel) develops from a ruthless killer in transit to a maximum-security prison to helping the heroine escape. In *The Fast and the Furious*, Toretto (Diesel) goes from highway robbery to helping the cop investigating the robberies. Diesel's protagonist in *XXX*, a notorious renegade, faces conscription into the National Security Agency, then warms up to the duty. *The Scorpion King* tells the story of the sole survivor of his ethnic group who rises to lead a coalition of darker minorities to overthrow a distinctively Anglo-Saxon despot—to become ruler himself. The story lines are devoid of illicit behavior, and often result in pro-law, pro-patriarchy, and nationalist messages, even if the main character starts out as a rebel.

13. Mary Beltrán's "The New Hollywood Racelessness" has been instructive in describing the "aesthetic trappings of cultural creolization." "The New Hollywood Racelessness: Only the Fast, Furious, (and Multiracial) Will Survive," *Cinema Journal* 44, no. 2 (2005): 50-67.

14. Street teams have been groups of volunteers, usually fans, who hand out flyers and plaster messages on billboards. Professional firms have co-opted this originally grassroots tactic in recent years, offering prizes in exchange for the labor to promote music, movies, and DVD releases. Patrick Goldstein, "Multiethnic Action Heroes Prove Brown Is Beautiful," *Los Angeles Times*, June 9, 2002.

15. Internet Movie Database, "Business Data for *Shaft*" (1971), 2006, www. imdb.com/title/tt0067741/business (accessed December 12, 2006); Guerrero, *Framing Blackness*, 95; Pierre Perrone, "Obituary: Ron O'Neal; Emblematic Star of Blaxploitation Films," *Independent*, January 20, 2004; John Petkovic, "Home Video; Long Condemned, 'Superfly' Really Tells a Complex Story," *Plain Dealer*, January 25, 2004; Petkovic, "Ron O'Neal, Star of Film 'Superfly,' Dies; "Remembering the Original Real Superfly—Ron O'Neal," *Free Press*, February 4, 2004.

16. Interview on *Super Fly* DVD.

17. Donald Bogle, *Blacks in American Films and Television: An Encyclopedia*, Garland Reference Library of the Humanities, vol. 604 (New York: Garland, 1988), 436.

18. For further discussion on the tragic mulatto, see Werner Sollors's *Neither Black Nor White Yet Both: Thematic Explorations of Interracial Literature* (New York: Oxford University Press, 1997), the end-all, be-all on the mulatto in literature; as well as Bogle, *Toms, Coons, Mulattoes, Mammies, and Bucks*; Sterling A. Brown, "Negro Character as Seen by White Authors," *Journal of Negro Education*

2, no. 2 (1933): 179–203; Manthia Diawara, *Black American Cinema*, AFI Film Readers (New York: Routledge, 1993); Jane Gaines, *Fire and Desire: Mixed-Race Movies in the Silent Era* (Chicago: University of Chicago Press, 2001).

19. Petkovic, "Home Video"; interview on *Super Fly* DVD.

20. Wil Haygood, "As 'Superfly,' Ron O'Neal Played All Too Well," *Washington Post*, January 17, 2004, Esther Iverem, *Bet.Com—Ron O'Neal of Superfly Was No Ordinary Negro*, BET.com, 2004, www.bet.com/articles/1,c5gb8512-9363,00.html (accessed May 12, 2004); Petkovic, "Ron O'Neal, Star of Film Superfly, Dies."

21. Quoted in Petkovic, "Ron O'Neal, Star of Film Superfly, Dies."

22. Iverem, *Bet.Com—Ron O'Neal of Superfly Was No Ordinary Negro*.

23. "Remembering the Original Real Superfly—Ron O'Neal."

24. David Walker, "Remembering Ron O'Neal: 1937-2004," Willamette Week Online, 2004, www.wweek.com/story.php?story=4739 (accessed May 12, 2004).

25. In Hollywood casting, this practice of interchangeable ethnicities has existed since the era of silent film (for example, in movies starring Ramón Novarro, in which he played Spanish, Egyptian, and Roman ethnicities, among others) and persists to this day (for example, with Samoan actor Cliff Curtis, who has played Dominican, Italian, and Iraqi characters). However, mixed black actors have only recently been part of this phenomenon, perhaps because of segregation in the industry, or because of black racial pride that would compel them to want black roles only. "Ron O'Neal," IMDB.com, 2004, www.imdb.com/name/nm0641938/ (accessed May 12, 2004).

26. Louis B. Hobson, "Diesel Power," *Calgary Sun*, February 13, 2000.

27. Anne Crémieux, "Vin Diesel: A Colorless Actor for a Colorblind America?" Africultures, 2005, http://africultures.com/index.asp?menu=affiche_article&no=3781 (accessed December 12, 2006); "Vin Diesel Shifts Acting Career into High Gear in `The Fast and the Furious,'" *Jet*, July 9, 2001.

28. David Denby, "Action!" *New Yorker*, August 19, 2002; Robertson, "The Robertson Treatment"; Kam Williams, "Hollywood Action Star and Sex Symbol Remains a Modest Guy from New York," *Afro-American*, August 23, 2002.

29. Quoted in Williams, "Hollywood Action Star and Sex Symbol Remains a Modest Guy from New York."

30. Ibid.

31. Ibid.

32. Hobson, "Diesel Power."

33. Ibid.

34. "Buffed, Bold and Bad: Hollywood's Black Action Heroes," *Jet*, July 29, 2002; Hobson, "Diesel Power."

35. Gil Robertson, "The Chameleon," *Savoy*, September 30, 2002, 56; Kam Williams, "Ron O'Neal of Superfly Was No Ordinary Negro," *Afro-American*, August 23, 2002, B1.

36. Jess Cagle, "The Next Action Hero: It's Not Just Vin Diesel's Brawn but His

Multiethnic Background That Gives the *XXX* Star Mass Appeal," *Time*, August 5, 2002; One Race Films, www.oneracefilms.com/ (accessed June 5, 2006); "Halle's Big Year!" *Ebony*, November 2002; Robertson, "The Chameleon"; Robertson, "The Robertson Treatment."

37. Kerry Ann Rockquemore, "Deconstructing Tiger Woods: The Promise and the Pitfalls of Multiracial Identity," in *The Politics of Multiracialism: Challenging Racial Thinking*, ed. Heather M. Dalmage (Albany: State University of New York Press, 2004), 129–30.

38. Erik Hedegaard, "Oh Mummy! Wrestling's Top Baby Face Goes All Out to Put Hollywood in a Headlock," *Rolling Stone*, June 7, 2001.

39. Terry Lawson, "The Rock Sticks Up for Himself in 'Walking Tall' Remake," *Free Press*, March 2004.

40. Andrew Corsello, "I Am the Rock," *GQ*, October 2003' Hedegaard, "Oh Mummy!"; Wesley Morris, "The Rock by Any Other Name? Dwayne Johnson, Movie Star, Is Serious about His On-Screen Career. But That Doesn't Mean the 'Walking Tall' Actor Is Leaving the Wrestling World Behind," *Globe*, March 28, 2004.

41. Corsello, "I Am the Rock."

42. Ibid.

43. Zondra Hughes, "The Rock Talks about Race, Wrestling and Women," *Ebony*, July 2001, 32.

44. "Nation of Domination Lyrics—We Are the Nation Lyrics," STLyrics.com, www.stlyrics.com/lyrics/wwfforceableentry/wearethenation.htm (accessed May 12, 2004); Rock and Joseph Layden, *The Rock Says—: The Most Electrifying Man in Sports-Entertainment* (New York: Regan Books, 2000); "WrestleView.Com— Nation of Domination FAQ," WrestleView.com, www.wrestleview.com/info/FAQ/nod.shtml (accessed May 12, 2004).

45. Rock and Layden, *The Rock Says*.

46. Yolanda D. Boone, "The Rock," *Ebony*, September 2001.

47. Ironically, one writer calls the original, 1973 version of *Walking Tall* "hixploitation." Doug Mosurak, "Plot Summary for Walking Tall" (1973), Internet Movie Database, www.imdb.com/title/tt0070895/plotsummary (accessed June 22, 2006).

48. John Arlidge, "Focus: The New Melting Pot: Forget Black, Forget White. The Future Is Generation E.A.," *Observer*, January 4, 2004.

49. As Ron Berger, the chief executive of Euro RSCG MVBMS Partners in New York, an advertising agency and trend research company whose clients include Polaroid and Yahoo, says, "Today what's ethnically neutral, diverse or ambiguous has tremendous appeal. . . . Both in the mainstream and at the high end of the marketplace, what is perceived as good, desirable, successful is often a face whose heritage is hard to pin down." Ruth La Ferla, "Generation E.A.: Ethnically Ambiguous," *New York Times*, December 28, 2003.

50. Jon Stewart, Ben Karlin, and David Javerbaum, *America (the Book): A Citizen's Guide to Democracy Inaction* (New York: Warner Books, 2004), 171.

*Part IV*

||||||||||||||||||||||||||||||||||||||||||||||||||||

# Generation Mix?
## *Shifting Meanings of Mixed Race Figures*

III

# Detecting Difference in *Devil in a Blue Dress*
## *The Mulatta Figure, Noir, and the Cinematic Reification of Race*

### *Aisha D. Bastiaans*

The debate among critics as to whether or not film noir can be regarded as a genre and, if so, how to periodize the genre, has yet to be resolved.[1] When frustrated film scholars assert that film noir can be most easily identified by academics and audiences alike as a visual style, those scholars suggest that difficult though film noir may be to articulate as an idea, *you know it when you see it*. A similar tension between a slippery definition, on the one hand, and characteristics that are easily and instantly recognizable, on the other, animates race as a mode of perception and ideology of difference that persists despite inconsistent logic and troubled classifications. How do *we know race when we see it*? In this chapter I examine how the neonoir film *Devil in a Blue Dress* (1995) engages the viewer in the reification of race by taking for granted the legibility of tropes of difference.

I am most fascinated with the subtle and quotidian ways in which race is reified in popular film, how we breathe life into racial categories from moment to moment through a dynamic exchange between film and viewer. Film noir, a genre with visual characteristics as readily recognizable as its defining historical and narrative boundaries are fuzzy, relies heavily on a viewer's familiarity with conventions of narrative, characterization, and visual and verbal style. Film noir depends upon a habituated visual and narrative logic in which the viewer keeps a watchful eye for clues that promise to reveal a greater truth and through which the viewer is driven to expose hidden meanings.[2]

Film noir's cultural legibility and will to knowledge acquire deeper significance when grafted, as they are in *Devil in a Blue Dress*, onto race as a
mode of perception and ideology of difference. The habituated visual and
narrative logics of race similarly rely upon a viewer's careful observation
of clues. In *Devil in a Blue Dress*, the well-known noir tropes that engage
a viewer in the film's mystery imbricate the wonted—and wanted—tropes
of difference requisite to cinematic processes of racialization that are also,
at base, searches for truth. I interrogate the peculiar confluence between
investigatory modes of perception particular to the film medium, the film
noir genre, and the mulatta figure in *Devil in a Blue Dress* and the ways
in which these investigatory modes of perception conspire to (re)produce
race as an ideology of difference.[3]

Based on Walter Mosley's 1990 novel of the same name, *Devil in a Blue
Dress* introduces Ezekiel "Easy" Rollins (Denzel Washington), a black ex-
GI who has recently migrated from the South to Los Angeles hoping to
take advantage of the post–World War II boom to buy a house, work in
industry, and attain the American Dream. Easy falls into amateur sleuth-
ing when hired to find a missing white woman, Daphne Monet (Jennifer
Beals). He quickly finds himself in a dark underworld of criminals, corrupt politicians, and racist cops. We come to learn that the web of murder, blackmail, and counterblackmail in which Easy is caught turns on the
fact that Daphne is passing for white.

Before she disappeared, Daphne was engaged to a rich white man
named Todd Carter, who suddenly and inexplicably broke off the engagement and dropped out of the mayor's race. His opponent, Matthew Terell, has the unsavory Dewitt Albright hire Easy to find Daphne. Daphne,
it turns out, is acquiring photographs proving that Terell is a pedophile.
Daphne intends to use the photographs to counterblackmail Terell, who
knows Daphne is passing, so that she can resume her relationship with
Todd Carter and Carter can reenter the mayor's race. In his search for
Daphne, Easy is caught up in murders, betrayals, and cover-ups. The concealment of Daphne's true racial identity precipitates confusion and death
even in this already violent and perverse noir landscape.

Film noir concerns the solving of mysteries, often mysteries linked
to mistaken, dual, or secret identities. The mulatta figure, especially the
woman who passes for white, bears a vexed relationship to racial classification, inciting the search for signs of racial identity. Framed by the
detective's gaze, Daphne Monet is cast as a mystery to be solved. How
does *Devil in a Blue Dress* engage the viewer in this attempt to solve the

problem of the mulatta's place in the racial order? If hard-boiled detective fiction is about the pursuit of knowledge, what are the implications of this will to knowledge for the reification of race? If, as the film's trailer asserts, "Ezekiel Rawlins is searching for the truth," how does he, and the viewer, uncover racial truths? How does film, as a medium that relies on visual and discursive shorthand, depend upon the viewer's desire for, and adeptness in, perceiving racial difference? And what is the role of the mulatta figure in this process of reifying race?

Close reading *Devil in a Blue Dress*, I explicate cinematic representations as dynamic processes that involve film and viewer in a cultural exercise of discerning racial and gendered characteristics, particularly when these social markers are obscured. I examine the ways in which the film engages the viewer-as-detective to demonstrate that race, as a mode of perception and ideology of difference, must continually discover and expose signs of the very difference it presumes. In elaborating how crucial the cultural legibility of film noir tropes and tropes of difference are to the viewer's participation in the racialization of Daphne Monet, I consider the implications of Daphne's transformation from femme fatale to tragic mulatto. I conclude by establishing a tension between the ideological work performed by the mulatta figure and the critical work the figure enables. I argue that although the mulatta figure is deployed in popular culture to reinscribe racial boundaries, the figure can be critically taken up to expose how race obscures its own contradictions and contingency.

## Detecting Difference

Adapted and directed by black filmmaker Carl Franklin, based on a hard-boiled detective novel by black author Walter Mosley, featuring a largely black cast, and starring Denzel Washington, *Devil in a Blue Dress* is set in post–World War II Los Angeles. This City of Angels oozes with the atmospheric characters, costumes, and cadences of classic film noir, but the film's nostalgia is held in tension with the film's post–civil rights critique of racism and segregation. *Devil in a Blue Dress* seems, then, to typify, and traverse, two trajectories: the 1990s ascendance of neonoir and the 1990s black film wave.

Heralded by the film *Body Heat* (1981), neonoir production increased steadily throughout the 1980s and peaked in the early to mid-1990s. [4] The neonoir trend included contemporary noirs, featuring established noir

*Still of Jennifer Beals in* Devil in a Blue Dress.

character types and narrative conventions but set in the present and shot in a contemporary visual style,[5] and "retro noirs," set in the past, featuring the narrative conventions and visual style of noir, and evoking nostalgia for the forties and fifties.[6] These remakes of classic film noirs, adaptations of hard-boiled novels, and original films cast in the noir mold share "a quality of deliberate allusiveness . . . a certain wit or sophistication about the cinematic past."[7]

From the early to mid-1990s, black-directed films and films featuring black actors in prominent roles constituted what film critics have dubbed a "black film wave," with the number of films in "1990 and 1991 alone easily [surpassing] the total production of all black-focused films released since the retreat of the Blaxploitation wave in the mid-1970s."[8] The black film wave in Hollywood was signaled by increased production of mainstream black-focused films, which included comedies and romances but was most visibly marked by social realist pictures focusing on the coming of age of black men amid "harsh urban realities: drugs, crime, violence, death on the streets."⁹ *Boyz N the Hood* (1991), a critical and box office triumph, remains the ensign of this direction in nineties film.¹⁰

Framing *Devil in a Blue Dress* with the 1990s ascendance of neonoir and the black film wave is a classificatory strategy supported by the trajectory of Daphne Monet's characterization, which shifts from femme fatale to tragic mulatto. The invocation of the tragic mulatto figure, however, also places the film within the history of Hollywood representations of mixed race. From the spate of early silent films demonizing the mulatto as a sexually deviant, ambitious threat¹¹ (D. W. Griffith's *Birth of a Nation* (1915) is the best-known example), to the "problem films" of the post–World War II era, which used a more sympathetically rendered mulatto figure to address the issue of integration (Douglas Sirk's 1959 remake of *Imitation of Life* is the best-known example),¹² films depicting mulatto characters or the issue of race mixing at times constitute a subcategory of black-focused film that frequently incorporates melodrama.

The noir revival, black film wave, and problem pictures are painted in very broad strokes here at a level of generalization that runs counter to the type of detailed reading I think is necessary to elaborate the microlevel processes of representation that reify black racial difference and interest me in this chapter. For my purposes, outlining these relevant cinematic contexts for *Devil in a Blue Dress* is primarily useful in establishing the fact that, for a viewer, much of the film is *familiar*. In the pages that follow, I focus on the taken-for-granted moments, those moments in which the film can work in shorthand or through fill-in-the-blank exercises because it trusts to the viewer's recognition of generic tropes and tropes of difference. Contextualizing *Devil in a Blue Dress* with neonoir, black social realism, and the problem pictures is valuable not because it prescribes conclusions about the historical and cultural significance of the film but because it opens up questions about how a viewer might recognize and engage this film, about the implications of genre film for the reification of race, and about the ways in which the mulatta figure troubles categories of many sorts.

If the integration of neonoir and social realism renders Easy Rawlins both the iconic gumshoe and a black ex-GI struggling against institutional racism such that *Devil in a Blue Dress* presents a unique twist on the private detective, then this combination also uniquely creates the viewer-as-detective. The film's formal dependence upon visual and aural shorthand and the film's transparent allusiveness especially draw the viewer into its mystery. Though in the tradition of classic film noir Easy assists the viewer in sorting out complicated plot twists through a voice-over narration, as in most films, characters' inner thoughts, feelings, motives, and moral attributes can only be inferred through accustomed visual and aural clues: facial expressions, body language, camera angles, focal lengths, music, and so on. The film's allusiveness further presumes a viewer's familiarity with noir characterizations, narrative conventions, and mise-en-scène. Thus both the formal devices for representing subjectivity in *Devil*, which are delimited by intrinsic qualities of the film medium itself, and the film's particular invocation of classic film noir tropes rely to varying degrees on a viewer's familiarity with those devices and tropes.

A brief discussion of the scene in which Dewitt Albright first presents Easy with his missing person's case illustrates how the film simultaneously teases the viewer by presenting clues that cannot yet be understood and relies on the viewer to recognize certain culturally resonant tropes. An analysis of this tension demonstrates that the film's representations are dynamic interactions between film and viewer in which the viewer must flesh out the film's visual and aural shorthand.

Much of the dialogue in *Devil* is the type of terse dialogue characteristic of hard-boiled detective fiction. This pared-down dialogue depends upon innuendo and double meanings for its economy. The following coded exchange between Albright and Easy is typical:

ALBRIGHT: I'm just looking for somebody, for a friend. Daphne Monet. Fiancée of Todd Carter. She's been gone two weeks. It upset the poor man so much, he stopped running for mayor.
EASY: I never laid eyes on her.
ALBRIGHT: That's a shame. See, Daphne has a predilection for the company of Negroes. She likes jazz, pig's feet, and dark meat—know what I mean?
EASY: Predilection.
ALBRIGHT: Yeah. I'd go looking for her myself, but I'm not the right persuasion, so to speak.

"Predilection" and "persuasion," are words that do not make any sense unless the viewer places in their stead the words "sexual preference" and "race." And when Albright rhetorically asks, "know what I mean?" we do. "Jazz," "pig's feet," and especially "dark meat," are code words for black cultural and sexual difference. By relying upon the viewer to supply the double meaning, the film asks the viewer to participate in the reification of such differences.

Conversations like this one are characterized by implications and hints because of illicit activities, implicit racial codes, and the fetishization of black vernacular expression;[13] much is communicated through meaningful looks and tense silences. Most viewers have found themselves drawn into similar scenes, watching men in fedoras pour whiskey into tumblers and discuss the unknown whereabouts of a mysterious woman though clouds of cigarette smoke. Genre fiction by definition promotes a feeling of pleasure in the viewer because he or she is familiar with plot structure, stock characters, and other conventions that enable one to anticipate what will happen next.[14] *Devil's* investment in enticing the viewer with a privileged look into the seamy noir underworld and black subculture of 1940s Los Angeles especially promotes the desire to feel one is "in the know."

Of concern is the fact the engagement of the viewer in the production of meaning is concentrated in the exercise of detecting racial truths; the fulfillment of generic expectations and the pleasure of recognition in *Devil in a Blue Dress* reifies racial difference to resolve the destabilizing effects of the passing figure. It is significant that in moments such as this one, the film can take for granted a viewer's recognition of euphemisms for blackness, sexual desirability, and transgression rather than turning to expository devices such as the voice-over narrative that is provided to help the viewer follow the labyrinthine plot. The film reifies race and gender precisely by taking for granted the cultural legibility of tropes of difference.

The viewer is not simply expected to recognize or interpret, however, but is offered a more active role as detective. The viewer's identification with Easy conspires with cinematographic devices, such as the camera's tendency to linger on objects and personal details in a way that suggests but does not reveal their significance, to frame the mise-en-scène with the detective's gaze. This gaze renders everything that comes under its watchful eye a potential clue, a sign of deeper meaning. Thus the investigatory mode of perception in which *Devil* is watched has interesting consequences for the passing figure, which is necessarily concerned with the disjuncture between appearance and reality. The enigmatic Daphne is not actually introduced until thirty-seven minutes into the film; displaced signifiers, however, provide clues to Daphne's character long before her racially ambiguous body appears.

The tension between appearance and reality so vital to cultural fascination with the mulatta figure is roused by the opening credits, during which the camera pans a painting depicting Chicago's black nightlife circa 1948: Archibald Motley Jr.'s *Bronzeville at Night*. The camera cranes up from the hustle and bustle of the street to a second-story window in which a light-skinned woman in a white dress stands with her back to the window. Returning to street level, the camera then lingers on a woman in a blue dress, again with her back turned. The woman in blue, a streetwalker perhaps, remains at the center of the frame throughout the final pullback reveal. The ostensible contradiction of the bedroom rendered public through the voyeur's gaze and the woman of the street rendered private through the concealment of her face establishes a tension between appearance and reality and gives this tension erotic import. Daphne, we will come to learn, is a woman dressed in white, so to speak, and, like the streetwalker, is an object of exchange in the political contest between two wealthy white men running for mayor. During the opening credits, T-Bone Walker sings the blues about his "West Side baby" who "lives way across town" and sets his "soul on fire." In the racial landscape of 1940s Los Angeles, inquiries into Daphne's geographic location are always inquiries into her social location. The sound track emphasizes Daphne's geographic and social separation, "way across town," and links this marginality to her sexual desirability. Thus the visual and aural backgrounds of the opening frames both initiate a *process* of representation, at work even in the absence of Daphne's on-screen presence, which casts the mulatta as a figure of contradiction, transgression, and marginality.

The first night that Easy searches for Daphne, he casually asks around the last place she was spotted, an illegal club on Central Avenue. Easy's friend Dupree and Dupree's girlfriend, Coretta, initially deny having heard of Daphne Monet. But once Dupree passes out, Coretta comes on to Easy and insinuates that she does indeed know Daphne. When Easy inquires, "Do you know her?" Coretta responds nonverbally, indirectly giving Easy a suggestive look in the reflection of a compact mirror she has pulled from her purse. The reflection of her own colored self in the compact mirror implies that to "know" Daphne means to perceive the colored woman concealed within, and this enigmatic response provokes the viewer's curiosity and suspicion. Later, Easy and Coretta have sex on her couch, while Dupree sleeps clueless in the bedroom. Coretta's transgressive infidelity and promiscuity become part of the constellation of associations with Daphne.

In the midst of their lovemaking, however, Coretta pulls away, protesting, "Easy, Easy, Easy, I can't give up that much . . . it ain't right . . . all you doin' is nosin' after my friend, Daphne." Coretta "has the nerve to charge [Easy] ten dollars" for what turns out to be an outdated address while literally pumping Easy for information about his employer. Information about Daphne is extremely profitable, and as Easy says, "everybody was in business in Los Angeles." Inordinate amounts of money are spent to find, protect, and bargain for Daphne in the deadly political game between Carter and Terell and the attempts of working-class black migrants to make a little money in its extralegal interstices. Six scenes include shots of money changing hands, which correspond to inquiries into Daphne's location and identity. In four scenes Daphne herself is supposed to physically pass from one man's custody to another's. These exchanges objectify Daphne, rendering her a commodity in the most literal sense.

In the scene preceding that in which Daphne finally appears in the flesh, the viewer receives a final clue to her character. As Easy dreams, haunted by the voice of the murdered Coretta, the handheld camera pans the darkened bedroom and comes to rest on the image of a calendar girl. The island woman holds forth an immense pink orchid, almost grotesque in its excessive sensuality. Symbolizing female genitalia, the orchid is held out to the viewer; the handheld camera work and the fitfulness of Easy's sleep give this offer immediacy. The image's luminous blue background and the prominence of the girl's blue hoop earrings evoke Daphne as "the girl in the blue dress." The woman leans forward, emerging from the indistinct blue background such that the only things visible are exaggerated markers of generic island beauty: her sensuous face framed by cascading waves of black hair parted down the middle, large hoop earrings and a sizable string of Tahitian black pearls, and the massive orchid. Once the phone rings, startling Easy from his nightmares, the viewer has been primed by the extreme close-up of the calendar girl to imagine inflections of sexual deviance in Daphne's upper-class enunciation. The image brings the historical weight of the colonial fantasy of mixed race women as sexual exotics to bear on the invitation Daphne extends to meet her at the Ambassador Hotel.[15]

It is worth mentioning that by all accounts watching *Devil in a Blue Dress* is a pleasure.[16] The production design by Gary Frutkoff and the cinematography by Tak Fujimoto have been highly praised by critics. Combined with Carl Franklin's well-regarded direction and decision to film entirely on location, they give *Devil* aesthetic appeal, a notable level of historical detail, and atmosphere. With the exception of the exotic calendar girl, the visual and aural clues heretofore discussed quite seamlessly blend in with the story's unfolding and the development of Easy's character. The *Bronzeville* women, T-Bone Walker's "West Side Baby," Coretta, and the wads of cash, which establish the viewer's sense that Daphne is a known racial and gendered subject before Daphne herself appears on screen, are all the more effective clues for their subtlety. These rather simple details exemplify the quotidian ways in which signs of racial and gender difference derive power from their very taken-for-grantedness. They demonstrate that representation is a *process* that operates in the absence, or displaced presence, of racial and gendered subjects. This process of cinematic representation, which is a process of cinematic racialization, involves a dynamic interaction between film and viewer in which tropes of difference are reified through the repetitive act of recognition.

The use of clues to construct Daphne's racial and sexual character in her very absence bespeaks the added significance that the film's reliance on the viewer's adeptness in perceiving signs of difference poses for the passing figure, in whom the most reliable visual markers of race are obscured. But these minor details also raise broader questions about the implications of the film's reliance on visual and aural shorthand to flesh out inner character for the reproduction of race and gender as modes of perception that perceive evidence of presupposed difference. Here the involvement of the viewer in the reification of black racial difference through the repetitive act of recognition illumines how the investigatory modes of perception common to race and film overlap to make the cinema such an important site for the production of racial meaning. Should a viewer ultimately choose to reject the tropes of difference proffered by the film or to "disidentify" with the racialization of Daphne Monet those tropes of difference enact,[17] the viewer's familiarity with and recognition of those tropes is nonetheless overdetermined; recognition precedes and is a precondition for negotiated or oppositional readings.

Briefly juxtaposing the oblique techniques of characterization discussed earlier in this chapter with the subjective techniques through which Easy Rawlins is developed as a character demonstrates that Daphne Monet is not so much *identified with* as she is *identified*. Interestingly enough, the first scene proper, which introduces Easy, parallels the *Bronzeville at Night* scene. Just as it does during the opening credits, the camera cranes up from busy Central Avenue to a second-story window through which we see Easy reading the classifieds in an undershirt. Dressed in white, as the *Bronzeville* woman was, Easy sits similarly with his back to the window. The next shot, however, cuts to a medium close-up of Easy and then zooms in to an extreme close-up of his face as his first-person narration begins. Whereas Daphne does not appear on screen for thirty-seven minutes, in just the first five minutes of the film, the viewer is introduced to Easy as narrator and protagonist. The viewer is further aligned with Easy's perspective through a flashback sequence, explaining that Easy is unemployed because he has refused to capitulate to his white boss's racism, and a point-of-view shot as Easy pulls into his driveway, constructing him as a property owner with middle-class aspirations. These cinematic devices establish Easy's integrity. Though the opening credits, which obliquely introduce Daphne through displaced visual and aural signifiers, and the first scene introducing Easy are similar, the subjective techniques that operate on Easy create empathetic identification between him and the viewer that is fundamentally different from the detective's gaze that structures the viewer's relationship with Daphne. Easy's character is *developed* through subjective techniques, whereas Daphne's character is *discerned* through an investigatory mode of perception.

The first face-to-face dialogue between Easy and Daphne exemplifies how the viewer-as-detective participates in the reification of difference at the very moment in which difference is called into question. The primary discourse at play in this encounter is the "discourse of seduction."[18] The discourse of seduction effaces dominative relations by disingenuously casting women as seductresses who wield an inordinate amount of sexual power and whose desire directly or indirectly initiates sexual encounters. The discourse of seduction thereby displaces responsibility for acts of sexual violence onto the victim. The hotel setting offers Daphne up to Easy and viewer alike, and a number of visual and aural cues incite the viewer to search for signs of desire and consent in Daphne's verbal expression and body language.

A sultry, saxophone-dominated jazz instrumental begins the moment Easy enters the room. Of course the fact that Daphne receives Easy in a hotel room in the middle of the night suggests her availability. Her blue dressing gown and the teasing manner in which she feigns modesty by crossing her legs so as to first reveal and then conceal her thigh draw attention from Daphne's surface to her interior. The repartee between Daphne and Easy assumes the viewer will actively seek out a subtext to Daphne's words:

DAPHNE: Easy, if you're thinking that Frank had anything to do with Coretta's death then obviously you don't know very much about him. Frank doesn't go around beating people up; he prefers to use a knife as his weapon.

EASY: And what do you prefer to use, as your weapon?

DAPHNE: Well, why don't you search me and find out?

EASY: Mind if I have another drink?

DAPHNE: Help yourself.

In this encounter between Daphne and Easy, just as in the encounter between Albright and Easy, to make sense of the conversation the viewer must flesh out the double entendres. The film expects the viewer to recognize certain tropes, and in fulfilling that expectation by interpreting the proffered hints and suggestions, the viewer reproduces those tropes; what is assumed within the viewer is rewritten into the film. Implying that Daphne's weapon is her manipulative sexuality, the dialogue casts Daphne as a femme fatale. The notoriety of the femme fatale as a figure who uses her sexuality to tempt, lead astray, and even kill men draws attention to the threat posed by Daphne's body in a way that elides the inequitable social relations that force her to manipulate her status as an object of exchange and to strategically engage the discourse of seduction.

The detective's gaze and the discourse of seduction establish a perceptual premise from which Daphne's words and body language must be regarded as indicators of some deeper truth. As Kate Stables points out, the gendered characteristics of the femme fatale in nineties films are almost cartoonishly exaggerated.[19] Furthermore, keeping her racial identity a secret requires Daphne to manipulate tropes of gender difference; she plays the lady, the seductress, and the victim by turns. The investigatory mode of perception in which the film is watched, the film's self-conscious engagement with noir, and Daphne's own motivation as a character thus conspire to emphasize the markers of Daphne's gender difference.

I would further suggest that Daphne's destabilized racial identity, as a result of either her transgressive "predilections" or a viewer's extratextual knowledge, leads her gendered characteristics to be exaggerated. In the absence of—which must always be the conjecture of—an identifiable racial classification, Daphne's gender difference is disproportionately responsible for her legibility as a subject. Because of Daphne's racial ambiguity, she must be socially located through notions of gender and sexual difference that rely in turn on notions of racial difference.

At this point in the film, the first-time viewer presumably does not yet know that Daphne's valuable and deadly secret is her blackness. We can consider how the exercise in discerning this secret is differently impacted by whether or not a first-time viewer has read the novel, by whether or not he or she is aware of actress Jennifer Beals's racial background, and by repeated viewing. Indeed, director Carl Franklin worried that casting Beals might give away the major plot twist:

Jennifer Beals approached me to play Daphne Monet, called me on the phone and I was concerned about her playing the role not because I did not trust her acting ability but because I knew that she was part African-American and I was concerned that it would tip off the secret that we were holding in the film.[20]

Yet Daphne's gender identity is racialized in complicated ways for all viewers even before the revelation of her blackness in the course of the film or through extratextual knowledge about Beals and the story line. Though at this point Daphne is ostensibly white and upper class, the suggestion that she has a sexual relationship with the "small time colored gangster named Frank Green," her "predilection" for "jazz, pig's feet, and dark meat," and Coretta's role as sexual proxy lend a sense of deviance to Daphne's sexuality because miscegenation and infidelity both connote transgression. Thus, before we know that Daphne herself is black in the diegesis, she is tainted by her association with blackness and her transgression of the color line. Daphne's racial identity, as well as her femininity, is suspect by virtue of her "predilections" long before the revelation of her blackness incites the viewer to search her physical features for black racial characteristics. In the circular logic of race and gender, the viewer must pit Daphne's body as reliably *gendered* evidence against her body as failed *racial* evidence to draw out her exotic sexuality—which is, of course, racial at base.

What happens to the viewer's participation in the racialization of Daphne once her secret is actually exposed? What indeed happens to Daphne? She is kidnapped and tortured. Moments after Daphne confesses to Easy that she is passing, that Frank Green is actually her half brother, and that she is indirectly responsible for Coretta's death, she is kidnapped by Albright and taken to a remote cabin. Albright knocks her around while questioning her about the location of the pictures she is using to counterblackmail Terell. In a desperate attempt to save Daphne and clear his own name, Easy sneaks up to the cabin and peeks through a window. We see Daphne sitting in a chair in front of a fireplace, surrounded by Albright and his goons. Albright circles her menacingly and asks,

Are you a liar? I know you're a liar. You lyin' about being a nigger? Tell me the truth. What part of you is nigger? Is your leg a nigger? Your arm a nigger? Maybe your face is a nigger. What part of you is nigger, huh? You know what I'm gonna do? I'm gonna burn it out of you!

Albright picks up a red-hot poker from the fireplace and approaches her. Our perspective on the scene is Easy's perspective, peering through a crack in the window. As Daphne begins to scream, all we see are her legs kicked up, her dress hiked with the garters showing, and the poker.

Albright's determination that he can identify the "nigger" part of Daphne through a figurative sexual penetration suggests that the "nigger" part of Daphne is the locus of her sexuality. The exoticization of Daphne as a mulatta depends upon just such a fantasy that Daphne's "one drop" of black racial difference is a drop of black sexual difference. The trope of the femme fatale, a woman who uses her sexuality to manipulate men, is colored, as it were, by the notion of black sexual deviance.

How, in this scene, is the viewer complicit with the racialization of Daphne's sexuality and with the sexual violence to which she is subjected? Our gaze is the voyeur's gaze. The provocative view of Daphne through the window with the phallic poker aimed between her legs puts the desire enacted by that gaze at odds with our horror at the spectacle of torture and at odds with the sympathy we might feel for Daphne. The extent to which we can empathize with her has already been compromised by the investigatory modes of perception analyzed earlier. Moreover, having earlier extended the offer to Easy, and to the viewer by extension, to "search" her and "help [him]self," Daphne cannot retract that offer; she can never quite be an innocent victim of sexual violence. And at the end of the day, Albright asks the question, "What part of you is nigger?" that we must all ask in our attempt to reconcile Daphne's apparent whiteness with the fact of black racial difference.

The mulatta figure's intrigue, I argue, lies precisely in the invitation to scrutinize her body and her mannerisms for signs of racial and gender difference. The mulatta typifies the body's vexed relationship with race because she exposes the ways in which the body is regarded as the best and most obvious evidence of innate differences and, particularly but not exclusively in passing narratives, of the ways in which the body is regarded as unreliable evidence of innate differences, suspect and at times downright deceptive. The mulatta figure is thus a fascinating vehicle for exploring race as a mode of perception and ideology of difference with a mutable discourse that obscures its contradictions and contingencies.[21] Daphne's contradictory characteristics, as she switches from calculating seductress to helpless victim, create intrigue and the desire to know, but to know in a specifically sexual way. Daphne is to be discovered, but we seek to discover a truth we already know. The thrill of exploration and the promise of revelation constitute the special desirability that has been the province of the mulatta. The mulatta seems to expose the falsity of oppositional racial categories but in a way that can ultimately be dismissed as a (sexual) fantasy of transgression. Gender difference stabilizes the mulatta figure when racial categories are subverted; possessing the mulatta through sexual conquest disciplines the figure.

At the very moment in which Daphne's blackness is exposed at the tip of Albright's poker, her heretofore intriguing sexuality loses its power, and Daphne's representational mode switches from femme fatale to tragic mulatto. After she is rescued, Daphne has Easy take her to meet and make up with Carter, certain that the pictures proving Terell is a pedophile will keep him from exposing her. Daphne is naively "convinced . . . that her Negro blood didn't matter now that Terell couldn't use it to keep the man she wanted to marry out of the mayor's race." But as Easy explains, "Even though we had fought a war to keep the world free, the color line in America worked both ways, and even a rich, white man like Todd Carter was afraid to cross it." Rejected by Carter, Daphne returns to her half brother and to the proper side of town.

Daphne's silence throughout the scene in which Easy drops her off, devastated, at her brother's apartment is crucial to completing Daphne's transformation from femme fatale to tragic mulatto. It is Easy who through his voice-over narration explains Daphne's motivations for passing:

> I dropped her off at her brother's apartment, a fourplex on Dinker Street. She had told me her story on the way home like a sinner who wanted to confess. Her name was Ruby Hanks from Lake Charles, Louisiana. And I suppose all she really wanted was a place to fit in. A few days later, my conscience got the best of me, and I went by her place to bring back my half of her money. I was kind of excited about seeing her again, but when I got there, she and her brother had picked up and gone.

Easy's narration recapitulates stereotypes of the mulatta's destructive sense of ambition and longing for social acceptance.[22] His description of Daphne as "a sinner who wanted to confess" likens the social transgression of the color line to a moral transgression and suggests that Daphne recognizes her own folly as such.

The very qualities that have heretofore made Daphne more of a noir trope than a developed character have become ridiculous in Daphne's final scene. Her blue wardrobe now seems like a childish dress-up game or, less innocently, the costuming of an actress. The disclosure of Daphne's homely real name, "Ruby Hanks," further divests her of mystery and allure. Instead of the name "Daphne Monet," sounding like a somewhat overzealous neonoir creation—something to gently chide the author for—the name now sounds like Daphne's own foolish attempt to be classy. Such noirish exaggerations have benefited the film by creating atmosphere, but as soon as these generic conventions become liabilities, Daphne takes the blame. She momentarily transforms from two-dimensional stock character to subject only when blameworthy.[23] The viewer thus experiences the double pleasure of indulging generic expectations and of disdaining them. Daphne's transformation from femme fatale to tragic mulatto absorbs criticisms of genre fiction as formulaic once the pleasures of that formula have run their course.

It is crucial to consider the shifting significance of Daphne's blackness in this regard. As a hidden aspect of Daphne's identity, blackness was signified by erotic transgressions and intimations of deviant sexuality. As the racial marking of Ruby Hanks, however, blackness domesticates Daphne. From being continually described with longing as "somethin' else" (in the dual sense of being physically attractive and different), Daphne has come to be described as any common black migrant would be described. Daphne's blackness functions alternately as a sign of the unknown and exotic and a sign of the utterly known and familiar.

Daphne's desirability, I contend, derives from her proximity to whiteness on what must be regarded as a *spectrum* of difference in which the terms of black racial difference are contingent. The equally inconstant and insistent interpolation of Daphne into the broader category of blackness reveals that the black racial difference at stake in our search for Daphne does not bear a fixed, binary relationship to whiteness.[24] Daphne's special allure and problematic mobility expose, rather, the underlying recognition that there are degrees of black racial difference and that the terms of this difference are contingent and contextual. The shifting terms on which Daphne is racialized as black offer an interesting example of what Saidiya Hartman calls the "figurative capacities" of blackness, the way in which blackness can be made to embody myriad meanings and cultural tensions.[25] Attending to the shifting and contingent iterations of blackness is of the utmost importance because blackness can be made to signify different differences in different moments.[26] The difficulty of constantly attempting, and failing, to play catch-up with the representation of blackness when the representations keep changing is the work of race. If we look for one signification or usage of black racial difference, we will be always two steps behind race in its wily mutability. The mulatta figure plays a crucial role in reifying blackness as a racial category that represents itself as fixed but operates most effectively as a shifting marker of difference.

Changing Daphne's characterization reifies both racial and gender difference. In the broadest terms, Daphne's trajectory is from femme fatale to tragic mulatto. This generic trajectory corresponds to her racial trajectory from white to black, compelling a consideration of the neglected question of the femme fatale's whiteness.[27] *Devil* presents a fascinating example that conjoins the femme fatale and the explicitly racialized tragic mulatto. It is complicated both to account for the legibility of these two notoriously formulaic characterizations in thinking through the question of their efficacy in the economy of the cultural work they perform, *and* to expose the nuances and contradictions in the representations of these tropes whose pretense to fixity conceals the ways in which race and gender must adapt and studiously reproduce themselves in different contexts.[28] *Devil*, however, employs the femme fatale and the tragic mulatto in remarkably conventional ways such that their combination disciplines both. The combination, or more specifically the succession, of the two figures arrests the subversive effects of the passing figure as a figure who initially troubles racial boundaries and the subversive effects of the femme fatale as a figure who initially troubles gender boundaries.

The tragic mulatto's inevitable ruin undercuts the femme fatale's power, duplicitous depiction of sexual power that it is. Both the femme fatale and the mulatta figure are marked by their intriguing sexuality, but whereas the femme fatale uses her sexuality to victimize others,[29] the tragic mulatta is sexually victimized.[30] In *Devil*, the aberrant femme fatale is disciplined through her racialization. The film ultimately concludes that the powerfully manipulative sexuality of the femme fatale is the mark of black sexual difference *and* that the ruin of the tragic mulatta and her sexual victimization are just punishments for the femme fatale's attempt to strategically use her sexual objectification to attain money and power. The treatment of Daphne Monet thus demonstrates how racial difference and domination and gender difference and domination bolster one another when in crisis.

The discourse of seduction and the stereotype of mulatto ambition conspire to make Daphne responsible for her own victimization. Daphne further takes the blame for the many wrongs perpetrated in the story. As Dupree says, "I know it was on account of her that Coretta got killed . . .

everything between Daphne and Coretta was always such a damn secret."
By concluding Easy's involvement in the noir underworld with Daphne's
abbreviated life story, the film enables us to forget that the many deaths
that have occurred are the collateral damage of a political contest between
two wealthy white men and, ultimately, of the white patriarchal order that
contest represents.[31] Finally, Daphne Monet is not cast as a mystery to be
solved but cast off as nothing much to speak about.

How can we track and account for what seems to be a dual usage of
the mulatta figure, the impulse to understand her as liminal and enjoy the
pleasures of transgression, on the one hand, and the desire to understand
her as reducible to black racial difference and enjoy the pleasures of categorization, on the other? How can we account for Daphne's exotic allure
and pathetic distastefulness? And how can we account for the abrupt shift
in Daphne's representation from femme fatale to tragic mulatta, which is
not experienced by the viewer as abrupt at all but rather as the reassuring
recognition of another *known*? It seems to me that when we reach such
moments of stuttering, such unresolved attempts to account for the "she
is but she isn't" quality of the mulatta, we should identify these as crucial moments in which the inner workings of race are exposed. The very
moment in which we struggle to resolve and connect the dots between
representational modes is the moment in which race's contradictions and
contingencies are visible. Race's great success is in creating a discourse of
absolutes and fixity that accomplishes race's *certitude* rhetorically and, in
the structures of our thought, to the extent that it can never accomplish
*certainty* in the reality of our experience, we are led to expect more de-
finitiveness and consistency in our deconstructions of race than race itself
has ever been able to achieve.

## Conclusion

Film's reliance on visual and aural shorthand raises questions about the
limitations of the medium for the representation of racial subjects whose
characteristics are overdetermined through displaced signifiers of difference that are not confined to the body but may accrue to objects, contexts,
and motifs. As I have argued, cinematic representation is a *process* that involves the viewer, and viewer involvement is necessarily concentrated in
those cinematic moments in which a discourse or iconography is assumed
to be shared, those moments that are familiar. Tropes of difference are

among the most culturally legible of cinematic devices; as viewers, we are
relied upon to flesh out tropes of difference and thus to reify difference in
each instance of recognition. *Devil in a Blue Dress* further suggests that
certain genres of film, such as film noir, raise the stakes for the representation of racial subjects and for blackness as a particular racial category. If
as an audience we come to a genre film wanting what we already know to
be affirmed or reproduced, how does this conservative investment in and
allegiance to generic convention affect our investment in and allegiance
to racial convention, to established practices of racial perception, classification, and hierarchy? My analysis suggests that the will to knowledge
operating in all genre film, and to its greatest degree in detective fiction,
exacerbates the will to knowledge operating in processes of racialization.

Daphne Monet comes to be known through clues that are at pains to
make up for the fact that her body, which should be the most obvious and
reliable clue to racial identity, is deceptive. These cinematic devices, which
establish her black racial difference through a constellation of associations
articulated through sexual and gender difference, clearly work overtime to
contain the subversive effects of the passing figure. But if Daphne incites
an investigatory mode of perception in which race is discerned beneath a
lack of visible difference, that very effort to discern her blackness exposes
the inconsistencies and failures of race. Of great significance is the fact
that the discovery of Daphne's black racial difference is a *process*.

At the outset Daphne is not different enough, momentarily exposing
race's operation on a spectrum of difference that is occluded by race's
vocabulary of absolutes. The treatment of the mulatta, as exotic and unknown, familiar and utterly known, different from authentic blackness
and reducible to that fundamental category of blackness, reveals that the
terms of black racial difference are shifting and contingent. Reducing the
figure's provocative destabilization of boundaries to a (sexual) fantasy of
transgression, and punishing the figure through sexual violence, scape-
goating, and exile might be regarded as an admission of sorts. These strategies for containment and the contradictory treatment of the passing figure as both race's worst problem and race's best evidence indicate just how
very hard race as a mode of perception and ideology of difference must
work to sustain its circular logic.

To call attention to the contradictions and contingencies in race's multiple ideologies of difference, however, is not enough. Race is articulated
through a vocabulary of absolutes that is every day contradicted by the
reality of our experience yet still provides a sense of surety. As critics we

must attempt to understand how race as a mode of perception and ideology of difference is highly adaptable precisely because of the contradictory discourses and iconographies that can address a vast and evolving array of problems, anxieties, and contexts.

If overdetermined, the *process* through which cinematic representations contain the subversive potential of the mulatta figure is also prismatic. Separating race into its multiple, contradictory, and relational constituent postulates—which are mutually referential precisely because they are individually insubstantial—the mulatta figure opens a point of entry for scholars of race that is not speciously cleaved by race's own classifications and logic. The mulatta figure warrants more *nuanced* critical attention from scholars interested in generating analytic frameworks for race and blackness. Critically taking up the mulatta figure to further our understanding of race requires both acknowledging how the mulatta functions in popular culture as a containment figure, and how disciplining that figure might constitute race's oblique acknowledgment of its own inadequacy.

### NOTES

1. Foster Hirsch sums up the debate: "Indeed, to this day, there is heated debate about whether or not noir ought to be considered a genre, a style, or a movement. Those who argue against noir as a genre maintain that it is defined by elements of style, tone, and mood that are easily transported across generic boundaries. . . . But films retroactively given the noir label are identified not only by 'elements of style' but also by such generic markers as repeated patterns in narrative structure, characterization, and theme. If, however, noir is considered a movement rather than a genre, its link to a particular era is enforced. As a movement, noir thrived at a certain time and place: Hollywood in the 1940s and 1950s." *Detours and Lost Highways: A Map of Neo-Noir* (New York: Limelight Editions, 1999), 2. In *More Than Night*, James Naremore concludes that "debates over whether specific films are 'truly' noir, or over the problem of what makes up a film genre, have become tiresome" (276), since "noir itself is a kind of mediascape—a loosely related collection of perversely mysterious motifs or scenarios that circulate through all the information technologies, and whose ancestry can be traced at least as far back as ur-modernist crime writers like Edgar Allan Poe or the Victorian 'sensation novelists'" (255). Naremore, *More Than Night: Film Noir in Its Contexts* (Berkeley: University of California Press, 1998), 276, 255.

2. Joyce Carol Oates asserts that detective fiction's "premise is that mystery, the mysterious, that-which-is-not-known, can be caused to be known and its

malevolent power dissolved." "Inside the Locked Room," review of *A Certain Justice: An Adam Dalgliesh Mystery*, by P. D. James, *New York Review of Books*, February 5, 1998.

3. I use the term "mulatta" to refer to a mixed race woman whose ancestors are classified as black and white. My analysis of the film *Devil in a Blue Dress* necessarily concerns the mulatta as both a historical subject and a cultural icon but focuses on the latter. There are important distinctions between literary and cinematic representations of the mulatta figure as a visibly mixed race woman and as a woman who can pass for white. In this chapter, I examine both valences of the mulatta figure and attempt to specify when necessary the peculiarities of the passing figure.

The term "classic film noir" is used in specific reference to films of the 1940s and 1950s. The term "neonoir" refers to films of the 1980s and 1990s. The shared characteristics of films from these two distinct historical periods are designated by the more general terms "film noir" and "noir."

4. Hirsch, *Detours*, 19.

5. Two of the primary features distinguishing contemporary visual style are fast-paced editing and explicit sex. Though a number of scholars have cited the explicit sex scenes in neonoir as significant departures from classic film noir, Kate Stables provides a particularly interesting analysis of this shift in which she considers the verbal dimensions of contemporary graphic cinematic sexuality as well as the visual dimensions. "The Postmodern Always Rings Twice: Constructing the *Femme Fatale* in 90s Cinema," in *Women in Film Noir*, 2nd ed., ed. E. Ann Kaplan (London: British Film Institute, 1998), 164-82.

6. James Naremore uses the term "retro noir" to distinguish neonoir films that are set in the past from neonoir films that take place in the present. Naremore, *More Than Night*, 203.

7. Ibid.

8. Ed Guerrero, *Framing Blackness: The African American Image in Film* (Philadelphia: Temple University Press, 1993), 158. Donald Bogle calls the increase in productions featuring blacks in prominent roles, directed by blacks, or addressing black issues "a new black wave." Bogle, *Toms, Coons, Mulattoes, Mammies, and Bucks: An Interpretive History of Blacks in American Films*, 3rd ed. (New York: Continuum, 1994), 342. Ed Guerrero uses the term "black film wave."

9. Bogle, *Toms, Coons, Mulattoes, Mammies, and Bucks*, 347. Bogle notes that these films' focus on the coming-of-age of black male characters results in the marked underdevelopment of black female characters. Manthia Diawara's description of what he calls the "new black realism" is very similar to Bogle's. However, Diawara makes the additional point that the black male characters of this new black realism, unlike the black male characters of Blaxploitation in the 1970s, develop over the course of the narrative rather than remaining "static." Diwara, "Black American Cinema: The New Realism," in *Black American Cinema*, ed.

Manthia Diawara (London: Routledge, 1993), 24. Though both Bogle and Diawara mention that the spate of black-directed mainstream films in the early nineties marginalized black women at best and objectified them at worst, neither of them provides a sustained consideration of this marginalization and objectification. Jacquie Jones, however, pulls no punches in her assessment of the ways in which the "new ghetto aesthetic" recapitulates black stereotypes and depicts black women as "bitches and ho's." Jones, "The New Ghetto Aesthetic," *Wide Angle* 13, nos. 3 and 4 (July–October 1991): 32-43.

10. The production of black independent films, such as Julie Dash's *Daughters of the Dust* (1990), also increased. Black independent films frequently explored positions of disenfranchisement within the broader category of blackness. Both Bogle and Guerrero subdivide the black film wave into independent cinema and mainstream cinema. Employing the dubious term "emergent groups," Guerrero notes that independent black cinema depicted "expanding black heterogeneity and 'difference,' with such emergent groups within the community finding voice as gays and women." Guerrero, *Framing Blackness*, 160.

11. Cedric J. Robinson and Luz Maria Cabral, "The Mulatta on Film: From Hollywood to the Mexican Revolution," *Race and Class* 45, no. 2 (October-December 2003): 7.

12. Barbara Tepa Lupack, *Literary Adaptations in Black American Cinema: From Micheaux to Morrison* (Rochester, NY: University of Rochester Press, 2002), 37.

13. In interviews, when discussing his motivations, Walter Mosley frequently explains that as a black writer he feels a sense of responsibility for creating texts that enable black people to read and affirm their own language: "One of the reasons I write books is so black people can just read black language." "Walter Mosley Sounds Out the True Detective Novel," *Jacksonville Free Press*, September 11, 2002.

14. According to Christine Gledhill, the pleasure of knowing what to expect when watching a genre film is held in tension with the desire for "novelty" and "innovation." She explains, "Hollywood genre production tended both to foreground convention and stereotypicality in order to gain instant audience recognition of its type—this is a Western, a Gangster, a Woman's Picture, etc.—and to institute a type of aesthetic play among conventions in order to pose the audience with a question that would keep them coming back—not 'what is going to happen next?' to which they would already have the answer, but 'how?.'" "Klute 1: A Contemporary Film Noir and Feminist Criticism," in Kaplan, *Women in Film Noir*, 24.

15. For more on the perception of "mixed blood" women as sexually deviant and the importance of native and "mixed blood" prostitution and concubinage to the colonial project, see Ann Laura Stoler's *Carnal Knowledge and Imperial Power: Race and the Intimate in Colonial Rule* (Berkeley: University of California Press,

2002); and Stoler, *Race and the Education of Desire: Foucault's History of Sexuality and the Colonial Order of Things* (Durham, NC: Duke University Press, 1995).

16. Even film reviewers' criticisms of the formulaic plot and characterizations of *Devil in a Blue Dress* tend to be qualified by testimonials about the pleasurable experience of viewing the film. Roger Ebert, for example, praises its "rich atmospheric style," admitting that he actually "liked the period, tone and look more than the story." Roger Ebert, "'Devil' Dances Out of the Past," review of *Devil in a Blue Dress* (Tristar movie), *Chicago Sun Times*, September 29, 1995, 33. Similarly, *Los Angeles Times* reviewer Kenneth Turan shrugs off what is unoriginal about the film in order to praise "the considerable visual sophistication of Tak Fujimoto," asserting that "the pleasant air of newness and excitement that 'Devil in a Blue Dress' gives off isn't due to its familiar find-the-girl plot. Rather it's the film's glowing visual qualities." Kenneth Turan, "Having a 'Devil' of a Time," review of *Devil in a Blue Dress* (TriStar Pictures), *Los Angeles Times*, September 29, 1995, 1.

17. "Disidentification" is José Esteban Muñoz's term for the way in which racially and sexually marginalized groups find a critical space for themselves within hegemonic representations. Muñoz, *Disidentifications: Queers of Color and the Performance of Politics* (Minneapolis: University of Minnesota Press, 1999). Though Muñoz's focus is more on artists and performers than on spectators, and though he focuses on queer subjectivities, I find his term to effectively describe the type of "critical spectatorship" discussed by scholars such as bell hooks in specific reference to cinematic representation and black female viewers. bell hooks, "The Oppositional Gaze: Black Female Spectators," in Diawara, *Black American Cinema*, 290.

18. I am heavily indebted to Saidiya Hartman for my understanding of the "discourse of seduction." Hartman explicates the ways in which slave women were made to seem not the victims but the perpetrators of their own sexual abuse through "the discourse of seduction," which recast the bonds of slavery as bonds of mutual affection and thus ascribed subjectivity and agency to slave women only to the extent that they could be made responsible for their own sexual violation. Saidiya Hartman, *Scenes of Subjection: Terror, Slavery, and Self-Making in 19th Century America* (New York: Oxford University Press, 1997), 88-89.

19. Stables, "The Postmodern," 170.

20. Carl Franklin, "Director's Commentary," *Devil in a Blue Dress*, dir. Carl Franklin, 101 min., TriStar Pictures, 1995, DVD.

21. In arguing that race is a mutable and contradictory discourse, I draw on Robert Lee's argument that the racial trope of the Oriental is able to persist across time and speak to a broad range of cultural anxieties precisely because that trope is made up of contradictory images. Robert G. Lee, *Orientals: Asian Americans in Popular Culture* (Philadelphia: Temple University Press, 1999), 13.

22. Sociologist Edward Byron Reuter's study *The Mulatto in the United States* (1918) exemplifies the pseudoscientific analyses of the mulatto that influenced the stereotypical portrayals of the mulatto in literature and film. Among the

distinctive—and dangerous—characteristics of the mulatto discussed by Reuter are the mulatto's self-destructive ambition and longing to be white. Reuter, *The Mulatto in the United States: Including a Study of the Role of the Mixed-Blood Races throughout the World* (New York: Haskell House, 1968), 315-16.

23. Hartman, *Scenes of Subjection*, 80. My argument here (that for most of the film Daphne Monet is not developed as a character but rather conforms closely to the generic convention of the femme fatale and that her transformation into a tragic mulatto type temporarily renders her a bit more legible as a subject only to the extent that speculations as to her motivations lead one to conclude she is blameworthy) is patterned after Saidiya Hartman's argument in *Scenes of Subjection* that slave women were recognized as subjects only to the extent that they could be made culpable for their own rapes.

24. Naomi Pabst articulates the nuanced and paradoxical ways in which the black-white mixed race subject "is both fully black (if inauthentically) and only one drop black coterminously." Pabst, "Mixedness/Blackness: Contestations over Crossing Signs," *Cultural Critique* 54 (2003): 204.

25. Hartman, *Scenes*, 25. It is important to note that Hartman's argument about the "figurative capacities of blackness" is a historical one about the slippage between property and person in the slave body. Though Hartman is specifically elucidating the figurative and literal uses to which black slaves could be put under nineteenth-century slavery, she is also making an argument about the constitution of blackness itself, which is a racial category and figurative device whose meanings both persist and evolve over time.

26. Mary Pratt's argument that ideologies of difference and domination can be reified through seemingly contradictory discourses and in fact depend upon the proliferation of meanings of difference informs my thinking here. Mary Louise Pratt, "Scratches on the Face of the Country; or, What Mr. Barrow Saw in the Land of the Bushmen," *Critical Inquiry* 12, no. 1 (Autumn 1985): 119-43.

27. Attention to film noir and detective fiction by scholars of race has steadily increased over the last decade. See, for example, Megan E. Abbot, *The Street Was Mine* (New York: Palgrave, 2002); Frankie Y. Bailey, *Out of the Woodpile* (New York: Greenwood Press, 1991); Samuel Coale, *The Mystery of Mysteries* (Bowling Green, OH: Bowling Green State University Press, 2000); Manthia Diawara, "Noirs by Noirs: Towards a New Realism in Black Cinema," in *Shades of Noir*, ed. Joan Copjec (London: Verso, 1993); Adrienne Johnson Gosselin, ed., *Multicultural Detective Fiction* (New York: Garland, 1999); Helen Lock, *A Case of Mistaken Identity* (New York: P. Lang, 1994); Eric Lott, "The Whiteness of Film Noir," *American Literary History* 9, no. 3 (Autumn 1997) 542-66; Maureen T. Reddy, *Traces, Codes, and Clues* (New Brunswick, NJ: Rutgers University Press, 2000). Race and the femme fatale is clearly a topic on which more work must be done.

28. Werner Sollors, Naomi Pabst, and others have rightly cautioned against the danger of treating the tragic mulatto as a type. By missing important variations

on the type, they contend, critics have inadvertently participated in undercutting the figure's subversive potential. Pabst, "Mixedness/Blackness," 195; Werner Sollors, *Neither Black Nor White Yet Both: Thematic Explorations of Interracial Literature* (New York: Oxford University Press, 1997), 242.

29. Chris Straayer, "*Femme Fatale* or Lesbian Femme: *Bound* in Sexual *Différance*," in Kaplan, *Women in Film Noir*, 153.

30. In his discussion of the novelistic treatment of the tragic mulatto, Glenn Cannon Arbery points out that the mulatta's a priori victimization, as the product of "erotic transgression," "slavery," and "bastardy," coupled with the promise of future victimization, as a concubine, was central to her special sexual desirability. Glenn Cannon Arbery, "Victims of Likeness: Quadroons and Octoroons in Southern Fiction," in *Interracialism: Black-White Intermarriage in American History, Literature, and Law*, ed. Werner Sollors (New York: Oxford University Press, 2000), 400-401.

31. The tragic mulatto, George Hutchinson and Werner Sollors argue, is often made a scapegoat in such a way that she—as an individual—is blamed for her ruin rather than the structural racial oppression that compels her to pass. Sollors, *Neither Black Nor White Yet Both*, 259; George Hutchinson, "Jean Toomer and American Racial Discourse," in Sollors, *Interracialism*, 374.

# Mixed Race in Latinowood

*Latino Stardom and Ethnic Ambiguity
in the Era of* Dark Angels

## Mary Beltrán

Scholars of the status of Latinas and Latinos in the U.S. entertainment media tend to be cautiously optimistic in this postmillennial era about opportunity and visibility.[1] Latinos are being featured in more nuanced and compelling roles, while a growing number of actors and actresses, among them Jennifer Lopez, America Ferrera, and Benicio del Toro, are gaining the publicity and popularity that qualify them as full-fledged members of the Hollywood star system.

A less understood wrinkle of contemporary Latino stardom that speaks to both the permeability and the permanence of imagined racial borders is in regard to how a number of contemporary stars identify with respect to ethnicity and race. More specifically, many successful Latino performers are of mixed racial heritage and choose to highlight this *mestizaje* in their publicity. Actors such as Jessica Alba (who is of Mexican, French Canadian, Danish, English, and Italian descent) and Freddie Prinze Jr. (who is Puerto Rican and Hungarian on his late, famous father's side, and Irish, English, and Native American on his mother's) are just two members of this growing contingent; they are joined by such performers as Rosario Dawson (who is Puerto Rican, Afro-Cuban, Irish, and Native American), Salma Hayek (who is Lebanese and Mexican), Jimmy Smits (Puerto Rican and Surinamese), and Cameron Diaz (Cuban and German American).

That is not to say that there is not a great deal of diversity among this contingent. Some stars of partial Latino descent foreground their Latin American ancestry (such as Rosario Dawson, who has been always forthcoming about her heritage), while others choose not to dwell on it in their publicity but are nevertheless "claimed" by the Latino-oriented entertainment news media and Latino fans (as was the case for Freddie Prinze Jr. for some years before he publicly embraced his Puerto Rican heritage). Irrespective of the many differences among what I term "mixed Latino" stars—to highlight that they have public images both as mixed race and as Latino—their careers have much to teach us about how notions of Latinidad and of racial categories more generally are evolving. Has something shifted in "Latinowood," as some Hollywood insiders dub the Latino creative professional community,[2] or in the industry's racial politics of casting that currently privileges actors of partial Latino heritage?[3] And what are the implications of this phenomenon with respect to imagined racial borders and notions of what it means to be Latina or Latino in U.S. popular culture today?

In this chapter I consider the implications of this shift and speculate in particular on the impact of the increasing emphasis on *mestizaje*, which I define for the purposes here strictly as racial hybridity, on Latina and Latino opportunity and star promotion in Hollywood media productions. To do so, I analyze the public image and career of one of the most successful actresses of mixed Latino background today, Jessica Alba, and to a lesser extent that of her contemporary, Rosario Dawson. Alba and Dawson, who have experienced radically different careers in the last decade, serve as apt case studies for this exploration, given that their multiracial heritage has occasionally figured as a topic of discussion in their interviews with the press. Their careers and the promotional texts that have contributed to their public images, including critics' reviews, promotional materials, and interviews, thus provide rich texts for the study of discourses circulating on mixed race and Latino identities in the mass media and U.S. social life.

Jessica Alba got her start as a young teen in a variety of small film and television roles and has since become a star of enough notoriety to play herself on HBO's satire of Hollywood stardom, *Entourage* (2004+). Interestingly, Alba's breakout role, and the one for which she arguably is best known, was that of racially mixed and genetically enhanced Max Guevara in the science fiction television series *Dark Angel* (2000–2002). This character, a heroic warrior of the future with a Hispanic last name and the DNA of multiple individuals of diverse racial heritage, is part of the new wave of mixed race characters that have become increasingly visible in Hollywood film and television texts in recent years.[4] Jessica Alba and

*Dark Angel* thus offer a rich case study of contemporary mixed race representation. In Alba's career trajectory since the series end, she also has had an increasingly visible profile that sheds additional light on the treatment of a mixed Latina star in contemporary Hollywood.

To further explore these casting and promotional tendencies, I compare Alba's career and public image with that of Rosario Dawson. Dawson arguably is seen as a more serious actress, as surveys of her films and film reviews bear out; she has acted in and has been well received by critics in a number of low-budget independent films, as well as having worked for such respected directors as Spike Lee, Robert Rodriguez, and Oliver Stone. She does not appear to be considered for the same roles as Jessica Alba, however, at least when it comes to bigger-budget and/or studio-driven films. In such films Dawson often has small roles amid large ensemble casts, as was the case in *Alexander* (2005), *Sin City* (2005), and *Rent* (2005), or has been stuck in thankless "best friend" roles, as in *Down to You* (2000) and *Josie and the Pussycats* (2001). This is beginning to shift as Dawson is cast in more lead roles, however; her work in *Men in Black II* (2002) and *Clerks II* (2006) is a case in point. Another important distinction between the two actresses is that Dawson has typically played Latina and African American characters, whereas Alba has been cast in a number of "ambiguously white" roles over the years, the dynamics and the consequences of which I explore in more detail later in this chapter.

In this exploration, I interrogate how the actresses' public images have developed over the years, and in particular how they have been received by media gatekeepers such as critics and journalists. How has the mixed ancestry of each actress been treated in their press coverage, and what has been the impact of their evolving images on their casting opportunities? With these questions in mind, can it be said that all *mestizaje* is the same when it comes to mixed Latino (or, in this case, Latina) stars? Through interrogating these questions, I aim to shed light on the boundaries and implications of mixed race and Latina identities as articulated in Hollywood films, star promotion texts, and both mainstream and ethnic-oriented news coverage.

## Latinos, Always "Ethnically Ambiguous"?

This is not to say that it is new for Latina and Latino stars to be mixed race. Given the privileging of fair skin and other European phenotypal features in Hollywood, Latino actors and actresses with some European ancestry have traditionally had an advantage with respect to being considered for lead roles, a paradigm that is only recently beginning to lose power.[5] Hollywood producers' casting of Spanish actors and actresses such as Antonio Banderas, Penelope Cruz, and Paz Vega in Latin American and Latino roles is just one manifestation of this preference. But while many Latino stars have been of mixed ancestry, stars of partial Latino descent often did not admit to or heavily publicize it prior to the 1990s, the decade in which mixed race births boomed in this country. Those who chose not to "out" themselves as mixed race likely were hoping to avoid being typecast in ethnic roles or, alternately, wanted to maintain the careers that their "Latin look" enabled.[6] Mixed Latino actors and actresses of past eras include the late Anthony Quinn (who was Mexican and Irish), *Wonder Woman's* Lynda Carter (who is half Mexican), and Raquel Welch (of half-Bolivian heritage). Notably, some previously "closeted" mixed Latino actors and actresses who have "come out" regarding their Latin heritage have found new acting opportunities with the move. Raquel Welch, born Jo Raquel Tejada, for example, was quickly cast in Latina film and television roles.[7]

The apparent vogue for mixed Latino stars follows the more general popularity in Hollywood and U.S. popular culture since the 1990s for ethnically ambiguous looks. Mixed race actors and models in particular are being centrally featured in advertising and media productions, alongside ethnically inflected and "multicultural" products and aesthetics. These trends have been prompted, among other catalysts, by increasing ethnic diversity and cultural curiosity in this country. In the realm of Latino-oriented media outlets, this has translated to a focus on mixed Latino celebrities "getting back to their roots" through such devices as interviews and photo shoots that take place in their ancestors' country of origin, as in *Latina* magazine's photo shoot with model Christy Turlington in January 1999, complete with the headline "*Nuestra* Christy returns to El Salvador." As scholars such as Marilyn Halter and Leon Wynter have discussed in relation to these trends, and as Danzy Senna aptly remarked, the "mulatto millennium" is upon us.[8]

Within these new formations, Latino icons and images have been centrally featured. This is likely because of the Latino legacy of *mestizaje*: Latinos, though often not acknowledged as multiracial, are of widely mixed ethnic and racial descent with respect to indigenous and Spanish ancestry and heritage that can be traced to African and other origins. As Gregory

Velasco y Trianosky notes, "The central racial and cultural reality of Latino life is that everyone is *mestizo*."[9] This legacy of amalgamation, among
other things, has historically been interpreted as reasoning for the racialization of and discrimination against Latinos in legal policy and by U.S.
social institutions.

It comes as somewhat of a surprise, then, given this long history and
statistics which indicate that the rate of Latino outmarriage is 1 in 3,[10] that
scholarship on mixed race in the United States has often neglected to focus on mixed race families or individuals of partial Latino descent. In
part this is because of continued confusion and debate regarding whether
Latinos are a race or an ethnic group[11]—and, thus, whether Latino-white
relationships or individuals can be viewed as interracial. Recently scholars
such as George G. Sánchez, Gregory Velasco y Trianosky, and Angharad
Valdivia have begun to remedy this gap through critical attention to Latinidad in relation to hybridity and/or mixed race;[12] I build on their work
here. My approach is based on the understanding that Latinos, while not
defined by the government as a race, are a racialized ethnic group—as
Chon Noriega notes, "legally white but socially black,"[13] as evident in their
historical and contemporary treatment by social institutions.

Perhaps most important when it comes to the predominance of individuals of full or partial Latino descent among the new wave of multicultural figures in U.S. popular culture, some (though certainly not all) Latinos possess an appearance similar to that of more clearly biracial or multiracial individuals. As Clara E. Rodríguez argues, the "look" historically
popularized for Latinos and Latinas in Hollywood includes a light tan,
café au lait complexion that falls between stereotypical norms of white
and black skin tones,[14] while some Latinos also possess other phenotypic
features that defy easy racial categorization. An illustration of how this
look can be construed for a trendy multiracial appearance: in 2003, a *New
York Times* article on the new vogue for racially ambiguous models and
actors in the realms of fashion, advertising, and media—what it termed
"Generation E.A. (Ethnically Ambiguous)"—opened with the story of Leo
Jiménez, a young model extremely popular with designers and club pro-
moters because of his multiracial good looks. The model's "steeply raked
cheekbones, dreadlocks, and jet-colored eyes" were the result not of being
the child of biracial parents, however, as the article went on to reveal, but
simply of being Columbian.[15] As Leo Jiménez aptly illustrates, Latinos are
already mixed race and as such have at times become trendy in the midst
of the vogue for the multiracial figure.

Performers of partial Latino ancestry such as Jessica Alba and Rosario Dawson thus are at times pulled into the wave of popular interest, gaining acting and promotional opportunities in the midst of the Mulatto Millennium, at least in part because of their ethnically ambiguous appearance. Among their contemporaries are countless lesser-known actors and actresses who, like Leo Jiménez, are also being cast in minor, nonspeaking, and extra roles to help flesh out the multicultural ethos of film and television storyworlds set in both present and future settings. Examples include *The Fast and the Furious* (2001) and the films of the futuristic *Matrix* trilogy (1999–2003). As such they are possibly portraying Latinos, but just as likely are meant to be interpreted as Filipino, Samoan, half African American or Asian, or simply light-skinned "ethnic" types. While it could be argued that this amounts to increased casting opportunities for Latino actors and actresses and thus should be interpreted as a progressive development, it is important to examine what happens to the representation of Latinidad, or Latinness, in the process. To begin to explore these dynamics, the case studies of Jessica Alba and Rosario Dawson illuminate how Latinidad has come to be framed in the careers and public images of two actresses of partial Latino descent.

## Jessica Alba and Max Guevara, Mixed Race Icons

According to biographies of Jessica Alba, the actress was born in 1981 in Pomona, California. She has related to interviewers that her mother is of Danish, French-Canadian, English, and Italian descent, and her father is Mexican American. Notably with respect to her Mexican heritage, Alba's father, Mark Alba, has been described in drastically diverse ways by the news media, some of which seem to attempt to avoid the label of Mexican American. He was described by *Marie Claire* magazine as "Mexican-Indian and Spanish," for example.[16] At the other extreme, he was described as "dark Mexican" in a *Rolling Stone* interview with Alba in 2005.[17] Such odd treatment of Alba's paternal heritage likely reflects the historical colonization and related denigration of Mexican Americans in the United States, as Pérez-Torres, Valdivia, and others argue regarding the continued privileging of certain types of Latinidad in sociopolitical spheres and popular culture.[18]

Alba was fairly young when she began acting; reports state that she started taking acting classes was twelve. She got her first, minor film role a year later in the children's comedy *Camp Nowhere* (1994); other roles followed in commercials and children's television series such as Nickelodeon's *The Secret World of Alex Mack* (1994–98), on which she appeared in 1994, and *Flipper* (1995–2000), on which she had a recurring role from 1995 to 1997. A survey of her work in these years reveals that she likely benefited from the newly multicultural ethos and casting of Nickelodeon, Disney, and other children's media producers, trends that Angharad Valdivia discusses in another chapter of this volume. Ambiguously ethnic roles that the young actress appeared in during these years include her role as Maya on *Flipper* and tomboy Samantha Swoboda in the children's techno-geek action film *P.U.N.K.S.* (1999).

With regard to star promotion, the publicity that Alba received was negligible at this stage in her career. While critics at times made mention of Alba as attractive, as in reviews of the teen horror-comedy film in which she played a girl-next-door type, *Idle Hands* (1999),[19] in none of the publicity that could be found for Alba from these years was ethnicity mentioned. Apparently it was seen as prudent to promote Alba merely as an "American" teen, even while she found much of her opportunity in nonwhite roles. Perhaps another reason for this lack of ethnic specificity was due to her audience—more specifically, due to a perceived lack of attention on the part of young audiences to performers' racial identities. Advertising firms were finding in 1990s studies that this was often the case, and likely media producers were taking notice.[20] According to this research, it likely did not matter to the same degree for Jessica Alba's young viewers as it did for their parents whether she was white, Latina, mixed, or all of the above.

When Jessica Alba was eighteen, her career underwent a dramatic turn. She was given her first major role when she was cast by *Dark Angel* executive producers James Cameron and Charles H. Eglee to play Max Guevara, a genetically enhanced (or in *Dark Angel*–speak, transgenic) female in a dystopic future. More than a thousand young women reportedly were considered in the producers' search for an actress with an appearance and stage presence suitable to portray Max. In this search a multiracial look was definitely part of the producers' vision. "If you're really going to assemble the best of humanity, why not cross the whole genetic spectrum?" Eglee asserted in an interview with *Entertainment Weekly* in 2000. "We wanted someone with a transgenic look."[21] Casting director Robert Ulrich has contributed that the series was cast to support the multiracial aesthetic the producers were aiming to create:

"It was in the future when everyone was going to be mixed and hopefully mixed in together. And obviously that was a very important part to casting the character of Max. And I think one that was one of the most wonderful things about Jessica, because it's hard to tell what exactly Jessica's ethnic background is."[22]

After the series debuted in the fall of 2000, Alba was quickly noticed by viewers, particularly young male fans. News stories about the series make note of the boom in Jessica Alba–dedicated Web sites and other signs of popularity that the young actress quickly received, even though *Dark Angel* did only moderately well in the ratings in its two seasons and was panned by some reviewers. For instance, at the culmination of the 2000–2001 season she was awarded a 2001 Teen Choice Award and the 2001 *TV Guide* Award for Breakout Star of the Year. She began to get offers to star in films and other projects.

*Max Guevara (Jessica Alba) is multiracial but also raceless in the Fox television series* Dark Angel *(2000–2002). Photo courtesy of Movie Market, Ltd.*

An interesting question here is the impact of Alba, as a mixed Latina star, rising to stardom in her portrayal of a mixed race and part-Latina character. Max Guevara is not so neatly categorized, however, as her backstory complicates how she can be read with respect to racial or ethnic identity. One could argue that the character is coded as Latina according to Hollywood traditions of racial marking, with Alba's olive complexion and dark brunette hair and makeup in the role contributing to this construction. This proves difficult to sustain, however, given that Max does not identify as Latina in the narrative. She never, for instance, questions the origin of her seemingly Hispanic last name, while the series producers reveal in commentary that accompanies the season 1 DVD set that her first name is short for the ethnically generic "Maximum." We also learn early in season 1 that Max's mother, who by appearance in flashback could be Latina, was not her biological mother.

And while Max has DNA that can be traced back to multiple individuals, such that she undeniably is multiracial, the series does not explore mixed race identity on more than a metaphoric level. Perhaps most important in this regard is the fact that Max's genetic mélange was manufactured in a laboratory and thus is removed from any connection to ethnic history or communities. Max also is characterized as so mixed that any one possible identity is nullified. "With my DNA, I'm pretty much a blood relative to everybody who's been anybody, ever. Winston Churchill . . . Einstein . . . Pocahontas," she shares with her compatriot and love interest Logan Cale in a season 1 episode.[23] Max's racial identity, rather, is one of affiliation, demonstrated in her sense of responsibility to her "family" of similarly engineered X-5s. Her X-5 brothers and sisters, a virtual United Colors of Benetton corps of genetically manufactured supersoldiers, while providing a visible metaphor for multiracial identity, also symbolize the elision of race. Max Guevara is the most developed case in point; in her case, Latino culture, history, and community were effaced in her creation.

Interestingly, despite her character's ambiguous but primarily mixed race status, early publicity for the series seldom made mention of Jessica Alba's multiethnic roots. Readers today are likely used to hearing of Alba's "smoky multicultural looks" and heritage of "ethnic mélange,"[24] but little mention of Alba's mixed ancestry was made in the articles that heralded the debut of *Dark Angel*. The first publicity for the series in *Entertainment Weekly*, for example, described only Alba's beauty (more specifically, her "mouth-agape beauty and swollen lips").[25] Other journalists chose to focus on *Dark Angel*'s similarity to other sexy and hard-fighting female characters on television, such as Buffy of *Buffy the Vampire Slayer*.[26] When Alba's ancestry was mentioned, it was at times reported incorrectly, often with her Mexican heritage downplayed or left out entirely. For instance, in an article in *Entertainment Weekly* in 2001, journalist Benjamin Svetkey described her as "a genetics experiment all her own. Part Spanish, part Danish, part Canadian, and part Italian."[27]

The Latino-oriented press was quick to notice the actress, however, and to trumpet her arrival as a new Latina star. This is unsurprising, given that the casting of a Latina, whether of full or partial descent, as the lead in a network television series was almost unprecedented in 2000. Alba and the *Dark Angel* series were mentioned in news outlets that reported on Latinos in Hollywood media projects, such as *Latina, Hispanic, People en Español,* and *Latin Heat*, an industry trade journal, with Alba touted as a rising star. Alba later was awarded a 2001 ALMA (American Latino Media Arts) Award as Breakthrough Star of the Year. This was followed by a second ALMA Award for Outstanding Actress in a Television Series in 2002. It would appear that Alba was fully embraced as a Latina actress within Latino-oriented media circles, even while she was clearly promoted in the mainstream press as mixed race. Schisms could occasionally be noted in reaction to this dual promotional strategy, such as in coverage in the Latino-oriented media that prodded the actress for not embracing her *Mexicanidad* more fully. For instance, a news item reported by *Latina* magazine in the spring of 2006 described her as "Mexican-American Alba (you can keep denying it, mi'ja, but we know the truth!)."[28]

Notably, in the period in which *Dark Angel* was broadcast, multiraciality was garnering a great deal of attention in popular culture. Films such as *The Fast and the Furious* (2001) and *The Scorpion King* (2001) were being released, while their mixed race stars, Vin Diesel and Dwayne "The Rock" Johnson, respectively, were prompting discussions of what Valdivia has termed the increasing "ethnification" of popular culture.[29] By 2001, news coverage of Jessica Alba often focused on her diverse ethnic background, now usually more correctly described. One especially blatant example was *Entertainment Weekly*'s quiz on its EW.com Web site, titled "What Nationalities Are in Jessica Alba's Ancestry?" Given *Dark Angel*'s lower ratings in 2001–2, Alba appeared to be receiving attention in part simply because she was seen as appealing to many fans. What would become of Alba's career and public image when she no longer was cast in a role that placed multiraciality at its crux, however? Exploration of the actress's post–*Dark Angel* career and image sheds additional light on mixed Latino stardom.

## A Place for Ethnic Ambiguity in "Real" Storyworlds?
### Alba after Dark Angel

Jessica Alba's career has taken new turns in the years since *Dark Angel* was canceled in 2002. While the actress has appeared in a handful of films since then, a survey of these films reveals that producers and casting directors were at least initially unsure of how to cast her outside of futuristic and/or fantastic settings. This is not to say that they may not have had high expectations with respect to her ethnic versatility—as long as the characters she was portraying were not white. For example, in 2003 Alba portrayed both a native Iban woman in 1930s Malaysia in the period drama *The Sleeping Dictionary* and a brash Puerto Rican dancer from the Bronx in the urban dance drama *Honey*. Unfortunately, Alba appears out of her element in both roles, particularly with respect to her attempt to proximate believable accents for her characters. Ella Shohat and Robert Stam's discussion of white-centrism as reinforced in studio-era Hollywood through lack of attention to realistic language and accent of nonwhite characters, particularly those from regions deemed third world, seems still relevant when considering Alba's verisimilitude in these roles.[30] Although *Honey* earned some respectable early box office and did fairly well in DVD sales, *The Sleeping Dictionary* was never released in theaters; both films were panned by critics.

Alba fared better with respect to story lines set in more fantastic surroundings. Two of her more recent roles involved portraying comic book figures, the superhero Sue Storm/Invisible Girl in *Fantastic Four* (2005) and a sweet stripper in Frank Miller and Robert Rodriguez's *Sin City* (2005). Controversy initially arose among comic book fans over the casting of Alba as the historically Nordic Sue Storm, which she supposedly muted when she appeared in dyed blond hair and impressed fans in the film. *Sin City*'s Nancy Carruthers, as portrayed by Alba, also appears to be ambiguously white. Similarly, Alba was cast opposite Paul Walker in the deep-sea-diving thriller *Into the Blue* (2005), in a case of color-blind casting that had the actress don various bikinis and allowed her to utilize her scuba-diving skills.

In the meantime, Jessica Alba has been consistently lauded in the press for her beauty and even more so for her perceived sexiness. To list a handful of her recent achievements in this regard, Alba was named one of *Teen People*'s 25 Hottest Stars under 25 in 2005, while her performance in

*Sin City* was awarded Sexiest Performance by the MTV Movie Awards. In 2006 she also topped *Playboy's* Hottest Celebrities list. This celebration of Alba's body has accompanied her rising status as an actress. Perhaps the most noticeable sign of this development in Alba's career, in June 2006, she was named "Must Girl of the Summer" by *Entertainment Weekly*, headlining its 2006 "It List." In its story on the star, the magazine declared Alba to be "on the brink of Hollywood domination," despite the fact that she was appearing in no films to be released that summer.[31]

Notably, as Alba has become increasingly successful as a Hollywood actress and visible as a public figure, she has spoken more candidly about her mixed race identity. As she described her childhood to *Rolling Stone* journalist Allison Glock, "I never really belonged anywhere. . . . I wasn't white. I was shunned by the Latin community for not being Latin enough."[32] Her discussions with interviewers in recent years have addressed elements of Latina identity that go beyond appearance, such as language and cultural habits. For instance, Alba has mentioned how her life has been impacted by not being given the opportunity to learn Spanish when she was growing up. "My grandfather was the only one in our family to go to college. He made a choice not to speak Spanish in the house. He didn't want his kids to be different," she has noted.[33] Alba added that she is currently taking lessons in Spanish.

## *Ambiguously Ethnic, Not the Same as Ambiguously White: Rosario Dawson*

Alba's off-white appearance and the advantages it brings her as a Hollywood actress become more apparent when her opportunities and promotional texts are compared with those of her peer Rosario Dawson. As noted previously, while Dawson has had a busy career and is also widely praised as attractive, she has experienced very different acting opportunities than Alba. We can surmise that this is in part because the two actresses have made different career choices. Arguably, however, it is also because Dawson's more markedly ethnic appearance and urban image have translated to media industry perceptions that her marketability to film audiences is not as broad as Alba's.

A comparison of the two actresses' promotional texts and filmographies reveals the pivotal importance of how a performer's appearance and early career choices are "read" by critics and journalists and ultimately contribute to the construction of racialized star images. This is particularly noticeable in the case of mixed race actors, who may be marked with a racialized image that actually differs from their ethnic origins and/or identity. For example, Halle Berry is interpreted by journalists as African American even when she brings her Euro-American mother with her to the Oscars, Cameron Diaz is perceived and promoted as unambiguously "white," and Salma Hayek simply as "Latina," even though their mixed racial heritage, which belies this simplicity, is known to much of the public. Mixed race is increasingly an identity category available to stars, but one that is unstable when it comes to its impact on their careers.

In this regard, Jessica Alba's initial lack of ethnic self-labeling in her career and her light tan, not brown, skin, and perhaps even her perceived girlishness have contributed to the perception that she is ethnically ambiguous to the degree most preferred by Hollywood producers and casting directors in casting lead roles. In other words, Alba has achieved an "off-white" image, to borrow the term coined by Diane Negra to describe the liminal racial status of white ethnic actresses since Hollywood's silent film era.[34] Dawson, in contrast, has somewhat darker skin and dark hair that does not look as natural when dyed blond (as has recently been a favored look of Alba's), has a more womanly and urban image, and has been associated with her mixed heritage since she began her acting career. Given Hollywood's ongoing, unwritten racial paradigms of casting, which still often dictate a color line between whiteness and nonwhiteness, it comes as no surprise that she has typically been cast only as Latinas, Latin Americans, and ambiguous ethnic types, and in one case, as Persian (in *Alexander*). She also has been much less likely than Alba to be cast in nonethnic specific ("white") roles. On the other hand, Dawson has received opportunities to portray the romantic partners of characters played by African American actors, including Will Smith in *Men in Black II* (2002) and Eddie Murphy in *The Adventures of Pluto Nash* (2002)—a casting paradigm that can be seen as a holdover from classical Hollywood's reluctance to portray mixed couples on screen. The rise of male actors of color who are seen as "having box office" and thus as able to headline a film has in this regard been a boon to Rosario Dawson's career.

Dawson also is viewed as more "urban" than Alba, which arguably has contributed to this racialization of her public image. A preponderance of Dawson's films have been set in New York City, beginning with *Kids* and subsequently including *He Got Game* (1998), *Light It Up* (1999), *Sidewalks of New York* (2001), *25th Hour* (2002), and *Rent* (2005). In these films her

*Rosario Dawson in one of the roles that contributed to her urban, ethnic image. She starred with Usher Raymond (left) and Robert Richard in the urban teen drama* Light It Up *(1999). Photo courtesy of Edmonds/Fox 2000 and the Kobal Collection.*

major costars have often been other actors of color. Such was the case in *Light It Up*, a drama about New York City high school students in a standoff with police in an effort to force improvements at their school; Dawson plays a brainy student who is convinced to take part. In addition, the story that is often repeated about Dawson's entrée as an actress is that *Kids* director, Larry Clark, "discovered" Dawson on her Lower East Side tenement stoop when she was fifteen.[35] This and the predominance of New York–centric roles that Dawson has portrayed since have contributed to a public image that is strongly rooted in the city and its polyglot, distinctly "ethnic" cultures. Common associations of Nuyorican and Afro-Cuban cultures with African American culture in the United States also arguably have an impact in this regard. Puerto Rican culture has historically been intertwined and strongly associated with African American culture in New York City in particular,[36] leading to an association with "blackness" in the public imaginary to a degree distinct from that of other Latino groups.

It is important to note that this process of the differing racialization of Alba's and Dawson's public images has taken place not only in Hollywood but to a large degree in the Latino- and African American–oriented news media and by ethnic advocacy groups that monitor media representation. More specifically, Alba and Dawson have been embraced by their overlapping ethnic communities, but to different degrees. A review of their mention in Latino-oriented magazines and nominations for awards such as the ALMAs supports that while both have been claimed at various times as Latina stars, Alba appears to have received more attention from the Latino-oriented press and especially from Latino advocacy groups. On the other hand, Dawson has been additionally "claimed" by and lauded for her acting by African American–oriented media outlets such as *Essence* and *Jet* magazines and groups such as the National Association for the Advancement of Colored People, which has honored her at its annual Image Awards ceremony.

Over the years, Dawson has received positive reviews from film critics (she has been described, among other things, as a "rising starlet" and "a lovely and appealing screen presence"),[37] and she was recently part of the ensemble cast of *A Guide to Recognizing Your Saints*, awarded a Special Jury Prize for best ensemble performance at the Sundance Film Festival in 2006. Her "diverse as downtown" image[38] has likely affected how she is viewed by Hollywood producers, who appear to still often be guided by white-centric norms, however. Interestingly, the few directors that have cast her as a romantic lead opposite a white male have in fact been New Yorkers. They include Edward Burns, who cast Dawson in both *Sidewalks of New York* and *Ash Wednesday* (2002), and Spike Lee, who cast her opposite Edward Norton in *25th Hour*.

## Hierarchies of Mestizaje: Mixed Latino Stars and Racialization

It is worth exploring the fact that Alba's *mestizaje* appears more desirable than Dawson's not only to Hollywood producers but also to Latino media outlets. While it is important not to read too much into this supposed difference, it does underscore the vagaries of contemporary Latinidad as defined within Latino communities and particularly by media outlets. What factors determine whether a star of partial Latino ancestry will be embraced by the Latino community? Notably, not all types of racial ambiguity are necessarily embraced equally. As Gregory Velazco y Trianosky argues, while *mestizaje* is very much a part of Latino and Latin American history, it still is not necessarily acknowledged or celebrated.[39] Indigenous and African ancestry continues to be denied and denigrated in casual talk and actions (my own mother, who likes to be reassured that her tan is not too dark when she has spent time in the sun, is just one example), while fair skin is typically celebrated. Similar patterns at times can be discerned in the Latino-oriented media when it comes to coverage of mixed Latino stars. In this regard, the historical "one-drop" rule, which dictated that any African ancestry meant an individual was black, still appears to be in effect, both in Latino-oriented realms and in Hollywood casting circles: Rosario Dawson has to contend with an association with blackness in her image, whereas Jessica Alba does not. Arguably for mixed Latina stars their approximation of the expected "Latin look" is still a necessity, while the more they can play with whiteness within these parameters, the better.

An illustration of the importance of perceived "assimilability" to whiteness to being viewed as a bankable Hollywood actress can be seen in the career of Jessica Alba, who is currently constructed as the Millennial Girl Next Door. The complexity of this construction should be acknowledged, however. Her public image arguably is coming full circle as she is seen simultaneously as mixed race *and* as the average U.S. American girl. As she noted to *Entertainment Weekly* in June 2006 in response to her popularity, "People today, especially this next generation of kids, they don't look like middle America anymore. They're not all blond and blue-eyed. They're more ethnically mixed. Today, the girl next door looks more like me."[40] This can be viewed as a strategic, assimilationist move in the development of her public image, but also as a sign of an increased broadening of ethnic notions in the popular imagination. Moreover, it is paying off. Alba appears to be following in the path set by Jennifer Lopez as she begins to be cast in a number of non-ethnic-specified roles in her upcoming films, a definite shift from how she was cast a few years ago. The films she has in production include the medical drama *Awake*, the romantic comedy *Good Luck Chuck*, the Ten Commandments–inspired satire *The Ten*, and the comedy *Bill*, in addition to *Fantastic Four* and *Sin City* sequels.

## Mestizaje *and Mixed Latino Stars: Conclusions*

Both in the mainstream and at the high end of the marketplace, what is perceived as good, desirable, successful is often a face whose heritage is hard to pin down.

—Ron Berger, chief executive, advertising firm Euro RSCG Worldwide[41]

In exploring Jessica Alba's and Rosario Dawson's evolving careers and public images, it becomes clear that in many ways Max Guevara's ambiguous but deracialized identity serves as an apt metaphor for how the actress who portrayed her was initially sold to the U.S. American public, and how Rosario Dawson, running up against what we might call the "one-drop rule of color-blind casting," has not and likely will not any time soon be given this opportunity on the big-budget film playing field. More recently, Alba has begun to complicate her image, however, as she shares increasing information about her struggles and achievements as a mixed race individual and actress. This ambiguity, as is foregrounded in Max Guevera's characterization and in Alba's public image, still can offer a challenge to Hollywood and the nation's imagined constructions of race, placing into question why anyone can be neatly categorized.

But while Alba, Dawson, and other mixed Latino actors provide a reminder of the constructed nature of racial and ethnic categories, and may publicly identify in a manner that emphasizes a mestiza or multiracial identity, they cannot fully avoid the process of cultural racialization that typically takes place in the realm of star promotion, which often reiterates a white-black or white-nonwhite color line. As the comparison of these two actresses illuminates, this process is dependent on the media industries' interpretation of an actor's appearance and acting choices, and, to a lesser extent, on how the star identifies him- or herself. Through these dynamics performers are subtly or not so subtly racially classified by production companies, publicists, and the entertainment news media, a process that has ultimate sway in an actor's career and public image. Performers can attempt to influence this process through their choice of news outlets in which to give interviews and other declarations of racial and ethnic affiliation, but ultimately they cannot change age-old paradigms that have guided how Hollywood film actors have been labeled, cast, and publicized.

Although her success does increase Latina visibility, Alba notably has had many doors open to her that are still not available to other Latinas, in large part because of her off-white appearance and image. As Ron Berger, chief executive of the advertising firm and trend research company Euro RSCG Worldwide, notes in the quotation at the beginning of this section, the most desirable look today is often one that is hard to pinpoint with respect to race and ethnicity—that is, as long as some of that heritage appears to be European American. From this perspective, is Alba's success reflective in any shape or form of a rising status of Latinos in the

United States or in Hollywood with respect to casting opportunities? Not necessarily, considering that in this process Latinidad is often nullified, construed merely as a hint of ethnic possibility that is never made meaningful.

Notably, while ambiguity and approximation of whiteness can result in increased opportunity in contemporary media projects, Latino representation as constructed by Hollywood still rests on notions of distinctive Latino elements and traits, which include an inherent *mestizaje*. This *mestizaje* is in danger of being submerged in movements to whiten and deny African and indigenous ancestry and appearance while exalting the multiethnic, however. In this regard the "multiculti" wave needs to be viewed critically, particularly regarding how it may threaten to halt progress toward increasingly diverse and dimensional Latino images. But much of the responsibility in this regard lies with Latino communities and media outlets. As Gloria Anzaldúa famously has argued, the challenge for Latino communities is to embrace the contradictions of our mixed ancestry in all its permutations. In this regard, mixed Latina stars such as Jessica Alba and Rosario Dawson serve as important symbolic tropes, whose future careers will have a great deal to say about the racial borders that affect Latinos more generally.

## Acknowledgments

I would like to thank Camilla Fojas for her astute suggestions, particularly regarding the assimilable mixed race star, in her review of drafts of this chapter. I would also like to thank LeiLani Nishime for organizing the American Studies Association conference panel in 2006 at which this chapter was first presented, and my *comadre* Becky Lentz for introducing me to the guilty pleasures of *Dark Angel*.

### NOTES

1. I hereafter use the term "Latino" in a gender-inclusive manner to refer to both Latinas and Latinos, rather than the more unwieldy Latina/o or Latin@.

2. I first heard this term used by Bel Hernandez, CEO and publisher of *Latin Heat*, a media industry trade journal, where I interned to conduct research in 2000. Hernandez in fact has since trademarked it. *Latin Heat*, which reports on

the deals made by Hollywood media companies with Latino actors and creative professionals, utilizes it in its recurring "LatinoWood™ USA: The Inside Chisme" column.

3. See Ella Shohat and Robert Stam, *Unthinking Eurocentrism: Multiculturalism and the Media* (New York: Routledge, 1994), for a foundational discussion of the racialized paradigms of casting in the Hollywood film industry.

4. For discussion of the new centrality of mixed race actors and models in film, television, and popular culture, see my essay "The New Hollywood Racelessness: When Only the Fast, Furious (and Multi-racial) Will Survive," *Cinema Journal* 44, no. 2 (Winter 2005): 50-67; as well as Marilyn Halter, *Shopping for Identity: The Marketing of Ethnicity* (New York: Schocken Books, 2000); Leon E. Wynter, *American Skin: Pop Culture, Big Business, and the End of White America* (New York: Crown, 2002); Danzy Senna, "The Mulatto Millennium," in *Half and Half*, ed. Claudine O'Hearn (New York: Pantheon, 1998), 205-8, and Caroline A. Streeter, "The Hazards of Visibility: 'Biracial' Women, Media Images, and Narratives of Identity," in *New Faces in a Changing America: Multiracial Identity in the 21st Century*, ed. Loretta I. Winters and Herman L. DeBose (Thousand Oaks, CA: Sage, 2003), 301–22.

5. For further discussion of the film industry's long-term preference for Latino and Latina actors of fair skin and appearance, see Clara E. Rodriguez, introduction, *Latin Looks: Images of Latinas and Latinos in the U.S. Media*, ed. Clara E. Rodríguez (Boulder, CO: Westview Press, 1997), 1–12; Charles Ramírez Berg, *Latinos and Film: Stereotypes, Subversion, and Resistance* (Austin: University of Texas Press, 2002); Antonio Ríos-Bustamante, "Latino Participation in the Hollywood Film Industry, 1911–1945," in *Chicanos and Film: Representation and Resistance*, ed. Chon Noriega (Minneapolis: University of Minnesota Press, 1992), 18–28; and Mary Beltrán, "The Hollywood Latina Body as Site of Social Struggle: Media Constructions of Stardom and Jennifer Lopez's 'Cross-Over Butt,'" *Quarterly Review of Film and Video* 19 (2002): 71–86.

6. Clara E. Rodríguez points out that fair, blond, and blue-eyed Latino actors and actresses typically are not considered for Latino roles; by Hollywood standards they do not have what she terms the preferred "Latin look" (*Latin Looks,* 4). Such rules regarding the "type" of Latino who might be considered for a lead role are beginning to shift, but only slightly.

7. Since she began to publicly promote herself as half Bolivian, Welch was cast in the Latino-themed *Tortilla Soup* (2001) and in *American Family* (2002), a television series about a Mexican American family written and produced by Gregory Nava.

8. Senna, "The Mulatto Millennium"; Halter, *Shopping for Identity*; Leon E. Wynter, *American Skin*.

9. Gregory Velasco y Trianosky, "Beyond *Mestizaje*: The Future of Race in America," in Winters and DeBose, *New Faces in a Changing America*, 176.

10. For discussion of the current rates of out-marriage in the United States, see Michael A. Fletcher, "Interracial Marriages Eroding Barriers," *Washington Post*, December 28, 1998, A1.

11. See Elizabeth M. Grieco and Rachel C. Cassidy, "Overview of Race and Hispanic Origin: Census 2000 Brief," '*Mixed Race' Studies: A Reader*, ed. Jayne Ifekwunigwe (London: Routledge, 2004), 225–43, for an overview of the problematic way in which Hispanics are currently tallied on the census. This discussion provides evidence for why Latinos continue to hold an indeterminate status in relation to racial categories and group identity.

12. Velasco y Trianosky, "Beyond *Mestizaje*"; Angharad N. Valdivia, "Latinas as Radical Hybrid: Transnationally Gendered Traces in Mainstream Media," *Global Media Journal* 3, no. 4 (Spring 2004), http://lass.calumet.purdue.edu/cca/gmj/sp04/gmj-sp04-valdivia.htm; George C. Sanchez, "Y Tú Que? (Y2K): Latino History in the New Millennium," in Ifekwunigwe '*Mixed Race' Studies*, 276–82.

13. Chon Noriega, *Shot in America: Television, the State, and the Rise of Chicano Cinema* (Minneapolis: University of Minnesota Press, 2000), xxvi.

14. Rodríguez, introduction, *Latin Looks*.

15. Ruth La Ferla, "Generation E.A.: Ethnically Ambiguous," *New York Times*, December 28, 2003, sec. 9, p. 1.

16. Dennis Hensley, *Marie Claire*, August 2005, par. 4, http://magazines.ivillage.com/marieclaire/mind/celebinterview/articles/0,,673522_673618-2,00.html.

17. Alba appears to be quoted in this article by Allison Glock, "The Body and Soul of Jessica Alba," *Rolling Stone* June 30, 2005, 76–83, par 6. The paragraph in which the quotation appeared is not listed in the excerpted article on *Rolling Stone*'s Web pages, but the complete article can be found in its reprint version. See "Fantasy Figure," *Guardian*, July 17, 2005, http://film.guardian.co.uk/interview/interviewpages/ 0,,1530103,00.html.

18. Rafael Pérez-Torres, *Mestizaje: Critical Uses of Race in Chicano Culture* (Minneapolis: University of Minnesota Press, 2006); Valdivia, "Latinas as Radical Hybrid."

19. See, for example, Marc Savlov, "Idle Hands," *Austin Chronicle*, April 30, 1999, www.austinchronicle.com/gbase/Calendar/Film?Film=oid%3a142862; and Ron Wells, "*Idle Hands*," *Film Threat*, April 26, 1990, www.filmthreat.com/index.php?section=reviews&Id=710.

20. BBDO New York, "TV Viewing Habits Differ in Black Households," *Minority Markets Alert* 7, no. 5 (May 1995): 2.

21. Eglee cited by Benjamin Svetkey, "The Terminatrix," *Entertainment Weekly*, March 16, 2001, par. 14, www.ew.com/ew/article/0,,280327_1,00.html.

22. *Dark Angel: Genesis* (Twentieth Century Fox, 2000), featurette, *Dark Angel: The Complete First Season* DVD set.

23. *Dark Angel*, season 1, episode 10: "Art Attack."

24. Benjamin Svetkey, "Jessica Alba Is Our Must Girl of the Summer," *Entertainment Weekly*, June 30, 2006, 45–51, par. 9; and Allison Glock, *Rolling Stone*, June 30, 2005, par. 7, respectively.

25. Dan Snierson, "Back to the Future: EW Goes behind the Scenes at Fox's Latest Foray into Sci-fi Drama," *Entertainment Weekly*, March 28, 2000, n.p., par. 3, www.ew.com/ew/ article/0,,85597,00.html.

26. For example, see Lewis Beale, "Attack of the Sexy Tough Women," *New York Daily News*, October 19, 2000, 52.

27. Svetkey, "The Terminatrix," par. 12.

28. Latina.com, "Jessica Alba to Host MTV Movie Awards," www.latina.com/latina/searchresults.jsp;jsessionid=2A538684F558A74579BCED3D09A6A9B8.

29. Valdivia, "Latinas as Radical Hybrid."

30. Ella Shohat and Robert Stam, *Unthinking Eurocentrism* (New York: Routledge, 1994*)*.

31. Svetkey, "Jessica Alba Is Our Must Girl of the Summer."

32. Glock, "The Body and Soul of Jessica Alba," par. 7.

33. Ibid.

34. Diane Negra, *Off-White Hollywood: American Culture and Ethnic Stardom* (London: Routledge, 2001).

35. This information has been confirmed by Dawson in multiple published interviews, including Logan Hill's "Avenue A-Lister" in *New York Magazine*, September 5, 2005.

36. See Juan Flores, "Qúe Assimilated, Brother, Yo So Assimilao: The Structuring of Puerto Rican Identity in the U.S.," in *Challenging Fronteras: Structuring Latina and Latino Lives in the U.S.*, ed. Mary Romero, Pierrette Hongdagnu-Sotelo, and Vilma Ortiz (New York: Routledge, 1997), 175–86.

37. *Love in the Time of Money* (review), *Hollywood Reporter*, January 14, 2002; Andrew O'Hehir, "Movie Reviews: *The Rundown*," Salon.com, September 26, 2003, www.salon.com.

38. Hill, "Avenue A-Lister."

39. Velazco y Trianosky, "Beyond *Mestizaje*."

40. Svetkey, "Jessica Alba Is Our Must Girl of the Summer," par. 8.

41. Quoted in La Ferla, "Generation E.A.," par. 4.

# Mixed Race on the Disney Channel

## *From* Johnnie Tsunami *through* Lizzie McGuire *and Ending with* The Cheetah Girls

*Angharad N. Valdivia*

Nearly everyone who has grown up either within U.S. culture or influenced by it elsewhere is familiar with the Disney canon.[1] Whereas the average U.S. person can easily name two or even all of the seven dwarfs, few of them can name any, let alone two, of the Supreme Court justices, as proved to be the case in my popular culture class this term, where out of sixty-three upper-division undergraduate students, nearly all could name all of the dwarfs, and only five could name more than two of the justices. Moreover, showing Disney film segments, even to these jaded and oh-so-hip and quite intelligent twenty-year-olds, turns them into mushy children. Just a clip from *Beauty and the Beast* or *The Little Mermaid* can literally bring tears to their eyes, not to mention that they know all the words to the theme songs. The reach of Disney is broad, and it has to be acknowledged as contributing to the national imaginary that implicates us all. We can all remember the Disney that teaches us through themes of love conquers all, including class differences, and anthropomorphized animals that sometimes represent or stand in for ethnic difference, happiness will reign, and the Mickey Mouse ears will fade into that blue cosmic sunset at the end of every Disney movie.

The classic Disney canon was and remains immensely popular and profitable. But at the level of the body, this pedagogy of innocence, as described by Henry Giroux,[2] remains if not entirely white at least privileging and normalizing whiteness. Moreover, Griffin has also written about the queer politic of classic Disney.[3] Disney products and cultural forms, such as theme parks,[4] movies,[5] comic books,[6] business,[7] television,[8] and even whole towns,[9] have been the subject of scholarly inquiry for decades. Given their global cultural reach and undeniable popularity, Disney films have received the most attention. Fast forward to 2006, or not even that far but to the early 1990s, and we get a different set of circumstances, technological options, economic logics, and demographic reality. Mixed race in Disney is a fairly new phenomenon. It is influenced by at least three overlapping sets of influence. First, there is undeniable growth not only in the racialized population of the United States but also in its mixed race component. Given that this population has disposable income, it makes sense to begin including some form of representation to generate some form of recognition, attention, and audience loyalty to the Disney brand.

In 1995 Disney sought to expand its synergies and convergence through the merger with Capital Cities/ABC. This resulted in some administrative shifts in order to maximize profit and revenues from its television holdings. One such way was to target the "tween" audience, which has been only recently identified as a new and profitable age segment. Tweens are that in-between age-group between childhood and adolescence. The gendered component of tweens, accomplished mostly through the consumerist messages and assumed interests of the tween girl audience, make the production of Disney-branded cultural forms all the more attractive to the media conglomerate. These influences help us to understand the three shows/movies analyzed in this chapter.

Thus in the contemporary situation, we must turn our critical eye to particular Disney cultural forms, especially the increasingly successful Disney television channel. Never one to fall too far behind the curve on these issues,[10] Disney has gingerly begun to address issues of difference as it seeks to maintain ratings prominence and economic returns in the form of increasing revenues and profits for its shareholders. Thus the representation of difference cannot be discussed outside of the political economy of the contemporary media giant. With Disney television making up a vibrant location of revenues for the parent company, this chapter addresses the representation of difference within this cable option. In particular I focus on three Disney television and movie franchises: *Johnny Tsunami* (1999), a made-for-TV Disney movie; the *Lizzie McGuire Show* (2000–2004), a television show, and the related *Lizzie McGuire Movie* (2003), a wide-release Hollywood film; and *The Cheetah Girls* (2003, 2006), yet another set of made-for-TV movies. While it is true that *Johnny Tsunami* and *The Cheetah Girls* are far more about mixed

*Disney's* Johnnie Tsunami, The Cheetah Girls, Lizzie McGuire.

race than *Lizzie*, discussing them in relation to each other allows us to explore Disney marketing and representation issues in tandem. All three of these Disney brands exhibit some form of attempt to deal with issues of difference against the political economy of demographic growth and targeted audiences.[11]

## Stages of Ethnic Representation

Once a bastion of whiteness, the Disney television channel has begun to expand its offerings to include a broader range of representations. For example, Celeste Lacroix studies the relational construction between heroines in the second set, post-1986, Michael Eisner era of Disney global animated hits.[12] She finds that in the representation of the oriental Disney princesses, such as *Pocahontas* (1995), Ariel from *The Little Mermaid* (1989), Esmeralda from *The Hunchback of Notre Dame* (1996), and Jasmine from *Aladdin* (1993), whiteness, as represented by Belle from *Beauty and the Beast* (1991), remains a normalizing strategy. The "brown"[13] heroines are much more embodied, physical, and assertive than the demure and intellectual Belle in *Beauty and the Beast*. In this strategy, Disney is no different than many other contemporary media giants. As I have written elsewhere,[14] the history of ethnic representations in the United States appears to be in a fourth stage. The first stage was one of absence—with the predominant form of representations being white. At that stage (dating roughly back to the 1700s), the visual was not as broad a category as it is now. Printed materials were not as widely available, and when they were, they were likely to contain more word than image. Visual materials for individual distribution were scarce and largely out of the reach of the general population. Publicly available large visual images were likely to reproduce white hegemony. Given that identity and difference are relational, even in this stage available representation normalized the white subject.

The second stage, dating back loosely to antebellum and postbellum politics, was mostly a binary one, with heavy tints of symbolic annihilation. In the United States the binary component, of course, was white and black, accomplished through the relative underrepresentation of the black subject as well as the victimization, marginalization, and ridicule of this subject when it was present. At this stage, which lasts until the civil rights era in the United States, and which also coincides with the Chicano movement and other redistributive political ethnic and gender movements, we get the deployment and widespread adoption of stereotypes that signify both difference and inferiority. Whether looking at Latinas and our spitfire señorita or dark lady or at African American mammies and coons, all of these stereotypes relied on narratives that symbolically annihilate populations of color in mainstream popular media.

The third stage—post–civil rights and up to the present—takes up "multiculturalism" as fashion. Here we have a broader range of ethnicities, though by and large many of the representations remain black and white. In the multicultural moment in the United States one is also likely to see forms of Latina/o and Asian American representations and much less often Native Americans. Post-9/11 Arab Americans and anyone who "looks Muslim"[15] are added to the hit list of minorities to be included in the multiculturalist recipe. Much research on multiculturalism (such as that of Ellen Seiter)[16] suggests that in such forms of representations, whiteness continues to be foregrounded and normalized. Multiculturalism is seen by many as a way to sidestep very real economic and political inequalities in favor of a visually pleasing, and not terribly threatening, cosmetic democracy.

Finally, the fourth stage is one of ambiguity and hybridity, which represents both an acknowledgment of the lack of purity at the levels of culture, the body, blood, and DNA, as well as an effort to reach as many segments of the audience as possible with one economical image. A case in point is that with an ambiguously brown image an advertiser can potentially appeal to a broad range of ethnicities ranging from white to Latina, Native American, Asian American, Indian, Middle Eastern, and even black if the signifiers are ambiguous enough.[17] The marketing effort in this case can claim a keen sensitivity to multiculturalism without alienating the white audience, something that remains important in a culture where whiteness is still hegemonic. This fourth stage is different from the third one in that in multiculturalism easily identifiable ethnicities are replaced by one or more ambiguous body that can sign in for more than one ethnicity. What also deserves note is that all of these stages are still present, though the last two are more prominent than the first two. Disney represents all four of these stages, as its older material is still widely available and globally circulated, and its newest stuff engages the third and fourth stages. Children continue to be introduced to all stages through Disney industry engagement, as classic Disney products continue to be recycled, quoted, and thus widely circulated.

## Disney Television Marketing

Nevertheless, the preceding representational path is also abetted by a set of industry exigencies that have forced Disney to change its marketing strategy. Like other companies targeting the children and youth audience, Disney entered into the cable television market in the eighties. However, Disney entered as a premium channel, meaning that subscribers did not get Disney in their basic package and that therefore the bulk of subscribers did not get Disney. In an effort to increase its audience and support some form of economic viability, in the early nineties Disney switched to basic package status in cable. This, as you might imagine, was not easily accomplished because Disney was far more expensive to cable operators than Nick Jr. or the Cartoon Network (at a ratio of roughly 73 to 33 to 8). Great parental demand made this a feasible shift as middle-class parents sought to provide their offspring with "quality" programming.[18] Part of the quality characteristic was tied to yet another difference. Whereas Nick Jr. and Cartoon Network are commercially supported, the Disney Channel is not. While this may have garnered more parental approval, it did not help the bottom line. Thus Disney television floundered for the early part of the nineties as one of the weaker components of the Disney empire. Its traditional audience of preschool and elementary-aged children did not return the profits sought by such a dynamic conglomerate and its demanding shareholders.

In the mid-1990s two major moves made a total difference in the marketing of Disney television products. First, Disney, under the leadership of Michael Eisner, sought to expand its global reach through a time-tested strategy of merger and acquisitions. In 1995 Disney purchased Capital Cities/ABC for $19 billion and thus moved "from being a dominant global content producer to being a fully integrated media giant."[19] While it is widely acknowledged that Disney practically wrote the book on media synergy and convergence, this merger geometrically expanded such possibilities. The reorganization and increased program and product delivery options enabled by this move meant that Disney television programs could now also be broadcast on ABC television channels in general and in the lucrative Saturday morning cartoon hours in particular. However, that Disney kept its noncommercial Disney Channel also meant the company had the freedom to develop shows outside of the rigorously formulaic Saturday morning time slot.[20] Second, Disney hired a proven veteran of children's television, formerly of Nick Jr., Anne Sweeney, as president of ABC Cable Networks Group and Disney Channel Worldwide. The acquisition, reorganization, and new management propelled the, until then, tepid returns of Disney television offerings into another dimension of profitability.

## Revenge of the Tweens

While family-oriented products, from classic Disney movies through the *Winnie the Pooh*–type entertainment on the Disney Channel, offered profits and synergistic potential, Anne Sweeney sought to strengthen the position of Disney Television vis-à-vis other Disney holdings as well as vis-à-vis other children's networks, namely, Nick Jr. and Cartoon Network.[21] The strategy was to expand the target audience to tweens, that elusive nine- to fourteen-year-old demographic of youth whose attention was eagerly sought simultaneously as their disposable income was acknowledged.[22] Creating the category of tweens opened up a new market of those who were not yet teens yet no longer children. These in-betweeners turn out to have a sizable amount of aggregate spending money and time to watch television. Sweeney was keenly aware of competitors for her desired audience, yet she wanted programming for those too old for Nick Jr. and too young for MTV.[23] As a result of Sweeney's mandate to create such programming, two shows rose to the top, *Lizzie*

*McGuire* and *Evens Stevens* (2000–2003), both of which focused on the travails of a group of junior high school students. Begun as *Zoog Weekendz* programming, the shows soon went into Disney prime-time daily rotation. Of these two I focus on *Lizzie McGuire* because it generated a much more profitable franchise and attempted to include some issues of difference.

Tween focus is an age, gender, and racial affair. Tween successes Mary Kate and Ashley Olson, for example, are young, female, and white. Most of the synergistic possibilities of tween cultural programming rely both on the disposable income of that affluent younger demographic—that is assumed to be white—and the added component that as girls with the assumed economic advantage and focus on image of white audiences, this target cohort will spend more money on appearance, clothing, and general lifestyle products. As girl culture literature documents, girls are big business, and postfeminist constructions actually rest on consumerism.[24] Disney estimates that the aggregate disposable income of this group of girls is between $40 and $60 billion.[25] Disney continues to attempt to replicate the tween girl monster hit *Lizzie*. Given the size of that disposable income figure, it is not surprising that Disney is not alone in trying to reach that target audience. Thus, as Melanie Lowe says of tweens in popular culture:

> In terms of media representations and constructions of possibility, it's a pretty good time to be a middle-class, twelve-year-old girl in suburbia, United States. . . . And several of the careers they envision themselves pursuing bear a striking resemblance to those of female characters on their favorite television shows—from doctor (*ER*) to lawyer (*Ally McBeal*) to forensic scientist (*The X-Files*). They see these careers as true possibilities. After all, they have, in their words, "good role models"—from Mom, who is a lawyer, to MTV's Daria, who will surely become one.[26]

In fact, much of tween culture seems to be a blend of this age/gender/race strategy and a serious dose of postfeminist politics that foreground style and consumption over political and social gender politics.[27] As feminist media scholars have noted, television has been at the foreground of the representation of this new white subjectivity,[28] and the migration of this postfeminism to children's and tweens' television and film is entirely expected. There is money to be made from tweens, especially girls, though the potential for a liberatory praxis cannot be entirely discounted.[29]

By 2003 the results of Sweeney's strategy were evident—Disney television, alongside its theme parks, was making up an increasing share of the revenues and profits of the parent company. The growth of the Disney Channel revenues even peaked at 47 percent in 2004. *Lizzie McGuire*, its cash cow, spawned off a seriously profitable set of synergistic ventures, ranging from books to music to video games to clothing to toys. So profitable was this venture that Disney made a wide-release *Lizzie McGuire* movie in 2003, which debuted in the number two spot as a new release and generated a healthy $50 million in revenues,[30] and an additional $5 million in DVD and VHS sales. The sound track from the movie went platinum, and the first album (and the only one Disney was able to secure from Hilary Duff, the actor who played Lizzie), entitled *Metamorphosis*, also went platinum. Duff was pronounced a tween queen in magazines ranging from *Time* to *Vanity Fair*, which placed her in one of its collages of young Hollywood covers in July 2004. Duff promptly severed her *Lizzie* contract and launched what she hoped would be a successful solo artist career, with more music and movie projects in the making. At this point (fall of 2006), Duff remains one of many Hollywood starlets who regularly show up in celebrity culture circuits such as *People* magazine and E! and the occasional movie, mostly targeted at a tween audience. *Lizzie* and Hillary are both represented as the quintessential good girl next door—that is, middle-class and white.

Predating this gendered and racialized tween effort in the late nineties, *Johnny Tsunami* (1999) was shown and circulated without great fanfare. Postdating this effort, *The Cheetah Girls* (2003) was shown and released to great fanfare with all sorts of synergistic options already being exercised, including the release of a second movie, *The Cheetah Girls, When in Spain* (2006), and the *Cheetah-licious Christmas Album* (2005). Currently (fall 2006), the *Cheetah Girls*, minus Raven, are on a national music concert tour that showcases another Disney young star/ TV show, Miley Cyrus of *Hannah Montana* (2006+), as the warm-up act.[31] To be sure, *Cheetah Girls* had an advantage over *Johnny Tsunami* beyond Disney Channel's realization of the tween market and the commodification of difference, that being that the movie is based on a bestselling sixteen-book series by Deborah Gregory. So in a sense this was an eagerly awaited movie by an already preformed tween girl of color audience that crossed over into the mainstream—read, white and middle-class—audience, thanks to Disney. One can purchase *Cheetah Girls* music, clothes, video games, and toys in addition to the books, movies, and sound tracks. According to industry figures, *The Cheetah Girls* is the second most profitable made-for-TV movie shown by the Disney Channel, with the first being *High School Musical* (2005), whose $4 million production budget is well on its way to generating a billion dollars in revenues.[32] Apparently Disney has yet to max out the audience and profit potential of the tween market.

## The Shows

As one would expect from Disney, all three movies/shows are very similar in important ways. Most prominently, all three are about upper-middle-class protagonists in mostly upper-middle-class suburban settings. Johnny Kapahaala, the protagonist of *Johnny Tsunami* (the show is actually named after his grandfather, a champion surfer), has an overachieving and overbearing father whose transfer to Vermont separates Johnny from his Hawaiian waves and his surfing friends and grandfather. Johnny's father pursues a quest of upward mobility that lands him and his son in far more elite settings than they had in Hawaii. Lizzie McGuire lives in a very upscale house in an undetermined neighborhood, with an apparently stay-at-home mom and a dad whose well-paying job nonetheless allows him to spend plenty of time around the house, and equally wealthy friends. Main Cheetah Girl Galleria, played by Raven, formerly Raven-Simoné, from *The Cosby Show* (1984–92) and the hit Disney TV show *That's So Raven!* (2002+), is also a privileged child living in an upscale Manhattan loft. Two of the other Cheetahs are equally well-off, while the presence of working-class Dorinda allows for issues of class and wealth to enter the narrative.

Issues of difference range from the overt in the movies to the more subtle themes on the television show. *Johnny Tsunami* is about difference. Johnny Kapahaala is the child of a Hawaiian father and a Caucasian mother. He hangs with an ethnically mixed group of fellow surfers. His grandfather, Johnny Tsunami, is inescapably ethnic and countercultural—he is, after all, a surfer into his sixties. Much of the movie plot is driven by the father-son struggle between Johnny Tsunami and his careerist son Pete, and, in turn, between Pete and his son Johnny Kapahaala. Once he gets to Vermont, Johnny Kapahaala experiences racial prejudice from most of his classmates in his elite prep school. He is different. His clothing, hairstyle, slang, indeed his brownness all stand out in a nearly Nazi-like white setting of the prep school in which he finds himself. Befriending a girl who turns out to be the schoolmaster's daughter spells trouble. When Johnny befriends an African American boy, the child of a military father, who goes to the local public school, Johnny finds community with him. As a signifier of difference, the prep school teens go skiing on the better side of the mountain while the public school kids go snowboarding on the other side of the mountain. Johnny finds snowboarding much more similar to surfing, and thus this cements the cross-racial and cross-class friendship.

Similarly, *Cheetah Girls* is about difference. In a typical postfeminist setting, Cheetah Girls are all about materialism, girl power, multiculturalism, and song and dance. Like Johnny Kapahaala, Galleria, the protagonist, is a child of a biracial marriage, with an African American mother and Italian father. The other Cheetahs come from a range of backgrounds—Chanel is "a little bit of this and a little bit of that,"[33] but all of it U.S. Latina and Latin American heritage. While Chanel exhibits subtle signifiers of Afro-Latina traces, her mother, who might be Argentinean, is very Caucasian, with only a thick Spanish accent to sign for her Latinidad. Aqua appears to sign in for prehybrid African American identity, though the narrative of both movies includes the fact that she is from Houston, Texas. Thus her sartorial choices always include western-style boots and country skirts. Dorinda, who in the books is of mixed heritage, appears in the movies as a white girl. In the first movie, she lives in a mostly African American foster home. She does not really know who her parents were, so neither she nor we are really sure of her background. As well, Dorinda is the working-class Cheetah, living in the superintendent's house, whereas all the rest of the Cheetahs live in very upscale condos.

"Cheetah" functions as a metaphor for mixed race. The songs are simultaneously about girl power and the acceptance, indeed celebration, of difference. The conflict in the first movie revolves partly around these issues. The theme song underscores the three main themes of sisterhood, difference, and success. Entitled "Cheetah Girls Cheetah Sisters," it functions as an anthem for multiculturalism:

> Cause we are sisters, we stand together
> We make up one big family though we don't look the same.
> Our spots are different, different colors
> We make each other stronger, that ain't ever gonna change.
> We're cheetah girls, cheetah sisters.

All of the songs foreground these three themes, often recasting or rejecting popular culture scenarios such as the following lyrics to their song called "Cinderella":

> I don't wanna be like Cinderella, Sitting in a dark, cold, dusty cellar,
> Waiting for somebody to come and set me free (Come and set me free)
> I don't wanna be like someone waiting,
> For a handsome prince to come and save me
> Oh I will survive, Unless somebody's on my side
> Don't wanna be, No, no, no one else.
> I'd rather rescue myself.

Similarly in "Together We Can!" the Cheetahs reaffirm their bond and goals:

> Together we can!
> Shoot the moon, Stop the rain, Even ride a hurricane!
> If we wanna!
> Together we can!
> Walk into space, Save the human race,
> Do ya think we oughta, oughta?
> Together we can!

I provide these lyric samples because song and dance are such a central part of the Cheetah Girl experience. Tween fans, and their unwitting mothers and relatives, learn the catchy lyrics and sing along. As Randall puts it:

> The messages in the songs are laudable, too: Dreams can come true if you work hard; love and friendship are essential parts of life; racial unity is a good thing. The bouncy closing number, "Amigas Cheetahs," presented the Cheetahs' case succinctly—"We can all be ourselves and still be one"—while managing not to seem preachy.[34]

The sound track sales to the first movie have gone multiplatinum. The sound track to the second movie debuted at number five in the Billboard 200 (Martin). And while it is undeniable that Cheetah Girls are not original in the sense of being a prefab girl band, the difference lies in the tween target audience and the inclusion of ethnicity.

*Lizzie McGuire,* as a television show, although not primarily about difference, nonetheless includes it in subtle ways. Lizzie's sidekick, Miranda Sanchez, is ambiguously Latina. (Raven's sidekick in the African American *That's So Raven!* is ambiguously white.) Her Latinidad is not foregrounded, though in a couple of episodes her Spanish-accented mother appears, and we hear that her grandmother lives in Mexico. Lizzie's other sidekick, Gordo, is Jewish. Much is made of his psychoanalyst parents who implicitly trust him and generally play out the stereotype of the over-analyzing, absent parents. As with Miranda Isabela Sanchez,[35] Gordo's religious ethnic status is not foregrounded, though in one episode he decides to embrace his religion and prepare for his bar mitzvah. Of course Lizzie and Miranda help him out. In Lizzie's high school, kids of all races occupy the stereotypical teen roles. For instance, one of the mean cheerleaders, and Kate's best friend, is an African American girl. Nonetheless, the head cheerleader, and Lizzie's nemesis and former best friend, Kate, is white, as is her and Miranda's heartthrob, Ethan. Teachers and students are primarily white, though the occasional African American teacher shows up. Matt's best friend, Lanny, is an African American boy who does not speak. Somehow Matt is the only one who always knows what he's "saying," thus acting as his interpreter and interlocutor. As an interesting aside, Lizzie's father, Sam, is played by Robert Carradine, younger brother of David Carradine, who once played the iconic Asian American character in the television series *Kung Fu.* In fact, David Carradine guests stars as Sam's older brother in an episode about martial arts. *The Lizzie McGuire Movie* largely writes difference out of the picture. Both Miranda and Lennie disappear, and the narrative focuses on Lizzie, Gordo, Kate, and Ethan—that is, the white cast.

## Difference in Disney

As mentioned previously, *Johnny Tsunami* predates Disney's realization of the profitability of the tween market and the commodification of ethnicity. It does not have its own official Web site or any ancillary products. As a result, it languishes in occasional rerun status on the Disney Channel. *Lizzie McGuire* and *The Cheetah Girls,* on the other hand, both have Disney-supported "official Web sites," as well as independent fan clubs and other Web sites. *Lizzie McGuire* is still on daily rotation, and *The Cheetah Girls* gets daily coverage as the three touring Cheetahs make their way around the country. Disney stores abound with merchandise from both franchises, and although neither Hillary Duff nor Raven has decided to pursue the original narrative in another form with the Disney Channel, the syndicated rotation and product placement of their franchises continues to generate more than healthy returns for Disney. In fact, Disney banks on the development of young talent to build and extend its brand.

Beyond economic return, difference is deployed very carefully by Disney. After all, its wholesome image is at least partly informed by the politics of whiteness. Difference has to function in relation to and in deference of whiteness. Difference also has to be G-rated and have a happy ending. Given all these formulaic structures, producing cultural products with the inclusion of difference is already a highly restricted and limited process. Thus none of the analyzed shows proposes any type of revolutionary option, yet; as is sometimes the case with cultural production, the resulting shows and movies may represent more difference and fluidity than the parameters of the genre and the industry delineate.

Of the three shows, *Johnny Tsunami* is the only one about a boy. Johnny, a mixed race person, tries to resolve racial and class dilemmas through communication and collaboration. Rather than get into fights, he tries either the proposition of physical challenges or simply running away. The intergenerational conflict stands in for the mixed race and hybrid identity. Fully Hawaiian Johnny Tsunami, the grandfather, is fully coded as an island person—the type that surfs all day, indeed all his life, and has a "don't worry, be happy" life philosophy. He also is very "natural," thus reaffirming the Hollywood and mainstream U.S. popular culture coding of the ethnic as closer to nature and the white as closer to culture. His skills include reading the stars. Pete, the father, on the other hand, is a hard-driving school administrator who welcomes a move to Vermont, because of the career mobility and the distance it will put between him and his laid-back father. Johnny Kapahaala tries to reconcile his mother's loving ways and his father's distancing manners, as well as the pursuit of a top-notch education and the search for the perfect wave. In a sense, his mother represents wisdom while his father represents stubbornness. This is quite gendered, as the wise mother is a stay-at-home mom and the stubborn father is a rugged individualist in the masculine paradigm. As well, Johnny's snowboarding friend is African American and a child of a soon-to-relocate military family. Thus class and race are collapsed into the coding of "less affluent." Johnny Kapahaala is the body through which mixed race and hybrid cultures must be negotiated. Tween pursuits of sports, buddies, and girls dominate his interests. Understanding and communication are reached by the end of the movie as his father and grandfather reconcile, and a working plan is made to have Johnny return to his waves every once in a while. In his Vermont environment, upper-class skiers reconcile with townie snowboarders, and race and class are superseded by goodwill and cheer. By the movie's end all get along—the natives from Hawaii, the Vermont kids, and our mixed race hero, Johnny Kapahaala.

*Lizzie McGuire* certainly evokes Seiter's research of the foregrounding of whiteness in children's advertisements.[36] Lizzie herself epitomizes of whiteness—she is a lovable, healthy, affluent blonde. Her nemesis, Kate, and crush, Ethan, also have blond hair. Her buddies are ambiguously ethnic, but the overall feel of the series is one of white affluence. The tween themes taken up revolve around issues of popularity, shopping for the first bra, getting one's picture in the yearbook, sibling conflict, trying out for cheerleader, and so on. Sometimes Gordo rethinks his masculine place as best friend of two girls, but such episodes are resolved with his coming to terms with both his girl friends and his male identity. These are not incompatible. None of the episodes are about solving or addressing issues of racial or ethnic difference, although the theme of geek difference is sometimes taken up. Not only is Lizzie a geek in comparison to Kate, her nemesis, but there also is a regular character named Larry Tudgeman who is the paradigmatic math and science, greasy hair, awful clothing geek. In a couple of episodes Tudgeman is originally excluded, but Lizzie and her buddies end up doing the right thing by including him and apologizing.

Since the bulk of the action takes place either in Lizzie's house or at school, we do not really get to see or experience her friends' home life. Her own is affluent, happy, and collaborative, as is the wonderful world of G-rated Disney. The few times we glimpse Miranda's home, there is no discernible difference, though her hair and clothing styles are decidedly more eclectic and colorful than Lizzie's. This dovetails with the fact that people of color in the show only seems to appear for the sake of visual diversity. At no point in the series does race as an issue come up, although in many shows racialized children and adults pass through as part of an episode. One could say that *Lizzie McGuire* is both postfeminist and postracial, as both vectors of difference appear to have been settled in Lizzie world.

The only and most peculiar manifestation of racial difference is Lanny, the best friend of Lizzie's younger brother. His muteness reminds one of several other African American males who have played supporting roles in television series in which they were missing one of the five senses. For example, LeVar Burton played blind lieutenant Geordi La Forge in *Star Trek: The Next Generation*. Lanny is not as regular a character as the protagonist, but his appearance always has to be accompanied by Matt, who is the only one who can understand him. In one episode, Matt and Lanny try to get walkie-talkies to work, even though Lanny does not speak. Lanny is cute but silent and plays the role of moral compass for Matt, who tends to be a typical rambunctious as well as unethical little brother. Lanny's muteness is a metaphor for the discussion of the issues of race in *Lizzie McGuire*.

As mentioned previously, the successful *Lizzie McGuire Movie* leaves the diverse cast in the United States as all the white characters travel to Rome. Miranda is explained away by the comment that she went to Mexico City to visit her grandmother. Neither Lenny nor Kate's best friend makes it to Italy. In this movie all the Italians are slightly tanned Caucasian actors. Italy, like all of Europe in the U.S. imaginary, signs in for a land of whiteness.

By far the most explicit version of Disney difference among the three is *The Cheetah Girls*. This might have something to do with the fact that the movie is set in Manhattan, in a school for artistically gifted children. The students and the faculty at the school are racially diverse. Three of the four Cheetahs, Galleria, Chanel, and Aqua, are ethnically coded. Two of the three ethnics, Galleria and Chanel, are of mixed race. Chanel knows she is of mixed race, and she is very proud of it. Galleria never mentions it, nor do her parents. The comfort level with both girls of mixed race is demonstrated in that none of the conflict, or indeed the plot, revolves around mixed race issues. Mixed race composes part of the spots that make up *The Cheetah Girls*. Nor are biracial couplings discarded. In fact, Galleria ends up with her white, blond, blue-eyed love interest. The Cheetah mothers, despite their racial and class differences, also get along without conflict. Even the record company producers are racially diverse, composing a *Cheetah Girl* universe wherein racial identity is varied and not a source of conflict.

Among the Cheetahs, Dorinda, the white-looking one, is the one who is different. A subplot about identity crisis in the first movie revolves about Dorinda, who, because she is adopted, does not know who her parents are or what her racial mixture is. This reversal is also at the level of class. In *The Cheetah Girls*, the poor girl is the white girl who lives with black foster parents. To add yet one more layer of role reversal, it is

Dorinda, the poor white girl, who is the best dancer. Once in Barcelona, Dorinda falls in love with Joaquin. Originally she believes he is rich, but he turns out to be poor, and talented, like her, extending that reversal of expectation begun in the first movie wherein the beautiful white character actually turns out to be poor and a great dancer. Thus *Cheetah Girls* turns on their head dominant narratives about race, class, and bodily expression.

Other than Dorinda, the *Cheetah Girls* movies follow a pretty familiar scenario: girls sing and dance; girls break up when in the midst of success; girls get back together and pledge allegiance to each other and commitment to artistic integrity. Throughout the first movie, song, dance, and friendship illustrate the engagement with diversity. The second movie is less concerned with difference and more with individual work ethic and a love subplot. Still, some of the songs in the second movie foreground difference, and some include lines in Spanish or are fully in Spanish, celebrating the location, Barcelona, Chanel's Latina heritage, and the introduction of Marisol, a local pop singer from Barcelona. In real life this is a way for Disney to introduce Belinda, a Mexican singer-actress. The closing song, "Amigas Cheetahs," returns the Cheetahs to their spotted roots and adds the fifth Cheetah to what will supposedly become the third installment in this profitable franchise:

> Amigas Cheetahs, Friends for life
> The rhythm and each other
> That's what keeps us tight
> Amigas Cheetahs, Livin' the dream
> Nothin' is ever gonna come between amigas
>
> . . .
>
> Ya que estamos juntas
> Estamos en un mundo
> Donde somos uno [sic] por la musica
> If we just believe it
> You know we can be it
> Nothin' can stand in our way

This is the closest that the second movie comes to themes of unity and difference. Although the girls continue together, their attention has shifted to fame, individual pursuits, and love. By the time they get to Barcelona, the Cheetahs have outgrown difference.

## Conclusion

Exploring the mixed race issues in these three shows reveals contemporary trends as illustrated by a rather conservative cultural force, Disney. Whereas the creation of a new marketing subjectivity, tweens, allows for an increase in profits, indeed a long-awaited rise of Disney Television Channel as the most highly rated among its peers, the success of *The Cheetah Girls* and the newer entry *High School Musical* suggests that multicultural and ethnically ambiguous characters can lead to more successful outcomes than the racially coded whiteness of *Lizzie* and newcomer *Hannah*. Still, it appears that Disney will acknowledge this popularity and commercial success but locate them in the made-for-television movie while whiteness and difference remain part of the daily rotation. Normalized mixed race is spectacular. Normalized whiteness is quotidian.

*Johnny Tsunami* not only precedes the acknowledgment and full-throttle pursuit of tweens but also focuses on a boy. Thus messages of consumerism, other than in surfing and snowboarding paraphernalia, are not as prominent. Lack of further marketing of *Johnny Tsunami* as a branded product may have something to do with the date and gender issue—not to mention that after the real tsunamis of 2003, it would be in poor form to title a Disney movie using this word. Nonetheless, *Johnny Tsunami* took up themes of mixed race, albeit in a Disney format, and turned them into a feel-good movie, signaling that even the big mouse ears had noticed that there are mixed racial audiences, or at least that there is some money to be made from representing mixed racial youngsters.

*Lizzie McGuire* both represents some racial diversity yet reiterates the discursive location of whiteness in the Disney universe. In Lizzie land there are no mixed race people, though there are plenty of ethnically ambiguous characters. Yet in Lizzie land the white ones rule—and they are the only ones who get to travel to Europe. The fact that the heir apparent to Lizzie is Hannah Montana (Miley Cyrus), another blonde/brunette,[37] reaffirms Disney's vision of its stars and audience as it seeks to reproduce the Lizzie tween machine.

*The Cheetah Girls* continues the profitable venture of tween programming. The ratings success of both movies, with the quick sales of ancillary products, serves to cement the profitability of the girl tween market. In fact, by the time that *Cheetah Girls 2* was released in 2006, tween popular culture was nearly synonymous with girl culture.[38] Tweens are girls. Tweens watch television, go to the movies, and purchase tons of products, including massive amounts of clothing and makeup. Cheetah as a metaphor for difference appears to strike a chord not only on the basis of ethnic difference but also in a form of connoting girl power. That girl power has also been recruited to consumerist subjectivity does not hurt in the marketing effort. What better way to demonstrate tween girl power than to purchase cheetah spot underwear? To be serious, while we cannot make authoritative statements about reception prior to a grounded research project using that methodology, we can find that *The Cheetah Girls* proposes a universe where difference is both commonplace and normalized. Mixed race identity is neither abnormal nor marked. Mixed race couples are neither criminal nor outcasts. Mixed race belongs in that fourth category of ethnic representation. Mixed race has made it to Disney prime time; it's profitable; and it will be another sequel. But the daily stuff remains in the binary or multiculturalist world, which is safer and less threatening.

Disney has come a long way since its lily-white days. To be sure, Disney does not pursue new representational strategies unless it is certain that profits will increase without alienating the bulk of its audience. The pursuit of mixed race has been conducted in gingerly steps and in concert with other social demographic forces and marketing categories. For every *Cheetah Girl* movie set in a mixed race universe, there is a whole television series along the lines of *Lizzie McGuire* in which whiteness reigns supreme. We are not quite sure where the boys fit in, but we can rest assured that Disney will find a way to reap profits from that audience as well.[39] That consumerism is foregrounded is to be expected from one of the top five media conglomerates in the world. However, the fact remains that there have been representational changes that, at least temporarily, normalize an ethnically diverse universe with a happy ending. In the wonderful world of Disney, that is revolutionary but not quite yet a happy ending.

NOTES

1. While Disney comprises a huge range of industries and products, I choose to use this generalized term because I am talking of marketing efforts that pervade the distribution of Disney media materials.

2. Henry Giroux, *The Mouse That Roared: Disney and the End of Innocence* (Lanham, MD: Rowman and Littlefield, 1999).

3. Sean Griffin, *Tinker Belles and Evil Queens: The Walt Disney Company from the Inside Out* (New York: NYU Press, 1999).

4. Christopher Anderson, "Disneyland," in *Television: The Critical View*, 5th ed., ed. Horace Newcomb (New York: Oxford University Press, 1994); Ramona Fernandez, "Pachuco Disney," in *From Mouse to Mermaid: The Politics of Film, Gender, and Culture*, ed. Lynda Haas, Elizabeth Bell, and Laura Sells (Bloomington: Indiana University Press, 1995); Alan Bryman, *Disney and His Worlds* (New York: Routledge, 1995); The Project on Disney, *Inside the Mouse: Work and Play at Disneyworld* (Durham, NC: Duke University Press, 1995).

5. Haas, Bell, and Sells, *From Mouse to Mermaid*; Celeste Lacroix, "Images of Animated Others: The Orientalization of Disney's Cartoon Heroines from the Little Mermaid to the Hunchback of Notre Dame," *Popular Communication* 2, no. 4 (2004): 213-29.

6. Ariel Dorfman and Armand Mattelart, *How to Read Donald Duck: Imperialist Ideology in the Disney Comic* (New York: International General, 1975).

7. Janet Wasko, *Understanding Disney: The Manufacture of Fantasy* (Cambridge: Polity Press, 2001).

8. Cindy White and Elizabeth Hall Preston, "The Spaces of Children's Programming," *Critical Studies in Media Communication* 22, no. 3 (2005): 239-55.

9. Andrew Ross, *The Celebration Chronicles: Life, Liberty, and the Pursuit of Property Value in Disney's New Town* (New York: Ballantine Books, 1999).

10. For example, Disney was quite adroit, indeed enlisted, to participate in the Good Neighbor Policy of the 1940s. *The Three Caballeros* (1944) was an effort to move beyond "banana republic" politics into a celebration of cultures and trade with our southern neighbors.

11. Although they begin as either movies or television shows, these Disney products are quickly, indeed simultaneously, turned into a wide range of products that are marketed across the entertainment and lifestyle spectrum; in other words, they are marketed as brands rather than a single show or movie.

12. Lacroix, "Images of Animated Others."

13. Here I use the term "brown" in the contemporary usage to refer to any racially marked population, not just to a particular color.

14. Angharad N. Valdivia, *Latinas in Popular Culture: Uses and Abuses of Hybridity* (Malden, MA: Blackwell, forthcoming).

15. I use this phrase in quotation marks because it is such an impossibility to decide what actually looks Muslim. Therefore, once more, policing and regulatory forces have to rely on stereotypes about the Other.

16. Ellen Seiter, "Different Children, Different Dreams: Racial Representation in Children's Advertising," *Journal of Communication Inquiry* 14, no. 1 (1990): 31-47.

17. Angharad N. Valdivia and Sarah Projansky, "Feminism and/in Mass Media," in *The Sage Handbook of Gender and Communication*, ed. Bonnie J. Dow and Julia Wood (Thousand Oaks, CA: Sage, 2006); Sujata Moorti, "Out of India: Fashion Culture and the Marketing of Ethnic Style," in *A Companion to Media Studies*, ed. Angharad N. Valdivia (Malden, MA: Blackwell, 2003).

18. Ellen Seiter, *Sold Separately: Children and Parents in Consumer Culture* (New Brunswick, NJ: Rutgers University Press, 1993).

19. Robert McChesney, "The Global Media Giants: We Are the World," *FAIR: Fairness and Accuracy in Reporting*, November/December 1997, http://www.fair.org/index.php?page=1406 (accessed June 12, 2007).

20. Ellen Seiter and Vicki Mayer, "Diversifying Representation in Children's TV," in *Nickelodeon Nation: The History, Politics, and Economics of America's Only TV Channel for Kids*, ed. Heather Hendershot (New York: NYU Press, 2004).

21. Julia Boorstin and Alynda Wheat, "Disney's Tween Machine: How the Disney Channel Became Must-See TV—and the Company's Unlikely Cash Cow," CNN, http://money.cnn.com/magazines/fortune/fortune_archive/2003/09/29/349896/index.htm (accessed September 29, 2006).

22. Dallas Smythe, *Dependency Road: Communications, Capitalism, Consciousness and Canada* (Norwood, NJ: Ablex, 1981).

23. Denise Martin, "New Tween Scene: Disney Nets Close in on Viacom in Youth Niche," *Variety*, www.variety.com/article/VR1117951880.html?categoryid=14&cs=1 (accessed October 15, 2006).

24. Anita Harris, *All about the Girl: Culture, Power and Identity* (New York: Routledge, 2004); Sarah Projansky and Leah R. Vande Berg, "Sabrina the Teenage . . . ? Girls, Witches, Mortals and the Limitations of Prime Time Feminism," in *Fantasy Girls: Gender in the New Universe of Science Fiction and Fantasy Television*, ed. Elyce Rae Helford (Lanham, MD: Rowman and Littlefield, 2000).

25. Martin, "New Tween Scene."

26. Melanie Lowe, "Colliding Feminisms: Britney Spears, 'Tweens,' and the Politics of Reception," *Popular Music and Society* 26, no. 2 (2003): 130.

27. Valdivia and Projansky, "Feminism and/in Mass Media."

28. Bonnie J. Dow, *Prime Time Feminism: Television, Media Culture, and the Women's Movement since 1970* (Philadelphia: University of Philadelphia Press, 1996); Sarah Projansky, *Watching Rape: Film and Television in Postfeminist Culture* (New York: NYU Press, 2001).

29. Lowe, "Colliding Feminisms."

30. Number one that week was *X-Men*.

31. *Hannah* is the number one tween show currently on the air and the heir apparent to *Lizzie McGuire* (Martin, "New Tween Scene"). *The Cheetah Girls*, like Lizzie, have an official page in the Disney Channel Web site.

32. Brett Pulley, "Disney Bursts into Song, Profits," *Forbes Media*, www.forbes.com/digitalentertainment/2006/06/02/disney-musical-itunes_cz_bp_0605musical.html (accessed June 5, 2006).

33. These are her exact words when she is talking about her ethnicity to her friend Dorinda.

34. Marc Randall, "Disney's Prefab Cheetahs Hit Their Mark," *Newsday*, www.newsday.com/entertainment/music/nycheetah494491600ct23,0,5092467.story (accessed October 23, 2006).

35. We get to know her full name in an early episode when the three buddies get in trouble and Miranda tells the other two that when her mother is really angry she calls her by her full name.

36. Seiter, "Different Children, Different Dreams."

37. The plot of this television show revolves around the fact that Hannah plays a brunette girl next door during the day, and at night she is a blond singing star.

38. Dave Itzkoff, "Multimedia Synergistic Slumber Party," *New York Times*, September 24, 2006, 1, 32.

39. On June 8, 2007, Disney Television aired the premiere of *Johnny Kapahaala: Back on Board* as a sequel to *Johnny Tsunami*, with the same main actor older and now on a skateboard. Another actor, Corbin Bleu, has already been featured in *Jump In!* and *High School Musical*, as well as in regular rotation as a hip-hop artist on the Disney Channel.

# *The Matrix* Trilogy, Keanu Reeves, and Multiraciality at the End of Time

## *LeiLani Nishime*

The film *The Matrix* (1999) ends with a monologue by the film's protagonist Neo, played by Keanu Reeves.[1] He promises that he will show everyone caught in the Matrix "a world without rules and controls, without borders or boundaries. A world where anything is possible." This fluid world of possibilities is also the world promised the filmgoer. Trailers and advertising for the film emphasized its mixture of live action and computer-generated special effects, as well as its melding of low-budget Hong Kong kung fu action and big-budget Hollywood bang. Most important, Reeves, the film's multiracial star, provided a visual metaphor for the hybrid future. The danger and allure of crossed boundaries pervade every aspect of the film, from its plot to its visual punch.

However, like Reeves himself, the film is unable to transcend all boundaries into a utopic future "without rules and controls." Despite its cutting-edge fashions and its casual talk of artificial intelligence and postapocalyptic angst, the film remains embedded in contemporary debate about the meaning ascribed to multiracial peoples. Both the narrative, which unfolds over the trilogy, and its arresting visual style offer up conflicting representations of hybridity, echoing the bifurcated view, both utopic and dystopic, of mixed racial and cultural identities in the United States. Are mixed race people a sign of the beginning of a new, stronger, better race or the harbinger of a coming racial apocalypse? Do multiple cultural allegiances lead us "beyond" identity politics, and is this a cause for alarm or celebration?

Rather than prioritizing a single dominant representation of multiraciality, this analysis compares the multiple and conflicting portrayals of mixture and hybridity in the film. Beginning with the narrative deployment of the racially ambiguous figure of Reeves himself, the film veers between valorizing and isolating the hybrid Neo in its story line and characterizations. Visual representations of hybridity are equally complicated. Graphic portrayals of cyborg technology, which emphasizes the merger of man and machine, inspires unease and disgust. On the other hand, the film's explicit melding of computer animation and live action and its crossing of national boundaries to blend Hong Kong and Hollywood cinematic traditions flamboyantly and almost gleefully point to its own hybrid filmmaking.

The immensely popular *Matrix* trilogy, which consists of *The Matrix* (1999), *The Matrix Reloaded* (2003), and *The Matrix Revolutions* (2003), presents a snapshot of the role of representations in the contemporary construction of racial categories and dominant racial narratives. Tracing these representations through the trilogy reveals the extent to which static and essentialist notions of race underwrite both utopic and dystopic representations of hybridity in the films. What emerges from such an analysis is a more nuanced understanding of both emergent and residual responses to hybridity and the ways that, despite the use of multiracial representations to express the different and the new, these narratives of multiraciality are implicated in hegemonic ideas of race.[2]

## Is Neo Multiracial?

Although many film audiences do not read Reeves as multiracial, the film speaks much more powerfully to those who do. For fans of Reeves, his appearance on screen begins a metonymic chain of associations between Asia, science fiction, the future, and multiraciality. Through his appearance in *The Matrix* and *Johnny Neumonic*, a film based on work by author William Gibson, Reeves has become associated with cyberpunk, a genre steeped in Asian references and discussed in more detail later in this chapter. Take, for instance, the "10 Reasons Keanu Rules" that appeared in the March 2006 issue of *Wired*.[3] Reason 1 is "He's the Face of Globalization," which is explained with the lines, "Born in Beirut to an English mother and a father of Hawaiian and Chinese descent, he's a citizen of the world." For those who can read the signs, globalization is written on Reeves's body, or at least his face. Through his body, multiraciality becomes conflated with globalization, making Reeves a "citizen of the world." Reason 2, "He's Now Hollywood's

Sci-Fi Guy," and reason 8, "He's Hipper Than a Japanese School Girl," connect his multiple races with a futuristic vision of global culture. The article elaborates on reason 8, explaining, "Reeves the fanboy has an impressive record for spotting what's next in everything from music to movies." The article highlights the easy slippage between race and nation, or more specifically, between the nation-state and racial "purity," on the one hand, and its opposite, globalization and multiraciality, on the other. The crossing of racial and national boundaries, embodied by Reeves, is then linked to whatever is cutting edge and modern. As this chapter will demonstrate, *The Matrix* trilogy capitalizes on these associations by presenting idealized models of national and technological hybridity and simultaneously denigrating and marginalizing bodily manifestations of hybridity in ways both coded and overt.

At first glance *The Matrix* seems to follow familiar generic narratives of man against machine. The film's hero comes to realize that his everyday reality is merely a construct of an artificial intelligence, a virtual space called the Matrix. In reality humans are slaves of the machine. Even more horrifying to Neo is the true function of humans as organic batteries that power a giant computer. Neo then pledges his allegiance to the human rebels and dedicates his life to battling the Matrix. The plot hinges upon the need to distinguish between human and machine, and the ultimate battle at the film's climax pits Neo, who has aligned himself with the fully human rebels, against the Matrix's cyborg agents. While the plotline's logic owes little to the laws of physics, it does make sense within sci-fi's long history of antimiscegenation narratives. As many film and science fiction critics have pointed out, science fiction does not show us the future.[4] Rather, it projects contemporary anxieties onto alien or fantastic worlds.

Despite the genre-bending prominence of nonwhite performers in the trilogy, academic writing on these films has largely ignored race. The few scholars that do address race in the films note that the overwhelming majority of people residing within the matrix are white, whereas those fighting the matrix are a mix of races and ethnicities. The people who enforce the reality of the matrix appear as stereotypical white, male, corporate drones, whereas the rebel forces are a conglomeration of various ethnicities and white women who have rejected traditional gender assignments. The only white character of note who lives outside the matrix ends up betraying the rebel group. This racial dichotomy becomes even more explicit in the second and third films in the trilogy. As we enter the world of Zion, we see a profusion of multiply raced bodies, while within the matrix Agent Smith

(Hugo Weaving) continues to replicate himself as identical white males in suits.[5] As Lisa Nakamura succinctly states, "There are inhuman agents and Architects, who are always white pricks; mentors, Oracles and Operators, who are always black, and benign software programs like Seraph, the Keymaster and the displaced information-worker's South Indian family depicted in *The Matrix Revolutions*, who are often Asian."[6]

Moreover, a number of critics view Neo as simply another white male.[7] When Richard King and David Leonard ask, "Is Neo White?" the answer is a resounding yes. They state, "Without any other clues, one must assume that Neo is destined to save, and lead the battle against the machines, *because of his whiteness*" (original emphasis).[8] Another writer, Thomas Forster, in critiquing the use of kung fu in the film, argues, "This appropriation of an Asian male action star's corporeal style reduces Asian-ness to a generalisable and appropriable set of signifiers, while also implying that such appropriations are attractive to both white and black men [Keanu Reeves and Laurence Fishburne] and that both whiteness and blackness might be subject to similar transformation."[9] His argument attaches a multiply qualified footnote that says, "This is *assuming* that Keanu Reeves' *somewhat* ambiguous racial persona is *generally* received as passing for white" (my emphasis).[10]

If, however, we take a different tack and recognize Reeves as multiracial, our readings of the racial dynamics of the film can become more richly textured and complex. In arguing for a multiracial reading of Neo, I do not claim to have a more accurate understanding of the intentions of the film's writers and directors, the Wachowski Brothers. Reeves was not, in fact, the first choice for the role of Neo. Other actors, including Will Smith and Brad Pitt, first passed on the script.[11] Once Reeves assumed the role, however, embedded narratives about multiraciality gained in depth and prominence. If we understand film, particularly genre films, as a way of collectively working through cultural anxieties, then the overwhelming popular response to the film compels us to ask what racial questions and narratives it invokes. In what ways does the film reflect or express conflicted notions of racial hybridity?

While Reeves's multiracial ancestry may be the most easily identifiable mark of hybridity in the film, the representation of Neo as multiracial is woven into the plot, the visual representation of his body, and even within the spatial logics of the film. In the narrative of the film, Neo is reborn twice. His first awakening from the Matrix is portrayed as a literal birth. He is seen encased in a mechanical uterus, floating in an amniotic pool of

*Neo is reborn naked, hair-less, and helpless, in* The Matrix *(1999).*

liquid, attached by computer cables/umbilical cord. Then he is expelled, naked and hairless, from the pod and shoots through a long narrow tube that clearly resembles a birth canal

When he regains consciousness in the "real" world, he looks up to see his "parents," Trinity (Euro-American actor Carrie-Anne Moss) and Morpheus (African American actor Laurence Fishburne). He barely survives the process and must be brought to life, Frankenstein-style, by Morpheus. Then, at the end of the movie, he is again reborn, or maybe resurrected, by the love of Trinity. Thus, within the film's metaphoric family, Neo is the child of a black father and white mother, doubly reinforcing a sense of Neo as biracial.

Reeves as Neo occupies a liminal space within the film. Following in the tradition of portraying multiracial people as "between two worlds," Neo is literally displaced from the world of the Matrix and its real-world opposition, Zion.[12] In fact, in the first film his entire experience in the real world takes place in transit, on a ship. Neo's constant movement denies him a singular or permanent space of identification. Samira Kawash, in her analysis of *Autobiography of an Ex-Colored Man*, argues that constant geographic alienation enables the construction of a multiracial self that does not fit into existing racial classifications.[13] Neo's liminality similarly is characterized by his ability to easily move between the white and racially marked worlds of the matrix and Zion; he is distinctive due to his superhuman ability to enter the matrix without the aid of technological prostheses. The emphasis on "motion over position," in Kawash's words, means that Neo is never completely enmeshed in either society.[14] Furthermore, his dislocation from both spaces motivates the story line. When Neo joins with Morpheus, he forfeits his casual acceptance of his place in the Matrix. As the perpetual newcomer to the ship Nebuchadnezzar and later to Zion, he never sheds his unease or completely learns the codes of behavior.

In a crucial scene in *Matrix Reloaded* (2003), the people of Zion have a gigantic rave. As the camera pans over the crowd and then pulls away to an extreme long shot of the entire group, we see the whole population in sync, dancing and moving to the same rhythm. Meanwhile, Neo and Trinity leave the crowd, and shots of them having sex are intercut with scenes of the communally writing bodies, all shown without plugs. The plugs, in the movie's parlance, are ports embedded in the bodies of the "human batteries" powering the matrix. At first, the dancers and the couple of Neo and Trinity are in concert, but then Neo has a disturbing vision, pulls away from Trinity, breaks the rhythm of the crosscuts, and abruptly ends their sexual tryst. The scene concludes with the camera moving away from their two intertwined bodies. We see Neo's body from behind, with the plugs that line his back prominently displayed. Thus we are reminded of his hybridity and isolation in contrast to the communal, "purely" human residents of Zion. This scene visually reinforces the narrative separation of Neo from the crowds of Zion; he is both a stranger and revered as "The One," a quasi-religious figure who fulfills prophecies of a savior of Zion able to battle the Matrix. As the trilogy ends, Neo is neither in the Matrix nor in Zion. We last see him in the no-man's-land of Machine City, with no indication of what will happen to him next and no place to call home.

## Multiraciality, Cyclical Time, and the Beginning of History

One of the mysteries that propels the plot of the trilogy is whether or not Neo is The One. If critics read Reeves/Neo as unambiguously white, then the film simply reiterates familiar racist and patriarchal notions of the great white hope come to save the "little brown brothers."[15] As Claudia Springer states, "It is a distinctly Hollywood conceit to suppose that a style produced during centuries of black suffering should be bequeathed to a young white man [Neo] who alone has the ability to use its powers to save humankind from extinction."[16] However, by reading Neo as mixed race, the films resonates with another, different, racial narrative.

The positioning of Neo as The One follows a long history of "positive" representations of multiracial people. While the story of the bad old days of antimiscegenation laws and the persecution of multiracial people as contaminated or as race traitors may be more familiar within our national narrative of progressive racial relations, there has also been an equally resilient counternarrative promoting racial mixing. For instance, Greg Carter documents the spread of the theory of hybrid vigor, which in the period from 1864 to 1926 drew from the plant world to argue for the notion of multiracial people as stronger, smarter, and more beautiful than their "pure" predecessors.[17] David Hollinger typifies contemporary liberal sentiment in his celebration of multiracial people as the leading edge of a "post-ethnic" America.[18] Gloria Anzaldúa, in her seminal work on racial and cultural hybridity, declares, "This mixture of races, rather than resulting in an inferior being, provides hybrid progeny, a mutable, more malleable species with a rich gene pool."[19] In keeping with these messianic visions of a new multiracial vanguard, Neo, with his extraordinary and unexplained powers, seems to be an evolutionary leap forward. Even his name, Neo, meaning new, and his multiple births discussed earlier gesture toward the idea of a new race or breed. Agent Smith, Neo's archrival, cannot violate the physical rules of the matrix, yet inexplicably, Neo can. At the end of the second film, he controls the machines in the "real world," a feat that prior to this moment in the trilogy could be accomplished only inside the matrix. The third film begins with Neo inside the matrix, but, unlike all other humans, he does not need to jack-in to enter the machine world.

As the embodiment of a new (mixed) race, Neo promises a new racial order. We learn at the end of Reloaded that the battle between the white-dominated matrix and the racially marked Zion is repeated endlessly as a bug in the programming of the machine. Since the inhabitants of Zion are wiped out at the end of each cycle, there is no memory or history of previous civilization, and each new generation is doomed to repetition. In this formulation, racial antagonisms do not arise out of a specific set of power relations, nor do they change over time. The "new" multiracial

category represented by Neo marks a break from this regressive and repetitive past and promises the start of a progressive and linear history. In
much the same way, popular narratives of racial progress in the United
States cast racial differences and hierarchies as anachronistic remnants of
an old system of classification. The utopic possibilities attributed to multiracial bodies rely on a fantasy of new beginnings, free from the weighty
legacy of racial history.

Ironically, what appears to be a celebration of Neo and, by extension,
hybridity both racial and technological, depends upon conceptions of
both racial and bodily purity and difference. The racial politics of the film
adhere to cultural dichotomies to create distinct boundaries between the
empowered, technological, mostly white matrix and its first world metropolis and the oppressed, natural-fiber-wearing, mostly brown Zion and
its third world, crowded, messy agoras. The film echoes similar attempts
to reinforce a sense of absolute difference in the face of globalization's
homogenization of culture. What is often unrecognized in the mourning
over lost, native innocence are the ways in which the rush to "protect"
the other's culture limits, idealizes, and stereotypes those cultures in contrast to a dynamic and aggressive West. Trinh T. Minh-ha points out how
the impulse toward imposing cultural boundaries serves the needs of the
West far more than those it, the West, is "saving." She says:

> Authenticity in such contexts turns out to be a product that one can buy,
> arrange to one's liking, and/or preserve. Today the "unspoiled" parts of
> Japan, the far-flung locations in the archipelago, are those that tourism
> officials actively promote for the more venturesome visitors. Similarly, the
> Third World representative the modern, sophisticated public ideally seeks
> is the *unspoiled* African, Asian or Native American, who remains more
> preoccupied with his/her image of the *real* native—the *truly different*—
> than with the issues of hegemony, racism, feminism, and social change.
> (original emphasis)[20]

The film also posits a vision of racial Others as "primitive" and "natural" in its depiction of the geographically and culturally isolated people of
Zion. Their environment, replete with rocky outcroppings and mud floors,
is in sharp contrast to the Matrix, with its futuristic depiction of concrete
high-rises and ubiquitous technological gadgets. The reification of absolute difference allows for the fantasy of a new breed or race to emerge as
a third term.

If we recognize the intimate connection between celebrations of multi-raciality and nostalgia for purity, the bifurcated representation of hybridity in the film becomes more comprehensible. The film figures miscegenation and multiracial bodies as heroic, thrilling, and progressive while simultaneously coding them as signs of colonization, rape, and contamination. Hybridity is both celebrated and reviled, both encouraged and persecuted. How can such seemingly contrary views exist within the same ninety minutes? The explanation lies partly in the larger debate. Since the film in no way attempts to address the issue of mixed race identity head-on, it can be read much more fruitfully as a reflection of the currently fractured discourse. The film plays out the contradictions inherent in current debates in which fear of the catastrophic/apocalyptic results of racial mixing exists at the same time as the lived experience becomes more common. We are dropped in the middle of a discourse in which Tiger Woods is both promoted as a pioneer and marked as a race traitor for refusing the single label of African American.

This simple explanation of the conflicted representation of hybridity brings up the more difficult issue of how these dichotomies exist simultaneously within a largely hegemonic culture. The answer lies in the assumptions that underlie the conflict. For even though there seem to be two opposing views expressed, they both function within a narrative of racial difference and racial essentialism. This adherence to codified notions of race is most clearly demonstrated in one of the major turning points of the first movie. In the moment just before Neo learns the truth about the matrix, he is given one more chance to back out. Morpheus hands Neo two pills, asks him to choose one, and tells him "This is your last chance. After this there is no turning back." This choice is particularly poignant because, as I noted earlier, the film racializes the world of the matrix and the "real world." In essence, Neo must choose between man or machine, black or white. Loyalty is measured by how absolutely the characters reject either world.

Even though conflicts over the significance of multiraciality coalesce around the body of Keanu Reeves, its complicated meanings finds multiple expressions in the trilogy. The breach of the boundaries between man and machine, between "real" bodies and special effects, and between national cultures address interrelated aspects of race and identity. The splintering of multiracial discourse across several representational levels mirrors the competing and intertwined narratives that guide our understanding of multiraciality. Questions of bodily integrity parallel, intersect, and diverge from questions of national integrity. Cultural cross-fertilization is set against racial mixing. As these discourses of hybridity are set into motion, the limits and possibilities for the figure of the multiracial hero emerge.

## Hybridity as Dystopia

For all the celebration of Neo's liminality and the eye-popping thrill of a cinematography that seamlessly blends special effects and "reality," the *Matrix* trilogy also demonstrates a deep, almost unconscious, disdain for hybridity. Like the valorization of hybridity, the denigration of hybridity takes place both at the narrative and at the visual and formal level. In this regard, the film not only reflects an alternative, liberatory rhetoric of multiraciality but also participates in the discourse of racial separation. Within the trilogy's story line, the clearest example of the preference of purity over hybridity is the contrast set up between the two sides battling over Neo's soul, the Agents of the matrix and the citizens of Zion. On a more emotional and visual register, the most grotesque imagery is reserved for moments when boundaries between man and machine blur.

The film creates two central and diametrically opposed factions and enacts familiar narratives of neocolonialism. At one extreme are the fascist, white, male enforcers of the matrix, and at the other are the heroic and indeterminately multiracial denizens of the Nebuchadnezzar and Zion. In a reversal of expectations, the white Agents of the matrix come to represent the uncontrolled menace of the invasive Other while the multiracial community of Zion promotes the values of purity and stabilized boundaries. When Neo meets the brothers Tank (Marcus Chong) and Dozer (Anthony Ray Parker), he is surprised to learn that they do not have the plugs that line Neo's body. Tank proudly announces that he is "100 percent pure, old-fashioned, homegrown human. Born free, right here in the real world. A genuine child of Zion." The absence of plugs not only proves their humanity but also prevents them from entering the matrix. Their minds have never been taken over by the machines. Without the threat of miscegenation and cross-contamination inherent in all colonial encounters, the audience can depend upon the "genuine child of Zion." On the other hand, the cyborgs, those with embedded plug-ins, are potential traitors whether by choice, in the case of the turncoat Cypher (Joe Pantoliano), or by force, in the case of the assimilated Bane (Ian Bliss).

Agent Smith, particularly in the second and third parts of the trilogy, plays out the threat posed by an unfettered interchange between unevenly positioned groups. If earlier, nineteenth-century concerns about colonization centered upon the fear of "going native," of the European colonizer losing himself through contact, sexual or otherwise, with the colonized, then early twenty-first-century anxieties about globalization often stem from worries about the loss of the native in the face of the dominant and dominating force of the colonial power. Native cultures are essentialized as natural, pure, and exotic and under pressure from a powerful, transnational, irresistible, and modern West. Like Agent Smith, these forces of globalization are imagined to be technological, male, and bent on endlessly replicating themselves at the expense of the individual. In the film, Smith accomplishes his goal by pushing his hand into the bodies of other people and transforming them into literal duplicates of himself, transgressive encounters that figure contact as destructive and invasive.

Hybridity is also mapped directly on Neo's body through cyborg technology. As I have argued elsewhere, cyborgs in science fiction film have often served as metaphors for racial mixing.[21] The narrative concerns over the breach of the boundaries of the body, representing white purity, by the inhuman machines, representing the racial Other, echo contemporary worries about and hopes for multiracial people. Neo's body, like all bodies of the characters that can move between the white-dominated world of the Matrix and the multiracial "real" world, is embedded with computer hardware.[22] These plugs once attached bodies to the machines that kept them alive and constructed their cyber-reality. Like belly buttons, they mark the bodies that were "nurtured" by machine, and they literally meld human and machine. In the birth scene described earlier and in the first scenes after Neo is reborn, the camera lingers over and presents close-ups of the plugs. Although the crew operate on his body to close up most of the plugs, they cannot be removed and remain a part of him, a visual reminder of his hybrid origins.

If the introduction of cyborg technology in the film presents a way to visually enact an otherwise invisible racial mixture, then it also offers a disturbing vision of hybridity. Agent Smith's violent remaking of man into matrix is only one example of the unease the film displays toward the merging of human and machine. For instance, while the film's heroes live in a ship that is no more than a means of transport, the ships sent by the matrix swim through space organically like eels, actively looking for the rebels in a threatening marriage of animal and machine. And while the meeting of man and machine that preserves bodily integrity, for example, the robot "suit" used by soldiers in *Revolutions* (2003), is presented as heroic and powerful, the bodily intersection of these two opposites is another thing entirely. In another example early in the film, Neo's body is invaded by what appears to be an organic machine. The scene resembles a gang rape scenario as Neo is kidnapped and taken into a room. He tries to scream as two agents rip open his shirt and hold him down, spread eagle, on a table. They pull an inert mechanical device from a box, and as they dangle it over his belt buckle, it comes to life and begins to wriggle like worm. The three men watch as the long, detached phallus burrows into Neo's navel. In another key example, when we first see Neo in the "real world," he is attached to machines by tubes and wires plugged into sockets embedded in his skin. Here both the borders between man and machine and the borders between inside and outside the body are breached. As a result, Neo is a slave to the machines and is presented as physically repulsive. The audience is meant to experience unease at the sight of the black industrial tubing invading his pasty skin. As Morpheus tugs at the plugs, pulling at the connection between skin and machine, it fills the entire screen, prompting a physical, sympathetic recoil from the sight.

## Hybridity as Utopia

Despite the grotesque imagery and narrative rejection of hybridity in the films, the trilogy simultaneously promotes the crossing of boundaries with its visual style, particularly in terms of its star, its special effects, and most prominently in its national cinematic idiom. If the movie presents a spectrum of responses to multiraciality, then Neo represents its most celebratory and utopic extreme. At the most obvious level Neo, who represents multiraciality, is The One. He is the long-awaited leader/messiah. Neo, like the infamous SimEve, "the new face of America," who graced the cover of *Time* magazine's 1993 special issue on immigration, is promoted as the path to the future.[23] He is literally The One who will deliver the people of Zion from an existence of constant struggle with the machines. Like Neo, the woman who appears on the cover of *Time* is only made possible through the intersection of material and virtual reality; she was created by morphing together images of several people of different races.

The film's use of special effects is one of its most prominent and noted elements, and the Wachowski Brothers fully exploit the intersection of the flamboyantly manufactured effects and the "real" actors and settings. For all the hand-wringing over the mixture of machine and humans within the film's narrative, the biggest draw of the film is, arguably, the computer-generated action sequences and the elaborate fight scenes—as *Newsweek* termed it, "the combination of Chinese martial arts and American special effects." The special effects in *The Matrix* trilogy emphasize, rather than hide, their disruption of the film narrative, recognizing the wide appeal of the visual mix of live action and animation. The special effects sequences in the trilogy are so distinct that fans, following the lead of the Wachowski Brothers, have names such as "Burly Brawl" and "Freeway Chase" for the most extended of these scenes. Instead of hiding these manipulations, the fantastic nature of the fights in *The Matrix* trilogy are highlighted, freeze-framed, and given the full 360-degree treatment. Iconic images such as the slow-motion bullets that Neo manages to dodge or the actors' physics-defying leaps from high buildings invite the viewer to marvel at the merger of technology and human actors. As the trilogy continues, the action scenes become ever more elaborate and fantastic. The distortions of time and space through the use of CGI, according to Aylish Wood, create another visual narrative in the film. Woods argues, "Thus, rather than the conflict being evident simply through the actions of the human actors, the manipulation of timespace through special effects introduces conflict at the level of organization of the visual images."[24] However, the special effects do not only signal conflict, they also celebrate the intersection of man and machine. While the movie's overt narrative rails against the simulated world of the matrix, its visuals tell another story.

Notably, SimEve is only made possible through the crossing of both technological *and* national boundaries. She represents an American future made possible through waves of global migration. As the face of *Time*'s issue devoted to immigration, she, like so many other multiracial icons before her, embodies the fraught relationship of race and nation. From early stories of Native American miscegenation through hysterical accounts of widespread racial mixing following the Civil War to contemporary fantasies of the "new face of America," the history of racial mixing is also the history of the formation and re-formation of national identities in the United States. For example, Asians, who were specifically targeted as "aliens ineligible for citizenship," were also subject to particularly stringent antimiscegenation laws. The Cable Act of 1922 effectively stripped white women who married Asian men of their citizenship, explicitly linking racial purity to national citizenship.[25] On the other hand, Native American and Euro-American intermarriage was often held up as a means to successfully assimilate racial others into the new nation.[26] Whether seen as a threat or as a solution to the racial future of the nation, multiracial people are an integral part of the narrative of nation and national boundaries.

In *The Matrix* trilogy, the celebration of hybridity moves beyond the metaphoric in its explicit play on the cultural and cinematic meeting of Asia and the United States. If, as the *Wired* article would have us believe, Keanu Reeves is the new face of globalization, then in *The Matrix* he marks the space where Hollywood and Asian national cinemas intersect. The film's references to Asian culture and to Hong Kong cinematic traditions follow a trend in science fiction toward "techo-orientalism." The term, first coined by David Morley and Kevin Robins, refers to the anxiety experienced in the West when, in the 1980s and early 1990s, Japanese technology appeared to eclipse Western technology, as Japan emerged as an economic powerhouse.[27] Instead of the familiar Asia that remained mired in a distant and static past, Japan suddenly came to represent modernity or even postmodernity. While late-century representations of Japan grew out of earlier stereotypes, Morley and Robins cite representations of Japan in cyberpunk fiction such as William Gibson's *Neuromancer* (1984) and the film *Blade Runner* (Ridley Scott, 1982) as examples of the transformation of those stereotypes into a dystopic vision of an Asian future. The importance of this reconfiguration of a global cultural imaginary is the breakdown of simple divisions between East and West.

The end of Japan's economic dominance coincided with the equally vertiginous decline in the popularity of cyberpunk fiction. However, the 1990s saw a resurgence of cyberpunk reformulated for a new economic age. Jane Park argues that both Neal Stephenson's *Snow Crash* (1992) and *The Matrix* are a response to the (first and greatly exaggerated) demise of cyberpunk.[28] This second generation is distinguished by a less overtly orientalist and more, one might say, integrationist perspective on Asia. As Nakamura notes, "While the first generation of cyberpunk texts hold racial and ethnic hybridity at bay by asserting the solidity of orientalist cybertypes, second generation texts such as *Snow Crash* and *The Matrix* acknowledge racial hybridity, even if at times this acknowledgment is covert."[29] The shift in representations of Asia in cyberpunk must be attributed, in part, to the rise in prominence of Hong Kong as an economic power as Japan declined. Hong Kong, which loomed large in the global public eye as it was "handed over" from Great Britain to China in 1997, began appearing in cyberpunk fiction as well. *Snow Crash*, for instance, imagines a future in which sovereign franchise "quasi-national entities" replace nation-states, one of the most powerful of which is Mr. Lee's Greater Hong Kong.

The looming economic power of China occupies a great deal of psychic space in the West, but the specific focus on Hong Kong in science fiction points to a fascination with the fusion of East and West. As Poshek Fu and David Desser assert,

> Hong Kong: East or West, Chinese or British, traditional or modern, colonial or postcolonial? Issues of identity continue to plague the territory and have been especially poignant since the announcement in 1984 of the Sino-British Joint Declaration announcing the handover of Hong Kong to China in 1997.[30]

Imagining Hong Kong as the future skips over the current uncertainty over its ultimate fate as we attempt to divine the lessons of a bloodless decolonization. Hong Kong, a British protectorate, was an island of Western, old-style colonialism in Asia. With its large English-speaking population, the significant presence of expatriates, Western-style capitalism, and cosmopolitan architecture, it seemed an island of Western culture in the midst of the cultural force of the massive country that surrounded it. The handover of power from Great Britain to China literalized Western anxieties about the redistribution of power and wealth from the West to the East. By the time the ninety-nine-year lease was up, China, with its population of more than a billion, was emerging as a political, military, and economic powerhouse, a country capable of setting rather than acquiescing to global policy. This history seemed to allegorize the larger shifts of world power, but it also exemplified a U.S. ideal of the marriage of Western capitalism and Eastern culture, technology, and labor.

*The Matrix* trilogy follows this trend by not simply incorporating references to Hong Kong but actually using the vernacular of Hong Kong cinema. With Fishburne as sensei and Reeves as his student, part of the film follows the generic story line of the making of a kung fu master. The films quote liberally from the most famous of the Hong Kong cinema directors, John Woo, from his patented two-handgun, flying shoot-out to the overhead shot in a dominatrix club scene in *Matrix Revolution* in which Morpheus, Trinity, and the Seraph and the Merovingian's thugs engage in a standoff, everyone's gun's drawn and pointing at an enemy's head. The inclusion of Chinese martial arts is nothing new in Western cinema, of course, as the careers of Jean-Claude Van Damme and Steven Seagal will attest. It was the use of wires and the disregard for the laws of gravity and physics long characteristic of Hong Kong, kung fu films that proved so visually arresting to Western critics and fans. Like the Hong Kong martial arts films that depict classical eras, the movie employed Chinese trainers (noted fight choreographer Yuen Wo Ping) to stage fight sequences. The flamboyant acrobatics and use of frozen poses to accentuate movement in the trilogy thus borrow heavily from Hong Kong kung fu rather than the awkward realism of Hollywood.[31] Even the pacing of the films, particularly the second and third installments, echo the extended, seemingly endless kung fu duels common to Hong Kong action films. Unlike earlier cyberpunk films such as *Blade Runner*, in which Asia is simply represented as the future within the context of classical Hollywood film, *The Matrix* trilogy uses Hong Kong cinema aesthetics to inform the visual style of the film. Asia is not merely the message but the medium as well.

### Race without Bodies

Although the film begins by promising a world "without borders or boundaries," in fact, the trilogy repeatedly reiterates the act of crossing boundaries. We witness the jump from the real world into the matrix and back again several times in each film, just as we experience the movement between the outside and inside of Zion as a passage over a clear and important threshold. In order to cross boundaries, the film first must construct or at least reinforce them. Neo embodies the "positive" representation of multiracial people by embodying the utopic promise of a new breed of people. However, this vision of a new, mixed race ethnic group draws a line between a futuristic multiracial world and an old, racially pure society. It ignores the fact that we have always already been mixed race. Like *Newsweek*'s SimEve, which can only show a "new face of America" in contrast to an earlier, static, and, presumably European version of America's face, representations of multiracial people as new retroactively construct former, pure races. As Suzanne Bost argues, the *Newsweek* issue "reflects the attitude that life was simpler back when America was 'an unhyphenated whole,' a fictitious, mythic monoculturalism that exists only in ethnocentric imagination."[32] Thus, the hybridity so celebrated in the trilogy trades upon the thrill of friction, of the clash between absolute differences.

Take, for instance, the promotion of the film as a blending of Hong
Kong and Hollywood cinemas. This characterization depends upon an
earlier understanding of the two categories as singular and distinct. Yet,
the notion of two formerly "pure" forms creating a new mixture ignores
years of cross-fertilization. In his article on the American influence on
Hong Kong cinema, Law Kar finds links to the United States in Hong
Kong cinema's "first golden age" between 1937 and 1941. U.S. kung fu films
of the 1970s also demonstrate the influence of Hong Kong cinema, particularly the work of American-born Bruce Lee. The influence was most
strongly felt in the legacy of Blaxploitation films such as *Super Fly* and the
recently remade *Shaft*. The resulting internationalization of kung fu genre
films in turn revitalized and remade the once-dominant Mandarin-lan-
guage Hong Kong cinema.[33] In the 1980s, David Bordwell argues, Hollywood action films such as *Raiders of the Lost Ark* (1981), *48 Hours* (1982),
and *Die Hard* (1988) had a major impact on Hong Kong cinema.[34] During
this period Hong Kong director John Woo moved to Hollywood, while
U.S. directors such as Quentin Tarantino borrowed freely from Hong
Kong film. These early adopters created a cinematic tradition of borrow-
ing from Asian cinema that paved the way for the Wachowski Brothers.
These cross-cultural influences do not even begin to trace other international influences such as Japanese anime. As this very abbreviated genealogy demonstrates, while dichotomies such as Asian/Western make for
good copy, such distinctions rely on unsustainable conceptions of purity.

The introduction of multiraciality into the struggle over racial meaning
offers the possibility of a radical reconception of race. By destabilizing our
commonsense ideas about what defines race and racial identities, multiracial people might and have put pressure on the validity of racial divisions.
However, rather than using that skepticism about racial categories as a
first step toward uncovering the nonbiological origins of racial difference,
multiracial bodies are more often used to evacuate meaning from race, to
restart history. In this work, race and racial mixing are turned into metaphor; through the surrogates of cyborg technology and hybrid filmmaking, the messy social and historical memory that haunts racially marked
bodies falls away. Like the meeting of Hollywood and Hong Kong cinema,
the representation of the split and/or melding of the two worlds, white
and nonwhite, functions through the repression of history.

Allucquere Rosanne Stone warns against the impulse to forget the
body in the flush of new technology. Before rendering the human body or
"meat" as obsolete, we must remember the costs. She argues, "Forgetting

about the body is an old Cartesian trick, one that has unpleasant consequences for those bodies whose speech is silenced by the act of our forgetting; that is to say, those upon whose labor the act of forgetting the body is founded—usually women and minorities."[35] By displacing most of the representational work of hybridity onto machines and onto the filmmaking technique itself, we can simplify and neutralize racial differences. Without the bodily reminders of racialized bodies we can ignore uneven development, power imbalances, and sedimented histories of racial mixing and segregation. We can imagine that these histories and the consequent structural racism, what Omi and Winant call "racial formations," will disappear along with race itself. However, if we reassert the presence of racialized bodies, we might be forced to recognize that the future is now, and race and racism haunt us still.

When differentiating horror and science fiction, Vivian Sobchack claims, "Terror is replaced by wonder. . . . The SF film is not concerned with the animal which is there, now for always, within us. It produces not the strong terror evoked by something already present and known in each of us, but the more diluted and less immediate fear of what we may yet become."[36] Those times when *The Matrix* moves into the territory of the horror genre such as the birth scene detailed earlier in this chapter are also when we are confronted with the presence of bodies, bodies that invoke the terror of contamination and remind us that it is too late. The film reproduces a terror of the racial Other who is already within us even though the vision of a multiracial society is always posited as a future world. By continually predicting a multiracial future, magazine articles and social commentators ignore the fact that multiraciality is not a new phenomenon. "Racial mixing" has a long history, and there are no pure races, and yet we still have racial divisions and racial inequality. The promise of a simple elimination of race and racial hierarchies through miscegenation has historically failed to deliver. Rather than abstracting bodies and freezing them in a timeless past or a utopic future, these moments of terror mark the entrance of multiracial bodies into present time, as participants in contemporary racial narratives. Thus, the scenes that force us to confront the bodily disruptions of boundary crossing, the moments when we see the interface of human flesh and machine, are difficult to watch, tempting us to turn away from the sight.

The body at the direct center of the film narrative, that of Keanu Reeves, seems strangely absent. Racially speaking, Reeves's body remains mute for much of the viewing audience. As Kim Hester-Williams argues:

Keanu Reeves is himself mixed race and the idea that he is the key to the future fate of humanity implies that race will not matter in the future. . . . Neo "looks" white so, without the knowledge of his racial history, he must be read as "white." Or more to the point, he can escape the question of "race" all together since he does not visibly wear its "mark."[37]

Although I argue that reading Neo as multiracial opens up many rich interpretive possibilities, it is true that for many viewers Reeves's body does not "speak" its race. For all the promise of a hybrid future invested in the figure of Neo, he is neither the leader nor the voice of the people. Morpheus, who is more clearly and definitively marked racially, fills that position. Morpheus leads the Nebuchadnezzar and gives the rousing speech to rally the people of Zion in their final battle, just as it is Morpheus who knows the lore of The One, and Morpheus who is active in the politics of Zion. As both Hester-Williams and coauthors King and Leonard point out, the African American characters in the film come to represent authenticity and true racial grievance. Hester-Williams argues, "Given the presence of black bodies and black codes that appear in *The Matrix*, the film's discourse of slavery cannot be disavowed from the larger historical context of American slavery."[38] Neo, on the other hand, is, in the words of the Oracle, "not too bright." His ignorance, however, positions him as the savior of humanity in a way that Morpheus, mired as he is in a cyclical history, cannot. Neo is a clean slate that carries the residue of race but does not embody it.

## "A World without Borders or Boundaries"

Like the supposed opposition between Hollywood and Hong Kong cinemas, the oppositions set up between white/technological and brown/natural begin to break apart as the trilogy progresses. According to Peter X. Feng, Tank, ironically one of the "100 percent pure" children of Zion, is played by the multiracial (African American and Asian American) Marcus Chong.[39] More crucially, as the trilogy continues, clear distinctions between the machine world of the matrix and the human flesh world of Zion are occasionally questioned. In the second film, Neo meets up with one member of the Zion Council, a white man. The two view the machines that power Zion, and Councillor Hamann (Anthony Zerbe) comments on the interdependence of man and machine, saying, "I like to be reminded how the city survives because of these machines. These machines are keeping us alive."

At the end of *The Matrix Reloaded* and the beginning of *The Matrix Revolutions*, Neo suddenly develops the ability to move into the matrix without jacking-in. At the same time, Agent Smith invades the avatar of a human fighter in the matrix, which enables him to enter into the real world encased in a human body. It is tempting to speculate that the downward slide in popularity of the trilogy may be due to the ever more complex and ambiguous divisions between the worlds. The resulting story may be narratively unsatisfying because it tells an unfamiliar tale, one that begins to dismantle the binaries that dominate depictions of mixed race.

Despite these hopeful signs, the film ultimately leaves the opposition of the matrix and Zion intact. At the trilogy's climax, we do not see the expected final destruction of the matrix and the ultimate triumph of Zion. Rather, the two broker an uneasy and impermanent peace and maintain their separate spheres. However, this final movement forward, this linear history, comes at the cost of Neo's body. In Neo's final scenes he is blind, bruised, and bleeding, having endured a near-fatal beating and a crash landing in Machine City. Yet his abused body also becomes less and less important because he no longer needs his eyes to "see" the computer code that creates the matrix; once inside the matrix for the final battle, his avatar can stand in for his "real" body. As the trilogy ends, Neo is nowhere to be found. His broken, motionless body is laid out, alone in Machine City, and the people/renegade programs within the matrix wonder when or if he will return. Peace and racial progress come only at a price, and the price is the multiracial body. In this new order, the line between the Matrix and Zion has been solidified, and bodies that cross those boundaries have no place. As the credits roll, the film itself seems unable to imagine "a world without borders or boundaries."

### NOTES

1. I would like to thank Theresa Velcamp-Alfaro, Lisa Nakamura, Kim Hester-Williams, and the editors of this volume for reading and responding to earlier versions of this chapter.

2. This chapter's interpretive frame is strongly influenced by Fredric Jameson's description of cultural forms as internally contradictory. These cultural objects read in the context of broader historical and economic shifts will, like the society that gave rise to it, express ideologies of both past and future modes of production.

3. Reeves's appearance in *Wired* magazine also signals his connection to futuristic technology. *Wired* targets the computer industry and consistently champions

both globalization and science fiction. Its hip image is marketed toward a digital cultural intelligentsia, the so-called technorati. Michelle Deveraux, "10 Reasons Keanu Rules," *Wired*, March 2006, 133.

4. See, for instance, Scott Bukatman, *Terminal Identity: The Virtual Subject in Post-modern Science Fiction* (Durham, NC: Duke University Press, 1998); Annette Kuhn, ed., *Alien Zone: Cultural Theory and Contemporary Science Fiction Cinema* (New York: Verso, 1990); Adam Roberts, *Science Fiction* (New York: Routledge, 2000); Vivian Sobchack, *Screening Space: The American Science Fiction Film* (New York: Ungar, 1987); J. P. Telotte, *Replications: A Robotic History of the Science Fiction Film* (Urbana: University of Illinois Press, 1995).

5. For further discussion of the ways in which race is used to signify the distance and difference between the artificial, oppressive, and exploitative Matrix and the freedom-loving, authentic, gritty rebels in Zion, see Claudia Springer, "Playing it Cool in *The Matrix*," and Lisa Nakamura, "The Multiplication of Difference in Post-millennial Cyberpunk Film: The Visual Culture of Race in the *Matrix* Trilogy." Both essays appear in *The Matrix Trilogy: Cyberpunk Reloaded*, ed. Stacy Gillis (New York: Wallflower Press, 2005).

6. Nakamura, "The Multiplication of Difference in Post-millennial Cyberpunk Film," 132.

7. Notable exceptions to these characterizations of the film come from Peter X. Feng, "False and Double Consciousness: Race, Virtual Reality and the Assimilation of Hong Kong Action Cinema in *The Matrix*," in *Aliens R Us*, eds. Ziauddin Sardar and Sean Cubitt (Sterling, VA: Pluto Press, 2002), who says, "While Reeves reportedly describes himself as white, Asian American spectators frequently label Reeves as Asian Pacific passing as white. Neo's passing diegesis to another occasions leaps in consciousness; Reeves passing for white implies the heightened awareness of double consciousness" (155). Nakamura also recognizes Reeves as multiracial when she says, "Neo, played by Keanu Reeves, is not included as white for two reasons: firstly, the actor has self-identified as multi-racial, and secondly, the character he plays loudly disavows whiteness in a key scene from *The Matrix Reloaded*, during which he has a long dialogue with the Architect" (*Matrix*, 130), and the chapter by Jane Park included in this collection.

8. C. Richard King and David J. Leonard, "Is Neo White? Reading Race, Watching the *Trilogy*," in *Jacking into the Matrix Franchise: Cultural Reception and Interpretation*, ed. Matthew Kapell and William G. Doty (New York: Continuum, 2004), 40.

9. Thomas Forster, "The Transparency of the Interface: Reality Hacking and Fantasies of Resistance," in *The Matrix Trilogy: Cyberpunk Reloaded*, ed. Stacy Gillis (New York: Wallflower Press, 2005), 71.

10. Ibid., 73. For more on the politics of the visual assignment of racial identities, see Robyn Wiegman, *American Anatomies: Theorizing Race and Gender* (Durham, NC: Duke University Press, 1995); and Sarah Chinn, *Technology and the Logic of American Racism* (New York: Continuum Press, 2000).

11. J. J. Goodrich, *The Keanu Matrix: Unraveling the Puzzle of Hollywood's Reluctant Superstar* (Boca Raton, FL: American Media, 2003), 162.

12. See also Valerie Rohy, "Displacing Desire: Passing, Nostalgia and *Giovonni's Room*," in *Passing and the Fictions of Identity*, ed. Elaine Ginsberg (Durham, NC: Duke University Press, 1996).

13. Samira Kawash, *Dislocating the Color Line: Identity, Hybridity, and Singularity in African-American Literature* (Stanford, CA: Stanford University Press, 1997).

14. Ibid., 139.

15. "Little brown brothers" was the colloquial term for Filipinos during the Spanish American War and reflects the paternalistic public face of U.S. imperialism.

16. Springer, "Playing It Cool in *The Matrix*," in *The Matrix Trilogy: Cyberpunk Reloaded*, ed. Stacy Gillis (New York: Wallflower Press, 2005), 89. Springer later acknowledges and then dismisses Reeves as multiracial, saying, "Although Keanu Reeves is biracial—Asian and White—the film does not present him in those terms, and his role in relation to the film's black characters evokes the 1950's paradigm of white malcontents learning from black trendsetters" (91).

17. Greg Carter, "America's New Racial Heroes: Mixed Race Americans and Ideas of Novelty, Progress, and Utopia" (Ph.D. diss., University of Texas, Austin, 2007). See also Suzanne Bost, *Mulattas and Mestizas: Representing Mixed Identities in the Americas, 1850-2000* (Athens: University of Georgia Press, 2003), who reads nineteenth- and twentieth-century novels and race theorists as "revealing the common tendency to theorize mixture as a resolution to social problems" (21).

18. David Hollinger, *Postethnic America* (New York: Basic Books, 1995).

19. Gloria Anzaldúa, *Borderlands/La Frontera: The New Mestiza* (San Francisco: Aunt Lute Books, 1987), 77.

20. Trinh T. Minh-ha, *Woman, Native, Other: Writing Postcoloniality and Feminism* (Bloomington: Indiana University Press, 1989), 88.

21. For a fuller discussion of the relationship of cyborgs and representations of multiraciality, see LeiLani Nishime's "Mulatto Cyborg," *Cinema Journal* 44, no. 2 (2005): 34-49.

22. One of the central concerns of *The Matrix* trilogy is what constitutes the real world. I have put the term "real" in quotes here to denote the tenuous claim the non-Matrix world has to reality. However, for the rest of the chapter I will, for the sake of brevity and clarity, dispense with the quotation marks and hope that they will still be implied in the mind of the reader.

23. *Time*, October 18, 1993. For further discussion of SimEve, particularly in terms of her gender and national identity, see also Bost, *Mulattas and Mestizas*; and Donna Haraway, *Modest_Witness@Second_Millennium.FemaleMan©_Meets_OncoMouse: Feminism and Technoscience* (New York: Routledge, 1997).

24. Aylish Woods, "Timespaces in Spectacular Cinema: Crossing the Great Divide of Spectacle versus Narrative," *Screen* 43, no. 4 (Winter 2002): 384.

25. For a sustained examination of Asian Americans and citizenship, see also Sucheng Chan, *Asian Americans: An Interpretive History* (Boston: Twayne, 1991); David Palumbo-Liu, *Asian/America: Historical Crossings of a Racial Frontier* (Stanford, CA: Stanford University Press, 1999); and Susan Koshy, *Sexual Naturalization: Asian Americans and Miscegenation* (Stanford, CA: Stanford University Press, 2004).

26. For more on Native Americans, miscegenation, and nation, see Mary Dearborn, *Pocahontas's Daughters* (New York: Oxford University Press, 1986); and Eve Allegra Raimon, *The "Tragic Mulatta" Revisited: Race and Nationalism in Nineteenth-Century Antislavery Fiction* (New Brunswick, NJ: Rutgers University Press, 2004).

27. David Morley and Kevin Robins, *Spaces of Identity: Global Media, Electronic Landscapes and Cultural Boundaries* (New York: Routledge, 1995).

28. Jane Park, "Orientalism in U.S. Cyberpunk Cinema from *Blade Runner* to *The Matrix*" (Ph.D. diss., University of Texas, Austin, 2004), 25.

29. In her extended analysis of *The Matrix*, Nakamura notes that Reeves's mixed race hero "is marked as the only available corrective to the agents of whiteness" (77). However, the majority of her analysis focuses on the interaction between the multiple racial groups in the film. Nakamura, *Cybertypes: Race, Ethnicity, and Identity on the Internet* (New York: Routledge, 2002), 69.

30. Poshek Fu and David Desser, "Introduction," in *The Cinema of Hong Kong: History, Arts, Identity*, ed. Poshek Fu and David Desser (New York: Cambridge University Press, 2000), 9.

31. Here I am drawing heavily from David Bordwell's characterization of the filming of action scenes in Hong Kong kung fu cinema. Bordwell, *Planet Hong Kong: Popular Cinema and the Art of Entertainment* (Cambridge, MA: Harvard University Press, 2000).

32. Bost, *Mulattas and Mestizas* 2.

33. See Stephen Teo's "The 1970's: Movement and Transition," in Fu and Desser, *The Cinema of Hong Kong*, 90-110.

34. Bordwell, *Planet Hong Kong*.

35. Allucquere Rosanne Stone, "Will the Real Body Please Stand Up? Boundary Stories about Virtual Cultures," in *Cyberspace: First Steps*, ed. Michael Benedict (Cambridge, MA: MIT Press, 1991), 113.

36. Sobchack, *Screening Space*, 38, 39.

37. Kim Hester-Williams, "NeoSlaves: Slavery, Freedom, and African American Apotheosis in *Candyman*, *The Matrix*, and *The Green Mile*," *Genders* 40 (2004), par. 11, www.genders.org/g40/g40_williams.html (accessed August 8, 2006).

38. Ibid., par. 14.

39. Although the points of convergence and divergence between the representations of Asian-white and Asian-black multiracial people are a subject for another essay, the positioning of Chong as "100 percent pure" may echo the perception of multiracial African Americans as simply black, while multiracial Asian Americans appear to have more flexibility in claiming a multiracial identity.

# Contributors

HEIDI ARDIZZONE teaches American studies at the University of Notre Dame. She is the author of *An Illuminated Life: Belle da Costa Greene's Journey from Prejudice to Privilege* (2007) and coauthor of *Love on Trial: An American Scandal in Black and White* (2001). She has published articles and essays in *Visual Studies*, the *Journal of International Labor and Working Class History*, and the *Chicago Tribune*.

AISHA D. BASTIAANS is a Ph.D. candidate in American studies and African American studies at Yale University. She is completing a doctoral dissertation that examines twentieth-century literary and cinematic representations of the mulatta figure in the United States. Her research interests include African American literature, film studies, and cultural studies, with an emphasis on race, gender, and representation.

MARY BELTRÁN is an assistant professor of communication arts and Chicana/o-Latino/a studies at the University of Wisconsin–Madison, where she studies and teaches on topics related to race, ethnicity, and U.S. film and media history and representation. She is currently completing a book entitled *Latino Stars in U.S. Eyes: The Evolution and Racial Politics of Latino/a Stardom*, on the marketing of Latina/o film and television stars to the American public since the 1920s.

GREGORY T. CARTER is assistant professor in history at the University of Wisconsin–Milwaukee. His research interests include mixed race identity and representation. He received his Ph.D. in American Studies from the University of Texas at Austin.

CAMILLA FOJAS is associate professor in and director of Latin American and Latino studies and a member of the Asian American studies program at DePaul University. She has published in the areas of cultural studies and film in the Americas. Her most recent book, *Border Bandits: Hollywood on the Southern Frontier*, is forthcoming from the University of Texas Press.

ROBB HERNANDEZ is Ford Foundation fellow at the University of Maryland, College Park, in the Ph.D. program in American studies. His research interests include Latina/o visual culture, museum studies, and queer theory. He holds an M.A. in film and television from UCLA. He is author of *The Fire of Life: Robert "Cyclona" Legorreta* (2007) and *The VIVA Papers: Lesbian and Gay Latino Artists of Los Angeles*, forthcoming in the Chicano Archives series from the UCLA Chicano Studies Research Center Press.

ADAM KNEE is assistant professor and M.A. program coordinator in the Ohio University School of Film. His work on issues of racial identity in American film includes the essay "The Weight of Race: Stardom and Transformations of Racialized Masculinity in Recent American Film," in *Quarterly Review of Film and Video* (2002), and essays in the anthologies *Soundtrack Available* (2001) and *Representing Jazz* (1995). His writing on horror has appeared in the anthologies *Horror International* (2005) and *The Dread of Difference: Gender and the Horror Film* (1996).

LISA NAKAMURA is associate professor of speech communication and Asian American studies at the University of Illinois–Urbana-Champaign. She is the author of *Cybertypes: Race, Ethnicity, and Identity on the Internet* (2002) and *Visual Cultures of the Internet* (2007) and a coeditor of *Race in Cyberspace* (2000). She has published articles on cross-racial role-playing in Internet chat spaces; race, embodiment, and virtuality in the film *The Matrix*; and political economies of race and cyberspace.

LEILANI NISHIME is assistant professor of communication at the University of Washington. She has published in the areas of Asian American studies and mixed race cultural studies and coedited *East Main Street: Asian American Popular Culture*.

KENT A. ONO is director of and professor in the Asian American studies program and a professor in the Institute of Communications Research at the University of Illinois–Urbana-Champaign. He conducts critical and theoretical analyses of print, film, and television, specifically focusing on representations of race, gender, sexuality, class, and nation. He has contributed articles to numerous journals and anthologies. In addition to coauthoring *Shifting Borders: Rhetoric, Immigration, and California's Proposition 187* (2002), he has coedited *Enterprise Zones: Critical Positions on Star Trek* (1996) and edited *Asian American Studies after Critical Mass* (2005) and *A Companion to Asian American Studies* (2005). He is currently completing a book on films and videos about the incarceration of Japanese Americans during World War II, *Forgetting to Remember: Representations of Japanese American Incarceration on Film and Video.*

JANE PARK is lecturer in the Department of Gender and Cultural Studies at the University of Sydney. Her research focuses on representations of race and ethnicity, particularly of Asiatic peoples and cultures in film and popular media, including television, popular music, and video games. She has published in *Global Media Journal, World Literature Today,* and *East Main Street: Asian American Popular Culture,* edited by Shilpa Davé, LeiLani Nishime, and Tasha Oren (2004). She is completing her book, entitled *Yellow Future: Oriental Style in Contemporary Hollywood Cinema,* which examines the ideological role of Asiatic imagery in U.S. films from the 1980s to the present.

J. E. SMYTH teaches in the history department at the University of Warwick and is the author of *Reconstructing American Historical Cinema from Cimarron to Citizen Kane* (2006), as well as several articles on classical Hollywood cinema. Smyth is on the editorial board of the *Historical Journal of Film, Radio and Television.*

ANGHARAD N. VALDIVIA is research professor at the Institute of Communications Research, with appointments in media studies, gender and women's studies, and Latina/o studies. She also is affiliated with the faculty at the Center for Latin American and Caribbean Studies and the Women and Gender in Global Perspectives Program. Her research, teaching, and publications focus on the intersection of media studies with international and transnational issues, especially in the area of popular culture, foregrounding issues of gender and ethnicity. Her books include *Feminism, Multiculturalism and the Media* (1995), *A Latina in the Land of Hollywood* (2000), *A Companion to Media Studies* (2003, 2006), *Latina/o Communications Studies Today* (forthcoming), and *Geographies of Latinidad* (forthcoming).

# Index